CAPITALISM AND CLASSICAL SOCIOLOGICAL THEORY

CAPITALISM AND CLASSICAL SOCIOLOGICAL THEORY

JOHN BRATTON, DAVID DENHAM, AND LINDA DEUTSCHMANN

University of Toronto Press

www.utphighereducation.com

LIBRARY AND ARCHIVES CANADA CATALOGUING IN PUBLICATION

Bratton, John
Capitalism and classical sociological theory / John Bratton, David Denham, and Linda Deutschmann.

Includes bibliographical references and index.
ISBN 978-0-8020-9681-4

1. Sociology—Philosophy—Textbooks. 2. Capitalism—Textbooks. I. Denham, David, 1944– II. Deutschmann, Linda Bell, 1943-2008. III. Title.

HM436.B7915 2009 301 C2009-902017-3

North America
5201 Dufferin Street
Toronto, Ontario, Canada, M3H 5T8

2250 Military Road
Tonawanda, New York, USA, 14150

ORDERS PHONE: 1-800-565-9523
ORDERS FAX: 1-800-221-9985
ORDERS EMAIL: utpbooks@utpress.utoronto.ca

UK, Ireland, and continental Europe
NBN International
Estover Road, Plymouth, PL6 7PY, UK
TEL: 44 (0) 1752 202301
FAX ORDER LINE: 44 (0) 1752 202333
enquiries@nbninternational.com

We welcome comments and suggestions regarding any aspect of our publications —please feel free to contact us at news@utphighereducation.com or visit our internet site at www.utphighereducation.com.

This book is printed on paper containing 100% post-consumer fibre.

Recycled
Supporting responsible use of forest resources
FSC www.fsc.org Cert no. SGS-COC-003153
© 1996 Forest Stewardship Council

The University of Toronto Press acknowledges the financial support for its publishing activities of the Government of Canada through the Book Publishing Industry Development Program (BPIDP).

Cover and typesetting by Em Dash Design.

Printed in Canada

Dedicated to all my SOCI 320 Classical Social Theory students, past and present

and in memory of Eric Biddulph, avid cyclist, social activist and friend

—*John Bratton*

To my wife Ann, Steven and Jennifer, Sarah and Rick, and our beautiful granddaughters Georgia Elizabeth, Imogen Hope and Ella Rose

—*David Denham*

To Karl, Michael, Audrey of the Island & Audrey of the Lake

—*Linda Deutschmann*

In memory of Linda Deutschmann,
who died on 21 August 2008.

About the Authors

JOHN BRATTON is Professor of Sociology at Thompson Rivers University, Kamloops, Canada. His research interests traverse industrial sociology, and he is author of *Japanization at Work: Managerial Studies in the 1990s*; co-author of *Workplace Learning: A Critical Introduction* (2004); co-author of *Organizational Leadership* (2005); co-author of *Human Resource Management: Theory and Practice* (2007), now in its fourth edition; and co-author of *Work and Organizational Behaviour* (2007).

DAVID DENHAM is an Honorary Research Fellow at Wolverhampton University, England, where he taught a wide variety of sociology courses, including classical social theory, over a career of thirty-five years. He has published articles on the sociology of law, criminology, and the sociology of sport and is co-author of *Victimology: Victimization and Victims' Rights* (2008).

LINDA DEUTSCHMANN was Professor Emerita at Thompson Rivers University. Her research interest was in aspects of social control in the "risk society," such as penal politics, social exclusion, and innovative restorative justice. She is the author of *Deviance and Social Control* (2007), now going into its fifth edition, and *Triumph of the Will* (1991). She is co-author of *Social Problems: A Case Study Approach* (2007), now in its second edition.

Contents

Preface and Acknowledgements

MY REASON FOR WANTING to write this book arose from a common experience of university professors, that of teaching a course for which there seemed to be no adequate text that corresponded with the syllabus I had designed. I started thinking about writing *Capitalism and Classical Sociological Theory* when I was preparing my lecture notes for SOCI 320 Classical Social Theory, a new prerequisite course for the sociology major at Thompson Rivers University. This book is a direct outcome of my research of existing books and course syllabi, and of discussions with faculty who teach classical social theory in Canadian and U.K. universities. During the writing stage, I persuaded my colleague, Linda Deutschmann, to write the Georg Simmel and the gender chapters and an old friend, David Denham, to write the chapters on Emile Durkheim.

Since each of us began teaching, unsurprisingly, profound changes in paradigms and perspectives have taken place in the way that modernity is studied. Changes in the condition of modernity include the implosion of Soviet and East European communism and South African apartheid, the ascendancy of neo-liberalism, and the emergence of new major economic players such as the People's Republic of China and India. The diffusion of microelectronics has seen the emergence of the Internet and the virtual organization. Predictions of a so-called leisure society resulting from new technology have not materialized. Many managers and workers alike still work long hours, are constantly electronically connected, and appear to be suffering increased levels of work-related stress. And, in addition to movements of capital and goods, the migration of people to Western Europe and North America has made multiculturalism and the diverse workforce a reality. A key issue for sociologists is the effect of globalization on the workplace and beyond. An important theme in the literature is the *convergence* in capitalism, which affects production and employment practices in different regions of the world. The convergence debate has a long antecedence in neoclassical economic theory. Detractors, however, emphasize the existence of "varieties of capitalism" and *divergence* in capitalist behaviour as evidence of the importance of the power of local culture, politics, and agency. Over the last thirty years sociologists also have witnessed the ascendancy of rival intellectual approaches to the study of social phenomena. For example, under the rubric of postmodernism, the traditional approach to researching aspects of society, loosely described as positivism, has been challenged by *constructivists*. The constructivist's view challenges researchers to re-examine their frames of reference, the research process itself, and the production of knowledge.[1] Importantly, the postmodern approach, as Eagleton and Lyotard notably argue, eschews *meta-narratives* such as Marx's conception of history, whose function was to legitimize the illusion of a universal human history, and celebrates the triumph of local fragmented specificities over any kind of totality.[2]

In this intellectual climate, inevitably, there will be disagreement among sociologists over which classical social theorist should be included in a text on classical theory. The membership of the classical canon is important, for the canon provides a shared language, a focus, some kind of identity for the discipline, and it shapes both the intellectual discourse and the trajectory of sociological research. In writing *Capitalism and Classical Sociological Theory*, we have chosen to be more inclusive and have extended the coverage of the familiar sociological canon established around the 1970s—that is, the trio of Marx, Durkheim, and Weber—to include Georg Simmel and four women who theorized about gender roles, gendered work, and new patterns of family life that were the consequences of the emergence of industrial capitalism. Our choice is influenced by a common criticism of the classical sociological canon: the marginalization of gender in their theories. We examine the gendering of social theory in the nineteenth and early twentieth century through the work of Mary Wollstonecraft, Harriet Martineau, Charlotte Perkins Gilman, and Jane Addams. Our selection of male and female social theorists extends the classical sociological canon to provide a better understanding of capitalist modernity.

Capitalism and Classical Sociological Theory represents a departure from popular texts on classical sociological theory currently available on the market in several important respects. It aims to provide a balanced coverage of the sociological canon but is selective in its choice of other contributors to the expanded canon. Our aim is to provide the reader with *depth* of the most significant contributions, rather than a superficial outline of *all* sociological works in the classical period from 1789 to 1920. The familiar adage "Jack of all trades, master of none," when applied to a review of classical social theorists, may be rewritten as "knowledge of many, understanding of none." In our experience of teaching one-semester undergraduate courses in classical social theory, time permits only an adequate coverage of a limited number of social theorists in any depth. Consequently, students become aggravated because only a third of the required text is covered in lectures. Another feature of the book is the inclusion of extended passages from the classical texts. The point of this is to counter the prejudice that classical texts are particularly difficult, if not almost possible, to read and to encourage the readers of this book to experience the prose and thoughts conveyed by the original texts. With this in mind, we have endeavoured, as far as possible, to cite the readily available English editions of Marx, Durkheim, Weber, Simmel, and Wollstonecraft, which are referenced at the end of the book. When quoting from the canonical works we have deliberately not changed the words to be gender-neutral. When the classical writers use the word *man*, that is precisely whom they are usually referring to: a conspicuous deficiency in their theorizing as will be explained. Importantly, while attentive to the historical context, *Capitalism and Classical Sociological Theory* encourages the reader to reflect upon capitalism in the early twenty-first century, contemporary society and on their own life experiences, and to evaluate the relevance of classical sociological theory for our time.

Another important event has happened since I began working on *Capitalism and Classical Sociological Theory*. Linda Deutschmann unexpectedly died in August 2008 while we were completing the final changes to the manuscript. I spoke at Linda's Memorial Service. In rereading Linda's chapter on gender, I realized that in an important way she mirrored the social activism of the early sociologists such as Jane Addams. Linda was a social activist engaged in, among other groups, the John Howard Society and the Kamloops-Thompson AIDS Society. In addition to her involvement in the community, Linda demonstrated the best in university teaching: Her own research and social activism informed her classroom teaching. A dedicated teacher and a supportive colleague, she will be sorely missed.

On behalf of Linda and David, I wish to thank the many people for their assistance. I would like to thank Sue Hughes, Leeds Trinity and All Saints College, England, for her written comments and suggestions for improving chapters 1 and 2; Bruce Baugh, Thompson Rivers University, for his valuable feedback on an earlier version of chapter 3; and Carolyn Forshaw, my partner, for reading most of the manuscript. I also would particularly like to thank Dr. Ulrich Scheck, Dean, Faculty of Arts at Thompson Rivers University for his encouragement and for releasing me from a full teaching load to write this book at a crucial time in the winter semester, 2008. David Denham would like to thank Dr. Pauline Anderson, Subject Leader of Sociology at the University of Wolverhamption, for her support and encouragement over the years. Linda Deutschmann wanted to thank Sheila Brownly Hervey for her unfailing material, intellectual, and personal support. We are grateful for the feedback from the three anonymous reviewers of the manuscript, for the editorial work and improvements made to the text by Carolyn Jongeward, and for the patience and support from Anne Brackenbury at Broadview/University of Toronto Press.

John A. Bratton
Kamloops, Canada
November 2008

Notes

1 S. Clegg and C. Hardy, *Studying Organization: Theory and Method* (Thousand Oaks, CA: Sage, 1999); K. Charmaz, "Grounded Theory: Objectivist and Constructivist Methods," in *Handbook of Qualitative Research*, 2nd ed., eds. N. Denzin and Y. Lincoln (Thousand Oaks, CA: Sage, 2005), 509–35; Chris Grey, *A Very Short, Fairly Interesting and Reasonably Cheap Book About Studying Organizations* (Thousand Oaks, CA: Sage, 2005); Karen Legge, *Human Resource Management: Rhetorics and Realities* (Basingstoke: Palgrave Macmillan, 2005).

2 T. Eagleton, "Awakening from Modernity," *Times Literary Supplement* (February 20, 1987), quoted in David Harvey, *The Condition of Postmodernity* (Oxford: Blackwell, 1990), 9; J.F. Lyotard, *The Postmodern Condition* (Manchester: Manchester University Press, 1984).

PART I
CONTEXT

Introduction

> Things fall apart; the centre cannot hold;
> Mere anarchy is loosed upon the world.
>
> —W.B. Yeats

> The stories of *civilization* in any place at any time
> have this in common—individuals feel they understand
> the mechanisms of their society. —John Ralston Saul

IN *VICTORIAN CITIES*, ASA BRIGGS NOTES that most Victorian writers were both horrified and fascinated by new industrial cities that seemed to represent "a system of life constructed on a wholly new principle."[1] The discourse about large polyglot cities in nineteenth-century Europe was part of an intellectual debate about modern life that occurred in France, Germany, and the United States. Also, the conditions of the industrial society provided the context for the development of what is now called classical sociological theory, which has become the principal frame of reference for modern sociology.[2]

Theorizing about society has deep historical roots. Egyptian prophets, Greek philosophers, and medieval scholars in Western Europe all sought to understand and explain the operations of their society. In Western Europe during the eighteenth and nineteenth centuries—known as the modern period—there was an extraordinarily high level of philosophical engagement by male and female public intellectuals. In the eighteenth century, the writings of Montesquieu, Rousseau, Wollstonecraft, de Bonald, de Maistre, Adam Smith, Saint-Simon, Comte, and Martineau provided the intellectual context for theorizing about new forms of social life and society that came to prevail first in Britain and subsequently worldwide.[3]

Eighteenth-century social thought was broadly optimistic about social change, confident that the certainties of the natural sciences could be applied without problem to the study of civil society.[4] By contrast, the *classical* theorizing that emerged in the nineteenth and early twentieth centuries—most closely identified with Karl Marx, Emile Durkheim, and Max Weber—was generally pessimistic. The transition from the premodern to the modern era ushered in profound and unprecedented economic, ideological, cultural, political, and social changes.

This book is an introduction to classical sociological theory and its legacy. The objective of this chapter is to introduce the classical social thinkers, and to make the initial case for studying the classical sociological canon.

Classical Sociological Canon

A theory implies a set of concepts and ideas that, taken together, purport to explain a given phenomenon or set of phenomena. Sociological theory is above all a theory created to explain the modern industrial society. By classical sociological theory we mean a collection of published works that embodies a *canon*, a privileged set of texts, which defines the discipline.[5] As artifacts of what is most distinctively sociological, the canonical texts are essential reading for academics and students in sociology because they "systematically developed consciousness of society and social relations,"[6] they have relevance to modern sociology, and they are worth reading and rereading. They are classical not only in the sense that they provide an historical context for reading sociology, and are therefore a must-read for any serious student of sociology, but also in that they help us understand our own society. The classical canon remains at the centre of modern sociology and continues to inspire, influence, and guide sociological theory and empirical research.[7] Contemporary sociologists have gone as far as suggesting that the canonical social thinkers have "entered the air that we breathe."[8] It is not surprising, therefore, that the Marx-Durkheim-Weber triumvirate is to sociology what Shakespeare and Dickens are to English literature, what Tchaikovsky and Beethoven are to music, or what Adam Smith and John Maynard Keynes are to economics—the iconic "fathers" or founders of the discipline.

The surviving founders of sociology are also a product of *our* constructions, the result of translations largely by Anglo-Saxon scholars of selected classical authors.[9] As such, the community of sociologists constantly revises the membership of the canon. In early twenty-first-century sociology, Marx, Durkheim, and Weber are well entrenched within the classical canon, but this was not always the case. Sociologists in the early 1900s disagreed about which particular "founding thinker" was actually responsible for the founding of sociology. They cited possible contenders from a range of thinkers in a broad intellectual landscape, including Adam Smith, Auguste Comte, Marquis de Condorcet, Vilfredo Pareto, G.H. Mead, and Charles Darwin.

As late as the 1920s, the Chicago School listed Durkheim and Simmel as notable contributors to the new social science, but not Marx or Weber. Emile Durkheim's work on research methodology and his references to social unity and "bonds of interdependence" secured his place early in the sociological canon. He was also canonized by Robert K. Merton's account of anomie. Though Marx never held an academic position, his contribution to sociological theory is immense. Even so, his full membership in the sociological canon is relatively recent; it dates from the mid-1960s and the period of radicalization of the university student movement in Western Europe. In the late 1970s Marx was beginning to be introduced to American undergraduate students as "the first great radical sociologist."[10]

As for Max Weber, his early training was in law, and he was professionally an economist. Though he was a founding member of the German Sociological Society, his contemporaries never regarded him as a founding thinker of sociological theory.[11] It was the American sociologist Talcott Parsons who established Weber as a full-fledged member of the sociological canon. From Parson's reconstruction of Weber's work, it became the parlance that Weber intended his best-known work, *The Protestant Ethic,* as a refutation of Marx's thesis on capitalism. Thus Marx, Durkheim, and Weber—the "founding fathers" of sociology—became canonized by the Anglo-Saxon sociology community only forty years ago.

The Marx-Durkheim-Weber triumvirate became further entrenched after Anthony Giddens's book *Capitalism and Modern Social Theory* was published in 1971 and after new English translations and books of readings were released. The work of British sociologist David Frisby helped the late canonization of Georg Simmel. And a recent survey of the theorists studied in forty-six university courses placed Simmel fourth after the "holy trinity" of Marx, Durkheim, and Weber.[12]

Towards an Inclusive Canon

Given that the development of the classical sociological canon was predominantly the work of white male Anglo-Saxon sociologists, the calls for a more inclusive canon are not surprising. This book offers a review of a more inclusive canon by including the work of Mary Wollstonecraft, Harriet Martineau, Charlotte Perkins Gilman, and Jane Addams. The common, primary concern of writings of the classical sociological canon is to achieve an understanding of the distinctive features, and the tensions and paradoxes, of a new emerging form of social life—capitalist modernity. Since it is generally agreed that the understanding of the emergence of sociology relies on its purported relation to modernity, it is to the meaning of *modernity* that we shall first attend.

Modernism is very much an urban phenomenon. It has existed, since 1850, in a complex relationship with the experience of capitalism, explosive urban growth, and a confluence of urban-based intellectual ideas and political movements. *Capitalism* is a way of organizing economic activity. Capitalist activities and institutions began to develop throughout Europe during the Renaissance period, dating from the 1400s, and continued throughout the premodern era. The production and exchange of commodities, however, were restrained by traditional religious and political controls.

Capitalist modernity has come to define the vast and largely unregulated expansion of commodity production and related market and monetary networks. The need to maximize profit from commodity production and exchange, rather than to satisfy the material needs of the producers, is the leitmotiv of capitalism.

Well before the publication of Jane Jacobs's *Economy of Cities* or Richard Florida's *Who's Your City?* cities have been conceived as the epicentres of innovation, technological progress, and personal freedom. As emblematic of profound changes, cities are equated with modernity. They are "simultaneously the machinery and the hero of modernity."[13] The city, in Weber's *General Economic History*, is the crucible of modernity. It is primarily an economic space: the location of commerce and manufacturing. It is also a place of new occupations and where new things are made for exchange, which, in turn, leads to inventions, reinventions, and new kinds of work. The city alone is the primary place of cultural development, that is, clusters of artists, architects, poets, writers, and vast collections of ideas and cultural artifacts: generally, Western culture is associated with cities. They are primary places of scientific thinking and are the places of specific religious institutions that produce theological thought.[14] Cities have also long been acknowledged as primary places of personal freedom and development, that is, where urbanites can release their creative minds, give liberty to imagination and play, challenge orthodoxy, and discover their sense of identity.

In reality, modernity has two sides. The first is the spread of a new economic model located primarily in new urban centres. The second but less obvious side to modernity is its unrelenting change, its insecurity, and its totalizing chaos. Modernity is characterized by ephemerality, and by fragmentary, chaotic change and paradox. Berman provides an insightful description of modernity:

> To be modern is to find ourselves in an environment that promises adventure, power, joy, growth, transformation of ourselves and the world—and, at the same time, that threatens to destroy everything we have, everything we know, everything we are. Modern environments and experiences cut across all boundaries of geography and ethnicity, of class and nationality, of religion and ideology; in this sense, modernity can be said to unite all mankind. But it is a paradoxical unity, a unity of disunity; it pours us all into a maelstrom of perpetual disintegration and renewal, of struggle and contradiction, of ambiguity and anguish. To be modern is to be part of a universe in which, as Marx said, "all that is solid melts into air."[15]

The collage of capitalist modernity is a quilt stitched together with patches from both the premodern and the new industrial society. Patches of agriculture, small manufacturing, villages, kinship, landed interests, monarchy, religion, tradition, and with increasing dominance, new patches of factories, cities, individualism, business interests, democracy, science, and reason. Modernity signifies creativity, innovation, aestheticism, wealth, and individual freedom and identity. It also exhibits chaotic change, poverty, human degradation, and inequality.

The uneducated, by definition, leave few written accounts of their experiences in the metropolis. For the most part, historians have been the ones to exhaustively document the social reverberations of modernity. Working-class women and children suffered the brunt of the chaotic change and adjustment. As the labouring poor migrated to the old and new cities, the bottom layer of the mid-Victorian social pyramid witnessed growing numbers of paupers and prostitutes. Industrialization and urbanization was accompanied by an increase in homelessness, child prostitution, and a permanent underclass of extreme poor living in urban slums. The surveys of the late nineteenth century reveal a labouring poor "stunted and debilitated" by a century of unconstrained capitalism. On average, children from upper-class private schools were twelve centimetres taller than children from working class schools.[16] Victorian moralists apparently saw no connection between "streets infested with prostitutes"[17] and the human crisis caused by an absence of social spending and by unfettered industrial capitalism. Behind the picture of urban wealth is a story of the destitute, disempowered, dispossessed, and disinherited: those described by the poet Rainer Maria Rilke as "ones to whom neither the past nor the future belongs"[18] constitute the ugly side of modernity.

The collage of modernity appears similar to a well-known drawing in first-year psychology textbooks, an image that can be seen at the same time as a beautiful young woman and as an old crone.[19] Charles Dickens's *A Tale of Two Cities*, published in 1859, perhaps best captures the life experience of capitalist modernity: "It was the best of times, it was the worst of times, it was the age of wisdom, it was the age of foolishness, it was the epoch of belief, it was the epoch of incredulity, it was the season of Light, it was the season of Darkness, it was the spring of hope, it was the winter of despair, we had everything before us, we had nothing before us, we were all going direct to heaven, we were all going direct the other way."[20]

Writers from a wide range of perspectives and disciplines, as diverse as David Hume, Adam Smith, John Millar, Adam Ferguson, Saint-Simon, Auguste Comte, were all strongly influenced by European Enlightenment thinking; they viewed modernity through a conceptual prism of rationalism, positivism, universalism, and a belief in linear progress. Enlightenment thinkers welcomed the maelstrom of change as a necessary prerequisite for modernity and believed that the sciences would not only control and harness natural forces but also promote understanding of society and of the self.[21] In the early twentieth century, the *fixity* and optimism of Enlightenment thought and modernity was challenged in part by the male canonical writers, and also by early feminist thinkers, and by socialist movements, which introduced a class dimension into modernism.

The Legacy of the Classical Canon

Skeptical readers may very well ask what the classical thinkers, whose major works were published over a century ago, can tell us today. We believe they can inform us greatly not only about the nature of modernity but also about present society. The members of the classical sociological canon sought their own ways to confront and make sense of the processes of transformation and to explain the key characteristics of capitalist modernity as contrasted with premodern society. The overwhelming interest of Karl Marx, Emile Durkheim, and Max Weber, writes Anthony Giddens, was in "the delineation of the characteristic structure of modern capitalism as contrasted with pre-modern forms of society."[22] At the centre of Karl Marx's theorizing is the primacy of capitalist production and how this shapes the political and social life of society. For Marx, Victorian capitalism *is* modernity, and modernity is capitalism.[23] Marx emphasized the relations of production, that is, the way in which formally "free" wage labour is organized and exploited. Emile Durkheim theorized that industrial societies, with their complex division of labour and their diverse and conflicting interests, constitute a moral entity held together by shared norms and values. Durkheim emphasized the impact of modern capitalism on social and cultural life. Max Weber tried to understand modernity through the role of ideas in social change and, above all, the importance of rationality. Weber agreed with much of Marx's economic analysis but emphasized wholesale rationalization in all spheres of life, irreversible development of bureaucracy, growing pluralization of values and beliefs, and increasing secularization, which brought about disenchantment.[24] For Weber, these developments describe modernity.[25] With modern society's plurality of social groups and culture, Georg Simmel gave primacy to the complex interplay of cultural dynamics and how urban dwellers might respond to and internalize the incredible diversity and fleeting social interactions found in large cities.

By way of summarizing the selected sociological canon, and as a heuristic device, figure 0.1 depicts the theoretical dimensions of modernity. It shows the interplay of four major concepts probed by the canonical writers—*materiality* (Karl Marx), *morality* (Emile Durkheim), *rationality* (Max Weber), and *culture* (Georg Simmel).[26] It also shows a fifth dimension, *gender,* which we have added for theorizing about society.

FIGURE 0.1 The classical theorizing of society

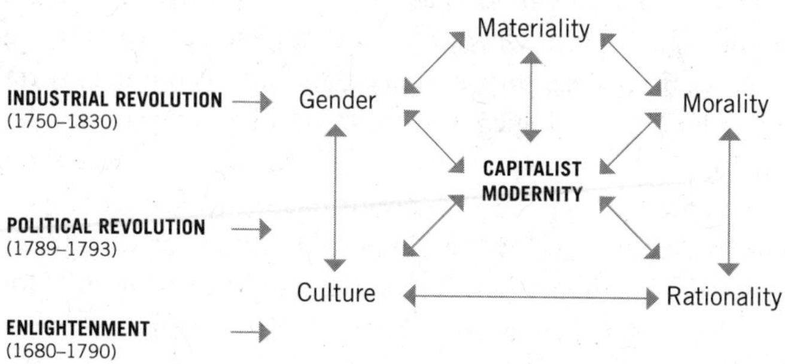

Over several decades *gender* has become a concept to be wrestled with, but here we use the word to refer to the classical theorists or theory that focuses on the processes of gender roles, inequalities in society, problems of power, and women's subordination and oppression. These problems were all addressed in different ways by early feminist thinkers. As we shall see in the respective writings of Mary Wollstonecraft, Harriet Martineau, Jane Addams, and Charlotte Perkins Gilman, the question of gender inequalities in society is explicitly addressed. These early feminists thinkers critically examined the plight of women oppressed through a variety of entrenched social processes, such as patriarchical strategies and sexism.

In *A Short History of Sociological Thought*, Alan Swingewood makes the valid point that "the history of sociology is never a history of a selective canon but a dialogue between the present and the past, how ideas born in different historical periods and cultures survive as active elements in contemporary sociological thought."[27] While there are limits to what can be reasonably portrayed in a diagram, figure 0.1 indicates the influences on the development of sociological thought provided by Europe's dual revolution—industrial and political—and by the intellectual thinking arising from the Enlightenment. The lines and arrows between the selected canonical theorists are not intended to suggest causal relationships, they are meant to convey to the reader that classical intellectual thinking is a complex, rich, interrelated set of accumulated knowledge and ideas. Thus, figure 0.1 refers to an arena of public discourse constituting the different perspectives and theoretical positions on capitalist modernity that defines classical sociological theory.

Since the construction of the Marx-Durkheim-Weber canon and the publication in 1971 of Anthony Giddens's seminal text, a number of sociologists have questioned the value of the classical canon and the concepts derived from studies of contemporary modernity. This skepticism has been fuelled by two main sets of arguments. First is the claim that advanced Western societies have shifted to a qualitative new form of society known as late modernity or postmodernity. Adherents of this standpoint argue that in view of the fact that society has undergone a noticeable shift in sensibility, practices, and also economic, social, and cultural orders,[28] sociological theories should be recast to make them relevant for the new postmodern world. In this intellectual climate, in general, and the political collapse of East European communism in 1989–90, in particular, the interest in postmodernism appears to question the intellectual credibility and status of Marx in the canon.[29] However, there is no necessary relationship between East European communism and Karl Marx's social theory.

As evidence of the new social world, critics have argued, for example, that the classical sociological theorists are irrelevant in the era of postmodernism: where increasing intervention of the state in the economy, as noted by Giddens, has been reversed by neo-conservative anti-state ideology; where the notion of nation state is openly challenged, appears anachronistic, and leads to a process of hollowing out of the state and government services;[30] where global competitive advantage stems from processing information and intellectual capital—the so-called knowledge economy—rather than from commodities and manual dexterity; and where economies and financial systems are closely integrated on a global scale .[31] Although globalization is a contested concept, arguably, it is about the unfettered pursuit of profit and the primacy of multinational power over local power.[32] There is nothing in the logic of profit-making corporations and capital accumulation to keep the manufacture of steel in Ontario, Pennsylvania, the Ruhr, or Sheffield, as many managers and workers have discovered.[33] Developments in transport and communication have meant that multinational corporations can increase their profits by relocating their operations beyond their parent countries. Moreover, the logic of unfettered globalization means that labour-intensive value-added activities migrate from high-wage to low-wage countries, that is to say, from the rich developed countries such as the United States and in Western Europe to the poorer developing countries such as China, Bangladesh, and India. It has been compellingly argued that the portability of capital in the era of globalization makes it possible for multinational corporations to select their production location in an endlessly variable geometry of profit searching.[34]

A significant body of literature connects globalization to postmodernity, particularly around themes of the ever more globalizing of capitalism, ideas of space-time compression, the concept of a global division of labour and power, and the globalization of mass culture. It also provides theoretical and empirical support for the thesis that postmodernity, and globalization in particular, is not simply a quantitative extension of modernity but a qualitatively new phenomenon. As McMichael explains, "As economic activity became embedded more deeply in global enterprise, the reach of the global economy strengthened at the expense of national economies. This situation is not unique to the 1980s, but the mechanisms of the debt regime institutionalized the power and authority of global management within states' very organization and procedures. This was the turning point in the story of development."[35] The problems and contradictions within global capitalism have been vividly demonstrated by the 2007–09 financial crises and recession in the United States. Despite healthy domestic economic performance indicators, economies and markets around the world have found it easier in theory than in practice to decouple from the United States, thereby reaffirming that "global markets are still clearly intertwined."[36] The nature of global capitalism and the depth of transformation are debatable, and sociologists remain divided on the merits of the first assertion.[37]

The skepticism surrounding the value of the classical theories has been fuelled by a second claim that these theories are, by-and-large, oblivious to problems concerning gender distinctions within employment, in particular, to male-dominated interests, and to social power. It is contended that Marx, Durkheim, and Weber "gazed upon a masculine world," and their works are said to be gender-blind.[38] Another notable related problem with these classical works is that they are ethnocentric and Eurocentric. Sociologists are less divided on the merits of this weakness. The classical theorists saw social transformation as a global phenomenon, but they saw it through a prism that defined modernity in terms of West European culture and religious models. However, colonization and its associated exploitation took place within the violent context of European religious norms, most notably the complicity in colonial genocides in South America and the aggressive proselytizing in Africa and Asia. As a result, analysis to examine the new society independently of the economics and politics of European colonialism and hegemony, and of its national repercussions on social mechanisms, becomes increasingly problematic.

The meta-narratives of Karl Marx, Emile Durkheim, and Max Weber can be summarized as referring to commodification, differentiation, and rationalization, respectively. In many mature or late-capitalist societies, there has been increased commodification, and each of these meta-narratives draws critical attention to the malfunctions of free-market societies. Marx's economic analysis emphasizes the process whereby goods and services that were formerly considered essential and collectively supplied—such as education, health care, drinking water, electricity, TV airwaves—are privately bought, sold, and operated as for-profit interests. Durkheim's sociology generates an interest in social regulation and the way in which market dynamics lead to rapid and unregulated social change. The deregulated market economies fostered by the New Right can be seen, in Durkheimian analysis, as amoral and as damaging to social solidarity. Even Weber, critical of socialist or communist societies for their potential for extending bureaucracy, was aware that rational market calculation brings its own social costs. He was aware that the rationality of markets could produce irrationalities. Simmel's sociology, which examines the processes of social differentiation and commodity culture, enhances interest and understanding of our "highly economized culture."[39] The legacy of Simmel's ideas on objective culture is reflected in the contemporary discourse on cultural globalization and "the stranger" in the metropolis. In diverse societies around the world an impact of cultural globalization is to force strangeness upon the whole of society. Without the early feminists' efforts, writes Rosemarie Putnam Tong, many women today could not have attained their newfound professional stature.[40] Even after the forty-fifth anniversary of Betty Friedan's *Feminine Mystique*, the early feminists writers still inspire[41] and provide sophisticated understanding into the gender-based, persistent, and pervasive injustices that women continue to experience in all areas of life. For example, were Mary Wollstonecraft to reappear today she would be outraged, but probably not surprised, that in the twenty-first-century Canadian women can be murdered and then victimized by "bland racist, sexist and 'classic' prejudices buried in Canadian society."[42]

Sociological theory attempts to make sense of society. We hope *Capitalism and Classical Sociological Theory* will help readers to better understand contemporary debates about the social world. In the context of a post-SUV economy and global capitalism, we seek to demonstrate that the works of Marx, Durkheim, Weber, Simmel, and the early feminist writers provide powerful conceptual tools for analyzing late modernity and for engaging in debates on globalization, global warming, Enlightenment thought, women's subordination and oppression, and multiculturalism.[43]

Capitalism and Classical Sociological Theory is divided into four parts and twelve chapters. The structure of the book will help instructors and students to align their lectures and readings. In part I we explore the context in which the classical theorists were writing. Chapter 1 provides an explanation of how early social theory not only is a response to but also is shaped by the industrialization and urbanization of nineteenth-century European societies. Chapter 2 examines the intellectual context of early sociological thought.

In part II we examine the classical triumvirate. Chapter 3 provides a biographical sketch of Marx and examines the antecedents of his philosophy and methodology. Chapter 4 further examines Marx's work through his conception of history, including alienation, class-consciousness, and the role of ideology. Chapter 5 examines Marx's economic analysis of capitalism, including the production of a commodity, the labour theory of value, and the theory of economic crises. Chapter 6 examines Emile Durkheim's work on the development of modern societies and analyzes how his theories differed from those of both Marx and Weber. Chapter 7 looks at Durkheim's rules of sociological method and his theory of suicide. Chapter 8 explains his theories on religion and education. Chapter 9 examines Max Weber's pronouncements on methodology and discusses how it differs with that offered by Marx and Durkheim. It also examines Weber's study of the Protestant ethic and its relationship with what he called the spirit of capitalism. Chapter 10 examines Weber's theory of legitimate domination and his treatment of social stratification.

In part III we expand the traditional canon through a selective review of the work of Georg Simmel and early feminist writers. Chapter 11 examines the work of Georg Simmel. Chapter 12 examines the influence of early feminist thinkers and women sociologists and the genesis of feminist social theory.

In part IV we argue that the ideas of the classical social theorists continue to be relevant and exert a profound influence on contemporary sociologists. These ideas have the power to help us analyze and understand contemporary capitalist societies and global capitalism. Indeed, we believe that the ideas of the classical social theorists should become part of every citizen's education. We hope that the readers of this book will gain an appreciation of this.

Notes

1 Asa Briggs, *Victorian Cities* (Harmondsworth, UK: Pelican Books, 1968), 12.

2 Anthony Giddens, *Capitalism and Modern Social Theory* (Cambridge: Cambridge University Press, 1971), xi.

3 See K.H. Tucker, *Classical Social Theory* (Malden, MA: Blackwell, 2002); L. Ray, *Theorizing Classical Sociology* (Buckingham: Open University Press, 1999); Alex Callinicos, *Social Theory: A Historical Introduction* (Cambridge: Polity Press, 2007).

4 Alan Swingewood, *A Short History of Sociological Thought* (New York: St. Martin's Press, 2000), viii.

5 R.W. Connell, "Why Is Classical Theory Classical," *American Journal of Sociology* 102 (1997): 1511–57.

6 Dorothy E. Smith, *The Everyday World as Problematic: A Feminist Sociology* (Boston: Northeastern University Press, 1987), cited by P. M. Lengermann and G. Niebrugge, "Early Women Sociologists and Classical Sociological Theory: 1830–1930" in G. Ritzer, *Classical Sociological Theory* (New York: McGraw-Hill, 2008), 300.

7 Ray, *Theorizing Classical Sociology.*

8 I. Craib, *Classical Social Theory* (Oxford: Oxford University Press, 1997), 2.

9 S. Eliaeson, *Max Weber's Methodologies* (Cambridge: Polity Press, 2002), 2.

10 R.W. Connell, "Why Is Classical Theory Classical," 1542.

11 Keith Tribe, ed., *Reading Weber* (London: Routledge, 1989).

12 Jan Thomas and Annis Kukulan, "Why Don't I Know about These Women? The Integration of Early Women Sociologists in Classical Theory Courses," *Teaching Sociology* 32 (2004): 252–263.

13 David Harvey, *The Conditions of Postmodernity* (Oxford: Blackwell, 1994), 26.

14 See M. Weber, *General Economic History* (1927; New York: Dover Publications, 2003), chap. 23.

15 M. Berman, "All that is solid melts into air," quoted in Harvey, *The Conditions of Postmodernity*, 10–11.

16 E.J. Hobsbawm, *Industry and Empire* (London: Weidenfeld and Nicolson, 1968), 137.

17 E.P. Thompson, *The Making of the English Working Class* (London: Pelican, 1968), 453.

18 The German poet Rainer Maria Rilke is quoted in Naomi Klein, *The Shock Doctrine* (Toronto: Alfred Knopf, 2007), 333.

19 D. Sayer, *Capitalism and Modernity: An Excursus on Marx and Weber* (London: Routledge, 1991), 148.

20 Charles Dickens, *A Tale of Two Cities* (1859; London: HarperCollins, 1952), 21.

21 See Harvey, *The Conditions of Postmodernity*.

22 Giddens, *Capitalism and Modern Social Theory*, xvi.

23 Sayer, *Capitalism and Modernity*, 12.

24 Ibid.

25 Bryan S. Turner, *Max Weber: From History to Modernity* (London: Routledge, 1992).

26 See Ray, figure 1.1, "Society as a multidimensional concept," in *Theorizing Classical Sociology*, 8.

27 Swingewood, *A Short History of Sociological Thought*, x.

28 See, for example, A. Huyssen, "Mapping the Post-modern," *New German Critique* 33 (1984): 5–52; and Harvey, *The Condition of Postmodernity.*

29 Bryan. S. Turner, *Classical Sociology* (London: Sage, 1999).

30 B. Jessop, *From the Keynesian Welfare to the Schumpeterian Workfare State*, University of Lancaster Regionalism Group Working Paper 45 (1992); Klein, *The Shock Doctrine.*

31 Giddens, *Capitalism and Modern Social Theory.*

32 See Hertz, *The Silent Takeover: Global Capitalism and the Death of Democracy* (London: Arrow, 2002); Joel Bakan, *The Corporation* (Toronto: Penguin, 2004); Klein, *The Shock Doctrine.*

33 Hobsbawm, *Age of Extremes 1914–1991* (London: Abacus, 1995).

34 M. Castells, "Information Technology and Global Capitalism," in *On the Edge: Living with Global Capitalism*, eds. W. Hutton and A. Giddens (London: Cape, 2000), 52–74).

35 P. McMichael, *Development and Social Change: A Global Perspective*, 2nd ed. (London: Sage, 2000), quoted in Leslie Sklair, *Globalization: Capitalism and Its Alternatives*, 3rd ed. (Oxford: Oxford University Press, 2002), 46.

36 Brian Milner, "A Safe Haven? Not All Emerging Markets Qualify," *The Globe and Mail* (April 12, 2008) B1.

37 See, for example, Z. Bauman, *Intimations of Postmodernity* (London: Routledge, 1992); A. Giddens, *The Consequences of Modernity* (Cambridge: Polity Press, 1990); J. Habermas, "Modernity versus Postmodernity," *New German Critique* 22 (1981); G. McLennan, "The Enlightenment Project Revisted," in *Modernity and Its Futures*, eds. S. Hall, D. Held, and T. McGrew (Cambridge: Polity Press, 1992).

38 Ian Macintosh, ed., *Classical Sociological Theory: A Reader* (Edinburgh: Edinburgh University Press, 1997).

39 A. Sayer, "Valuing Culture and Economy," in *Culture and Economy After the Cultural Turn*, eds. L. Ray and A. Sayer (London: Sage, 1999).

40 Rosemarie Putnam Tong, *Feminist Thought* (Boulder, CO: Westview Press, 1998).

41 Ayaan Hirsi Ali, *Infidel* (New York: Free Press, 2007), 295, states that Wollstonecraft's *A Vindication of the Rights of Women* inspired her.

42 See review of *The Pickton File*, Stevie Cameron (Toronto: Knopf, 2007) by Elliott Leyton, *The Globe and Mail* (June 16, 2007).

43 See Callinicos, *Social Theory.*

1. Modernity and Social Theory

> Manchester streets may be irregular ... its smoke may be dense... but not any or all of these things can prevent the image of a great city rising before us as the very symbol of civilization, foremost in the march of improvement, a grand incarnation of progress.
>
> —*Chamber's Edinburgh Journal* (1858)

> The city is simultaneously the machinery and the hero of modernity.
>
> —M. de Certeau[1]

CLASSICAL SOCIAL THEORY developed as a response to the advent and the conditions of modernity in Western Europe, which created unprecedented chaotic change and social upheaval. This great transformation from ancient times occurred over a period of about 135 years between 1776, when Adam Smith published his *Wealth of Nations* and Louis XVI still ruled France, and 1914, when Max Weber published his *Spirit of Capitalism Economy and Society* and Georg Simmel completed his work on *The Metropolis* and *The Philosophy of Money*. The historical antecedents of classical social theory can be found in what historian Eric Hobsbawm has called the dual revolution: the British Industrial Revolution (1780–1830) and the French Revolution (1789). This dual Anglo-French revolution cannot be understood without examining conditions many decades before 1780, but such analysis is well beyond the limits of this chapter. As ideas and theories about the great transformation developed, a transformation of vocabulary occurred: words took on new meanings or new words were formed to explain the historical changes. For example, the development of vocabulary is evident in the use of the word *social*. In the late seventeenth century it could mean either "associated" or "sociable" or be a synonym for "civil," as in social war. By the early nineteenth century there had been a decisive transition of *social* towards its most general and abstract sense: as in "man is a social creature." The word *sociology* was first used by Auguste Comte in 1830 and first appeared in English in 1843.[2] To appreciate the profound implications of the dual revolution for sociology, consider some of the dominant words that gained their modern meanings during that period: *factory*, *division of labour*, *proletariat*, *working class*, *capitalism*, *alienation*, *anomie,* and *ideology*. The development of vocabulary reflected an intellectual engagement in the debate about the nature of modernity.

Before retracing the economic and social transformation of Western Europe, we need to highlight some challenges this task presents. Studying social change from a historical perspective, and the use of the word *revolution* in particular, is problematic for a number of reasons. First, such an exercise involves a compression of time periods and a compression of different modes of social organization. The dialectic between past and present means we need to avoid presenting the emergence of new social forms as a coherent, orderly, and inevitable process of change. For example, someone looking back from the vantage point of the early twenty-first century might find it reasonable to talk of the emergence of the factory system. However, as others have pointed out, this development took place sporadically. Many features of paid work in premodernity survived well into the modern era. When compressing the specific into general historical trends, we have to avoid attaching a coherent pattern to these changes that are spurious.[3] The second problem is how to separate the empirical developments from the theoretical perspectives within which these developments are organized and located.[4] History is about interpretation, and much of what follows represents one synthesized account of historical events. How historians assemble and interpret a chosen sample of facts will depend mainly on what methods are chosen, how the data are analyzed, and by the kinds of facts he or she wants: "By and large, the historian will get the kind of facts he [sic] wants."[5] Each of the classical theorists selected and gave prominence to the empirical developments that they found most significant.

In this book we give prominence to the immense social changes that occurred primarily in Western Europe, or more precisely, in Britain, France, and Germany. This is not because the neglected histories of other countries are less interesting or less important, or for reasons of space, but because Marx, Durkheim, and Weber witnessed first-hand the maelstrom of chaotic social change, marked by industrialization and urbanization. In Britain, for example, by 1867, when Marx wrote *Capital, Volume I*, the factory system was well established and the majority of Britons lived in cities. And in Germany and France, by 1914, Max Weber, Emile Durkheim, and Georg Simmel could observe for themselves the triumph of industrial capitalism and the social effects of urbanization. This chapter aims to provide a general historical synthesis, to make sense of the social transformation of Western Europe—insofar as it's reasonable to do so in one chapter—in order to understand how and why European modernity influenced the classical sociological thinkers that we have chosen to study. Our treatment examines the social processes of industrialization, urbanization, and democratization in Britain, France, and Germany between 1780 and 1914.

The factory was a technological and social transformation of paid work, increasing labour productivity but imposing a routine and discipline quite unlike pre-industrial rhythms of work.

Industrialization

From 1780 traditional work rhythms and practices of pre-industrial society gave way to an industrial society and a new modus operandi of producing goods. We can define the Industrial Revolution as a fundamental change in the structure of the economy in which the capitalists' pursuit and accumulation of profit guided the mode of organizing work, harnessing technology, and determining the social relations of work. Britain was the classic theatre for the transformation of a pre-industrial agrarian economy into an industrialized and urban society. The British Industrial Revolution occurred roughly between 1780 and 1830.[6] In France the contours of a modern industrial society developed much later, between 1875 and 1914. Germany in 1790 was still essentially a collection of states sharing a common language, and seventeen million of her population of twenty-three million was engaged in agricultural rather than industrial activity. The German "destitution" was evident when compared with England, whose industrial sector economy was already well established, and even when compared to France, whose economy was transforming from agriculture to manufacture. Between 1800 and 1848 Germany's industrial production was rapidly expanding but still small compared to England and France. Typical of this expansion was the tripling of metallurgical output, the 50 per cent increase in the output of the coalmines between 1800 and 1830, and the construction of 2,500 kilometres of railways tracks between 1835 and 1847. The development of steam-machine production in Germany was still fifty years behind England in 1831. Some German states did industrialize faster than others. In Rhineland-Westphalia, for example, the province where Karl Marx was born, the Prefect of the Ruhr could plausibly claim that it was the most industrial region in Europe.[7] In the late 1840s the effect of industrialization in Britain, the effect of the French occupation of the Rhineland, and state support acted as the catalyst for social transformation in Germany. The unification of the country by force under Prussian leadership and an atmosphere of exacerbated nationalism gave German industrial capitalism its special character. Large-scale expansion of industry occurred in Germany between 1850 and 1900.[8] It would be monotonous to quote data on rates of economic growth; suffice to say that, whereas before 1800 virtually the only quantities measured in millions were populations, by 1890 the quantities of iron, steel, and manufactured goods produced in Britain, France, and Germany were measured in such magnitudes. By 1890 Western Europe was the region of advanced capitalism par excellence.

The common features of industrial capitalism are found principally in the economic forces that produce it. First, industrialization involved a more productive use of the factors of production—land, labour, and machinery—partly obtained by introducing new methods of organization to production: the factory, a combination of power technology, specialized machines, and specialized occupations. Before each Industrial Revolution, most manufacturing operated on a small scale, employed labour-intensive methods, and used little fixed capital. The factory was the most striking outward symbol of the new industrial society. Second, industrialization involved a great increase in the productivity of human labour, in terms of output per head. The factory system provided greater degrees of coordinative and controlling power on the part of the capitalist factory owner. The significance of the concentration of workers lay in the potential for increasing labour productivity by extending the division of labour, installing machines, regulating the flow of raw materials, and moulding workers' behaviour in the workplace. The factory offered the opportunity to increase production by innovation: "The very division of labour ... prepared the ground from which mechanical invention could eventually spring."[9] Third, industrialization required the existence of a reserve army of free labour, the people able and willing to work for wages because they had no other adequate means of support. As we shall explain, the effects of agricultural reforms and population growth created a large pool of cheap labour as people migrated to the new industrial towns.

The role of technology within the factory system has been long debated. In *Capital, Volume I*, Karl Marx's analysis of the industrial division of labour emphasizes how the process enabled the capitalist to control work processes in ways that were not possible with the traditional domestic, or the putting-out, system. Pre-industrial methods made it difficult for entrepreneurs to monitor and control the quantity and quality of the work performed by cottage-based workers because "the domestic weaver or craftsman was master of his time, starting and stopping when he [sic] desired."[10] The factory system provided new opportunities for controlling the pace and quality of work by means of the "discipline of mechanization"—the actual speed of the machine—and the hierarchy of direct supervisory control over the work process. Another aspect of the factory system was the need for workers to comply with a new rhythm of work. Factory owners demanded a new mentality towards work, one favourable to the exorable demands of factory rationality. Workers were taught the values of punctuality, obedience, and self-discipline. As noted by social historians, however, the process took several generations: "by fines; bells and clocks; money incentives; preaching and schooling; the suppression of fairs and sports—new labour habits were formed, and a new time-discipline was imposed."[11] For Marx, as we will explain, the industrial division of labour and its concomitant capitalist relations of production are the prime movers of conflict and social change.

Economic historians have long debated the role of the state in the transition from early modern, to modern, capitalist society. The modern state, which Marx famously summarizes in the *Communist Manifesto* as "a committee for managing the common affairs of the whole bourgeoisie,"[12] comprises the parliament, the judiciary, and civil service officials, whose authority is backed by the capacity to use the police and the military to implement its policies. The development of European capitalism depended on a new state apparatus to provide a broadly similar socio-economic environment: free markets, a structure of business laws and regulations, fiscal and currency control, a trained workforce and, if necessary, defence of commercial interests. In Britain the old Corn Laws, with which the agrarian interests sought to protect farming, were abolished in 1846. To create the most favourable conditions for industrial capital, the fixing of minimum wages was abolished, and the new Poor Law of 1834 became less generous. Its aim was to make payments to the destitute as cheap as possible, to encourage labour mobility, and to act as a social deterrent against the slothful. A precondition of the new industrial paradigm was a large supply of unregulated labour. This meant that the working classes had to abandon their traditional way of life and were compelled to enter the new occupations. Recognizing that a reservoir of free labour is a prerequisite for modern capitalism, Weber writes, "Persons must be present who are not only legally in a position, but are also economically compelled, to sell their labour on the market without restriction ... The development of capitalism is impossible, if such a propertyless stratum is absent, a class compelled to sell its labour services to live; and it is likewise impossible if only unfree labour is at hand. Rational capitalistic calculation is possible only on the basis of free labour; only where ... under the compulsion of the whip of hunger, offer themselves."[13] The British government established a system of mass elementary education in 1870 and state secondary education in 1902. The state is also of crucial importance in the workings of capitalism, not only as a major customer of private enterprise (war ships, armaments, etc.) but also, in the case of Britain in the nineteenth century and the United States in the twenty-first, in its readiness to protect business interests with military force. The triumph of British capitalism was achieved, as Eric Hobsbawm notes, "very largely because of the unswerving readiness of British governments to back their businessmen [sic] by ruthless and aggressive economic discrimination and open war against all possible rivals."[14] In Western Europe, state intervention supported the birth and growth of capitalism to the extent that it eventually became impossible not to be unaffected by the state's power and interventions in every aspect of modern life.[15]

Some of the classical social thinkers actually witnessed a double transformation in the structure and modus operandi of industrial capitalism.[16] On the one hand, by 1890 there was the concentration of capital, the emergence of big business and monopolies, and the control or dominance of a market by a single manufacturer or provider. On the other hand, there was the systematic attempt to rationalize production and manage business enterprises by applying scientific methods. The American Frederick W. Taylor (1856–1915) pioneered the so-called scientific management approach to industrial work; hence, the term *Taylorism* represents both a set of management practices and a system of ideological assumptions.[17] Taylor believed that workers were too stupid to develop the most efficient way of performing a task—the one best way. The role of management was to scientifically analyze all the tasks to be undertaken in order to eliminate waste. The centrepiece of Taylorism is the separation of tasks into their simplest constituent elements: the "routinization of work," and the transferring all decision-making functions to managers. In North America Henry Ford applied the major principles of Taylorism in his car plant but also added an important innovation, the assembly line. The assembly line intensified work through ever-greater job fragmentation and short task-cycle times. In 1922 Ford described his approach to managing workers: "The idea is that man ... must have every second necessary but not a single unnecessary second."[18] By measuring tasks managers gained even more control over the workers' performance. This form of work organization is called *Fordism*. A caustic satire on Fordism is presented in Charlie Chaplin's film *Modern Times*. The inherent problems associated with Taylorism and Fordism—alienation and industrial strikes—became a rich source of sociological inquiry in the twentieth century.

We have already noted that the canonical writers were, by and large, oblivious to the issue of gender. In Western Europe early industrial capitalism absorbed huge numbers of working-class women into the new factories, and this had a rapid effect on public attitudes towards gender roles and patterns of family life. As historians Annette Timm and Joshua Sanborn point out, European industrialization changed not only how people earned money and how they worked but also how they related to others socially and sexually.[19] Gender-based patterns of work and gender inequality were soon omnipresent in European capitalism. The factory owner's need for cheap labour provided new opportunities for working-class women to do paid work. In the later period of industrialization, the 1880s, large-scale food processing factories and bakeries were female dominated. Emerging stereotypes reinforced the belief that work and family life were two separate spheres: "images that depicted men as naturally suited to the highly competitive nineteen-century workplace and women as too delicate for the world of commerce."[20]

Did industrial capitalism segregate home from work and allocate women to the former and men to the latter? Space doesn't allow us to address this question fully, but the evidence suggests that gender-based patterns of work predate modernity: they are socially constructed and not the result of capitalist-induced social change.[21] Work tended to be labelled female or male on the basis of socially changeable expectations of how to view, judge, and treat the two sexes. Enduring patterns of gender inequality at work can be partially explained by the activities of trade unions. According to one union leader, the object of a trade union is "to bring about a condition ... where wives and daughters would be in their proper sphere at home, instead of being dragged into competition for livelihood against the great and strong men of the world."[22] Historian Stephanie Coontz argues that whenever women undertake paid work in large numbers, certain social processes unfold.[23] Women begin to challenge laws and customs that regulate their subordination in the public sphere and within the family. Many working-class women became early supporters and activists in the trade unions and in the women's rights movement. Working women also begin to marry later and have fewer children, especially when they have access to education and attain higher paying careers. The issue of gender roles and inequality at work remains a complex one, but there is no doubt that traditional assumptions about the family economy were undermined by the emergence of the notion of the "breadwinner's wage."[24] Consequently, throughout the nineteenth and well into the twentieth century, large numbers of working-class and middle-class women were effectively excluded from participating in many trade and professional occupations, while men succeeded by using patriarchal strategies to conceptualize and defend *skill* and *profession* as male property.[25]

Urbanization

The most obvious symbol of the new industrial society was not only the factory but also its inescapable attendant urbanization. Industrialization required housing for the new urban working class, transportation services, and financial institutions. At the heart of the question about the social effects of industrialization is the disjuncture between pre-industrial and industrial labour. Factory labour imposed a regularity and monotony quite unlike pre-industrial rhythms of work, and labour increasingly took place in cities, which prevented any means of supplementing family income, for example, by growing food. The new manufacturing towns grew exponentially. In Britain in 1750 there were only two cities with more than 50,000 inhabitants: London and Edinburgh. In 1851 there were twenty-nine, including nine cities with over 100,000. In 1831 the industrial city of Manchester had 238,000 inhabitants; Leeds had 123,000; Liverpool, 202,000; and Glasgow, 193,000. The growth of industrial cities was caused both by the general growth of population and the uprooting of people from the rural areas. Census returns show the extent of the migration. In 1851 less than 50 per cent of inhabitants of Manchester, Liverpool, and Glasgow had been born in these cities. London increased from 2.5 million in 1851 to 3.9 million in 1881; Paris from one million in 1849 to 1.9 million in 1875; and Berlin increased from 378,000 in 1848 to 1.6 million in 1888. With the rapid growth of cities came the most appalling standards of urban squalor known in nineteenth-century Britain. Urban conditions have to be related to their context before they can be evaluated. Public services—clean water supply, sanitation, street cleaning, and public spaces—were non-existent or of very poor standard before industrialization began. Comparisons must begin from here, not from twenty-first-century standards. Traditional living practices that were appropriate to the conventions and conditions of a pre-industrial society became carried into the new context, where the sheer numbers of people and the speed of urban development brutalized and degraded the older practices, which then appeared even more brutal and appalling in the new urban environment. Cities grew rapidly in a laissez-faire atmosphere that was without planning and the most basic public services, not to mention affordable housing. Air pollution and water pollution caused mass epidemics of contagious disease, notably cholera and typhoid, which swept through nineteenth-century European cities. Each industrial city had extensive working-class enclaves, which created the European division of the "good" west end and a "poor" east end of large cities. The pressure of profit-making shaped the living conditions of the urban working class, as developers and builders constructed railways into the city centres, preferably through the urban slums where the real estate costs were low. Most working-class people rented accommodation in high-density tenement houses, typically consisting of one and two rooms only. For the city's powerful social elite, the working-class enclaves were public health hazards. It was only after 1850, when epidemics spread from the slums and began to kill the rich also, and after mass agitation, that systematic urban planning and rebuilding was undertaken.

This 1872 engraving by Gustave Doré shows a typical industrial district of London with back-to-back townhouses built alongside factories. The majority of working people had to live in these squalid conditions. The city caused traditional patterns of human social relationships to change, as did the relationship between the individual and society.

Reflective contemporaries did not deny that the new cities were cauldrons of appalling squalor and misery. In Britain successive Royal Commissions, contemporary literature, and individual studies provided empirical evidence of working-class conditions. In 1835 the French liberal de Tocqueville wrote of Manchester, "From this foul drain the greatest stream of human industry flows out to fertilize the whole world. From this filthy sewer pure gold flows. Here humanity attains its most complete development and its most brutish, here civilization works its miracles and civilized man is turned almost into a savage."[26] In Friedrich Engels's classic study of urban conditions, *The Conditions of the Working Class in England*, published in 1845 in German, is a scathing account of filth and squalor of working-class housing: "Every great city has one or more slums, where the working class is crowded together ... The houses are occupied from cellar to garret, filthy within and without, and their appearance is such that no human being could possibly wish to live in them."[27] Describing the area of Manchester southwest of the city centre and known as "Little Ireland," Engels writes:

> Masses of refuse, offal and sickening filth lie among standing pools in all directions; the atmosphere is poisoned by the effluvia from these, and laden and darkened by the smoke of a dozen tall factory chimneys. A horde of ragged women and children swarm about here, as filthy as the swine that thrive upon the garbage heaps and in the puddles. In short, the whole rookery furnishes such a hateful and repulsive spectacle as can hardly be equalled in the worst court on the Irk. The race that lives in these ruinous cottages ... must really have reached the lowest stage of humanity.[28]

However, the industrial city, hailed as enterprising by bourgeois contemporaries, was not only more populous than pre-industrial settlements; the increasing atomization of peoples and the migration of large masses unanchored from stable social groups fundamentally changed the social structure. Not only did the new urban working class live in squalid urban enclaves but also their only relationship with their bourgeois employers was as a *cash-nexus*. And the social distance between the urban rich and poor classes widened. Writing about Manchester, which was viewed by some contemporaries as the very symbol of civilization and of the new age,[29] a clergyman in the 1840s exemplified this new sensibility: "There is no town in the world where the distance between the rich and poor is so great, or the barrier between them so difficult to cross ... There is far less personal communication between the master cotton spinner and his workmen ... than between the Duke of Wellington and the humblest labourer on his estate."[30] The city was not merely emblematic of the labouring classes' exclusion from human society; for them it was a social catastrophe. As a corollary to this, distinctive patterns of social norms and behaviour that characterize a modern industrial society became firmly established in industrialized Western Europe, particularly in Britain as early as the 1850s. This fast-paced urban life based on economic rationality, individualism, and a secular world view gave people a strong sense that they were living in a new age of constant change. As most introductory sociology texts explain, this experience provoked much contemporary discussion on the distinction between traditional and modern societies, a discourse formalized in the celebrated work of the nineteenth-century German sociologist Ferdinand Tönnies, who distinguished the foundations of rural and small-town community life—

what he called *Gemeinschaft*—from the foundations of large-city life, which he called *Gesellschaft.*

The clash between the pervasive influence of religion and the moral economy of the past and the principle of self-interest and rationality of the present was particularly apparent in the realm of social behaviour and welfare. The spending habits appropriate to rural life increased social problems when translated into the new high-density urban environment. In the city, the wage is the industrial family's *sole* protection against starvation and destitution, dependent as this is on the vicissitudes of the market. In contrast, although poverty among agricultural labourers was common, money did not usually have such unique importance for agricultural families that had the opportunity to supplement their income by growing food. In urban centres, when higher wages were fed into traditional spending habits, greater social problems resulted.[31] A companion of laissez-faire industrialization and urbanization therefore exacerbated existing problems of alcoholism, infanticide, crime, prostitution, and suicide.[32]

The urban bourgeoisie, supported by the maxims of liberal economics and utilitarian philosophy, believed that the rational man must make provision for accident, illness, and old age. The social mechanism of the new society was in the profoundest manner inhuman and inequitable, and it left an indelible mark on the emerging discipline of sociology. As the Marxist historian Eric Hobsbawm convincingly explains, the British Poor Law Act of 1834, which made all welfare *less* than the lowest wage offered in the market, forcibly separated husband, wives, and children into institutionalized workhouses in order to punish the poor for being destitute. Yet the gap between the rich and poor classes grew wider and "the poor suffered because the rich benefited."[33] In France and Germany despotic employers with a strong Catholic and paternalist tradition did, at least, partly offset the inherently insecure factory employment by providing education and welfare. The social relations of Britain's new industrial cities determined the pattern of social movements, as we shall soon discuss. As early as 1819, the year of the "massacre of Peterloo," *The Times* of London reported of the discontented Manchester working classes: "Their wretchedness seems to madden them against the rich, who they dangerously imagine engross the fruits of their labour without having any sympathy for their wants."[34] The development of classical social theory is inextricably tied to this debate about the social effects of urbanization.

Democratization

European industrial capitalism developed predominantly under the influence of the British Industrial Revolution; however, the French Revolution shaped its ideologies and greatly influenced the processes of democratization.[35] Democracy is a complex word derived from the Greek word *demokratia*: *demo* means "people," and *kratos* means "rule." In mid-seventeenth century England, the Leveller movement represented the aspirations of the working poor and campaigned for land reform, democracy, and equality.[36] By the 1790s democracy was understood as uncontrolled popular power. In 1790 Edmund Burke expressed the orthodox contemporary view that "a perfect democracy was the most shameful thing in the world."[37] Democracy was still considered a revolutionary term even in the 1850s. Only when it became defined in terms of the liberal tradition of open elections of representatives did it gain wide acceptance. It was the Enlightenment faith in reason and human progress that provided so powerful an impetus to the French radicals, and later the French Revolution helped spur the process of democratization. On July 14th, 1789, the Bastille, a state prison symbolizing the absolute authority of King Louis XVI, was captured, and by August the revolution had acquired its manifesto, the Declaration of the Rights of Man and Citizen. The French Revolution rather than the earlier American Revolution of 1776 inspired radical reform across Europe and ancient civilizations. It was "the first great movement of ideas in Western Christendom that had any real effect on the world of Islam."[38] Revolutions in nineteenth-century Europe were caused largely by the struggle both for and against the principles of 1789; this struggle was surpassed only by the immeasurably more radical ideology of the Bolshevik Revolution of 1917.

In his seminal book, *The Age of Revolution, 1789–1848*, historian Eric Hobsbawm gives what seems to be a convincing explanation of the origins of the French Revolution. He argues that it emerged because of the conflict between the absolute monarchy of Louis XVI and the rising new social forces represented by the middle classes. The bourgeoisie wanted to build a new society according to the maxims of reason and liberal economics. The ideology of the French Revolution, found in the famous Declaration of the Rights of Man and Citizen, is, in essence, a manifesto against the old hierarchical society of aristocratic privilege: "men are born and live free and equal under the laws" and "all citizens have a right to cooperate in the formation of the law."[39] In Hobsbawm's view these ideals are rooted in classical liberalism as formulated by such philosophers as Charles Montesquieu and Jean Jacques Rousseau and by liberal economists such as Adam Smith.[40] The leaders of classical liberalism believed in constitutionalism, an enlightened monarchy and a secular state with civil liberties, guarantees for private enterprise, and a government representing taxpayers and property-owners. Although the Revolution's manifesto opposed the aristocratic hierarchy, it was not supportive of a democratic society: no property-owners were disenfranchised, but women were. Major reforms occurred between 1789 and 1791. In the countryside, common land was enclosed, rural and small-town entrepreneurship was encouraged, the old guild system was abolished, and trade unions were banned. A second revolution of 1792, the Jacobin Revolution, led to the first People's Republic and inspired the dream of "equality, liberty, and fraternity." It led to the overthrow of the monarchy, to wars and to the rise to power of Napoleon Bonaparte (1769–1821). Napoleon Bonaparte brought stability to France and, during his reign, introduced a Civil Code and the most striking symbol of middle class stability, a National Bank.

From 1792 until 1850 Europe experienced almost continual war and three waves of revolution. The first wave occurred in 1820–24, which saw uprisings in Spain and Italy (1820) and Greece (1821). The second wave occurred in 1829–34 and 1837–42 and was confined to Western Europe, with uprisings in Britain, Belgium, Germany, Italy, and Poland. A third wave of revolution broke out in April 1848, shortly after the publication of Marx and Engels's *Communist Manifesto* in France, Germany, and Italy. In London a mass demonstration marched to Parliament to demand universal male suffrage. Though arguably the French Revolution inspired all these uprisings, post-1815 revolutions occurred because the political and social institutions were profoundly inadequate for the modern era. Throughout the second half of the nineteenth century, the state and the power-holders of finance and the big industrialists in Britain, France, and Germany were anxious to prevent revolution on the French Jacobin model. In Germany the desires of the commercial bourgeoisie—the real beneficiaries of industrialization—were an impetus for democratic processes and gave strength to the various currents of liberal thought. The more conservative German liberals rejected, equally, the idea that sovereignty resided in the monarch and the idea that it resided in the people. For some German liberals, the liberalism of England was more of a model than that of France. Radical ideas were confined to groups of German intellectuals, of which the most prominent was that of the Young Hegelians.[41] It was not until the 1880s that political oligarchs were seriously challenged by the agitations of the labour movement of trade unions and working-class political parties.

The French Revolution and industrial capitalism gave rise to another phenomenon of modernity: nationalism. In the literature of the politics of nationalism, the concept of national identity is often treated as the outcome of capitalist expansion, a development resulting from the pressure of industrial society to produce a large, centrally educated, culturally homogeneous population.[42] Nationalism helped create the notion that people share a collective history and destiny, expressed in the formulation by social elites of shared values and common narratives on the national past and national interest. In the new industrial age nationalism was a powerful social force in giving the people in advanced capitalist countries a strong sense of culture and social identity. The social experience of those most affected by industrial capitalism was moderated by the "imagined community" of the nation-state. Each nationalist movement tended to justify its principal concern with its own nation. Following the French Revolution and the three waves of revolution in Europe, nation-building and mass nationalism became an important feature of European politics.

Mass nationalism was pivotal to capitalist growth.[43] As the British, French, and German economies expanded, nationalism helped give rise to colonialism. In simple terms, *colonialism* refers to the economic, political, social, and cultural domination of an indigenous people by an outside foreign power. The long reign of the British Empire over parts of Africa, India, and Canada is an example of colonialism. The same can be said of German rule over parts of East and West Africa, and French rule over parts of North Africa. The alleged superiority of the advanced European nations, governed by superior moral and religious beliefs and the rule of law, and composed of literate citizens and inventors of superior technology, helped justify colonial expansion in those territories deemed to be lawless, illiterate, and inferior. The relationship between capitalist development and colonialism is complex. But in Hobsbawm's view, "it is undeniable that the pressure of capital in search of more profitable investment ... contributed to policies of expansion—including colonial conquest."[44] In Western Europe the confluence of economic and political forces created the conditions out of which the tensions and the First World War (1914–18) arose. The German industrialists wanted access to international markets for their increasing productive capacity, which only an expansionist foreign policy and colonialism could give. An expansionist foreign policy brought the demand for building a German navy. The economic development of Germany cannot be separated from the politics of colonialism and nationalism.[45] Ideas of colonial backwardness, and inferiority with Europe were buttressed by social science. Economists justified colonial expansion through theories of economic growth predicated on the international division of labour, and second-order Darwinism spuriously accounted for the division of races into advanced and backward.

England was not only the birthplace of industrial capitalism but also the cradle of new mass social movements. Disenchantment with the excesses of laissez-faire capitalism gave rise to the Chartist Movement, trade unions, and working-class political parties. The fundamental demand of Chartism was political reform, principally universal male suffrage. Universal female suffrage was never asked for, or conceded. In explaining the rise of the working-class Chartist Movement in the 1830s, Gammage wrote in 1854, “It is the existence of great wrongs which principally teaches the masses the value of political rights.”[46] A social movement is a sustained, organized challenge to existing authorities in the name of a deprived, wronged, and disenfranchised population.[47] For centuries before 1790, popular uprisings of one kind or another had challenged local employers and power-holders. But between the 1780s and the 1830s, a great transformation in the form and organizational base of British workers' collective action began: “British workers nationalized, developed a strong orientation to Parliament, and interacted increasingly with issues outside the workplace.”[48] Mass popular politics gave voice to ordinary people on a wide range of social issues and took several forms: mass national demonstrations, petitions, public statements, the lobbying of members of Parliament. These political repertoires greatly increased as a means by which members of the middle class and working class made collective claims on the ruling class. Participants and observers alike recognized the maturity of the sporadic surges of political militancy: a transition from relatively parochial to national popular politics. Marx and Engels's *Communist Manifesto* best captures the significance of this new political phenomenon: “All previous historical movements were movements of minorities, or in the interest of minorities. The proletarian movement is the self-conscious, independent movement of the immense majority, in the interests of the immense majority.”[49]

The British Industrial Revolution and the French Revolution and the Napoleonic wars profoundly changed the relative political power of the social classes. As industrial capitalism expanded, the ascendancy of the middle classes became manifest, as did the downward tendency of the aristocracy. War-driven taxation and debt increased Parliament's power and compelled the aristocracy to make concessions: To wage a war against the French Republics and to save themselves from an otherwise inevitable fate, it's argued, the British aristocracy “threw themselves into the arms of the monied class.”[50] The French Revolution gave both the middle class and the urban working classes confidence. The Reform Act of 1832, which enfranchised the British middle strata, was the Charter of the bourgeoisie. It was the first example in Europe of an *ancien régime* acquiescing peacefully to the forces of constitutional democracy.[51] For working-class reformers, the Reform Act was merely the beginning. After campaigning alongside the bourgeoisie to achieve their own political emancipation, they believed that the middle class would campaign in and outside Parliament for the extension of reform to include at least all adult males in the franchise. The fact that the new enfranchised bourgeoisie did not champion working-class rights became known as the great betrayal.

In the 1830s and 40s the growing disaffection of the poor was universal in Europe. In Britain, following the 1832 betrayal, the Chartists under the *People's Charter* united the working classes around six points of political reform: universal male suffrage, the secret ballot, payment of members of Parliament, the abolition of property qualifications for MPs, equal electoral districts, and annual parliaments. The Chartist Movement was the first national working-class movement in the world, but it was not a revolutionary movement. The movement demanded inclusion into the political system, not its abolition. It reached its peak during 1839–42, but its program of reforms gradually passed into the acts of 1867, 1884, and 1918. As late as 1880 Britain's Queen Victoria opposed political reform. She declared with emphasis that she "*cannot* and will not be Queen of a *democratic monarchy*.[52] In 1884 the newly formed Social Democratic Federation (SDF) attempted to win the working-class masses to socialism. In 1900, almost unnoticed amid the jingoism surrounding the South African War, the SDF joined the Labour Representation Committee. By 1914 an independent Labour Party, backed by trade unions and inspired by socialist ideology, was firmly established in Britain. Men and women reformers had long sought women's political emancipation, but it was only in 1918 that the first woman gained the right to vote and sit in the British House of Commons. In France and Germany the survival and prosperity of substantial sections of the peasantry retarded the development of working-class political movements, similarly to the British experience. In the first half of the nineteenth century, French and German intellectual elites and reformers were the followers of Saint-Simon and French utopian socialism, and they were not interested in organizing mass political agitation.[53]

From the eighteenth to the early twentieth century, conflict and collective action was further transformed as working-class activity progressed from machine breaking—commonly referred to as Luddism—to unionism. Trade unions have a history that goes back beyond the Industrial Revolution, but most unions were local and specialized. Until 1824 workers had no legal rights to organize unions to improve their working conditions. In the aftermath of the "great betrayal" there was an upsurge of trade unionism in Britain. In 1833 the Grand National Consolidated

Trade Union (GNCTU) was formed. The British government crushed the GNCTU when it sentenced six agricultural workers to seven years deportation to Australia—the Tolpuddle Martyrs. Examples of workers' resistance to employer control are legion. However, reflecting their more privileged position, it was skilled male workers—the "aristocracy of labour"—that created the first effective new model unions. In 1851 the Amalgamated Society of Engineers (ASE) had a membership of almost 12,000, large enough to compel employers to negotiate improvements to their working conditions. The leadership—the Junta—of these new unions were not the new factory wage labourers but skilled engineers, carpenters, iron founders, and printers. The most active and politically conscious of the leadership led the campaign for the legal recognition of unions in 1871 and 1875.[54]

By 1880 British trade unions had acquired a legal status and privileges so extensive that militant employers, conservative governments, and judges did not succeed in reducing or abolishing them until 1980.[55] The years following the 1880s saw a significant growth of trade unionism, both in numbers and character. General unions attempted to organize all workers, skilled and unskilled, and developed the general strike as a weapon of the working class. This new unionism represented an ideological and political "sharp turn to the left."[56] In Britain the novel phenomenon of *industrial unionism*, the organizing of all workers in a single industry with nation-wide strikes, appeared for the first time in the 1890s.[57] Elsewhere the situation was rather different. In France unionism might in theory be national, but in practice it was extremely localized. The French national trade union federation (CGT) required only a minimum of three local unions to constitute a national union. In Germany the strength of its Free Trade Unions was not to be found in the heavy industries of Rhineland and Ruhr. In France and Germany a wave of labour unrest and strikes did occur during 1868–71, which certainly frightened employers and governments. After 1870 the paternalistic attitude of the German employers was inspired by fear of socialism.[58] The raison d'être of trade unionism was, as it remains today, to secure through collective negotiation better terms for the sale of labour power. Exclusionary practices against working-class women persisted, however, and unionism largely remained the preserve of male workers throughout the nineteenth century.

Conclusion

The dynamic social changes occurring between 1780 and 1914 provided the context of the classical assemblage we have chosen to study. The works of Marx, Durkheim, Weber, and Simmel are inextricably bound up with the conditions of modernity. As we have attempted to capture, compared to the eighteenth century, Europe in 1914 was a qualitatively different Europe after experiencing colossal technological and social transformation in at least three respects.

First, economies were no longer predominantly agriculture-based. The large-scale industrial production symbolized by the factory and pioneered by Britain had migrated to the mainland of Europe and elsewhere, most notably to North America. In 1848 Britain was the superpower and the "workshop of the world," but the superpowers of 1914 included France, Germany, and the United States. Large-scale industrial production was a technological and social transformation of paid work, which increased labour productivity but imposed a routine and discipline quite unlike pre-industrial rhythms of work. Paradoxically, the period between 1780 and 1914, whose claim to have benefited humanity rests on the enormous triumphs of an industrial capitalism based on natural science and technology, ended with the new technology of mass-produced machine guns, artillery, armoured warships, and munitions slaughtering millions in the trench warfare of 1914–18. The second dynamic transformation, and in some ways more significant, was the unprecedented development of cities where wage labour increasingly took place. With urbanization, traditional social norms and patterns of human social relationships were abandoned, and this changed the relationship between the individual and society: society comprised unconnected individuals in the anarchy of competition pursuing only their own self-interest. Marx and Engels's description of the transformation of social structure is familiar: "The bourgeoisie ... has pitilessly torn asunder the motley feudal ties that bound man to his 'natural superiors' and has left remaining no other nexus between man and man than naked self-interest."[59] The third dynamic transformation was the process of democratization and the creation of mass national social movements that challenged despotism, the logic of capitalism, and inequality. Working-class emancipation and the institutions of working-class self-defence—the trade unions—had become firmly rooted by 1914.

These are some of the dynamic developments of humanity that Marx, Durkheim, Weber, Simmel, and the early feminist thinkers confronted. It was, simultaneously, a new world of perpetual collapse and renewal, extreme wealth and poverty, individual growth and alienation, liberal democracy and political exclusion, and contradiction and struggle. The classical theorists were preoccupied with trying to make sense of the *totalizing chaos* and with explaining the key characteristics of modernity as contrasted with premodern society. We will explore their works in future chapters, but before that we need to examine the intellectual forces that also shaped the theoretical thinking of the founders of sociology.

Notes

1 M. de Certeau, *The Practice of Everyday Life*, trans. Steven Rendall (Berkeley, CA: University of California Press, 1984), quoted in D. Harvey, *The Conditions of Postmodernity* (Oxford: Blackwell, 1994), 26.

2 Raymond Williams, *Keywords: A Vocabulary of Culture and Society* (New York: Oxford University Press, 1976), 291–6.

3 See C.R. Littler, *The Development of the Labour Process in Capitalist Societies* (London: Heineman, 1982); G. Salaman, *Class and the Corporation* (London: Routledge & Kegan Paul, 1981.

4 E.J. Hobsbawm, *On History* (London: Weidenfeld & Nicholson, 1997).

5 E. Carr, *What Is History* (London: Harmondsworth, 1961), 22–3; see also A. Marwick, *The Nature of History* (London: Macmillan Press, 1970).

6 Dividing social and economic history into periods can only be very approximate, and the date for the beginning of the Industrial Revolution is still a matter of dispute among historians.

7 For a short account of German economic, social, and political background of the period, see David McLellan, *Marx Before Marxism* (London: Harper and Row, 1971).

8 Tom Kemp, *Industrialization in Nineteenth Century Europe* (London: Longman, 1969).

9 M. Dobb, *Studies in the Development of Capitalism* (London: Routledge & Kegan Paul, 1963), 145.

10 D. Landes, *The Unbound Prometheus* (Cambridge: Cambridge University Press, 1969), 59.

11 Edward P. Thompson, "Time, Work-Discipline, and Industrial Capitalism," *Past and Present* 38 (1967), 90.

12 Robert Tucker, ed., *The Marx-Engels Reader* (New York: Norton, 1972), 475.

13 M. Weber, *General Economic History*, trans. F. Knight (1927; New York: Dover Publications, 2003), 277.

14 E.J. Hobsbawm, *Industry and Empire* (London: Weidenfeld and Nicolson, 1968), 196.

15 R. Miliband, *The State in Capitalist Society* (London: Weidenfeld and Nicolson, 1969).

16 E.J. Hobsbawm, *The Age of Empire 1875–1914* (London: Abacus, 1994).

17 C.R. Littler, "Internal Contract and the Transition to Modern Work Systems," in *The International Yearbook of Organizational Studies*, vol. 1, eds. D. Dunkerley and G. Salaman (London: Routledge & Kegan Paul, 1980), 51.

18 Quoted in H. Beynon, *Working for Ford* (Harmondsworth: Penguin, 1984), 33.

19 A. Timm and J. Sanborn, *Gender, Sex and the Shaping of Modern Europe* (Oxford: Berg Publishers, 2007), 55.

20 B. Reskin and I. Padavic, *Women and Men at Work* (Thousand Oaks, CA: Sage, 1994), 21, and quoted by M. Alvesson and Y. Due Billing, *Understanding Gender and Organizations* (Thousand Oaks, CA: Sage, 1997), 58.

21 See Alvesson and Billing, *Understanding Gender and Organizations*; M. Berg, "Women's Work, Mechanization and Early Industrialization," in *On Work*, ed. R.E. Pahl (Oxford: Blackwell, 1988); Jane Rendall, *Women in an Industrialized Society: England 1750–1880* (Oxford: Blackwell, 1990).

22 H.A. Turner, *Trade Union Growth, Structure and Policy: A Comparative Study of the Cotton Unions* (London: Allen & Unwin, 1962), 185, and quoted in K. Grint, *The Sociology of Work*, 2nd ed. (Cambridge: Polity Press, 1998), 72.

23 Stephanie Coontz, "Feminism Didn't Fail the Family," *The Globe and Mail* (August 25, 2008), A13.

24 Jane Rendall, *Women in an Industrializing Society*, 62.

25 D. Knights and H. Willmott, eds., *Gender and the Labour Process* (Aldershot: Gower, 1986).

26 Alex de Tocqueville, *Journeys to England and Ireland*, ed. J.P. Mayer (New Haven, CT: Yale University Press, 1958), 107–8, quoted in E.J. Hobsbawm, *The Age of Revolution 1789–1848* (London: Abacus, 1962), 44.

27 F. Engels, *The Conditions of the Working-Class in England* (Moscow: Progress Publishers, 1848), 66–7.

28 Ibid., 100.

29 See A. Briggs, "Manchester, Symbol of a New Age," chap. 3, in *Victorian Cities* (London: Pelican, 1968), 88–138.

30 Canon Parkinson, quoted in Briggs, *Victorian Cities*, 114.

31 Peter Mathias, *The First Industrial Nation* (London: Methuen, 1969), 208.

32 Hobsbawm, *The Age of Revolution*, 241–2.

33 Ibid., 247.

34 Briggs, *Victorian Cities*, 90.

35 Hobsbawm, *The Age of Revolution.*

36 C. Hill, *The Century of Revolution, 1603–1714* (London: Sphere Books, 1961).

37 Quoted in Williams, *Key Words*, 96.

38 B. Lewis, "The Impact of the French Revolution on Turkey," *Journal of World History* (1953): 105, quoted in Hobsbawm, *The Age of Revolution*, 76.

39 Hobsbawm, *The Age of Revolution*, 81.

40 See also Hill, *The Century of Revolution.*

41 See David McLellan, *Marx Before Marxism* (London: Harper and Row, 1971), 10–14.

42 E. Gellner, *Nations and Nationalism* (Oxford: Blackwell, 1983).

43 E.J. Hobsbawm, *The Age of Capital 1845–1875* (London: Abacus, 1977), 110–21.

44 E.J. Hobsbawm, *The Age of Empire 1875–1914* (London: Abacus, 1994), 45.

45 Tom Kemp, *Industrialization in Nineteenth Century Europe* (London: Longman, 1969), 117.

46 R.C. Gammage, *History of the Chartist Movement, 1837–1854* (London: Merlin Press, 1969).

47 See Charles Tilly, *Popular Contention in Great Britain, 1758–1834* (Boulder, CO: Paradigm Publishers, 2005), and Charles Tilly, *Social Movements, 1768–2004* (Boulder, CO: Paradigm Publishers, 2004).

48 C. Tilly, *Popular Contention in Great Britain*, xix.

49 Marx and Engels, *Communist Manifesto*, quoted in Tilly, *Social Movements*, 6.

50 Gammage, *History of the Chartist Movement*, 2.

51 Dorothy Thompson, "Chartism, Success or Failure?" in *People for the People*, ed. David Rubinstein (London: Ithaca Press, 1973, 90–97.

52 Henry Pelling, *The Origins of the Labour Party, 1880–1900* (Oxford: Clarendon Press, 1965), 1.

53 Hobsbawm, *The Age of Revolution*, 152.

54 For an extended account of early trade union history, see Peter Mathias, *The First Industrial Nation* (London: Methuen, 1969), and Henry Pelling, *A History of British Trade Unions* (London: Pelican, 1963).

55 Hobsbawm, *The Age of Capital* (London: Abacus, 1977), 124.

56 J. Lovell, *British Trade Unions 1875–1933* (London: Macmillan Press, 1977) 20.

57 Hobsbawm, *The Age of Capital*, 128.

58 J-F. Bergier "The Industrial Bourgeoisie and the Rise of the Working Class, 1700–1914," in *The Fontana Economic History of Europe*, ed. Carlo M. Cipolla (London: Collins/Fontana, 1973), 436.

59 E.J. Hobsbawm, *The Age of Extremes 1914–1991* (London: Abacus, 1995), 128.

2. European Enlightenment and Early Social Thought

> If the Enlightenment marks the most dramatic step towards secularization and rationalization in Europe's history, it does so no less in the wider history not just of western civilization but, arguably, of the entire world. —Jonathan Israel

> People come to the struggle for Enlightenment values from very different angles, and even when they find common ground, their aims may be less than enlightened. —Ian Buruma

> Faith in the power of reason—the belief that free citizens can govern themselves wisely and fairly by resorting to logical debate on the basis of the best evidence available, instead of raw power—was and remains the central premise of American democracy. This premise is now under attack. —Al Gore

SOCIAL THEORY DID NOT DEVELOP IN A VACUUM. It emerged from a complex set of philosophies that date back to the seventeenth century. In medieval Europe scholastic theories about humankind were dictated by the church and religious ideology. The Church of Rome denounced anyone a heretic who sought for truth independently of the church and religion. Views began to change in the seventeenth century when the educated classes adopted secular ideas to debate the nature of society and the direction it was going or ought to go. It is this unprecedented shift in social discourses, the sets of ideas that together form a powerful body of intellectual thought, which we associate with European Enlightenment. In reality, the intellectual movements cannot be separated from social forces, and the former was intimately related to modernity. The Enlightenment not only challenged religious doctrine but also negated all legitimation of monarchy, slavery, and woman's subordination to man. The Enlightenment heralded a new social discourse and, moreover, "a breakthrough in critical consciousness."[1] It is therefore of immense importance for understanding the rise of modernity and social theory.[2]

In this chapter, we provide a brief and selective survey of the core ideas of European Enlightenment to gain some insight into the philosophies that engaged Marx, Durkheim, Weber, Simmel, and the early feminist theorists. The start date of this synthesis, in 1648, marked the beginning of a restructuring of Europe's political powers and a secularization of knowledge. Intellectual theorizing became more rational and methodical. The end date, 1789, witnessed the French Revolution and the beginning of a sustained conservative reaction against the ideals of European Enlightenment. After defining *Enlightenment*, the chapter examines the ideas of key Enlightenment thinkers under three thematic headings that interlock and, in many cases, overlap: epistemology, human nature and civil society, and emancipation. Within each thematic group, the contribution of Enlightenment writers is organized in chronological order. The rest of the chapter considers the conservative reaction to Enlightenment ideals and the effects of these social discourses on early sociology. As we shall see, early sociology developed out of the warring catastrophe and the dynamic exchanges between Enlightenment and post-Enlightenment ideas.

The Enlightenment

Any coverage of the European Enlightenment that fails to acknowledge its antecedents within the centuries of other intellectual thinkers would be misleading. Enlightenment thinkers were conscious of their debt to the past and at the same time aware of the uniqueness of their own historical moment as an age of critique, reassessment, and transformation.[3] The ancient Greeks speculated on the nature of society. *Republic* by Plato (427–347 BCE)[4] describes an organic social division of labour. And *Politics* by Aristotle (384–322 BCE) contains one of the first attempts to systematically analyze different forms of government—tyranny, oligarchy, and democracy. In the two centuries dating from 1400 to 1600, European intellectuals and artists developed an interest in the ancient civilizations of Greece and Rome. With this, there began the Renaissance Movement, originating in Italy and extending progressively to the rest of Europe, which cultivated "a spirit of enthusiastic inquiry" in the fields of the arts, architecture, literature, philosophy, and politics.[5] However, neither ancient Greek philosophers nor Renaissance intellectuals conceptualize society as something distinct from government or the state. The crucial notion of society as a general and abstract concept had to await the Enlightenment.[6]

What is the Enlightenment? Since the seventeenth century, there have been many attempts to define *European Enlightenment*. The elasticity in the meaning of the term prompted an academic journal to hold a competition in 1784 on this question. The Prussian Immanuel Kant (1724–1804) entered the competition. In what is now a seminal paper, Kant wrote, "Enlightenment is man's release from his self-incurred tutelage.[7] It's understood here not only as a reaction against ignorance and superstition, but also in terms of acquiring the maturity to exercise moral authority."[8] Kant's description of Enlightenment, however, is not particularly helpful for understanding an intellectual phenomenon that's distinctive because of its complexity.

The frontispiece of the *Encyclopédie, or Reasoned Dictionary of the Sciences, Arts and Trades,* embodies one of the most common interpretations of the term "Enlightenment." It depicts Reason and Philosophy pulling away the veil from Truth, while clouds withdraw to open the sky to light. Imagination (left) offers Truth a garland on behalf of all the Arts and Sciences.

In the twenty-first century there is still no scholarly consensus about when, where, and who should be given preference. For some, such as Peter Gay, European Enlightenment represents a unified body of thought developed around the core principle of reason, and as the basis for human progress.[9] Similarly, for Zeitlin, the Enlightenment is about the advancement of humanity and ever-greater degrees of freedom through "reason and science." For others, such as Dupré and Callinicos, the Enlightenment is complex, contained ambiguities and is best seen as work in progress, involving a series of interrelated problems and social discourses on modernity. It has been interpreted in many different ways. In 1932 Ernst Cassirer's synthesis of European Enlightenment, *The Philosophy of the Enlightenment*, implies that the term refers to a desire for human action to be guided by rationality, rather than by faith, superstition, or revelation. Written in the immediate aftermath of World War II (1939–45),

Horkheimer and Adorno's 1947 *Dialectic of Enlightenment* is far less positive. The authors argue that at the heart of Enlightenment lurks political terror in the form of "rational" technological systems utilized to assure mass death in the Holocaust. In the early twenty-first century, scholars argued that Enlightenment ideals had inured people against uncritical acceptance of authority. And, moreover, in relation to social discourses on Christianity and Islam, they posited that Enlightenment is an embodiment of Western cultural imperialism. Enlightenment was a pan-European phenomenon and was pre-eminently a movement of ideas. The movement's leading thinkers were religious skeptics, cultural critics, and historians who shaped intellectual opinion across Europe. In the eighteenth century the French *philosophes* (a term used to refer generally to all kinds of Enlightenment thinkers) most fervently criticized religious orthodoxy. Some of Enlightenment thought as it relates to the development of social theory we consider next.

Epistemology: Rationalism and Empiricism

The significance of European Enlightenment for the evolution of social theory lies in large part in the Enlightenment's philosophical trait of rationality and the secular concepts of society and human progress as objective, collective forces. Philosophers ask questions about knowledge: How is knowledge acquired and how reliable is knowledge? Such questions are known as epistemology or the theory of knowledge. Rationality refers to a philosophical doctrine that gives primacy to the *a priori* (deductive) method of reasoning in the process of developing knowledge. Rationalism assumes that the human mind is the sole source of truth and hence must reject faith as a source of truth. As such it is opposed to empiricism, which is an epistemological doctrine that gives primacy to the *a posteriori* (inductive) method of reasoning to arrive at general truths, which is derived from experience, observation, or experiments.

Historically, rationalism is embodied in the works of two prominent seventeenth-century philosophers, Descartes and Spinoza. The French philosopher René Descartes (1596–1650) is often regarded as the originator of the rationalist method and had an important influence on early Enlightenment thinking. Descartes argued that strict deductive reasoning must be the only source of knowledge. In his 1641 *Discourse on Method and Meditations on First Philosophy*, Descartes sets out the conditions necessary for something to be *knowledge*. Descartes posits that, like the structure of a building, knowledge must rest upon secure foundations, and this foremost principle is based on self-consciousness: "I exist, simply because I am able to doubt my existence." All things that we can conceive of clearly and distinctly exist. In establishing self-consciousness as the basis of absolute certainty, Descartes rejects faith as a possible source of truth and celebrates the universal power of human reason.[10] Cartesian philosophy is part materialist and part idealist: the human is a machine but has a soul. Benedict (Baruch) de Spinoza (1632–1677) attracted notoriety in early Enlightenment Europe because he was the chief progenitor of the medieval Christian doctrine of Revelation.[11] In his 1674 *Ethics*, Spinoza conceives the reality of the universe both as the sum of all facts and as the ordering principle that determines the relationship of all those facts in the whole.[12] In other words, all things that exist, exist necessarily, and are modes of thought and extension. For Spinoza, reason in humans is akin to reason in nature; one order permeates everything. Reason enables rational human beings to understand themselves and the totality of the universe: it is the key to all of life.[13] The underlying assumption of Spinoza's philosophy is that reality and concept coincide, so that relations between ideas correspond exactly to relations in reality. Spinoza's materialist philosophy had the potential of producing a revolutionary ideology, which may be seen as a precursor of Marx's historical materialism.

Empiricism, which is an epistemological doctrine that gives primacy to the a posteriori method of reasoning, is most famously associated with the writings of Sir Isaac Newton, John Locke, David Hume, and Immanuel Kant. In contrast to the emphasis placed solely on deductive reasoning, the English mathematician Sir Isaac Newton (1642–1727) believed in the importance of data based on experience and observation. In *Optics* (1704) he persuasively puts his case for "experimental philosophy": "As in mathematics, so in the natural philosophy, the investigation of difficult things by the method of analysis ought ever to precede the method of compositions. This analysis consists of making experiments and observations, and in drawing general conclusions from them by induction."[14] Like Newton, John Locke (1632–1704) and the Scottish philosopher David Hume (1711–1776) emphasize the pivotal role of experience in all human understanding and knowledge. Locke's 1690 *Essay Concerning Human Understanding* provides the epistemological foundations of modern empiricism. An *idea*, according to Locke, is "whatsoever is the Object of the Understanding when a Man thinks."[15] Locke acknowledges that sometimes humans conceive of things outside their life experience. He asserts that when ideas do not appear to connect directly to experience, they are in fact fabricated by some kind of extrapolation from the ideas that *are* based upon sensory experience.[16] In *A Treatise of Human Nature* (1739), David Hume avers empiricism, and his radical approach involved him in deconstructing the identity of the self: "The true idea of the human mind is to consider it as a system of different perceptions of different existences which are linked together by a relation of cause and effect, and mutually produce, destroy, influence, and modify each other."[17]

The celebrated German thinker Immanuel Kant, arguably one of the most influential philosophers of European Enlightenment, established his international reputation through his trilogy of *Critiques*.[18] His seminal treatise on epistemology is found in the first *Critique* when he asks what can be known by a priori reasoning. While concurring with empiricists such as Locke and Hume that there were no innate ideas, he didn't accept that all knowledge could be derived solely from sense experience, which imprints impressions on the human mind. To understand the phenomenal world, humans have to rely upon their own inherent logic and concepts, such as causation, that enable us to make sense of the natural world. The human mind is equipped with several categories of understanding, including cause and effect, which are not learnt from sense experience. To Kant, the order of the natural world and the laws of nature are not then inherent in nature but are human *constructs* imposed upon it by human minds. The works of Descartes, Spinoza, Locke, Hume, and Kant offer an overview of the debate on the epistemological question of what is (or should be) regarded as acceptable scientific knowledge. The precise meaning and status of the words *positivism* and *empiricism* is something that later affected the emerging discipline of sociology.

Human Nature and Civil Society

The phrase civil society was central to the European Enlightenment as a description of the conditions of organized social life. The French and Scottish *philosophes* were preoccupied with the concept of civil society, its moral values, its development, and whether it could be shaped for the betterment of humankind.[19] They sought to extend Sir Isaac Newton's law of universal gravitation to the systematic study of morals, understood broadly to embrace human passions and social institutions.[20] In the "new science of man" human passions are to morals what movement is to physics. "Commercial society," the form of civil society that the Enlightenment philosophers analyzed, is what has been referred to since Marx as capitalism. At the centre of Enlightenment's ideas on civil society is the timeless concept of natural law. The concept had two meanings: prescriptive and normative. It referred to the universal order of nature, namely, that all humans share a common nature. This universal order also had a normative quality in that human freedom *ought* to conform to nature as all other things do.

The philosophers believed that the state of nature was antecedent to society. This approach, therefore, gave a privileged status to the concept of human nature. Two models of human nature are found in the work of John Locke and Thomas Hobbes (1588–1679). In *Two Treatises of Civil Government* (1690), Locke argues that individuals will readily abdicate their agency and live under the rules of civil society in order to protect and promote their God-given individual rights: "To avoid this state of war ... is one great reason of men's putting themselves into society."[21] In *Leviathan* (1651), Hobbes portrays humans as innately and wholly self-seeking and engaged in perpetual war. Hobbes work is pre-Enlightenment, but it did influence later *philosophes*, such as Rousseau. Both Locke and Hobbes distinguish between a pre-social state of nature characterized by peace, good will, and reciprocal relationships, and a state of social conflict and the growth of private property and social inequality.[22] In Hobbesian analysis the complex transition to civil society involves the interplay between society and state. Society is an association of free humans, who draw on the active senses of reason. The state, on the other hand, is an organization of power that draws on the senses of hierarchy and despotism.

It is suggested that the prominent Swiss philosopher Jean-Jacques Rousseau (1712–1778), was probably one of the first to use *société* as a key concept and explicitly to reason in terms of *social* relations.[23] In his *Discourse on the Origins of Inequality* published in 1755, Rousseau rejects both Hobbes position that life in the state of nature was "brutish and short," and Locke's view that property existed before the emergence of society. He declares, "The first man who, having enclosed a piece of ground, took it into his head to say 'This is mine,' and found people simple enough to believe him, was the real founder of civil society."[24] For Rousseau, social conflict is not the result of human nature, but of the social institutions of private property. In his view, the natural state was not the cause of human misery; it was the origin of society, principally private property, which placed new chains on the poor and gave new powers to the rich. Rousseau concludes: "The original

W. Hogarth, Gin Lane (engraving, 1751). The observation and celebration of the ordinary, imperfect world of "common nature" was typical of Enlightenment thinking.

man having vanished by degrees, society only offers to us an assembly of artificial men and factitious passions, which are the work of all these *new relations*, and without any real foundation in nature." [italics added][25]

The above passage from *Discourse* exemplifies social theory in the making.[26] In his deliberations on the notion of a covenant between individuals and the state, Rousseau presupposes a theory of social life involving new social relations, social institutions, and social processes. Whereas Hobbes in *Leviathan* represents human life as "solitary, brutish, and short," Rousseau in *Discourse* represents the savage in the state of nature as an innocent who becomes corrupted by the encroachment of civil society.[27] He contends that there must be two kinds of social inequality, one which is natural or physical, and hence beyond human control, the other moral or political, because it depends upon human choice. Claims to rule put forward by a few who govern the many can have no force unless they are acknowledged to be legitimate by others.[28] Rousseau's secular views, not astonishingly perhaps, influenced the French revolutionaries.[29]

In the *Social Contract* (1762), Rousseau argues that the inequalities established by humans themselves require each individual to enter into relations with other individuals. This creates a complex reciprocal arrangement—expressed in the commercial terminology of a *social contract*—that converts the mass into a coherent body and constituted a society. A social contract emerges as one of the fundamental concepts of Enlightenment thought. It was Rousseau's view that a social contract could not have been formed in the state of nature but must have been a hoax perpetrated by the rich upon the poor. In exchange for security, as he put it, "All ran headlong to their chains believing they had secured their liberty."[30] Rousseau conceived the history of humankind as beginning in solitude, with civil society gradually emerging: a solitary creator becoming social.[31] At a time of European economic expansion, social contract theory was an ideology for social change and a justification for the modern state.[32] In *Social Contract* can be found tensions. Poised between the ideal of the state based on reason and his declared reservations about democracy—"a Government so perfect is not suited for men"[33]—Rousseau expressed his own personal dilemma as well as that of the bourgeoisie. Marx read Rousseau as a bourgeois radical committed to the abstract natural rights of man. But others suggest that *Discourse* expounds a theory of the development of private property and social inequality that is analogous to Marx's own concept of history.[34]

Although the writings of Rousseau contain substantive sociological concepts such as society and inequality, they do not adequately conceptualize society as a complex structure of institutions and social processes shaped by specific historical development.[35] In this context *The New Science* by Giambattista Vico (1668–1774) and *Spirit of the Laws* by Baron de Montesquieu (1689–1755) attempt both to theorize society as an organic whole and to relate its different cultures, values, and institutions to specific stages of historical development. Montesquieu's *Spirit of the Laws* contains the genesis of social theory. In it he outlines a comparative analysis of different types of government, which is effectively a type of society.[36] Each political form has three aspects: nature, spirit, and object. *Nature* refers to its formal constitutional structure; *spirit* refers to its tendency to act in a particular way; and *object* refers to its ultimate purpose such as "liberty." He identifies three basic kinds of government: republican, monarchic, and despotic. His analysis examines the nature of government—that which makes it what it is—and its principles—that which makes it act. He argues that virtue, the thirst for glory and self-sacrifice, drives republics (e.g., Ancient Greece). Monarchies are driven by honour or status, meaning the ambition of titles (e.g., England). And despotism is founded on fear and the will of the despot (e.g., Asian societies).

Montesquieu attempts to formulate grand narratives of society. Human passions, each associated with a specific political form, make up part of a wider totality of interrelated conditions, institutions, and culture that underlie and sustain that form. Montesquieu calls this totality *The Spirit of the Laws*. Though society presents itself as a chaotic phenomenon, Montesquieu contends that beneath the surface exist a definite structure or laws comprising patterns of human behaviour. Thus, social institutions and processes are the product of definite material conditions, which can be discovered by empirical analysis. It was this aspect of Montesquieu's work that led Durkeheim and others to argue that Montesquieu founded sociology.[37] Others are less positive about Montesquieu's scholastic accomplishments. In particular, his controversial thesis that climate plays a central role in shaping society as well as the social institutions that support it—"The empire of climate is the first of all empires"—negates the possibility of explaining the roots of historical social change.[38] Explaining the roots of social change fell to the Scottish Enlightenment.

In the decades after 1750, a group of Scottish philosophers—Adam Ferguson, John Millar, and Adam Smith—produced works of genius in social theory.[39] In *An Essay on the History of Civil Society* published in 1767, Adam Ferguson (1723–1816) traces the development of society from primitive to capitalist forms: each stage of evolution being due to a dynamic interaction of social, technological, and psychological factors. In a rebuttal to Rousseau, he notes the absence of proof to substantiate his hypothesis on the state of nature and asserts there are societies because there are principles of union in human nature.[40] Also to be found in *An Essay* is the seed of C. Wright Mills's notion of the sociological imagination. Ferguson writes, "Mankind are to be taken in groups, as they have always subsisted. The history of the individual is but a detail of the sentiments and thoughts he has entertained in the view of his species: and every experiment relative to this subject should be made with entire societies, not with single men."[41] Ferguson was particularly interested in how economic pressures might affect the psychology of commercial society: for example, the beliefs underpinning the exchange agreement between individuals and their employers. He writes, "It is here, indeed, if ever, that a man is sometimes found a detached and a solitary being: he has found an object which sets him in competition with his fellow-creatures, and he deals with them as he does his cattle and soil."[42] The observations by Ferguson are remarkably akin to Marx's most pivotal sociological critique of the capitalist wage-effort bargain, namely that alienation is built into the nature of employment under a capitalist mode of production.

Adam Smith (1723–90) is probably the most influential figure in the Scottish Enlightenment movement. In his economic treatises, *The Wealth of Nations* (1776), Smith embraces the notion of internal laws of progress and benevolent capitalism. He identifies and explains the fundamental "natural" principles upon which economic growth, wealth, and societal development are, and should be, based. Motivated to promote their own economic welfare, all individuals are free to pursue their self-interests in the form of private economic gain. In Rousseau's *Social Contract* the state had absorbed within itself all social and economic spheres. In Smith's *Wealth of Nations* the state became a particular segment of civil society, namely, the institution that legalizes and protects property relations. Smith's fundamental notion is that markets allocate resources efficiently, are self-correcting, and best advance the interests of society. This market fundamentalism, what he famously called the "invisible hand," did not appeal to virtue but rather was an assumption that the unfettered pursuit of private economic gain contributes most to the common good: "It is not from the benevolence of the butcher, the brewer, or the baker that we expect our dinner, but from their regard to their own interest."[43] Through this process of economic individualism, society can be conceptualized simply as an association of independent individuals acting on the principles of economic exchange of self-interest.[44]

While Smith did not employ the concept of social class, *The Wealth of Nations* exhibits a rudimentary theory of social class. The new commercial society produced a social structure divided into three main classes: landowners, capitalists, and wage labourers. And according to Smith, property forms the basis of social differentiation; the natural source of influence and authority. It is easy to caricature Smith's economic treatises as a heartless justification of the inequalities of capitalism. But Smith, foremost a moral philosopher, did not mistake self-interest for greed and selfishness, and he never suggested that the serving of self-interest was a comprehensive view of the human endeavour.[45] Neither did he believe that industrial capitalism was a naturally occurring form of human life that required no government intervention. Before proposing his economic treatise in *The Wealth of Nations*, Smith wrote *The Theory of Moral Sentiments* (1759), in which he declares:

> The love of our country seems ... to involve ... an earnest desire to render the condition of our fellow citizens as safe, respectable, and happy as we can ... He is certainly not a good citizen who does not wish to promote, by every means in his power, the welfare of the *whole society* of his fellow-citizens ... Concern for our own happiness recommends to us the virtue of prudence: concern for that of other people, the virtues of justice and beneficence. [italics added][46]

The *sine qua non* of Smith's argument is that economic outcomes and the evolution of human life draw on the theory of political economy *and* moral personality. For this reason we need to be wary of interpreting his argument solely in terms of the "hidden hand" of modern economics and neo-conservative ideology.[47] That society constitutes a process that is the product of specific economic, social, and historical forces that can be identified and systematically analyzed, is the great legacy of the Scottish Enlightenment.[48]

Emancipation: Slavery and Women

In that new age, when philosophers and other public academics believed in a *universal* human being—one possessed of reason—and which gave primacy to equality and freedom, slavery and women's subordination is a paradox.[49] Though his work predates the main period of the Enlightenment, Hobbes, in his *Leviathan* (1651), declares that reason was found in equal measure in all men: "From this equality of ability [among men], ariseth equality of hope in the attaining of our ends."[50] Yet plantation owners legally treated slaves as private property. By treating humans as a commodity, colonial slavery raised questions about who was a person, who was inside, and who, such as slaves, was outside the boundary of the community. Slavery could exist without guilt or abhorrence if those who are totally subordinated can be seen as enslavable outsiders. As missionary activity in the colonies increased, more slaves were baptized and became Christians. The problem arose, therefore, of reconciling the ideological language of spiritual equality and legal inequality and servitude coexisting in one person. The fact that the abolition of colonial slavery involved the dismantling of a highly profitable economic structure heightened the intensity of the public discourse on slavery.

In Enlightenment thought, property holding and liberty were closely related. The right to possess property gave men a "stake in the country," which stabilized society. By this logic, property rights would be undermined if slaves were freed. Few of the middle class endorsed Rousseau's radical position that private property was the cause of harmful inequality among humans who were naturally equal. In Europe and the Americas it became easier for the bourgeoisie to justify colonial slavery by linking it to race. On the basis of "scientific" evidence it was argued that, for the African, slavery was natural to their being because they were inferior. The German philosopher, Johann Gottfried Herder (1744–1803) questioned the presumption of *white* racial superiority, as did the progressive Enlightenment thinker Baron de Montesquieu. After 1750, there began a sustained opposition to colonial slavery. In England evangelical Christianity drove abolitionism. In France it was driven by secular imperatives of the Declaration of the Rights of Man and the Citizen, which Condorcet helped to draft. Condorcet's *Reflections* of 1781 is the most radical treatise on the justification of abolition. He openly addresses the slaves as his brothers and recognizes in them an unreserved entitlement to full human rights.[51] The abolition of slavery took place in the French colonies in 1789, in British Caribbean colonies in 1834, and in the United States in 1865. The shift of societal consensus, or to use the German word *Zeitgeist*—"spirit of the times"—towards the abolition of slavery was due to the combined influence, directly or indirectly, of the French Revolution, Methodism, and Quakerism, and the writings of Montesquieu, Condorcet, and Wollstonecraft.

The standard history of the European Enlightenment, as Margaret Atherton's *Women Philosopher* [52] points out, is that it obscures the fact that women as well as men wrote and published philosophy during the period. One such woman was Mary Wollstonecraft (1759–1797), a product of Enlightenment and one of the first feminist thinkers. Her contribution is also considered in chapter 12, so we can afford to be brief here on her critique of Enlightenment. The problem of reconciling the ideological language of spiritual equality and legal inequality applied to European women in the same measure as it did to slaves. In seventeenth and eighteenth-century Europe, white women were baptized, but spiritual equality did not result in their legal equality with men. In her seminal work, *A Vindication of the Rights of Woman* (1792),

The Kneeling Slave: "Am I not a man and a brother?" This image is a typical Enlightenment representation of a slave asserting his common humanity.

Wollstonecraft persistently draws parallels between the status of slaves in the colonies and the status of white middle-class women in the metropolis.[53] She takes many of the ideals of the Enlightenment and applies them to middle-class women, arguing that it was hypocritical not to do so. In essence, she argues that if rationality is essentially human, it is irrational not to apply it to women too: Knowledge is learnable by all—men and women. In *The Rights of Woman* she provides a scathing critique of Rousseau's pedagogical treatise *Emile*, in which he proposes that woman's nature disqualified her from an academic education. The assumption that woman is essentially inferior to man, she posits, cannot be demonstrated as long as she is subjugated: "Man denies woman reason, shuts her out from knowledge."[54] Wollstonecraft persuasively argues that, excluded from reason and education, women are confined within the arbitrary power of beauty and sensual experience. In Western culture men constitute women as "the fair sex" by means of rituals of gallantry and courtesy, thereby separating women from the male world of reason. Once trapped within the sensual world of beauty, women's subordination is further strengthened as they are forced into both financial and emotional dependence on men, and a life of "petty" activity.[55] One effect of *Rights of Woman* is the questioning of any analysis of a capitalist society that segregates studies of paid work from those of family and gender divisions.

The Romantic-Conservative Reaction

The Enlightenment movement, as even this short selective survey should indicate, did not constitute a simple unitary body of doctrine; it assumed many forms. The term *liberal individualism* is used as a brief description of Enlightenment thought. By this we mean that the individual is seen as the location and source of all the important ingredients in the "liberated" society.[56] A number of core intellectual concepts, or what Richard Hadden calls "intellectual weapons," developed from Enlightenment and helped to undermine ecclesiastical authority and to change the way philosophers viewed the relationship between the individual and society. The Rousseauist notion of the social contract entailed *freedom* to engage in contract formation; *equality* between parties to the contract; *universality* in that the personal character of either party was considered irrelevant; *private property*, the right to acquire and dispose of it as the parties wish; and *religious tolerance*. The individual's religious convictions were considered irrelevant; put in crude commercial terms, religious intolerance was bad for business. The radical ideology of the philosophers was a change catalyst and therefore, not astonishingly, found support among the rising commercial and professional classes. The Enlightenment's confidence in the powers of reason, its often naïve optimism that through the application of knowledge the good society was to be secured, as well as its agnostic ideology were too partisan to remain unchallenged.

In the 1740s, dissenting voices against the Enlightenment project were beginning to bè raised, first in the German states, then in England.[57] Johann Gottfried Herder and Edmund Burke began the critique, which gathered momentum and became known as Romantic-Conservative Reaction. The influential Catholic critic Edmund Burke (1729–1797) appalled by the excesses of the French Revolution, linked morality and civil government closely to the divine order, and to the providential authority of God. In *Vindication of Natural Society* published in 1756, he argues that Rousseau's rejection of inequality meant nothing less than the rejection of the civil order and God-given natural law. In later publications Burke defended inequality and the consequent strata of aristocratic order as natural and progressive phenomena that guarantee the civil order. After 1815 French intellectuals engaged in wide-ranging debates on the nature of modernity. However, as the previous chapter noted, the dual revolution was not only criticized from the political right, such as Burke, but also from the left, such as Saint-Simon. And as a backdrop, we should note that in England in the 1830s the Chartist Movement was critical of the effects of industrial capitalism. Though initially a reactionary movement that defended the traditional view of the world, the Catholic counter-revolutionary movement developed propositions about modernity that greatly influenced Saint-Simon, Comte, and Durkheim.

The French Catholic intellectuals Joseph de Maistre and Louis de Bonald were the main dissident voices. Both dissidents rejected the rational core principles enshrined in the social contract; emphasized *natural* social hierarchy, duty, and collective good; and conceptualized society as an organic whole in which *rational* and also traditional elements played an active, constitutive role. Joseph de Maistre (1753–1821), a resolute opponent of the Revolution, asserted, "There is a satanic quality to the French Revolution that distinguishes it from everything that we have ever seen or anything that we are likely to see."[58] Like Burke, Maistre repudiated Rousseau's conception of the origin of society because it implied that it had been created without the intervention of divine Providence. His writings repeatedly affirm that human activities are governed by God: "Nothing happens by chance in this world, and even in a secondary sense, there is no disorder, for disorder is commanded by the sovereign hand that submits it to a rule and forces it to contribute to a good."[59] Maistre's work, like that of Burke, may be read as a sustained polemic against secular-rational Enlightenment thinking. But his work is a reformulation of the medieval doctrine of an infallible Church, and thus, in conceptual terms, there is very little that is new in Maistre.[60]

Louis de Bonald (1740–1840) was an influential figure in the Catholic counter-revolutionary movement. In his best-known work, *Théorie du Povoir*, Bonald presents a rebuttal of Montesquieu's *Spirit of the Laws* and Rousseau's *Social Contract*. Bonald contends that knowledge is not simply derived from individual reason, but is situated in a cultural community, and is a product of the social. Art and literature, for example, incorporate situated communities of practice and are expressions of the society that produces the artifacts. That knowledge is a social process is echoed more than a century later in Vygotsky's work on the cultural-activity theory of learning. For Bonald, the natural man is a meaningless abstraction: Natural man does not exist, only social man.[61] Like Maistre, Bonald argued that humans by their very nature are social, moral, and cultural beings, and he repudiated Enlightenment rationalist, humanist, individualist ideology. As Bonald expressed it, "The schools of modern philosophy ... have produced the philosophy of modern man, the philosophy of I ... I want to produce the philosophy of social man, the philosophy of we."[62] As an organism, society was defined in terms of its inner spirit or soul, and it was to be understood through intuition, not reason or science. Modernity was couched in terms of pre-industrial organic values, such as beauty and nature. Society, moreover, did not consist of simply an aggregate of individuals; rather it was the expression of a whole culture. Bonald argues that the individual cannot exist outside society, and as such, it is the individual, not society, that is an abstraction. The atomization of the collective could eventuate only in the collapse of social bonds and social disorder. Bonald believed that urban industrial capitalism undermined the most natural and scared of social units, the family, and he extolled the importance of the community and the binding influence of the Church.

While we can detect in the Enlightenment dissidents a strong anti-modernist sentiment, over decades the Enlightenment and Reactionary movements mutated into a new, more comprehensive humanism.[63] This essentially *dialectical* view of intellectual history, which was first grasped by Hegel, posits that European Enlightenment never developed into a simple rationalism or a simple anti-rationalism. Louis Dupré provides an insightful passage describing the dialectical relation between social change and the roles of ideas: "Whenever human thought has been dominated by some special interest [e.g., the dual revolution], the most fruitful philosophy of the age has reflected that domination; not passively, by mere submission to its influence, but actively, by making a special attempt to understand it and placing it in the focus of philosophical inquiry."[64]

What is most significant for our purposes is this: the ongoing engagement between Enlightenment thinkers and its detractors contributed substantially to the foundation of classical sociological thought. On the one side, we have Enlightenment individualism with its emphasis on reason and a reverence for science as a way to investigate society. On the other side, we have a conservative collectivism with its emphasis on extra-individual concepts and its conception of society as an organic whole. As Irving Zeitlin argues, once expunged of its theological assumptions, Bonald's polemic against Enlightenment ideology becomes the source of core sociological concepts and ideas.[65]

Positive Sociology

Sociology, it is argued, has always had an ambivalent relationship to the Enlightenment and post-Revolutionary conservative thinking. On the one hand, sociology emerged out of and extended Enlightenment thinking on reason and epistemology; on the other hand, it draws upon Counter-Enlightenment thinking for its subject matter, particularly the secular, collective concepts of community and culture, rather than the power of pervasive individualism. Thus, sociology is an amalgam of secular liberal ideology and conservative intellectual thought.[66] Elements of both the Enlightenment and the conservative reaction can be found in the works of French socialist Count Claude de Saint-Simon and Auguste Comte, two academics most closely identified with establishing sociology as a distinct discipline.

Saint-Simon (1760–1825) is credited for conceiving both the name and the essentials of positive sociology.[67] He was fiercely critical of the French Revolution. Although the Revolution had swept away feudal hierarchy and privileges, the French class system remained intact, and indeed, social inequalities widened due to the Industrial Revolution, he argued. Like de Bonald, Saint-Simon believed that knowledge is a product of a community of ideas. Further, he believed that knowledge is both the binding force of society and a moving power of progress. Like Marx after him,

Saint-Simon viewed the historical transformation of society as a result of forces that had been maturing in the old regime. In his view, the *philosophes* had contributed to the disintegration of the ancient regime, yet Enlightenment ideology gave little or no guidance for rebuilding the new industrial order. According to Saint-Simon, the new order needed to be built on a foundation of new intellectual principles. Science would replace religious dogma and, as a body of verified and established beliefs, would be the defining force of society. His view of French modernity consisted of *industriels*—those who produced society's wealth—and *oisifs* (idlers)—the social parasites who lived off the producers. The new social order would remain essentially hierarchical: the new scientific-technological elite and the property owners replacing the old priests and feudal elite, and science replacing religion as the binding force holding society together. Saint-Simon, then, envisioned what historian Eric Hobsbawm calls "a Rousseauist cult of the supreme being."

Auguste Comte (1798–1857) was born in the French city of Montpellier. Both his parents were devout Catholics and ardent royalists. He attended the École Polytechnique in Paris, and later held a minor appointment at the École. His most famous work, *Philosophie Positive*, was published in 1830. Comte was a marginal figure in French intellectual culture,[68] and the originality of his social theory is contested. Zeitlin writes, "Auguste Comte ... appropriated virtually all of Saint-Simon's ideas."[69] In *Philosophie Positive* Comte attempts to understand what was conceived as a crisis of modernity following the French Revolution of 1789, its excesses, the implosion of the ancient regime, and the creation of a new economic regime—industrial capitalism. Comte claimed to be the champion of intellectual positivism, broadly understood as an epistemological position that advocates the application of the methods of the natural sciences to the study of society and social life. For Comte, positivism and the new science of sociology would provide the intellectual and moral basis of the new social order. He argued for giving up the metaphysical search for causes and instead advocated the search for invariable relations between things—the regular patterns in social phenomena.

Comte's Law of Three Stages is one of his most well-known propositions. In the context of social turmoil in nineteenth-century France, Comte endeavoured to discover the causes of this social phenomena. He claimed to have discovered a great fundamental law, to which the human mind evolves through a series of stages, each of which marked a different way of thinking or philosophizing. These three theoretical states are the theological or fictitious state, the metaphysical or abstract state, and the scientific or positive state. Comte believed that, in the positive state, "the human mind, recognizing the impossibility of obtaining absolute truth, gives up the search after the origin and hidden causes of the universe and a knowledge of the final causes of phenomena. It endeavours now only to discover, by a well-combined use of reasoning and observation, the actual laws of phenomena—that is to say, their invariable relations of succession and likeness."[70] Comte believed that metaphysical thought was a rational attempt to explain all worldly phenomena that are beyond the physical, that is, not observable. Catholic theology represented *meta*-thought, and in Comte's opinion, the human mind during the period of European industrialization was leaving the metaphysical and entering the positive or scientific stage. The crisis in modernity, then, occurred because too many features of the metaphysical remained to sustain the new regime, which should embrace the positive philosophy. Comte wrote, "We are theologians in childhood, metaphysical in youth, and natural philosophers in virility."[71]

In *Philosophie Positive* Comte's positive doctrine attempts to reconcile two mutually antagonistic principles: *order* and *progress*. Order or *static* describes the functioning of a society and its culture that binds society together. The principle of order was derived from Catholic theology. Progress or *dynamics* describes the "functional pre-requisites" for historical development. The principle of progress was derived from the Enlightenment. As Larry Ray points out, although the concept of static passed out of use in the twentieth-century sociology, the concept still informs many theoretical approaches, particularly functionalism.[72] Though Comte's account of modernity neglects the role of colonialism and vastly overestimates the decline of militarism and religion in modern societies, his insights remain influential. Most important is the "centrality of the social" and his insistence that people are significant only as social beings, that society is an organic necessity which "commands all times and places." He emphasized the cohesive nature of culture and the importance of language to transmit cultural mores and values across generations. Comte laid the foundations of sociological positivism, which was the dominant paradigm throughout the nineteenth century. Sociologists, such as Zeitlin, have been highly critical of Comte, but others have given more favourable evaluations. Comte does not provide the insights offered by philosophers of the first rank, but he should be given credit for synthesizing the conceptual terrain of sociology and for rejecting metaphysics in favour of positive empirical methods.[73]

Conclusion

This chapter has covered a lot of material. The Enlightenment challenged religion's pre-eminent authority to both know and speak the truth. For

Kant, for example, reason was an intellectual tool to be used against the power of church or state. As authority generally prefers darkness, it was the self-appointed task of Enlightenment thinkers to shine light, to expose the abuses of power, to instill skepticism concerning omniscient clergy and the motives of government leaders. We have seen throughout this chapter, however, that European Enlightenment, like most intellectual movements, was not a unified body of thinking but was internally fractured and riddled by contradictions. The debate on slavery and women's rights is an example of its intellectual anomalies. The Enlightenment was essentially a dialectical movement, a process that saw philosophers and other public intellectuals taking particular positions in the debate about modernity. The intellectual legacy of this public engagement between rationalist, secular Enlightenment ideology and the post-Revolutionary, conservative, philosophical reaction is a number of propositions about society: Society has an organic nature, with internal laws of unity and development; it creates the individual, and individuals have no existence outside of a social context; it is composed of relationships and institutions; and it has institutions and customs that are positively functional in that they either fulfill human needs directly or indirectly by serving other essential institutions.

The intellectual legacy of Enlightenment ideology is, unsurprisingly, a masculine vision of the nature of human nature and of social life. Sylvana Tomaselli's essay offers a feminist view of women in history, which "linked women, not, as is all too swiftly done, to nature, but to culture and the process of historical development."[74] Similarly, Rosalind Sydie's *Natural Women, Cultured Men* has luminously explored the *sex-blind* nature of classical social thought. Canonical writers, she argues convincingly, overwhelmingly viewed the "natural" differences between the sexes based on the reproductive capacity of women to justify the hierarchical relations of female subordination and exclusion from the public sphere. The feminist critique of masculine interpretation of nature predates the Enlightenment era. Aristotle, for example, believed that the female was an incomplete version of the male. And one Renaissance writer opined that

> men are by nature of a more elevated mind than women. They are more suited to struggle with arms and with cunning against the misfortunes which afflict country, religion, and one's own children. The character of men is stronger than that of women and can bear the attacks of enemies better, can stand strain longer, is more constant under stress. Therefore, men have the freedom to travel with honour in foreign lands, acquiring and gathering

> the goods of fortune. Women, on the other hand, are almost timid by nature, soft, slow, and therefore more useful when they sit still and watch over things. It is as though nature thus provided for our well-being, arranging for men to bring things home and for women to guard them.[75]

European Enlightenment was grounded in the assumption that universal man in thought and practice becomes *rational* man, active and able to conquer the forces of the natural world, in stark contrast to *subjective* woman, passive, and a repository of the natural. Influential Enlightenment writers promulgated the widespread conviction that women were, by nature, less rational, less objective, more prone to hysteria, weaker than men in mind and body, best suited to the domestic sphere, and often inherently inclined to vanity, frivolity, and wantonness. The early feminists critiques of the masculinity of Enlightenment thinking exposed this irrational position, arguing that if rationality is essentially human, it was irrational to apply the term only to men. Throughout the nineteenth century, the socio-economic and cultural changes brought about by the dual revolutions and by urbanization in Western Europe had a significant impact on the lives of women. Many entered the paid-labour market as factory workers or as domestic servants to the growing middle classes. Though crucial to capitalist development, the discourse among the middle classes generally supported the idea that male wage earners should be the head of families, and it idealized woman's domestic role. There was also the work of Charles Darwin. His belief that men were "more courageous, pugnacious and energetic than women, and [had] a more inventive genius"[76] provided a "scientific" basis for sexual dichotomy and the resultant natural superiority of men over women. Contemporary feminist critiques have emphasized that the sociological canon generally accepted the idea of a sexual dichotomy and the resultant hierarchy of sex relations as a "natural" phenomenon. According to this meta-narrative, men inhabited the public world of business, competition, decision-making, and power, and ideally, women inhabited the domestic domain of child rearing and care giving and were the moral and religious fulcrum of family life. Although expunged of theological ideology and further theorizing by Saint-Simon and Comte, Enlightenment thinking about society, including the idea of a dichotomized social order as natural, became the foundation of sociological positivism, which remained the dominant paradigm until the early twentieth century.

Between 1900 and 1915 Enlightenment thought was increasingly challenged by late-modern thinkers and was ultimately dethroned by an emphasis upon divergent frameworks of thinking. In Germany writers such as Max Weber, Friedrich Nietzsche, and Georg Simmel no longer accorded Enlightenment reason and rationality a privileged status in the definition of the essence of human nature. Max Weber argued that universal freedom is suffocated by the growth of rationality, which creates "the iron cage" of bureaucratic control. Friedrich Nietzsche (1844–1900) placed aesthetics above science and rationality and attacked the accepted Enlightenment logic on linear progress, civilization, and morality. Georg Simmel, who is often labelled as a precursor of postmodern sociology, contemplated how individual city dwellers might respond to and internalize the aesthetic experiences and the fleeting, micro-social interactions in the city. Karl Marx, rebutting Adam Smith's optimism, inserted a class dimension into modernity.

In the twentieth century, the logic of Enlightenment rationality led to domination and oppression and the unparalleled institutionalization of state violence,[77] but for the classical social thinkers, these observations were made with the facility of hindsight. In the twenty-first century, there remains an ongoing need to instill skepticism about the motives of politicians. Scott McClellan's scathing memoir, *What Happened* (2008), describes his years at the White House and speaks of a culture of deception, the manipulation of public opinion, and lies to justify the Iraq war. In this context it's argued, convincingly, that given the abuses of power of world leaders such as George W. Bush and Tony Blair, the critical spirit of Kant and other Enlightenment thinkers is vitally important to us now.[78]

In summary, the chaotic transformation of European societies between 1700 and 1850 was due to what we have called three waves of modernity: the British Industrial Revolution, the French Revolution, and the contemporaneous Intellectual Revolution consisting of Enlightenment and post-Revolutionary thought. These three revolutions profoundly influenced and shaped the work of the classical canon to which we now turn.

Notes

1 Louis Dupré, *The Enlightenment and the Intellectual Foundations of Modern Culture* (New Haven and London: Yale University Press, 2004), xiii.

2 Jonathan I. Israel, *Radical Enlightenment: Philosophy and the Making of Modernity 1650–1750* (Oxford: Oxford University Press, 2001), vi.

3 David Williams, ed., *The Enlightenment* (Cambridge: Cambridge University Press, 1999), 1.

4 BCE means Before Common Era.

5 R. Kirkpatrick, *The European Renaissance* (London: Pearson Education, 2002), 1.

6 Alan Swingewood, *A Short History of Sociological Thought*, 3rd ed. (New York: St. Martin's Press, 2000), 4.

7 Immanuel Kant, "What Is Enlightenment?"(1784), and quoted in *The Enlightenment: A Sourcebook and Reader*, ed. Paul Hyland with O. Gomaz and F. Greensides (London: Routledge, 2003), 54.

8 Larry Ray, *Theorizing Classical Sociology* (Buckingham: Open University Press, 1999), 11.

9 Peter Gay, *The Enlightenment: An Interpretation* (New York: Norton & Company, 1996).

10 Dupré, *The Enlightenment and the Intellectual Foundations of Modern Culture*, 3; Hyland, *The Enlightenment*, 33.

11 Israel, *Radical Enlightenment*, 159.

12 Michael Morgan, ed., *The Essential Spinoza* (Indianapolis, IN: Hackett Publishing, 2006).

13 Don Garrett, ed., *The Cambridge Companion to Spinoza* (Cambridge: Cambridge University Press, 1996).

14 Quoted in Hyland, *The Enlightenment*, 35.

15 John Locke, Essay 47, section 8, quoted in Peter Sedgwick, *Descartes to Derrida: An Introduction to European Philosophy* (Oxford: Blackwell, 2001), 12.

16 Hyland, *Enlightenment*, 40.

17 David Hume, Treatise, Bks.1, 4, 6, quoted in Dupré, *The Enlightenment and the Intellectual Foundations of Modern Culture*, 49.

18 Immanuel Kant's trilogy is *Kritik der Reinen Vernuuft* (Critique of Pure Reason, 1781), *Kritik der Praktischen* (Critique of Practical Reason, 1788), and *Kritik der Urteilskraft* (Critique of Judgement, 1790).

19 See Alex Callinicos, *Social Theory: A Historical Introduction*, 2nd ed. (Cambridge: Polity Press, 2007), 4.

20 Ibid., 16.

21 John Locke, *Two Treatises*, vol. 2, chap. 3, paras. 16 and 21, quoted in Hyland, *Enlightenment*, 155.

22 Swingewood, *A Short History of Sociological Thought*, 4.

23 J. Heilbron, *The Rise of Social Theory* (Cambridge: Cambridge University Press, 1995), 88, quoted in Callinicos, *Social Theory*, 10.

24 Jean-Jacques Rousseau, *Discourse on the Origins of Inequality* (1755), quoted in Hyland, *Enlightenment*, 178.

25 Ibid., 179.

26 Swingewood, *A Short History of Sociological Thought*; Ray, *Theorizing Classical Sociology.*

27 Alexander Broadie, *The Scottish Enlightenment* (Edinburgh: Birlinn, 2001), 80.

28 Robert Wokler, *Rousseau: A Very Short Introduction* (Oxford: Oxford University Press, 2001), 47.

29 James Miller, *Rousseau: Dreamer of Democracy* (New Haven: Yale University Press, 1984), 1.

30 *Discourse*, pp. iii, 176–7, in *The Enlightenment*, Hyland, 52.

31 David Gauthier, *Rousseau: The Sentiment of Existence* (Cambridge: Cambridge University Press, 2006), 164.

32 Dupré, *Enlightenment and the Intellectual Foundations of Modern Culture*, 162.

33 Jean-Jacques Rousseau, *The Social Contract* (London: Penguin, 1968), 114.

34 Wokler, *Rousseau*, 68.

35 Swingewood, *A Short History of Sociological Thought*, 4.

36 Ibid., 6.

37 For example, R. Aron, *Main Currents in Sociological Thought* (New York: Doubleday, 1970), quoted in Ray, *Social Theory*, 26.

38 See Swingewood, *A Short History of Sociological Thought*, 26; Callinicos, *Social Theory*, 22.

39 See Swingewood, *A Short History of Sociological Thought*, 6–10; Broadie, *The Scottish Enlightenment*, 78–112; S. Copley and K. Sutherland, eds., *Adam Smith's Wealth of Nations* (Manchester: Manchester University Press, 1995).

40 Broadie, *Scottish Enlightenment*, 83.

41 Adam Ferguson, *An Essay on the History of Civil Society* (1767), in Hyland, *Enlightenment*, 189.

42 Broadie, *Scottish Enlightenment*, 84–5.

43 Adam Smith, *The Wealth of Nations*, edited and introduction by Andrew Skinner (London: Penguin Books, 1999) 119.

44 Ken Morrison, *Marx, Durkheim, Weber* (London: Sage, 2006) 22–26.

45 Knud Haakonssen, Introduction to Adam Smith, *The Theory of Moral Sentiments* (1759; Cambridge: Cambridge University Press, 2002), x.

46 Adam Smith, *The Theory of Moral Sentiments* (Cambridge: Cambridge University Press, 2002), 272, 309.

47 Noel Parker "Look, No Hidden Hands: How Smith Understands Historical Progress and Societal Values," in *Adam Smith's Wealth of Nations*, eds. Copley and Sutherland, 122–43.

48 Ibid., 7.

49 On slavery and enlightenment, see D. Outram, *The Enlightenment* (Cambridge: Cambridge University Press, 1995), chap. 5, 60–76, from which this section is largely based.

50 *Leviathan*, chap. 13, and quoted in Hyland, *The Enlightenment*, 9.

51 Williams, *Enlightenment*, 35.

52 M. Atherton, *Women Philosopher* (Cambridge, MA: Hackett Publishing, 1994).

53 Moira Ferguson, *Colonialism and Gender Relations: From Mary Wollstonecraft to Jamaica Kincaid* (New York: Columbia University Press, 1993).

54 Wollstonecraft, *The Vindication of the Rights of Woman*, 129.

55 Ibid., 116.

56 See R. Hadden, *Sociological Theory* (Peterborough, ON: Broadview Press, 1997); Ray, *Theorizing Classical Sociology.*

57 Isaiah Berlin, *The Age of Enlightenment* (New York: Mentor, 1956).

58 Ibid.

59 Ibid., 72–3.

60 Callinicos, *Social Theory*, 74.

61 See I.M. Zeitlin, *Ideology and the Development of Sociological Theory*, 7th ed. (New Jersey: Prentice Hall, 2001), 54.

62 Quoted in Swingewood, *A Short History of Sociological Thought*, 11.

63 Ibid., 4.

64 Dupré, *The Enlightenment and the Intellectual Foundations of Modern Culture*, 5–6.

65 Zeitlin, *Ideology and the Development of Sociological Theory*, 58.

66 See I. Craib, *Classical Social Theory* (Oxford: Oxford University Press, 1997), 3; Robert A. Nisbet, *The Sociological Tradition* (London: Heineman, 1967); and Zeitlin, *Ideology and the Development of Sociological Theory.*

67 See Zeitlin, *Ideology and the Development of Sociological Theory*, 65–77.

68 Swingewood, *A Short History of Sociological Thought*, 15.

69 See Zeitlin, *Ideology and the Development of Sociological Theory*, 77.

70 A. Comte, *Introduction to Positive Philosophy* (Indianapolis: Bobbs-Merrill, 1970), 1–2, and quoted in Callinicos, *Social Theory*, 65.

71 A. Comte, *The Foundations of Sociology*, ed. K. Thompson (London: Nelson, 1976), and quoted in Ray, *Theorizing Classical Sociology*, 45.

72 Ray, *Theorizing Classical Sociology*, 51.

73 See Ray, *Theorizing Classical Sociology*, 55, and Swingewood, *A Short History of Sociological Thought*, 15.

74 Quoted Hyland, *Enlightenment*, 400.

75 L.B. Alberti, *The Family in Renaissance Florence* (Columbia: University of Carolina Press, 1969), 207, quoted in R.A. Sydie, *Natural Women, Cultured Men* (Vancouver: University of British Columbia Press, 1994), 5.

76 Sydie, *Natural Women, Cultured Men*, 6.

77 See M. Horkheimer and T. Adorno, *The Dialectic of Enlightenment* (Amsterdam: Querido Verlag, 1947); John Ralston Saul, *Voltaire's Bastards: The Dictatorship of Reason in the West* (Toronto: Penguin, 1993).

78 See, for example, Susan Neiman, *Moral Clarity* (Toronto: Harcourt, 2008).

PART II

THE CLASSICAL TRIUMVIRATE

3. Karl Marx: Philosophy

> The history of Marxism is the history of nineteenth-century thinkers and twentieth-century politicians. —C. Wright Mills

> Marxian thought is not alone sufficient, but it is indispensable for understanding the present-day world. —Henri Lefebvre

THE LEGACY OF EUROPEAN ENLIGHTENMENT and the ideas of Saint-Simon and Auguste Comte informed the intellectual thinking of Karl Marx. Like Saint-Simon and Comte, Marx viewed human history as passing through stages of evolution and claimed to be applying scientific reasoning to human activity and development. Whereas Saint-Simon and Comte regarded a hierarchical society based on functionally differentiated class divisions in which all social classes worked for the common good, Marx envisioned capitalist society in permanent conflict due to irreconcilable class conflict, and he regarded social classes as representing an emergent social force for change. At the centre of Marx's social theory is the precept that the anatomy of civil society is to be found in the social and economic modes of production: society is produced rather than pre-arranged; cultural mores are learned, not given; and social conditions determine human consciousness and patterns of human history and development. This perspective has important ramifications for sociological theory.[1] Epistemologically, sociological theory must embody concepts that analyze the making, not the completion, of social structure, and it must include the nexus of social relations, cultural conditioning, and entrenched interests of powerful social elites. Marx prophetically states, "At the same pace that mankind masters nature, man seems to become enslaved to other men or his own infamy. Even the pure light of science seems unable to shine but on the dark background of ignorance."[2] Thus, he addresses a challenge that haunts all thinkers today: the balance between sustainable development and ecological catastrophe.

The analysis of capitalist society by Karl Marx and his lifelong confidant, generous benefactor, and intellectual companion, Friedrich Engels, is firmly rooted in the social and political changes stemming from the dual revolution in Britain and France and is organically bound up with the labour and political movements in Western Europe. In the 1880s Marx's doctrines gained widespread attention in European social movements. His views on how his theory was subsequently applied by various social movements, however, can be gauged from his comment on certain French "Marxists": "as for me, I am not a Marxist!"[3] His work inspired the Russian Revolution of November 1917, a cataclysmic event, which profoundly shaped global politics for seventy years. Since his death in 1883 various political leaders have reshaped the legacy of Marx, including Lenin and Stalin in Russia, Mao Tse-Tieng in China, and Ho Chi Min in Vietnam, and some of the things done in the name of Marxism would make Marx himself turn in his grave. Probably for these reasons Marx's name, whether revered or reviled, is known to all, and is likely the only classic social theorist the general public have a strong opinion about, without actually reading his voluminous works.

The purpose of the next three chapters is to survey Karl Marx's central themes with particular reference to his philosophy, history, and economics and to present a critical account of how these contribute to social theory. The profound intellectual content of Marx's works and chronological position means that the other classical social theorists are conventionally seen in relation to him.[4] Naturally, in three short chapters, we cannot elaborate all of Marx's theory, which would require a separate book. After first reviewing his life and published works, we shall explain Marx's critique of Hegel's philosophy and Marx's dialectic method. The next chapter examines what Karl Marx and Friedrich Engels had to say about the development of industrial capitalism, referred to as the materialist conception of history. The final chapter on Marx examines his economic theory, which, as we shall see, is a profoundly sociological theory.

Life and Works

Karl Marx was born in 1818 into a middle-class Jewish family in the predominantly Catholic city of Trier, Germany. The city had very little industry, and in the early 1800s falling agricultural prices caused growing poverty among the peasants. Liberal ideology had much support among large sections of the city's population, as it did in other regions of Germany. Karl Marx's father, Heinrich Marx, was born in 1782, the third son of Meier Halevi Marx, a rabbi in Trier. Little is known of the ancestry of Henriette Marx, Marx's mother, but like her husband she came from the rabbinic tradition. Born in the Netherlands, she was the daughter of Isaac Pressburg, a rabbi in Nijmegen. Unlike her husband, she was uneducated, indeed only semiliterate, and did not enjoy socializing with the city's upper-class elite. There were nine children in the Marx family, of whom Karl was the eldest. Relations with his mother were distant and "icy."[5] Anti-Semitism in the Rhineland, where Jews were often blamed for the peasants' increasing poverty, increased Jewish self-consciousness. It is a matter of conjecture how Marx's Jewish ancestry and the social context affected him, but it would be facile to disregard Jewish self-consciousness as a factor that influenced Marx's development. Marx's Jewishness made him an *outsider* in European society, and, it is argued, the experience of prejudice and discrimination are powerful arguments for changing society.[6]

Karl Marx was born in 1818 in Tier, Germany. In 1836 he married Jenny von Westphalan. The Marx family experienced financial hardship because of Marx's inability to manage his finances. In 1849, Marx was expelled from Paris, and he and his family moved to London, where he died in his study in 1883.

A lawyer to the high court of appeal in Trier, Heinrich Marx had a comfortable income, and the Marx family owned a house in a desirable part of town. Heinrich Marx had adopted the ideas of Enlightenment and had considerable influence on Karl Marx's development. As a civil servant Heinrich Marx was compelled to renounce Judaism and convert to Protestantism to keep his job, and he was baptized some time in 1817. Another important influence on the young Marx was the von Westphalen family. The Baron von Westphalen was inspired by the views of the eighteenth-century French Enlightenment thinkers, and he introduced the young Marx to Utopian socialism put forward by Saint Simon, as well as Shakespeare who remained Marx's favourite author all his life. Between 1830 and 1835 Karl Marx attended the Frederick William High School in Trier. The school introduced Enlightenment ideology and tried to reconcile faith and reason from a Kantian perspective. The earliest surviving documents in Marx's hand are three essays he wrote for his *Abitur*, the German school-leaving examination. The most interesting essay, entitled "Reflections of a Young Man on the Choice of a Career," shows some originality. Its underlying ideas, much like those of his fellow graduating peers, are the humanist ideals of the German Enlightenment, wherein the full development of the individual and the full development of the community of humankind are interdependent.[7]

In 1835 Karl Marx became a student of law at the University of Bonn. Although a diligent student in the first semester, he increasingly became distracted from his studies and was even imprisoned for a day for "disturbing the peace with drunken noise."[8] In 1836 young Marx transferred to the University of Berlin. Marx also became engaged and married Jenny von Westphalen, a friend from early childhood. Heinrich Marx wrote to his son, "Scarcely was the wild rampaging in Bonn finished; scarcely were your debts paid—and they were really of the most varied nature—when to our dismay the sorrows of love appeared."[9] At University of Berlin, Marx became a reformed character, reading widely in jurisprudence and philosophy. He made the intellectual transition from romantic idealism to Hegelianism, the philosophy of Georg Hegel. Marx's conversion to Hegelianism was probably the most profound intellectual step of his whole life. In 1838 Marx began working on his doctoral thesis, which compared the atomic theories of Democritus and Epicurus. Despite its apparently arid subject, his thesis set out to show that theology must yield to the superior wisdom of philosophy and that criticism will triumph over dogma. Many post-Hegelian philosophical themes that Marx was later to develop in his published works are to be found in his thesis.[10] In particular was the notion of *praxis* that was to become so central to his later philosophy. The concept of praxis has its origins in the work of a Polish writer, August von Cieszkowski. Whereas Hegel had only dealt with the present and the past, Cieszkowski argued, "philosophy must descend from the heights of theory into *praxis* ... Just as thought and reflection overcame the *beaux-arts*, so the deed and social activity will now overcome philosophy."[11] In 1841 Marx was awarded his doctorate in philosophy. At the early age of twenty-three, and before he had published anything, Marx was admired by many of his contemporaries. Moses Hess, a member of the Young Hegelians, said of Marx at the time: "Imagine Rousseau, Voltaire, Holbach, Lessing, Heine, and Hegel fused into one person—I say fused not juxtaposed—and you have Dr. Marx."[12]

After completing his doctorate Marx was unable to obtain employment as a university professor because of his incendiary ideas. Instead, he accepted the position of editor of *Rheinische Zeitung* (Rhine News), an opposition weekly financed by liberal industrialists. The German government suppressed the paper in March 1843 because of an article by Marx on rural poverty, an inquiry that led him "from pure politics to economic relationships and so to socialism," said Engels.[13] Marx emigrated to Paris where he began his lifelong friendship and collaboration with Friedrich Engels, the son of a German cotton spinner whose company had a factory in Manchester. Engels, who regarded "vile commerce" as a penance that had to be endured, was able to educate Marx with the practical workings of industrial capitalism. During this period, Marx wrote a series of searing essays critiquing Hegelian philosophy and industrial capitalism. He was expelled from Paris in 1845 for subversive journalism. Marx relocated in the city of Brussels. In the last three months of 1845 Marx and Engels wrote *The German Ideology*, which contains Marx's longest discussion of historical materialism. After a visit to London, the Communist League commissioned Marx and Engels to write the theory underpinning their political activities. The result was the classic *Communist Manifesto*, published in 1848. This was a period of social and revolutionary upheaval in France and Germany. Marx moved to Paris and later to Cologne in 1848, at about the same time as the Belgian government was issuing him an expulsion order for breaking his promise not to engage in political journalism. In Cologne Marx edited a new paper, the *Neue Rheinische Zeitung*, which advocated "a single, indivisible, democratic German republic" but made virtually no reference to working-class politics and refused to support working-class candidates for elections. Unsurprisingly this stance caused friction between Marx and labour leaders. Notoriety followed Marx everywhere. In July 1849 he returned to Paris but was expelled yet again, and the Marx family moved to London where he began what Marx called his "sleepless night of exile."

For the next decade Marx experienced financial hardship and personal tragedies. His letters to Engels describe his misery and impoverishment: "I am unable to go out for want of the coats I have in pawn, and I can no longer eat meat for want of credit ... My wife is ill. Little Jenny is ill ... I could not and cannot call the doctor because I have no money to buy medicine. For the past eight to ten days I have been feeding the family solely on bread and potatoes ... If possible, therefore, send me a few pounds."[14] We should note that the Marx family was never poor by ordinary standards. Even in 1851, one of Marx's most poverty-stricken years, his income was three times that earned by an average skilled British worker. Marx's difficulties arose from his unwillingness to seek full-time employment and his inability to manage his financial resources. During the thirty-four years he lived in London he sought gainful employment only twice. At heart, Marx was a traditional Victorian middle-class patriarch, with "inverted priorities," who lived beyond his means.[15] Despite his "sub-proletarian" way of life, as he put it, he thought it "unseemly" *not* to have a private secretary. What working-class families considered luxuries—regular holidays and new dresses for his wife, dance, piano, and foreign language lessons for the children, and attendance at a ladies' seminary—Marx considered "absolute necessities." Marx claimed that a purely proletarian household would not be appropriate for his daughters "to establish themselves socially with a view of securing their future."[16] He was often to muse in letters to Engels that while he spent so much time writing about *money*, he had little skill for managing it. A regular source of income came from his articles for the radical newspaper the *New York Tribune*. While he subcontracted much of this work to Engels, Marx apparently resented doing what he called "journalism muck" because it kept him away from his research. It was not until 1864, however, that a legacy brought financial relief. In the 1850s personal tragedies afflicted Marx; first his daughter Franziska died in 1852, and three years later his eldest son Edgar died. The *Grundrisse* (Ground Notes), a disconnected tome of his thoughts on political economy, was published midway between the *Communist Manifesto* (1848) and the first volume of *Capital* (1867). In the early 1850s Marx began working on his treatise on political economy, *Capital*, a manuscript for which, he acknowledged, he had "sacrificed health, happiness and family," but also that procrastination, multiple revisions, frequent bouts of ill health, personal digressions, and political activism (e.g., involvement in the International) delayed its completion. His publisher must have had monumental patience. In the summer of 1846 Marx wrote to the German publisher saying the revised version of the first volume would be complete at the end of November. Two decades later the manuscript was still unfinished.[17] Volume one of *Capital* was finally completed twenty-one years later in April 1867. After finishing the last proofs of the text, he wrote a note to Engels and acknowledged his support: "So, *this volume is finished*. I owe it to *you* alone that it was possible ... *Salut*, my dear, valued friend."[18] It was Engels who edited and published volumes two and three of *Capital* in July 1885 and November 1894 after Marx's death.

In the 1870s a generous annuity from Engels enabled Marx to adopt a comfortable upper-middle-class lifestyle. Free of financial worries Marx found the time to play with his grandchildren, but his writing productivity diminished. After a mild stroke in 1873, and suffering from bronchitis that was complicated by pleurisy, possibly from a vicious skin disease called hidradenitis,[19] his work became fragmentary as he spent more time travelling to recuperate. He did manage to write the second edition of *Capital, Volume I*, in 1873 and a critique of the first program of the German socialists under the title *Critique of the Gotha Programme*, published by Engels in 1891. In December 1881 Marx's wife died of cancer, and two years later his daughter Jenny also died. Two months later racked by bronchitis and suffering an abscess in the lung, Karl Marx died stateless in his armchair on 14 March 1883. His lifetime intellectual companion Friedrich Engels died of cancer on 5 August 1895. The rest of this chapter examines Karl Marx's philosophy.

Intellectual Influences

The philosophical context of Marx's early education was the rationalism of European Enlightenment and the school of German philosophy called idealism. It is not possible to understand Marx's ideas without understanding the work of Georg Hegel, and to understand Hegel we need to be familiar with the work of the German philosophers Immanuel Kant and Ludwig Feuerbach. The sequence was that Hegel improved Kantian idealism; Feuerbach transformed Hegel's dialectical mode of thinking; and Marx extended Feuerbachian dialectics.

German idealism emerged in part as a response to the academic discourse on *phenomenalism*, that is, the question of whether human knowledge was restricted to that provided by human impressions, as articulated by the Scottish empiricist David Hume, or whether there existed a reality independent of human experience. Hume was a skeptic. He questioned the power of reason to provide demonstration of aspects of reality that human beings believe, including miracles and religion. He cast doubt on the existence of God and on the frailty of reason to provide answers for which it is simply not capable. Historically, the occurrence of miracles is evidence for the existence of God. In his *Essay on Miracles* (1748), Hume challenges the likelihood of miracles actually occurring, because eyewitness testimony is insufficient to give credibility to accounts of events that the laws of nature and current day human experience contradict: "A wise man, therefore, proportions his belief to the evidence," wrote Hume.[20] In *Dialogues Concerning Natural Religion* (1779) Hume was also the author of one of the principal statements of religious skepticism in the period. He was denied a university teaching position for negating the deist argument for the Creator. The Enlightenment passion for achieving universal truth through the faculty of reason was challenged by Hume. In his *Treatise of Human Nature* (1739–40) and *Enquiry Concerning Human Understanding* (1748), he argues that human sense experiences can never demonstrate a necessary real connection between what humans routinely perceive as cause and effect. Hume wrote, "I venture to affirm of mankind, that they are nothing but a bundle or collection of different perceptions, which succeed each other with an unconceivable rigidity, in perpetual flux and movement."[21] He points out that causality is only a subjective expectation stimulated by the mechanism of association, and this is learned. The gist of his thesis on phenomenalism is that ideas extend no further than human experience. According to Hume, without the support of experience, reason hovers in an experiential void and actually takes us nowhere. Seemingly, in the absence of experience, knowledge of the universe is placed in a magical realm predicated on the faith that humans are mysteriously connected to it from within.

Immanuel Kant saw Enlightenment as a liberating process. Liberty is self-determination, meaning the subjection of one's self and its necessary functions to one's own conscious, rational choice. For Kant, what is real and what is not was a matter of great political importance and furtherance of self-determination. The Enlightenment insisted on the audacity of relinquishing traditional feudal law for abstract ideals of universal justice. Importantly, the Enlightenment also contested the reality of superstitions. As long as people believed that poverty and disease, for example, were God's punishment for human sin, they were unlikely to explore ways of tackling these social problems. In the political milieu of eighteenth-century Western Europe, Kant's philosophy was widely considered as reflecting the incendiary ideals of the French Revolution. Kant himself averred that his trilogy of major works, *Critique of Pure Reason* (1781), *Critique of Practical Reason* (1788), and *Critique of Judgement* (1790) effected a "Copernican revolution" in philosophy. His treatment of human faculties in the three *Critiques* sought to explain the workings of the human mind: its ability to reason, to form morally correct decisions, and to shape a satisfying aesthetics.

It was largely the writings of David Hume that inspired Kant to refute British empiricism and reaffirm the paramount importance of reason. While concurring with Hume that there were no innate ideas, Kant rejected the underlying premise that *all* scientific knowledge derives solely from experience, as some knowledge did not spring from experience. Thus, in his seminal work on epistemology the *Critique of Pure Reason*, he writes:

> There can be no doubt that all our knowledge begins with experience...[and] In the order of time, therefore, we have no knowledge antecedent to experience, and with experience all our knowledge begins. But ... it does not follow that [knowledge] all arises out of experience. For it may well be that even our empirical knowledge is made up of what we receive through

> impressions and of what our own faculty of knowledge supplies from itself. Any knowledge that is thus independent of experience and even of all impressions of the senses ... is entitled *a priori,* and distinguished from empirical, which has its sources *a posteriori*, that is, in experience.[22]

For Kant, the human mind is not simply a tabula rasa, a pristine blank slate, passively recording the sense impressions it receives from the external world; it is also an active agent in understanding those impressions in terms of certain categories and principles that it brings itself to bear on its experience and the multiple data coming to it. The human mind's immanent principles include, for instance, cause and effect. These innate principles or categories exist independently of and prior to sense experience. Kant's most creative intellectual idea is that the human mind does not view the external world in a random way; it imposes structure and order on sense experience: "The order and regularity in objects, which we entitle nature, we ourselves introduce."[23] For example, when we make a judgment such as "the sun caused the earth to become warm," we are not simply describing what we perceive, because all we perceive is that the sun appears and then the earth becomes warm. We make sense of what we perceive, however, by engaging the principle of causality that we apply to experience. Thus, for Kant, humans do not simply accept what is given to them by perception, but they are active, rational beings who understand what they perceive in terms of the mind's categories and principles. The individual human mind, therefore, does not derive the laws of nature *from* the natural world, but on the contrary, it imposes its own laws on nature. At least in part, individuals construct the natural world that they perceive. Thus, Kant gave primacy to the subject—the human mind—rather than to the objects of knowledge.

Kant's philosophy contains paradoxes. On the one hand, he is a materialist when he says we can only know the world as it appears to us and is experienced by us, that is, not as it is "in-itself." On the other hand, Kant is an idealist when he insists that ideals are not to be measured by whether they reflect reality: We adjudicate on what is real and what is not by whether it lives up to experience.[24] Contrary to Hume's thesis, if our ideas of what is possible are restricted by our ideas of what is reality, no new ideas can flourish. While providing a foundation for knowledge through reaffirming the validity of knowing by a priori reasoning, Kant also simultaneously defines limits to laws of reason by insisting that, for rational human beings, knowledge is restricted within the boundary of the phenomena. Although Kant says that we have no rational grounds, no proof, of any divine or mystic forces, the effect is to make cognitive space for faith in the existence of divine or mystic forces, beyond the boundary. According to Kant's analysis, human unhappiness or alienation results from the inability of a rational, but finite, being to realize the inner drive to be perfect, or from the failure to accept human boundaries. Escaping from the phenomenal world and entering the world of *noumenon* was achievable by an individual's own moral imperatives.

The German idealist Georg Wilhelm Friedrich Hegel (1770–1831) endeavoured to resolve the paradoxes introduced by Kant in his *Critique*—dichotomies between faith and reason, between the infinite and the finite.[25] Hegel's philosophy, which is, by universal acknowledgement, abstract and quite difficult, demands our attention for two important reasons. First, his thought is the most ambitious single attempt to demonstrate that modernity contains within itself the intellectual resources to justify, rationally, its rupture with the premodern era.[26] And second, he was the first philosopher to put contradiction and social change at the centre of thought itself. In his most celebrated work, *The Phenomenology of Spirit* (1807) Hegel provides a complex rational reconstruction of the entire prior movement of Enlightenment. He emphasizes that we cannot ever simply perceive the world, or what is, without preconditions or presuppositions—and here Hegel follows Immanuel Kant—because all human consciousness is informed by innate principles or categories of thought that mediate everything we experience.[27] While Hegel endorsed Kant's view on the importance of the human mind and mental instruments in the quest for truth about the world, of his criticisms of Kant, two are particularly important for sociological theory. First, for Kant, the conceptual mental instruments through which humans see the world are static and universal for all finite rational beings. The problem is the ahistorical character of Kant's conceptual framework. Kant's position is that the framework constitutes a timeless grid that gives to human experience a uniform conceptual structure that remains constant throughout history. The basic structure of the human mind is the same in all times and locations, whether in Aristotle's ancient Greece or Kant's early modern Germany.

From Hegel's perspective things are more complex. Some categories may well be universal, but others, for instance cause and effect, are understood by civilizations in different ways. In *The Phenomenology,* Hegel posits the existence of a universal Mind or Spirit (that is, *Geist* in Hegel's German) that knows itself as Spirit—which develops over time and may differentiate itself in different cultures that exist at the same time. Hegel's notion of Mind or Spirit is complex; in essence it is an activity or process involving self-expression, self-actualization, and self-knowledge.[28] For Hegel, the principles or categories of thought that mediate everything we experience constitute the changing *historical* preconditions of knowledge. The following dense and difficult-to-understand passage from the *Phenomenology of Spirit* contains the essence of Hegel's philosophy:

> The living Substance is being which is in truth *Subject*, or, what is the same, is in truth actual only in so far as it is the movement of positing itself, or is the mediation of its self-othering with itself. This Substance is, as Subject, pure, *simple negativity*, and is for this very reason the bifurcation of the simple; it is the *doubling which sets up opposition*, and then again the negation of this indifferent diversity and of its antithesis [the immediate simplicity]. Only this self-*restoring* sameness, or this reflection in otherness within itself—not an *original* or *immediate* unity as such—is the Truth. It is the process of its own becoming, the circle that presupposes its end as its goal, having its end also as its beginning; and only by being worked out to its end, is it actual.[29]

The Subject, or consciousness—Spirit—is conceived as a *relation*, not a discrete thing; over time "it is the process of its own becoming." Whereas Kant conceptualizes the mind's categories of understanding as being subjective forms that are imposed on the world and provided by sense experience, Hegel's conception of the self is *socially situated*, as each is a member of a historically specific community of self-conscious human agents. Hegel's idealism, therefore, provides the power to elevate the subject beyond immediate circumstances, by placing the individual outside the boundaries provided by empirical limitations. Moreover, his conception of Absolute Spirit, that is, truth in its totality, evolves and develops and has a circular structure: "a circle which returns upon itself, for mediation bends back its end into the beginning."[30] In Hegel's eyes, human history is the story of the gradual realization of reason or spirit in the world; it is a rational process that enables truth to unfold and make itself known to the human mind. This realization of reason or spirit involves the full articulation of its internal contradictions.

This brings us to Hegel's second and equally important criticism of Kant, that the human mind develops by grasping the interplay between potential opposites, which results in a third alternative or "unity of opposites."[31] For Hegel, the cognitive process by which we come to understand the world is a dialectical process. Dialectic is a concept that predates European Enlightenment. The etymology of *dialectic* comes from the Latin *dialectica* and Greek *dialecktike*, and for Plato the word described "the art of defining ideas." The essence of dialectical thinking, for Hegel, lay in its intrinsic contradictions as well as in a method of

Georg Wilhelm Friederich Hegel (1770–1831), a major European philosopher who provided a significant critique of Kantian idealism. His philosophy, particularly his use of the dialectic method to human history, profoundly influenced Karl Marx. Marx famously "stood on its head" Hegelian dialectic thought.

interrelated thinking that uses concepts of change, motion, and process. Dialectical thinking is the principle whereby apparently stable thoughts reveal their inherent instability; such thoughts turn into their opposites and then into new, more complex thoughts, as the thought of being is overcome by the thought of nothing and then is overcome by the higher thought of becoming. Through the negation of the antithesis and "the process of its own becoming" consciousness becomes aware of itself as Spirit, that is, becomes "conscious of itself as its own world, and of the world as itself."[32] The pinnacle of "absolute knowing" is the point at which Spirit reflects on the proceeding process and understands it as nothing other than its own self-development.

The dialectical principle, for Hegel, is "the soul of all genuinely scientific cognition," and it is what gives Hegel's thinking its distinctive character by making his thought dynamic. In his *Science of Logic* (1812) Hegel describes what he calls his "absolute method of knowing" that makes philosophy "an objective, demonstrated science."[33] The principle depicts three moments, or concepts, or categories of each logical reality: (a) Thought, (b) the dialectical moment and (c) the speculative moment or positive Reason. Hegel seeks to demonstrate that upon conceptual analysis, category A proves to contain a contrary category, B, and conversely that category B proves to contain category A, thus showing both categories to be self-contradictory. Hegel then seeks to demonstrate that this negative result has a positive outcome, a new category, C, which is referred to as the "negation of the negation" or the "determinate negation." Category C *unites* the preceding categories A and B. When analyzed, the new category C contains both A and B, but they are united in such a way that they are not only preserved but also abolished. Hegel's term for this paradoxical process is *Aufhebung*; that is, the categories A and B are preserved in the new C but only with their original meaning modified. This modification of their meaning renders them no longer self-contradictory. At a new higher level, category C plays the role that was formerly played by category A, and the reciprocal containment is repeated.[34] This triadic logic of understanding is often conveniently depicted as *thesis* (affirmation of Thought which is contradictory), *antithesis* (affirmation of its negation), and *synthesis* (a higher unity which itself becomes a thesis), but we must emphasize that Hegel never used these terms in his formulation. The dialectical method provides the necessary five scientific standards for Hegel's philosophical system. A philosophy must (1) have a method, (2) constitute an entire system, (3) examine the totality, (4) demonstrate the necessity of everything, and (5) give to the subject an a priori character.

The dialectical principle is somewhat abstract, but Hegel gave sociological form to his dialectical mode of thinking in his famous account of the mythical master-slave relation. Our treatment here is by no means exhaustive; our aim is simply to flesh out Hegel's dialectical thinking and, in so doing, to introduce the reader to its application in Marx's analysis of industrial capitalism. In *Phenomenology* Hegel sets out the "science of the *experience* which consciousness goes through"[35] and uses the master-slave relation to explain the mutation of two primitive consciousnesses into self-consciousness and its *logical* development into a higher unity of absolute knowledge. Through experience, simple sensuous certainty changes logically into perception and then mutates itself into *understanding*. Hegel then argues that consciousness turns logically into self-consciousness. Fully developed self-consciousness occurs only when two (or more) self-consciousnesses mutually recognize one another. We would not exist as a person unless another person acknowledges our existence. In Hegel's words, "Self-consciousness exists in and for itself when, and by the fact that, it so exists for another; that is, it exists only in being acknowledged."[36]

At the initial encounter the two primitive self-consciousnesses are perfectly symmetrical, neither would see the other as participating in Reason and committed to mutual recognition. Each demands to be recognized by the other as "being-for-itself," or having freedom, and wants to end the symmetry by dominating the other. "Absolute negativity" is what Hegel calls the freedom that is determined by the other. The symmetry of mutual recognition between the two self-consciousnesses is unstable; only one self is to be recognized, the other recognizes. One will be master; the other will be slave. Since each primitive self demands to be recognized by the other, a "life and death" struggle for recognition by the other ensues. Each combatant tries to prove to the other how free he or she is by killing the other and by risking his or her life in the struggle. The struggle contains a contradiction: if either combatant should actually be killed, the victorious self would be denied the desired recognition by the dead self-consciousness. The logical "experience" of self-consciousness shows that both combatants must emerge from the struggle alive. Indeed, one must surrender to the other self, if there is to be any conferral of the desired recognition. The self that surrenders out of fear of death, abandoning its effort to be recognized, will become the slave. The dominant self-consciousness, who is recognized by the slave, becomes the master. The slave labours for the master.

In the master-slave relation each self learns through experience that they are actually the opposite of what they initially take themselves to be. The master takes himself to manifest freedom and unfettered power. However, he does not learn the productive potential within himself; he does not produce but consumes, and, paradoxically, despite his freedom he is in fact *dependent* on the labour of the slave. Further, the master wants recognition from an *equal* other but obtains recognition only from a subordinate human being reduced to an object and a means, a slave. The slave, by contrast, takes herself to be wholly unfree, but learns that she does in fact experience an *independent* consciousness or spirit of her own. In *Phenomenology* Hegel writes: "Just as lordship showed that its essential nature is the reverse of what it wants to be, so too servitude in its consummation will really turn into the opposite of what it immediately is; as a consciousness forced back into itself, it will withdraw into itself and be transformed into a truly independent consciousness."[37] Through the process of labour the slave learns self-respect and realizes that he, too, has a certain power to transform things: "the bondsman [slave] realizes that it is precisely in his work wherein he seemed to have only an alienated existence that he acquires a mind of his own."[38] Albeit "a freedom which is still enmeshed in servitude ... it is a skill which is a master over some things, but not over the universal power and the whole of objective being."[39] Hegel's master-slave relation logically mutates to a new shape of self-consciousness that renders fully explicit the master's state of dependence and the slave's independent consciousness. This truth was always there, implicitly, unconsciously, or, in the Helegian language affected by Marx, "in-itself"; the *experience* renders it explicit, consciously, or "for itself." Thus, as each self learns of its reversed relation to being, it brings in its wake a new higher unity, one that is enriched and made self-conscious by the experience of contradiction and antagonism: Each self benefits more from mutual economic cooperation than from domination. For Hegel, the dialectic is a self-transformative process and, because it embodies a theory of social change—the slave is the driving force—provides the epistemological paradigm for understanding human history.[40] The philosophy of Hegel has been referred to as "the algebra of revolution."[41] While this is an exaggeration, his ideas, particularly the emphasis on social change, had a profound influence on Marx and a group of German intellectuals in the 1830s and 1840s known as the Young Hegelians.

The Critique of Hegel, Feuerbach, and Marx's Philosophy

Marx's early conversion from the romantic idealism of Kant to the dialectic idealism of Hegel is captured in a letter to his father written in 1837. Marx wrote, "A curtain had fallen, my holy of holies had been shattered, and new gods had to be found. Setting out from idealism ... I hit upon seeking the Idea in the real itself. If formerly the gods had dwelt above the world, they now become its centre."[42] Previously, Marx had read fragments of Hegel's work but did not like its "grotesque craggy melody." Converted to Hegelianism, Marx began to believe that the Idea was immanent in the real. Thus, he changed from a romantic idealist who viewed human history as an arena of contesting ideas or Spirit, shaping the course of civilization, to a materialist who viewed human history as propelled by material forces. On his conversion to Hegelian philosophy, Marx joined in 1836 a group of radical intellectuals, including Bruno Baurer, Ludwig Feuerbach, Moses Hess, Arnold Ruge, and Max Stirner known as the Young Hegelians of the Left.

Both Left and Right Hegelians accepted Hegel's central thesis that nothing is eternal or unchanging and the trajectory of human history could be understood by dialectic logic. The Young Hegelians of the Right stressed Hegel's belief that German culture was a synthesis representing the zenith of civilization. The Young Hegelians of the Left, however, rejected this interpretation of Hegel and championed engagement in the dialectic in history; they were the vanguard of intellectual revolutionaries. Isaiah Berlin summed up the politics of the Young Hegelians of the Left like this, "To promote revolution by the technical skills which he alone commands, that is by intellectual warfare."[43] Whereas Hegel held that philosophy and religion had different forms but the same content, the Young Hegelians argued that religion was irrational and, moreover, acted as an impediment to social progress. Thus, the Young Hegelians' intellectual climate was secular idealism, which is echoed in Marx's proclamation in the preface of his doctoral thesis: "Philosophy makes no secret of it. Prometheus' confession—in a word, I detest all Gods."

Marx's critique of Hegel's philosophy was strongly influenced by the well-known German philosopher and theologian Ludwig Feuerbach (1804–1872). While Feuerbach accepted Hegel's aphorism that human history contains an inner logic that is an intelligible dialectic process,

Lugwig Feuerbach (1804–1872), a German philosopher, criticized Hegel for maintaining a religious world view. Karl Marx acknowledged Feuerbach's intellectual achievements, particularly his views on religion and the limitations of the Hegelian dialectic.

his central criticism was that Hegel, like Kant, had mystified truth, because the mind and the world change only abstractly at the level of pure thought. In his *Essence of Christianity* (1841), Feuerbach criticizes Hegel's philosophy for preserving a religious world view. He argues that philosophy should not start from God or the Absolute but with the human being and the material world, the finite, the real, and acknowledge the primacy of the senses: "The essence of Hegel's logic is transcendent thought, exteriorised human thought."[44] Feuerbach uses the concepts of inversion and alienation to critique Hegel's philosophy. He argues that religion is an expression of mythical thinking that involves people unwittingly projecting their human essence onto a fictitious entity, whose image represents perfection. The human being, fearful and self-doubting, "sets God before him as the antithesis of himself … God and man are extremes: God is the absolutely positive, the sum of all realities; man the absolutely negative."[45] Thus, God represents the externalization of an idealized human being. As such, this amounts to a process of inversion in which the *subject*—a creative human being—is reduced to the status of a *predicate*—a dependent attribute—by a *mystic being*—God—the product of the human imagination. Further, Feuerbach conceives the dialectic as a process self-alienation because people divest themselves of their best qualities and make these qualities the property of a God or gods. Hegel's philosophy, according to Feuerbach, remained a repository of religion and, as such, had to be exorcized to end the deception. He asserts that there must be an "inversion of this inversion" so that human beings recognize themselves as the real subject of the process, thereby regaining control over human attributes, desires, and potentialities that they had ascribed to a God-ideal, and thus be in a position to restore to themselves their alienated "species-being" (*Gattungswesen)* or human nature. People would realize that *they* have created religion: when intellectuals understood the "true" relationship of thought to being; that is, "Being is the subject, thought is the predicate. Thought arises from being—being does not arise from thought."[46] Though critical of Hegel,

Feuerbach, like Bruno Bauer, still believed that alienation consists in, or is caused by, false consciousness, that human emancipation from religion and idealism is an intellectual process, and that the course of history is determined by the conceptual dialectic of the universal Spirit. As such, Feuerbach's thesis remained firmly within a Hegelian framework.[47]

In the winter of 1843–4, Marx criticized the metaphysical "fog" that, in his view, engulfed the Young Hegelians and developed his critique of religion, idealist philosophy, and political economy. In so doing, Marx substituted the Young Hegelians' idealism and liberalism with materialism and communism. Marx argues that religion gives expression to a mode of life that is empty, dehumanized, alienated; it serves the dual social function of compensation for material human suffering, which makes it *seem* tolerable, and gives expression to false or illusionary actualization of human's deepest desires. In the early article "Critique of Hegel's *Philosophy of Right,*" published in the *Deutsch-Französische Jahrbücher* (German-French Annals) in early 1844, Marx argues that religion served the purpose of reparation for self-alienation and economic alienation. Though agreeing with Feuerbach that "man makes religion; religion does not make man," Marx thought this observation was too abstract and ahistorical. Marx writes:

> *Man* is not an abstract being, squatting outside the world. Man is *the human world,* the state, society. This state, this society produce religion which is an *inverted world consciousness,* because they are an *inverted world*. Religion is the general theory of this world ... The struggle against religion is, therefore, indirectly a struggle against *that world* whose spiritual *aroma* is religion. *Religious* suffering is at the same time an *expression* of real suffering and a *protest* against real suffering. Religion is the sigh of the oppressed creature, the sentiment of a heartless world, and the soul of soulless conditions. It is the *opium* of the people.[48]

In other words, people live in such a world, such a system of social organization, that invoke feelings of reverence or religious consciousness, which become the dominant way of thinking about themselves and their world. It is easy to interpret the famous epigram in the sentence about religion being the "opium of the people" as meaning that religious consciousness produces human misery or that *opium* is the problem. Both interpretations are incorrect. To understand Marx's metaphor we have to know that opium was in common use in Europe as a relief from pain and other forms of distress and that it produces some form of ecstasy in those who use it. If we view the use of opium as a *response*—albeit not a wise one especially if used regularly—to human suffering, we have something approaching Marx's thesis. Religious illusions and the God Hypothesis give expression to a sense of emptiness and worthlessness of human life—to alienation. Its social function is to anaesthetize people to the misery of their social condition. The belief in the supernatural also offers solace for this alienation, by the false promise of a meaningful and unalienated life in the beyond. Religion, therefore, is an illogical reaction to the finitude of the human condition. Marx's conclusion is that it's necessary to change the material conditions that make false consciousness or illusion necessary: "The abolition of religion as the illusory happiness of men is a demand for the real happiness. The call to abandon their illusions about their condition is a call to abandon a condition, which requires illusions. The criticism of religion is, therefore, the embryonic criticism of this vale of tears of which religion is the halo."[49] The religious veil may conceal earthly misery, but the task of removing the veil is just a beginning. This is because the phenomenon of religion, the disease, is primarily alienated labour—a state of existence increasingly exacerbated by the division of labour and ever-sophisticated factory machinery in the hands of capitalists—as opposed to abstract ideas in the form of religion. Once alienated labour is abolished, and the cause removed, the symptom religion will wither on its own. Philosophers must be critical of material conditions, not only their religious reflection. Thus, in his *Theses on Feuerbach* (1845), Marx declares that the chief defect of all hitherto philosophers is that they "have only interpreted the world, in various ways; the point is to *change* it."[50] We can now begin to understand why religion is so important to Marx's critique of German idealist philosophy, for "the criticism of religion is the premise of all criticism."[51] His critique of religion ends with the categorical imperative to abolish all conditions that abase, enslave, and alienate human beings.

The concept of alienation figures prominently throughout his critique of idealist philosophy. Originating with Hegel, alienation has become a key concept in modern sociology. Central to Marx's notion of alienation is the idea that human beings progressively forfeit to something (e.g., God) or someone (e.g., capitalist) something that is the essence of their nature: principally, the control over their own attributes and activities. Marx addresses political alienation in another early article entitled "On the Jewish Question" (1844). In this Marx discusses how the state deprives people of the opportunity for attaining the essence of their nature, and this is a form of political alienation. Marx's old mentor Bruno Bauer had argued that Jewish emancipation could not be achieved without the state ceasing to be Christian. Marx, however, countered that the simple secularization of the state was insufficient because it did not entail the emancipation of men and women as human beings. He argued that specific social elements had to be defeated in order to achieve genuine emancipation: "The question of the relation between political emancipation and religion becomes for us a question of the relation between political emancipation and human emancipation."[52] For Marx, human emancipation necessitated the democratic control over all human activity.

The *Theses on Feuerbach* contains a critique of Feuerbach's account of materialism. While Marx accepted much of Feuerbach's critique of Hegel, he argued that the real relation of thought to human life was not Feuerbach's human nature, but the social and economic system of production. In Marx's inversion, thought is a product of these concrete conditions. The opening page of the first thesis contains the essence of Marx's criticism of Feuerbach's materialism: "The chief defect of all hitherto existing materialism—that of Feuerbach included—is that the thing, reality, sensuousness, is conceived only in the form of the object or of *contemplation*, but not as *human sensuous activity, practice*, not subjectivity."[53] Marx concludes that Feuerbach's critique of Hegel merely substituted one mystic for another. In the second thesis, Marx explains his principle of the unity of theory and practice: "The question whether objective truth can be attributed to human thinking is not a question of theory but is a practical question."[54] Theory without practice is a form of pure cognitive gymnastics—graceful perhaps, but ultimately sterile and of no consequence. And in the third, Marx identifies the agent of social change: "The materialist doctrine that men are products of circumstances and upbringing ... forgets that it is men who change circumstances and that it is essential to educate the educator himself."[55] The other theses elucidate Marx's rebuttal of the idealistic and static nature of Feuerbach's treatment of religious alienation.

After exposing religion as a product of social alienation, Marx applied himself to studying material conditions or political economy, the outcome of which was the *Economic and Philosophical Manuscripts* of 1844. Known as the *Paris Manuscripts*, these were not published until 1927. The documents contain a critique of the classical economists Adam Smith and David Ricardo, culminating with an analysis of "alienated labour," a description of communism, and a critique of Hegel's dialectic logic. Marx's discussions on communism and his analysis of the workings of industrial capitalism are examined in chapters 4 and 5. Here we examine how Marx extended Hegelian and Feuerbachian dialectics. Marx begins by acknowledging Feuerbach's achievements, particularly in having discovered the "true" materialist approach by making the social relationship of "man to man" the basic principle of the theory of human social development. Marx's concept of social reality is dialectical, but he never wrote a systematic treatment of dialectics; this was left to Engels. In *Anti-Dühring*, Engels wrote, "Dialectic is nothing more than the science of the general laws of motion and development of nature, human society and thought."[56]

The sociological implication of Marx's dialectical method is illustrated by Hegel's classic representation of the master-slave relation. Hegel understands mastery and enslavement as an inner dialectical movement: a struggle for recognition by the other. The slave discovers his *independent* consciousness through creative labour and servitude. For Marx, Hegel's master-slave dialectic was ambiguous, mystifying, and written from an idealistic standpoint. In the *Manuscripts* Marx recognizes the positive elements of Hegel's dialectic as found in the *Phenomenology of Spirit*: "The outstanding thing in Hegel's *Phenomenology* and its final outcome—the dialectic of negativity as the moving and generating principle—is first that Hegel conceives the self-genesis of man as a process, conceives objectification as loss of the object, as alienation and as transcendence of this alienation; that he thus grasps the essence of *labour* and comprehends objective man—true, because real man—as the outcome of man's *own labour.*"[57] However, Marx criticized Hegel's dialectic because it still harbours uncritical idealism: "The appropriation of man's essential powers, which have become objects, indeed alien objects, is only an *appropriation* occurring in *consciousness*, in *pure thought*, i.e., in *abstraction*."[58] While Hegel, according to Marx, only recognizes "abstractly mental labour," Marx defined his position as consistently humanist, avoiding idealism, which recognizes "real, corporeal *man*, man with his feet firmly on the solid ground, man exhaling and inhaling all the forces of nature."[59] Marx rejected Hegel's notion of Mind or Spirit [*Geist*] as an independent reality and replaced its supposed antithesis to the external world by the antithesis between human beings and their *social* being.[60] For Marx, Hegel's philosophy reduces human beings and history to an abstract mental process, which constitutes a form of alienation. Contrary to Hegel's thesis, the human mind is the totality of mental powers and human activities within a given society. Adopting Feuerbach's approach of secularizing the Hegelian dialectic, Marx explains his methodology in the afterword to *Capital* (1867): "My dialectic method is not only different from the Hegelian, but is its direct opposite. To Hegel, the life-process of the human brain, i.e., the process of thinking, which, under the name of "the Idea," he even transforms into an independent subject, is the demiurgos of the real world, and the real world is only the external, phenomenal form of "the Idea." With me, on the contrary, the ideal is nothing less than the material world reflected by the human mind, and translated into forms of thought."[61]

Human history is indeed, as Hegel averred, intelligible and an arena of human alienation, but Marx argues that the Mind or Spirit is not the creator of the universe, and the process of thinking does not forge human development towards self-realization. Marx, however, acknowledges he is extracting from Hegelian dialectic "the rational kernel within the mystical shell"[62] to develop a materialist dialectic. To demystify Hegel's *Logic* Marx believed it must be "inverted" or "turned upside down" before it can assume a rationale shape. For Marx, the "mystical shell" of Hegel's dialectic is his pantheistic metaphysics, and the "rational kernel" is Hegel's vision of the social as structured organically and characterized by inherent contradictions and tendencies to development. Thus, Marx accepts Hegel's vision of reality, but rejects the metaphysics that motivates his vision.[63] Marx's philosophical perspective, which he didn't change, is that any dialectical perception of nature is subordinate to the dialectic between human activities and nature, which arises from human beings satisfying their everyday economic needs through their physical and mental labour. He considered his dialectic method scientific because it went beyond superficial market relationships to explain these in terms of, what Marx referred to as, the *essence* of production relations: the material interchange between humans and nature.[64] Marx's dialectical method therefore offers an alternative epistemological paradigm for understanding modernity.

Criticisms

To write about the intellectual assault of Marx's philosophical concepts would be almost tantamount to writing a history of modern philosophy, and would go well beyond the aims of this chapter. This is not to say that we cannot identify a number of criticisms of Marx's early works.[65] Marx never studied religion in any detail, but his discussions underscore that religion is a product of social alienation; people create an imaginary figure known as God in order to find solace from their suffering in the real world; the cause of their suffering is alienation caused by a particular type of social organization; and religious beliefs and values provide justification of social inequality—the theory of ideology. One possible criticism to Marx's hypothesis on religion is that traditional theology is right and Marx is wrong. There is a God, who created all things and ordered us to worship him. For those who believe in God, or a higher force, and in the possibility of the salvation of one's soul through the acceptance of Christ as personal saviour, Marx is wrong. Critics also point out that while there is evidence to support the *secularization thesis* within post-modernity, new religious movements and Christian and Islamic fundamentalisms challenge the notion that religious commitment in all its manifestations is about solace or a bourgeois conspiracy to keep down the "lower orders."

An orthodox critique of Marx's dialectic method is that it lacks credibility because it denies the basic law of non-contradiction. This law holds that the presence of a contradiction in a statement or proposition invalidates its claim to truth. For example, we cannot simultaneously say that "it is snowing and that it is not snowing." Formal logic denies that contradictions exist in reality, and if they do exist in thought, they signify an error and have to be expunged in order to reveal truth. Marx's insistence that contradictions exist in capitalist reality is, critics claim, a repudiation of formal logic. Marx's use of the dialectic logic, critics argue, also exhibits a doctrinaire or "mechanical" use of the concept and a unidirectional notion of human history. This alleged doctrinaire dialectic is counter-posed against the *genuine dialectic* defined in terms of interaction, reciprocity, and multiple causation. In reply it may be said that dialectic contradictions are different from contradictions referred to in formal thinking. From this perspective, the principle of non-contradiction has limited value when studying a complex system in motion, and, thus, dialectic contradictions do not repudiate the laws of thought but augment and qualify them.

Conclusion

Marx's philosophical concepts are not original but were fashioned by an extraordinary constellation of philosophers and transformed through dialogue and imagination. Specifically, there was continuity in the thinking of Hegel, Feuerbach, and Marx that certainly began at least with Immanuel Kant. Hegel provided a major critique of Kantian idealism, and his account of the master-slave dialectic gave sociological form to his philosophy. He described the myth about self-discovery, showing how desire, consciousness, and self-consciousness, fear, conflict, alienation, and creative labour is bound up with the struggle for recognition. The paradigmatic account of the master and slave relation, with contradictory elements of antagonism as well as economic cooperation, resonates in Marx's analyses of social classes and the dynamics of social change in terms of the struggle of opposed class interests.[66] For Marx, the stimulant of social change and liberation is class-consciousness. Unsurprisingly, the sociological implications of Hegel's concept of recognition have provided inspiration for the feminist conception of gender relations and inequality, and for the Black Consciousness Movement. Through his critique of German idealism, Marx constitutes society in materialist terms. Thus, he argues that it's not human consciousness that determines the social being, but rather it is the material conditions and a purposive praxis that determines human consciousness. His conception of political, religious, philosophical, and economic alienation—a condition in which human beings progressively lose control and become estranged within the society that their labour creates—remain central to his writings.

As we have noted, there can be few social theorists whose fate it has been to be so persistently misunderstood as Marx. And, following the collapse of the Stalinist regimes in Eastern Europe in the late 1980s, we could be forgiven for assuming that Marx's philosophy has little to contribute to understanding the myriad challenges facing us in the early twenty-first century. There is, of course, a strong intellectual case for studying Marx's philosophy alongside the great philosophers such as Plato, Aristotle, Descartes, Hume, Kant, and Hegel. The works of these philosophers are read not because they have discovered the path to utopia but because they are valued for their insight, originality, rigour, vision, and so on. Marx's critique of Idealism is worthy of attention for more than historical reasons, however. Confronted with globalization, fragmented governmental responses to global warming, the manoeuvring by industrialized states to control the planet's remaining, diminishing fossil fuel reserves, and the public discourse on Christianity and Islam, his philosophical concepts are insightful, suggestive, and remain a fertile source for social theorizing.[67]

Turning to his commentary on religion, for example, Marx's concepts contain much insight for a world of diasporas and multiculturalism. Marx may well have said to followers of different faiths, "Your mind would be much more free if you critically examine your faith and think about the degree to which that faith is itself responsible for your own oppression." Without doubt, we are witnessing a revival of religion in local and global political conflicts.[68] Perhaps once people stop kneeling before an imaginary deity, humanity will be able to address cataclysmic issues such as war, epidemics, and global warming. As to the relevance of Marx's dialectic, it can be argued that despite all the knowledge and sophisticated information technologies we possess, we still don't know how to conceptualize the intensified conflict over the Earth's shrinking reserves of natural resources, and global warming, and how to make connections between apparently disparate processes and events. Marx's dialectic is the logic of post-modernity that provides us a way to think philosophically about the changes and innumerable instances of contradiction that lie at the heart of processes of globalization and global warming; for these reasons, we suggest Marx's dialectic is of lasting significance.

Notes

1 Alan Swingewood, *Marx and Modern Social Theory* (London: Macmillan, 1975).

2 David McLellan, *Marx* (London: Fontana Press,1975), 9.

3 Ibid., 72.

4 Ian Craib, *Classical Social Theory* (Oxford: Oxford University Press, 1997), 11.

5 Francis Wheen, *Karl Marx* (London: Fourth Estate, 2000), 8.

6 David McLellan, *Karl Marx: The Legacy* (London: BBC, 1983), 12.

7 Ibid., 35–6.

8 Ibid., 41.

9 Quoted in McLellan, *Karl Marx*, 14–15.

10 Wheen, *Karl Marx*, 32.

11 Quoted in McLellan, *Marx Before Marxism*, 65.

12 Ibid., 71.

13 Quoted in McLellan, *Marx*, 12.

14 Wheen, *Karl Marx*, 179–80.

15 Ibid.,180–95.

16 Ibid., 184.

17 Ibid., 234.

18 Ibid., 298.

19 Philip Jackson, "Marx's Skin Disease," *The Globe and Mail* (October 31, 2007), A2.

20 David Hume, *Enquiry Concerning Human Understanding* (1748), 110, quoted in A. Broadie, *The Scottish Enlightenment* (Edinburgh: Birlinn, 2001), 132.

21 David Hume, *Treatise of Human Nature* (1739), bks. 1 and 4, chap. 6, quoted in Dorina Outram, *The Enlightenment* (New York: Cambridge University Press, 2005), 100.

22 Immanuel Kant, *Critique of Pure Reason*, trans. Norman Kemp Smith (1781; New York: St. Martin's Press, 1965), 41–3.

23 P. Hyland, ed., *The Enlightenment: A Source and Reader* (London: Routledge, 2003), 53.

24 Susan Neiman, "Can and Kant," *The Globe and Mail* (May 10, 2008), D13.

25 Other German idealists such as Johann Gottlieb Fichte (1762–1814) and Friedrich Schelling (1775–1854) also addressed the paradoxes that Kant had enshrined in his works.

26 This section draws heavily from the chapter on Hegel in Alex Callinicos, *Social Theory: A Historical Introduction*, 2nd ed., (Cambridge: Polity Press, 2007), 39–56.

27 See Stephen Houlgate, *An Introduction to Hegel* (Oxford: Blackwell, 2005), 4–12.

28 Allen W. Wood, *Karl Marx* (London: Routledge, 2004), 199.

29 G. F. Hegel, *Phenomenology of Spirit*, trans. A.V. Miller (1807; Oxford: Clarendon Press, 1977), 10, quoted in Callinicos, *Social Theory*.

30 G.F. Hegel, *Science of Logic*, quoted in Callinicos, *Social Theory*, 52.

31 Hegel, *Science of Logic,* quoted in Wood, *Karl Marx*, 208.

32 Callinicos, *Social Theory*, 51.

33 Hegel, *Science of Logic*, quoted in M. Forster, "Hegel's Dialectical Method" in *The Cambridge Companion to Hegel,* ed. F.C. Beiser (Cambridge: Cambridge University Press, 1993), 131.

34 Ibid., 132.

35 Hegel, *Phenomenology of Spirit*, 21.

36 Ibid., 111.

37 Ibid., 117.

38 Ibid., 119.

39 Ibid.

40 Anelica Nuzzo, "Dialectic as Logic of Transformative Processes," in *Hegel: New Directions*, ed. Katerina Deligiorgi (Chesham: Acumen Publishing, 2006), 94–9.

41 A Herzen, *My Past and Thoughts*, abr. ed., ed. D. Macdonald (Berkeley: University of California Press, 1982), and quoted in Callinicos, *Social Theory*, 79.

42 David McLellan, *Marx Before Marxism* (New York: Harper Torchbooks, 1970), 48.

43 Isaiah Berlin, *Karl Marx: His Life and Environment*, 4th ed. (Oxford: Oxford University Press, 1978), 49–50.

44 L. Feuerbach, *The Essence of Christianity*, trans. George Eliot (New York: Harper 1957), quoted in McLellan, *Marx Before Marxism*, 107.

45 Feurerbach, *Essence of Christianity*, 33.

46 McLellan, *Marx Before Marxism,* 107.

47 Callinicos, *Social Theory,* 79–80.

48 Karl Marx, "On the Jewish Question," in *The Marx-Engels Reader*, 2nd ed., ed. Robert C. Tucker (New York: Norton, 1978), 31; hereafter cited as the *Marx-Engels Reader,* 53–4.

49 Ibid., 54.

50 Ibid., 145.

51 Ibid., 53.

52 Ibid., 31.

53 Tucker, *Marx-Engels Reader*, 143.

54 Tucker, *Marx-Engels Reader*, 144.

55 Ibid.

56 F. Engels, *Anti-Dühring* (1878; Moscow: Progress Publishers, 1959), 194; quoted in Swingewood, *Marx and Modern Social Theory*, 14.

57 Tucker, *Marx-Engels Reader*, 112.

58 Ibid., 111.

59 Ibid., 115.

60 David McLellan, *The Thought of Karl Marx*, 2nd ed. (London: Macmillan, 1980), 118.

61 Karl Marx, "Afterword to the Second German Edition," *Capital, Volume I* (1873), in *Marx-Engels Reader*, 301.

62 Ibid., 302.

63 Allen W. Wood, *Karl Marx,* 2nd ed. (New York: Routledge, 2004).

64 McLellan, *The Thought of Karl Marx*, 153–4.

65 See J. Wolff, *Why Read Marx Today*? (Oxford: Oxford University Press, 2002), 100–8; L. Wilde, "Logic: Dialectic and Contradiction," in *The Cambridge Companion to Marx*, ed. T. Carver (New York: Cambridge University Press, 1991) 275–95; Wood, *Karl Marx*; Swingewood, *Marx and Modern Social Theory*, 11–12.

66 Chris Arthur has argued that the alleged connection between the master-slave relation and Marx's conception of class-consciousness and class struggle, first popularized by Jean-Paul Sarte, is false. See "Hegel's Master-Slave Dialectic and a Myth of Marxology," *New Left Review* (Nov–Dec 1983): 67–75. Available at: http://marxmyths.org/chris-arthur/article.htm.

67 See Wolff, *Why Read Marx Today?*; Nuzzo, "Dialectic as Logic of Transformative Processes, 100.

68 John Gray, *Black Mass* (Toronto: Doubleday, 2007), 3.

4. Karl Marx: Theory of History

> They have the strength; they can subjugate us, but they cannot halt social processes by either crime or force. History is ours, and the people make it.
>
> —Salvador Allende[1]

> The concept of the fettering of the productive forces of society by its [therefore obsolete] relations of production, is at the very centre of the historical architectonic: social revolution occurs when and only when, and because, relations of production fetter the productive forces.
>
> —G.A. Cohen[2]

> Marx, more than any other thinker of his generation, was a connoisseur of paradox and contradiction—since it was these very contradictions which guaranteed capitalism's demise.
>
> —Francis Wheen

CENTRAL TO MARX'S PHILOSOPHICAL work is that humans have individual and collective material needs. The labour necessary to satisfy those needs leads to ever more complex forms of productive activity and social interaction. It is this philosophical view of human interaction with nature and each other that forms the rudiments of a theory of human history. At Marx's funeral, Friedrich Engels paid tribute to Marx for discovering the primary motive force in human history: "Just as Darwin discovered the law of development of organic nature, so Marx discovered the law of the development of human history."[3] Marx never used the term *historical materialism*, which was coined by Engels; instead he preferred to call his approach "the materialist conception of history."

A thorough treatment of Marx's materialist concept of human history is found in the first part of *The German Ideology*, and the most succinct statement of it is in the *Preface to a Contribution to the Critique of Political Economy*. The aim of *The German Ideology*, which Marx co-authored with Engels, was "to settle accounts with our erstwhile philosophical conscience."[4] As such, Marx's conception of history is a product of his critique of German philosophy; it is an amalgam of Hegel's *historical* idealism and Feuerbach's ahistoric *materialism*. The materialist conception of history provides an explanatory theory about society's different forms, class structure, ideas and belief systems, and development over time. As such, it constitutes one of the central elements in Marx's social theory. This chapter examines the core elements of the general theory. To begin to understand the materialist conception of history, however, we need to recognize the importance Marx gave to human nature and to labour in formulating his theory of history.

Human Nature and Alienation

Marx's understanding of human history is based on the fundamental premise that people must obtain their basic necessities of life—food, clothing, shelter, and so on—by cooperating with others and by entering into a conscious relation with nature: "The first fact to be established is the physical organization of these individuals and their consequent relation to the rest of nature."[5] Thus, the most important historical act is the act of productive labour; by this means men and women develop and exercise their human faculties to transform nature to satisfy their material needs.

The human species, according to Marx, is different from all other animal species because it alone produces its own means of subsistence and creates something in reality that previously existed only in an individual's imagination:

> We presuppose labour in a form that stamps it as exclusively human. A spider conducts operations that resemble those of a weaver, and a bee puts to shame many an architect in the construction of her cells. But what distinguishes the worst architect from the best bees is this, that the architect raises his structure in imagination before he erects reality. At the end of every labour process we get a result that existed in the imagination of the labourer at its commencement. He not only effects a change of form in the material on which he works, but he also realizes a purpose of his own that gives a law to his *modus operandi*, and to which he must subordinate his will.[6]

Marx calls this process whereby humans create external objects from their internal thoughts objectification. We can begin to understand Marx's concept of objectification by thinking of the work of an artist. An artwork is a representation of the artist's imagination—a representation of an idea that exists in the artist's head before the commencement of the project. Thus, the artwork is an objectification of the artist. During the creative process the artist's ideas about the object may change and prompt a new art form that needs objectification. Work, for Marx, provides the means through which humans can realize the fullness of their humanity. It is through work, an essentially social process, that humans transform nature, themselves, their consciousness, and in so doing, they transform society. This is the basis of Marx's materialism.

Marx believed that capitalism destroyed the pleasure associated with socially productive labour. Consequently, humans are alienated from their product, productive activity, species being, and other people. Under capitalism people are unable to exercise and experience the distinctively human capacity to make and remake nature critical for human freedom. All forms of alienation are located in the real world and it was necessary to change the conditions that cause alienated labour.

In the *Economic and Political Manuscripts* of 1844, Marx sets forth the fundamentals of his conception of history based on philosophical concepts, such as self-estrangement, derived directly from Feuerbach; ideas on communism, from French socialists Gracchus Babeuf and Charles Fourier; and his understanding of capitalism, derived from Adam Smith's political economy. Capitalism perverts the relation between human nature and productive power—thereby stultifying human creativity—and as such is the locus of *alienated labour*. The following tour de force contains Marx's classic statement on alienated labour under capitalism:

> The object which labour produces—labour's product—confronts it as *something alien*, as a *power independent* of the producer ... The worker is related to the *product of his labour* as to an *alien* object. For on this premise it is clear that the more the worker spends himself, the more powerful the alien objective world becomes ... the poorer he himself—his inner world—becomes, the less belongs to him as his own ... The alienation

> of the worker in his product means not only that his labour becomes an object, an *external* existence, but that it exists *outside him*, independently, as something alien to him, and that it becomes a power of its own confronting him; it means that life which he has conferred on the object confronts him as something hostile and alien ... But the estrangement is manifested not only in the result but in the *act of production*—within the producing activity itself ... Estranged labour turns man's *species being* into a being *alien* to him, into a *means* of his *individual* existence. It estranges man's own body from him, as it does external nature and his spiritual essence, his *human being*. An immediate consequence ... is the estrangement of *man from man*.[7]

This dense passage can be read in more than one way. What follows is the traditional interpretation in which Marx contends that humans experience four discrete but related types of alienation: alienation from their product, from their own productive activity, from their own nature or species being, and from other human beings.

The first type of alienated labour is from the *product*. Extensive use of division of labour and machinery means that workers have no creative input into how products are designed or made. In this sense, the product confronts the individual worker "as something alien, as a power independent of the producer." The more sophisticated the productive process becomes when narrower divisions of labour and machinery are applied, the less significant is the individual worker. In a less obvious way, humans collectively become alienated from the products they create because of two related concepts: mystification and domination. Everything individuals use or encounter in their daily lives is the result of accumulative learning. This process creates a mystery around products because few people have any real understanding of how everyday products actually work. Take, for example, the use of Internet and related electronic products that also dominate people's lives. The cumulative effect is that "we are strangers in our own world."[8]

The second type of alienated labour is "within the producing activity itself." Marx emphasizes the long-term tendency for extensive division of labour and machinery to make paid work repetitive and monotonous, with no intrinsic satisfaction: The worker becomes an "appendage of the machine."[9] Marx's notion of alienated labour is an extension of Feuerbach's analysis of religious alienation. In the *Manuscripts* he makes the parallel with Feuerbach explicit: "Just as in religion the spontaneous activity of the human imagination, of the human brain and the human heart, operates independently of the individual—that is, operates on him as an alien, divine or diabolical activity—in the same way the worker's activity is not his spontaneous activity. It belongs to another; it is the loss of his self."[10]

The third type of alienated labour is alienation from the human species. Marx uses the term *species being*, taken from Feuerbach, to refer to the free ability of humans to create a world to manifest their full creative nature. The human essence is not an abstraction, however, but is concrete and defined by the human capacity to create objects: "It is just in the working-up of the objective world, therefore, that man first really proves himself to be a *species being*. This production is his active species life. Through and because of this production, nature appears as *his* work and his reality. The object of labour is, therefore, the *objectification of man's species life*: for he duplicates himself not only, as in consciousness, intellectually, but also actively, in reality, and therefore he contemplates himself in a world that he has created."[11] But, under capitalism, work embodies the opposite qualities; labour is repetitive, boring, and mentally incapacitating. Work is, as a woman factory worker put it, "the blank patch between brief evening and the next."[12] Workers produce as animals do and feel human only when they are not engaged in paid work.

The fourth type of alienation is "the estrangement of man from man." Again, Marx draws on Feuerbach's analysis of religion to capture the experience. In the intellectual world, "religious self-estrangement necessarily appears in the relationship of the layman to the priest. In the real, practical world self-estrangement can only become manifest through the real practical relationship to other men."[13] The essential point is that capitalist production alienates workers from fellow human beings as well as from the communal aspects of their lives. This is because people are fixated with going to work to earn money and then going to shopping malls to spend it—a consumer culture in which humans are integrated into society, above all, as consumers.[14] By being continuously engaged in the individual aspect of a consumer culture, people have little time or interest for communal *species essence*. Alienation is an objective condition, and although it has subjective implications, a "happy" worker is no less alienated than a bored one. Marx's economic analysis of alienated labour is a central concept in his conception of the development of capitalism.

The General Thesis

The materialist conception of history explains how productive systems work and the underlying motive force in human history. It also had a political function. By applying "scientific" principles to history, it provided a theoretical basis for social revolution. The 1859 *Preface* is the canonical text that served as a "guiding thread" for Marx's work:

> In the social production of their life, men enter into definite relations that are indispensable and independent of their will, relations of production, which correspond to a definite stage of development of their material productive forces. The sum total of these relations of production constitutes the economic structure of society, the real foundation, on which raises a legal and political superstructure and to which correspond definite forms of social consciousness. The mode of production of material life conditions the social, political and intellectual life process in general. It is not the consciousness of men that determines their being, but, on the contrary, their social being that determines their consciousness.[15]

Three fundamental, central concepts of Marx's general thesis can be derived from this passage: productive forces, relations of production, and superstructure. The *productive forces* refer to two factors: the "means of production" and "labour power." Although there are some problems of definition, what qualifies as a productive force is an instrument or facility that must be ownable, progressively developed by humans, and capable of being utilized by labour power.[16] In every stage of history, men and women utilize non-human resources such as tools, machinery, and raw materials—the means of production—and harness human resources in the form of physical strength, skill, or knowledge—labour power—to satisfy their needs. The means of production vary with the different ways that human beings attain their subsistence. For example, a fisher needs a net, and a software designer uses more complex instruments of production. Concomitantly, the type of labour power used by the fisher or the software designer differs according to the specific ways these individuals attain their economic needs.

The *relations of production* may be defined in terms of ownership and non-ownership of the means of production,[17] but this also refers to the social relations and classes that are formed. Under capitalism, the relations of production that workers enter into, "indispensable and independent of their will,"[18] differ from feudalism. Workers are compelled to sell their labour power to the owner of the means of production in order to satisfy their own economic needs. In so doing they also enter into relations that place them under the control of the owner. The forces and the relations of production constitute the economic base of a society. According to Marx, it is people's economic activity, their "mode of production in material life," that primarily characterizes their social life, and the economic base determines both the institutions and prevalent ideas in the society. This is Marx's first premise: the level of development of the productive forces will determine the nature of its social form. Why should this be the case? As we have already discussed, factory production involved specialized machines and occupations that changed patterns of ownership and instilled new patterns of social behaviour. An equivalent transformation in present society is the new globally oriented communication technology of the so-called knowledge economy. The apparent primacy of economic affairs over social processes illustrates the materialist nature of Marx's theory of history.

The *superstructure* in Marx's socio-economic model includes the legal, political, religious, philosophical, and cultural processes and institutions of society. The legal and political architecture, for instance, embrace criminal and civil law, the law courts, and provincial and federal parliamentary systems. These non-economic features are different forms of human consciousness that correspond to the locus of economic forces. The nature of the relationship between the superstructure, or forms of consciousness, and the economic base introduces Marx's second premise: the economic base will "determine" (*bestimmen*) the social superstructure of a society, and, moreover, the superstructure and consciousness will change as the economic base undergoes change. Here lies the genesis of Marx's theory of ideology. The causal relationship embodied in Marx's theory and the process of change has been a central topic for debate and scholarship. For heuristic purposes, figure 4.1 shows Marx's socio-economic model that can be used to analyze any society.

FIGURE 4.1 Marx's triadic model of industrial capitalism

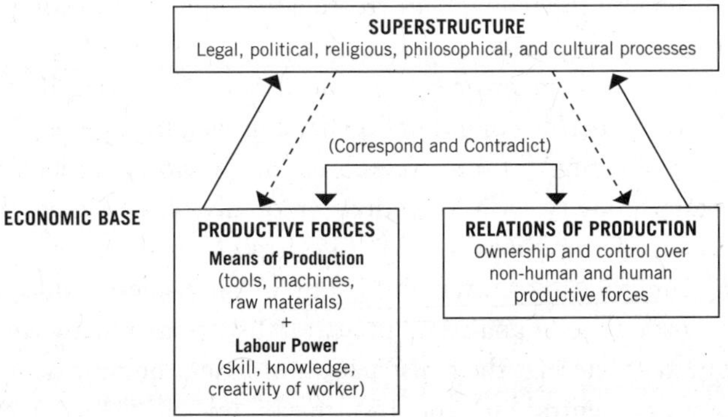

The notion of *mode of production* is not fully defined by Marx, but it conceptualizes the totality and richness of a society comprising both productive forces and relations of production and also its superstructure at each historical epoch. Thus, the pre-capitalist feudal mode of production subordinates ancient forms of production, such as the use of slaves, and the capitalist mode of production subordinates feudal forms of production, such as domestic handcraft workers, to the logic of factory production.

Stages of Historical Development

Like Saint-Simon and Comte in the early nineteenth century, Marx viewed human history as passing through stages of development. These various stages of social forms serve to test Marx's general theory. As Marx explains it, a particular system of forces and relations of production, and a class system that develops on the basis of these relationships, define different types of society. In *The German Ideology*, five social forms are described: tribal (*Stammeigentum*) or primitive communism, ancient, feudalism, capitalism, and communism. The pre-capitalist modes of production were conservative and underdeveloped because of low labour productivity. The first pre-capitalist mode of production is *tribal*, which describes a rudimentary system of social organization in which people live together principally by "hunting and fishing, by the rearing of beasts or, in the highest stage, agriculture ... The division of labour is at this stage still very elementary"[19] and the social structure is limited to family and kinship groups of "patriarchal family chieftains, below them the members of the tribe, finally slaves."[20] Property is communal and, therefore, there is no developed system of class relations. Tribalism did embody a degree of gender equality among non-slaves.[21]

The *ancient* mode of production, such as Rome and Greece, describes a form of society, in which tribes create cities and develop complex civil structures, "which proceeds especially from the union of several tribes into a city by agreement or by conquest, and which is still accompanied by slavery. Beside communal ownership we already find ... private property developing."[22] Productive forces are based on agricultural and rudimentary industry, with more division of labour. The social structure begins to change too. In particular, a system of class relations develops, and the "antagonism of town and country" intensifies.[23] Marx devotes relatively little time to analyzing pre-capitalist tribal and ancient societies, but he suggests that the construction of irrigation networks and the emergence of a central bureaucracy are examples of the primacy of the productive forces.

For Marx, different social forms throughout the centuries are to be explained by a changing complex interplay of productive and other material factors and the social and ideological spheres of society.

The *feudal* mode of production is still predominantly agricultural and community-based but "the directly producing class standing against it is not the slaves, but the enserfed small peasantry."[24] Whereas slaves were at the disposal of their owner, serfs had the right to life and access to common land. The feudal or "petty" mode of production was based on subsistence agriculture, with simple commodity production undertaken by a multiplicity of small capitalists and traditional, skilled, guild masters and artisans. Extensive rules governed the making and selling of commodities under the early craft guilds. In terms of relations of production, there was little differentiation between master and journeymen. One historian, describing the position of the journeyman to his master, goes so far as to state that it was "rather that of a companion-worker than a hired servant," with the journeyman working alongside his employer and often eating at the employer's table.[25] A distinctive social structure developed with "the differentiation of princes, nobility, clergy and peasants in the country, and masters, journeymen, apprentices and soon also the rabble of casual labourers in the towns."[26] The feudal legal system defined the ownership and privileges of the landowning aristocratic class. And religious ideologies indoctrinated people to view themselves as subjugated to nature, life as essentially preordained, and an attempt to change the inevitable as futile. The accumulated wealth of the town-based bourgeois class intensified the conflicts between rural and town interests. Marx notes, "As soon as feudalism is fully developed, there also arises antagonism to the towns."[27]

The *capitalist* mode of production, with its antecedents in the growth of a market-oriented economy, population growth, and improved domestic agricultural techniques spanning several centuries, became historically significant after the rise of the urban bourgeoisie and the decline of feudalism. In volume one of *Capital*, Marx explains the emergence of industrial capitalism by identifying the fettering of the productive forces by feudal relations of production:

> This [feudal] mode of production presupposes parcelling of the soil, and scattering of the other means of production. As it excludes the concentration of these means of production, so also it excludes cooperation, division of labour within each separate process of production, the control over, and the productive application of the forces of Nature by society, and the free development of the social productive powers. It is compatible only with a system of production, and a society, moving within narrow and more or less primitive bounds ... At a certain stage of development it brings forth the material agencies for its own dissolution. From that moment new forces and new passions spring up in the bosom of society; but the old social organization fetters them and keeps them down. It must be annihilated; it is annihilated.[28]

This passage illustrates the complexity of Marx's dialectic process. A highly complex and technical division of labour and the relation between formally free wage labour and private capital defines *industrial capitalism*. The transition to a large-scale mode of production also saw the development of new relations of production and modes of life. The new workforce were landless workers for whom selling their labour power was their sole source of subsistence, and the capitalists extracted a surplus of production through the dominance of the wage nexus. For the new urban bourgeoisie, with their own economic interests, the feudal system was archaic and socially rigid. The politically decisive urban bourgeoisie abolished the privileges of the rural aristocracy. They also enacted parliamentary legislation and created a legal system that reflected their power and suited the needs of a complex industrial society consisting of private ownership and geared towards the needs of the market. Wage legislation and welfare security, culminating in the Poor Law Act of 1834—which made all welfare relief less desirable than the lowest wage—forced long working hours and discipline on the working poor. There were also ideological changes. The most profound was secularization and the triumph of Enlightenment thinking, which encouraged a moral-individualism that stressed individual choice, responsibility, and a strong work ethic. Thus, under capitalism, the forces and relations of production changed, as did the forms of consciousness, which were part of the superstructure.

The three main elements of the totality, as depicted in figure 4.1, are in harmony again.

For Marx, capitalism is the last antagonistic society. The system's inherent contradictions become the driving force for its replacement by the communist mode of production. In Marx's words, "Communism is the position as the negation of the negation, and is hence the *actual* phase necessary for the next stage of historical development in the process of human emancipation and recovery."[29] Under communism there is no alienation because, writes Marx, "society regulates the production and thus human labour is fulfilling, free from coercion, and will correspond to humans' nature.[30] Thus "socialized production" makes it possible for humans to work and produce as artists would, allowing their creative powers to be expressed.

Dual Theory of Social Change

Marx's conception of history seeks to explain the underlying motive force in social change. He devotes little time to explaining the process of change in pre-capitalist societies, focusing instead on the transition from feudalism to capitalism in Western Europe. Marx identifies two fundamental drivers of social change. Social change is driven, first, by contradictions between the forces and relations of production and, second, by class antagonisms. Marx offers a highly complex account of his first position. A standard reading of the 1859 *Preface* and the historical chapters of *Capital, Volume I*, is that, at the initial stage of each mode of production, productive forces develop rapidly in society. The relations of production help this process of development as they complement, or *correspond*, to the productive force. Over time, the two reciprocally dependent forces and relations of production come into conflict, or *contradiction*, and turn into "fetters" on human progress. Marx explains his theory of social change like this:

> At a certain stage of their development, the material productive forces of society come in conflict with the existing relations of production, or—what is but a legal expression for the same thing—with the property relations within which they have been at work hitherto. From forms of development of the productive forces these relations turn into their fetters. Then begins an epoch of social revolution. With the change of the economic foundation the entire immense superstructure is more or less rapidly transformed. In considering such transformations a distinction should always be made between the material transformation of

> the economic conditions of production, which can be determined with the precision of natural science, and the legal, political, religious, aesthetic or philosophic—in short, ideological forms in which men become conscious of this conflict and fight it out.[31]

The first two sentences of this canonical passage introduce the notion of *fettering*, which has been interpreted two ways. The passage can be read as stating that by fettering relations of production, all further improvement in productive forces is prevented; this is the *absolute* conception of fettering. Alternatively, fettering occurs when existing relations of production are suboptimal for further development of the productive forces; this is referred to as *relative* conception of fettering. At the core of historical materialism is the notion that the system of production of a given society will eventually exhaust its creative and productive potential.[32] Marx also suggests—in the third sentence in the passage—that social revolution installs productively superior relations of production. However, an epoch of social revolution cannot be successful unless it follows from a real change in the economic base, as Marx argues in the *Preface*: "No social order ever perishes before all the productive forces for which there is room in it have developed; the new, higher relations of production never appear before the material conditions of their existence have matured in the womb of the old society itself."[33] The text, which taken literally, support the absolute conception of fettering, whereby a social revolution occurs when, and only when, and because obsolete relations of production fetter all further improvements in the productive forces of society.[34]

Competing with the notion that structural contradictions develop within the production system is the concept that the primary mechanism of historical change is class struggle. In each stage of development a particular antagonistic class is responsible for the transformation from one mode of production to another. The textual evidence shows that Marx believed that in the feudal mode of production it was the bourgeoisie who were responsible, whereas in capitalist society it was the proletariat. Marx states in the 1859 *Preface*, "Men become conscious of this conflict and fight it out."[35] And the *Communist Manifesto*, which shows Marx and Engels as joint authors but was penned by Marx alone, famously declares: "The history of all hitherto existing society is the history of class struggles. Freeman and slave, patrician and plebeian, lord and serf, guild-master and journeyman, in a word, oppressor and oppressed, stood in constant opposition to one another, carried on an uninterrupted, now hidden, now open fight, a fight that each time ended, either in a revolutionary reconstitution of society at large, or in the common ruin of the contending classes."[36] In the previous quote, Marx posits that in all societies the most distinctive form of social stratification involves class divisions. This universal feature is viewed in the economic terms of both those who own property and live off the labour of others and also those who do productive labour. Hegel's master and slave dialectic, with its inherent contradictions and antagonisms, finds resonance here in Marx's analyses of classes. Just as for Hegel, where master and slave define and implicate each other, for Marx, the capitalist and proletariat define each other by their *relation* to the means of production. Under capitalism historical change arises from the antagonistic relations between two opposing class interests, the bourgeoisie and the proletariat: "The bourgeois relations of production are the last antagonistic form of the social process of production—antagonistic not in the sense of individual antagonism, but of one arising from the social conditions of life of the individuals; at the same time the productive forces developing in the womb of the bourgeois society create the material conditions for the solution of that antagonism. This social formation brings, therefore, the prehistory of human society to a close."[37]

For Marx, classes are change agents, but the precise dynamics of how society is transformed through *class struggles* is ambiguous, and there is a tension in Marx's thought on the primacy of the productive forces to which he was committed by his general theory. For example, in pre-capitalist societies there were slave rebellions and serf riots in medieval feudalism, but action by *oppressed* slaves did not cause the collapse of the ancient society. Similarly, in feudal England, the antagonistic classes were not "lord and serf" but the rural aristocracy and the urban bourgeoisie. The serfs, the oppressed class, were rather marginal historical actors in the transformation process. Historical change occurred because feudalism imposed fetters on the further development of the economic system, and the merchant capitalists, not the serfs, were the revolutionary class who dismantled the fetters of the obsolete guilds and caused the demise of feudalism.

Did Marx believe that acute class struggles inevitably generate historical change? There is certainly textual evidence in his writings that support such an interpretation. Thus, describing the social revolution that transformed feudalism into capitalism, Marx declares, "The weapons with which the bourgeoisie felled feudalism to the ground are now turned against the bourgeoisie itself."[38] Yet, there is also textual evidence that Marx did not ascribe to a deterministic conception of historical change. His celebrated statement, "Men make their own history, but they do not make it just as they please; they do not make it under circumstances chosen by themselves, but under circumstances directly found, given and transmitted from the past"[39] recognizes that human agency is constrained by the structural limits constituted by a given society and that historic change is not the inevitable consequence of these limits. Neither is the human factor the isolated individual of Rousseau's philosophy. The individual is embedded in a particular social context and class.[40] Thus, Marx's dual theory identifies structure and agency as the prime drivers of social change. On the one hand, the tendency for the forces and relations of production to enter into a structural contradiction creates fetters on the productive forces. On the other hand, the class struggle is contingent on an unpredictable composite of economic, political, and social factors.

Social Class

As we have already seen, the guiding thread of Marx's general theory had convinced him that to understand human history and capitalist modernity it was essential to analyze the development of productive forces and relations of production of different societies. Marx's general theory holds that the internal dynamics of each mode of production predicts that class relations, class conflict, and ideology principally flow from the economic structure. For Marx, social class performs an essential role in the dialectic process; people, not productive forces, engage in revolution and develop societies when historical circumstances provide them with the motives and opportunities for doing so. His account of class is intended to explain the prevalence and forms of collective social conflict in terms of the *class position* and *common interests* of the people engaged in it.[41]

We have two questions: What are classes? How many classes are there? Unfortunately, Marx nowhere offers a systematic analysis of class devoted to the first question, but we know that Marx rejected the theory that class is stratified purely according to income and wealth. He wrote, "The size of one's purse is a purely quantitative distinction, whereby any two individuals of the same class may be incited against one another at will."[42]

As to the second question, in the polemical *Communist Manifesto*, society is characterized as divided into "two great classes," with wholly irreconcilable common interests, and class struggles are expressed purely in bipolar terms as a conflict between the bourgeoisie and the proletariat.[43] A salient point here, one frequently missed, is that the *Manifesto* was crafted primarily as a political document to inspire and energize European labour movements in a specific historical context; it was never intended as a treatise on social class. The beginning of a more complete answer to our second question can be found in *The Eighteenth Bruniaire of Louis Bonaparte* (1852), where Marx identifies seven classes: bourgeoisie, petty bourgeoisie, financiers, landlords, free farmers, proletariat, and the lumpenproletariat. In his more academic and historical studies, such as *Capital, Volume III*, Marx states that wage labourers, capitalists, and landowners constitute the "three big classes" of modern capitalist society, but he also mentions "middle and intermediate" classes.[44] As Marx conceives classes, they have a dynamic or subjective element: classes *potentially* develop or arise out of the experience of a given system of production relations. In the capitalist mode of production, each category of people constituting the capitalists and the proletariat is a *class-in-itself* because each class is defined by its common relationship to the means of production. As in Hegel's master-slave dialectic, however, only when a group of people share the same relationship to the means of production, share a common interest, and act together to discover a consciousness that promotes their common interests do they actually constitute a *class-for-itself*. Thus, class formation might be gauged by the development of social movements and ideologies that promote class interests. Based on these criteria, unsurprisingly, Marx was sometimes hesitant as to whether the proletariat had developed sufficiently to constitute itself as a class, and he observed, "The combination of capital has created for this mass a common situation, common interests. This mass is thus already a class as against capital, but not yet for itself."[45] He also noted impediments: "This organization of the proletarians into a class, and consequently into a political party, is continually being upset again by the competition between the workers themselves."[46]

It is common to read in many introductory sociology texts that Marx advanced a "simple two-class model" of social class. When the textual evidence demonstrates that Marx never articulated such a crude model, how can we explain this common misreading of Marx's ideas on class? In part it can be explained by the fact that Marx predicts the demise of capitalism through the triumph of class struggle, without an unambiguous theory of class itself.

Marx's account of class is intended to explain the prevalence and forms of collective social conflict in terms of the class position and common interests of the people engaging in it. For Marx, classes perform an essential role in the dialectic process. It is people, not productive forces, that engage in social revolution and develop societies when historical circumstances provide them with the motives and opportunities for doing so.

Marx's methodology also explains the misreading of his social theory.[47] Marx isolates the "essential" labour-capital relation to analyze capitalism's specific historical character, much as bourgeois economists use the concept of *ceteris paribus* to freeze all other determinate factors when isolating the price-quantity relation. Thus, *Capital, Volume I*, operates at a high level of abstraction with its assumption of a two-class model, while *Capital, Volume II* and *III*, extend and deepen the analysis by examining "many capitals," and, thus, industrial capitalism as an historical-empirical reality.[48] Marx did not discover classes in modern society; class structure was well known to historians and political economists. Marx's innovation was to construct a theory of how classes are related to particular historical epochs in the development of forces and relations of production in the society.[49]

Ideology and Consciousness

Marx's general theory not only supplies a conceptual framework through which to interpret past and present society and, through his conception of ideology, explains how people come to hold their erroneous views about society but also assigns a positive role to social factors in the transformation process. Marx held that, in all class societies, the dominant class develops and disseminates a web of social beliefs about how men and women relate to one another and how society should function, which provides legitimacy for its domination. Marx's treatment of ideology, as found in *The German Ideology* is part of his critique of Hegelian idealism. Whereas Hegel believed that ideas were manifestations of the Spirit, Marx believed that ideas or consciousness cannot have a life independent of practical activity; they are generated by and embedded in human activity or praxis like other social relations. This premise is indicated in figure 4.1 as solid lines. This is the meaning of the statement "The production of ideas, of conceptions, of consciousness, is at first directly interwoven with the material activity and the material intercourse of men, the language of real life."[50] In this sense, the social circumstances in which productive labour occurs condition the perception of the society in which people live and form the *practical consciousness* of human beings. Marx and Engels caution that ideologies are a distortion, which has the effect of inverting human perception of social reality: "In all ideology men and their circumstances appear upside down as a *camera obscura*."[51] The claim here is that ideas are like badly prescribed lenses; while allowing a person to view material conditions, they distort or obscure social reality. As an example, Marx and Engels posit that the liberal ideology of the French and United States revolutionaries, proclaiming the rights of man and equality, cannot be taken at face value and that political and legal freedoms are not eternal truths about humanity. Thus, the bourgeois ideology could only be understood with respect to the social relations of production in which it was embedded, that is, their pressing need to end feudal controls and their need for unfettered competition in economic life.

Marx's treatment of ideology also emphasizes that ideas do not evolve in a social vacuum; they do so as part of the consciousness of human beings living a particular mode of life, and, historically, they are propagated to serve a given class. In this way, Marx's theorem focuses on the connection between human consciousness, or thought, and praxis, or labour, which differentiates his view from Hegelian philosophy. In all class societies the purpose of the creation of ideas, as well as their dissemination, is to justify the rule of the dominant class over another class. In the words of Marx and Engels, "The ideas of the ruling class are in every epoch the ruling ideas: i.e., the class which is the ruling material force in society, is at the same time its ruling intellectual force."[52] The class that controls the means of production also controls the means of ideological production and its dissemination. For example, bourgeois economic theory of free trade is the principal ideology scaffolding capitalist globalization. Marx's generalization that the dominant ideas of any epoch are the ideas of the dominant class underscores the connection between the ideological superstructure and the forces and relations of production in a given society. The acceptance of the role of class domination arguably accounts for subordinate classes not recognizing their capacity to change society because of ideologies that obscure the injustice and inequality, but which fallaciously appear to be natural. Marx did not use the term *false consciousness*, a term used to explain the proletariat's general lack of interest for social revolution, but he may have implied it.[53] While some Marxist thinkers interpret Marx's conception of history as *closed*, whereby ideas are of secondary importance in the understanding of social change, others have convincingly reconstituted Marx's theory as an *open* theoretical perspective—an interpretation that emphasizes the relative autonomy of social factors and underscores the role of human consciousness in the shaping of history.[54] Marx's theory of ideology is complex and controversial, but it allows sociologists to explore the nexus among economics and culture and ideas.

Criticism

Marx's general theory provokes a cacophony of criticisms, raising issues that are complex and not easily settled.[55] The first critique relates to Marx's materialist account of human nature, which is predicated on a universal human being engaged in "creative" labour. Marx's ideal has been criticized both for being too materialistic and also for being utopian—requiring an impossibly total development of the individual when an extensive division of labour is necessary to meet the ever-demanding and sophisticated needs of people.[56] Under communism labour is free of alienation because, declares Marx, "society regulates the general production and thus makes it possible for me to do one thing today and another tomorrow, to hunt in the morning, fish in the afternoon, rear cattle in the evening, criticize after dinner, just as I have a mind, without ever becoming hunter, fisherman, shepherd or critic."[57] The question of who would collect the garbage, clean the toilets, or unblock the sewers was neither asked nor answered. Once asked who would polish shoes in a communist regime, Marx retorted, "You should." Critics rightly point to the adoption of a dehumanizing division of labour, embodied as Taylorism, in the failed Soviet Union and the Republic of China.[58] Against this criticism, it is argued that twentieth-century examples of socialized production deviate widely from what Marx envisioned, and his views on alienated free labour applied only when "world-historical" communism replaced capitalism.

Some of the most trenchant criticism of Marx's historical materialism has concentrated on its first premise, that the level of development of the productive forces will determine the nature of its social form. Critics accuse Marx of either economic or technological determinism, theories of history that are causally determined by either economic or technology factors entirely outside human control. The textual evidence for technological determinism is a frequently cited passage written by Marx in *The Poverty of Philosophy* (1847) in response to Pierre-Joseph Proudhon's book *The Philosophy of Poverty*: "The hand-mill gives you society with the feudal lord, the steam-mill gives you society with the industrial capitalist."[59] However, others argue against this criticism, saying it is a simple-minded misinterpretation of Marx[60] that not only interprets the passage literally, and in isolation, but also ignores his more thoughtful treatment of technology, as written twenty years later in the first volume of *Capital*. Marx writes: "Relics of bygone instruments of labour possess the same importance for the investigation of extinct economic forms of society, as do fossil bones for the determination of extinct species of animals. It is not the articles made, but how they are made, and by what instruments, that enables us to distinguish different economic epochs. Instruments of labour not only supply a standard of the degree of development to which human labour has attained, but they are also indicators of the social conditions under which that labour is carried on."[61] Here Marx understands that technology on its own—similarly to fossils excavated by archaeologists—allows only limited inferences to be made about the nature of society: it's not determinative. The level of technological development is a necessary but insufficient condition for the emergence of certain types of society.[62] Marx makes countless references to the idea that technology can never be separated from the economic, political, and social milieu in which it is embedded. The essence of Marx's dialectic thesis is the unity of the subjective and objective factors that are present throughout human history[63]: "Men make their own history."[64] Moreover, if human history is seen as technology contingent, this not only contradicts everyday experience but also is profoundly at variance with one of Marx's principal aims, the aim to educate and politicize the proletariat.

Although Marx's historical materialism gives primacy to the dialectic between forces and relations of production, critics argue there is a lacuna concerning gender. Insofar as Marx's analysis of capitalist society is a theory of oppression, his work is rightly criticized for failing to address gender, in general, and the position of women, in particular. For Marx, the essence of society is productive labour, and labour in the material world mediates people and nature. However, Marx's treatment of productive labour conceptually and empirically neglects the way that gender relations, men and masculinity, and, presumably, women and femininity are socially constructed. A related criticism is that Marx overanalyzes paid, productive work to the detriment of unpaid, domestic work performed mainly or exclusively by women. In this sense, his analysis of society is premised on a particular form of biological paradigm, one founded in sexual reproduction, and thus a particular version of sex and gender. One feminist interpretation of Marx's failure to consistently theorize female oppression, relations of production, and gender is an example of a European man writing about other European men and masculinity.[65] Marxist feminists took Marx's mental framework, however, to argue that women's exploitation and oppression is a symptom of capitalism. In this view, the family and the gendering of paid work are fundamentally shaped by the needs of the new industrial paradigm, and concomitantly, the family is the site of women's oppression. A rethinking of Marx's analysis emphasizes that labour power is itself a commodity produced and nurtured by the *unpaid* domestic labour of women.[66]

Conclusion

Marx believed that the mode of production of material life is central to social life. Bill Clinton's 1992 campaign slogan, "It's the economy, stupid," is an excellent summing up of Marx's argument that material forces profoundly affect social, political, and intellectual life processes far beyond the workplace. For Marx, different social forms throughout the centuries are to be explained by a changing, complex interplay of the productive factors and the social and ideological spheres of society. Society is not a stable constellation of essential factors, but a socially constituted structure with interconnected, contradictory tendencies and movements. Certain laws characterize human history, but it is people who ultimately build a society through their labour, or praxis, and change it. Marx argued that class-consciousness, not the unifying self-consciousness of Hegel's dialectic, in tandem with class struggle, is the stimulant for social change. But there is nothing inevitable about progressing to a higher form of society. Marx's conception of history provides a series of interrelated structural concepts through which to interpret the development of the past and to expose contradictory social phenomena in the present.

In the early twenty-first century, when grand narratives of history are considered passé,[67] what contribution can Marx's ideas make to contemporary social theory? First, his theory has taught sociologists to see the current society we inhabit in historical terms. The notion of the "sociological imagination" requires us to develop a historical consciousness, that is, to relate personal biographies and troubles to the broad sweep of human history. As the eminent American sociologist C. Wright Mills declared, "men do not usually define the troubles they endure in terms of historical change and institutional contradiction. The well-being they enjoy, they do not usually impute to the big ups and downs of the societies in which they live. Seldom aware of the intricate connection between the patterns of their own lives and the course of world history, ordinary men do not usually know what this connection means for the kinds of men they are becoming and for the kinds of history-making in which they might take part."[68] In addition, Marx's ideas about alienated labour under capitalism are extraordinarily rich and remain central to the contemporary study of work in the postmodern "new economy."[69]

The *Communist Manifesto* had a powerful affect on the thinking of many classical theorists and is arguably the most widely read political program. In North America its influence on William Du Bois is obvious in his call to Pan-African socialists: "You have nothing to lose but your Chains! You have a continent to regain!"[70] Its legacy is reflected also in *The Regina Manifesto*, adopted at the founding convention of the Canadian Co-operative Commonwealth Federation on July 20, 1933, which calls for extensive public ownership of the means of production, including all banks, communications companies, mining, and gasoline industries, and for the extension of rights for racial and religious minorities, but, regrettably, not for women.[71] Moreover, Marx's ideas on class still provide a skeletal framework for the basis of most contemporary sociological analysis of social class and stratification in capitalist societies.[72] What is truly astonishing about *The German Ideology* is that after more than 160 years Marx and Engels's ideas on ideology are still highly relevant in modern sociology, particularly studies of the relationships between the realm of ideas and those of economics. Canadian writer Naomi Klein, in *The Shock Doctrine*, illustrates how the ideology of U.S. laissez-faire capitalism serves a given class. The neo-conservative mantra of unfettered markets, privatization, and minimal regulatory controls was applied in South America in the 1970s and in Poland and Russia in the 1990s. The Chilean and Argentina economic elite, for example, supported by the military elite, systematically "cleansed" society of people who believed in competing ideologies other than laissez-faire capitalism and "pure profit." Finally, a historical perspective reminds us that capitalism is relatively new, and it's plausible to assume that a long-term alternative to capitalist globalization will develop. Understanding Marx's economics will give further insight into whether capitalist globalization will adapt itself, or eventually fetter the productive forces of society.

Notes

1 Salvador Allende, as quoted in *The Shock Doctrine: The Rise of Disaster Capitalism*, N. Klein (Toronto: Alfred A. Knopf, 2007), 122.

2 G.A. Cohen, *Karl Marx's Theory of History* (Princeton NJ: Princeton University Press, 2000), xxviii.

3 F. Engels, "Speech at the Graveside of Karl Marx," in *The Marx-Engels Reader*, 2nd ed., ed. Robert C. Tucker (New York: Norton, 1972), 681.

4 Tucker, *The Marx-Engels Reader*, 146.

5 Tucker, *The Marx-Engels Reader*, 149.

6 Ibid., 344–5.

7 Tucker, *The Marx-Engels Reader*, 71–77.

8 Jonathon Wolff, *Why Read Marx Today*? (Oxford: Oxford University Press, 2002), 32.

9 Tucker, *The Marx-Engels Reader*, 479.

10 Ibid., 74.

11 Ibid., 76.

12 Quoted in Keith Grint, *The Sociology of Work*, 2nd ed. (Cambridge: Polity Press, 1998), 1.

13 Ibid., 78.

14 See Paul Du Gay, *Consumption and Identity at Work* (London: Sage, 1996).

15 Tucker, *The Marx-Engels Reader*, 4.

16 Jon Elster, *Making Sense of Marx* (Cambridge: Cambridge University Press, 1985), 243–53.

17 Ibid., 254.

18 Tucker, *The Marx-Engels Reader*, 4.

19 Ibid.,151.

20 Ibid.

21 See F. Engels, "Origins of Family Property and the State," in *The Marx-Engels Reader*, ed. Tucker, 734–59.

22 Tucker, *The Marx-Engels Reader*, 151.

23 Ibid.

24 Tucker, *The Marx-Engels Reader*, 153.

25 Maurice Dobb, *Studies in the Development of Capitalism* (London: Routledge, 1963), 85.

26 Tucker, *The Marx-Engels Reader*, 153.

27 Ibid.

28 Ibid., 437.

29 Ibid., 93.

30 Ibid., 160.

31 Ibid., 4–5.

32 See G. A. Cohen, *Karl Marx's Theory of History* (Princeton, NJ: Princeton University Press, 2000), 326–40; Jon Elster, *Making Sense of Marx* (Cambridge: Cambridge University Press, 1985), 258–67.

33 Tucker, *The Marx-Engels Reader*, 5.

34 Cohen, *Karl Marx's Theory of History.*

35 Tucker, *The Marx-Engels Reader*, 5.

36 Ibid., 473–4.

37 Ibid., 5.

38 Ibid., 478.

39 Ibid., 595.

40 Alex Callinicos, *Social Theory: A Historical Introduction*, 2nd ed. (Cambridge: Polity, 207), 92–99.

41 See Allen W. Wood, *Karl Marx*, 2nd ed. (New York: Routledge, 2004), 82–100.

42 *Deutsche-Brusseler-Zeitung* (November 18, 1847), quoted in Elster, *Making Sense of Marx*, 336.

43 Tucker, *The Marx-Engels Reader*, 474.

44 Ibid., 441.

45 Ibid., 218.

46 Ibid., 481.

47 Alan Swingewood, *Marx and Modern Social Theory* (London: Macmillan, 1975), 47; Alan Swingewood, *A Short History of Sociological Thought* (New York: St. Martin's Press, 2000), 40.

48 Swingewood, *Marx and Modern Social Theory*, 46.

49 McLellan, *The Thought of Karl Marx*, 182.

50 Tucker, *The Marx-Engels Reader*, 154.

51 Ibid., 154.

52 Ibid., 172.

53 Larry Ray, *Theorizing Classical Sociology* (Buckingham: Open University Press, 1999), 71.

54 I.M. Zeitlin, *Ideology and the Development of Sociological Theory*, 7th ed. (New Jersey: Prentice Hall, 2001).

55 Wood, *Karl Marx*.

56 See Cohen, *Karl Marx's Theory of History*; C. Tausky, "Work is Desirable/Loathsome: Marx versus Freud," *Work and Occupations* 19, no.1 (1992): 3–17.

57 Tucker, *Marx-Engels Reader*, 160.

58 C.R. Littler, *The Development of the Labour Process in Capitalist Societies* (London: Heinemann, 1982).

59 Karl Marx, *The Poverty of Philosophy* (1847), in *Karl Marx: Selected Writings*, 2nd ed., ed. David McLellan (Oxford: Oxford University Press, 2000), 219–20.

60 See Wood, *Karl Marx*, chap. 5.

61 Tucker, *The Marx-Engels Reader*, 346.

62 Zeitlin, *Ideology and the Development of Sociological Theory*, 161.

63 McLellan, *The Thought of Karl Marx*, 137.

64 Tucker, *The Marx-Engels Reader*, 595.

65 See Susan Himmelweit, "Reproduction and the Materialist Conception of History: A Feminist Critique," in *The Cambridge Companion to Marx*, ed. T. Carver (New York: Cambridge University Press, 1991), 196–221; and Jeff Hern, "Gender: Biology, Nature and Capitalism," in *The Cambridge Companion to Marx*, ed. T. Carver, 222–45.

66 See R.A. Sydie, *Natural Women, Cultured Men* (Vancouver: University of British Columbia Press, 1994), 104–21.

67 See, for example, David Harvey, *The Condition of Postmodernity* (Oxford: Blackwell, 1990).

68 C.W. Mills, *The Sociological Imagination* (New York: Oxford University Press, 2000), 3–4.

69 James W. Rinehart, *The Tyranny of Work: Alienation and the Labour Process* (Toronto: Thomson-Nelson, 2006).

70 W.E.B. Du Bois, *The Autobiography of W.E.B. Du Bois: A Soliloquy on Viewing My Life from the Last Decade of Its First Century* (New York: International Publishers, 1968), 404.

71 See Gerald Caplan, "A Faith to Love, Free of Utopias," *The Globe and Mail* (July 19, 2008), A15.

72 Anthony Giddens, *Sociology* (Cambridge: Polity Press, 2009).

5. Karl Marx: Economics of Capitalism

[Marx's] meticulous scholarship gives an unrivalled account of capitalist modernization and the pathos and contradictions to which it is prone.
—David McLellan[1]

As long as capital endures, *Das Kapital* will never lose its resonance, or its power to bring the world into a new and sharper focus.
—Francis Wheen[2]

The leading economists of the day feared that if workers understood Marxist theory, the working class would realize how badly they were being exploited. Fearing this, economists sought to recast economic theory to neutralize the Marxist critique. They limited their neoclassical theory to looking at innocuous issues such as how prices change.
—Fred Lee[3]

ACCORDING TO MARX'S CONCEPTION of history, the different forms of society are to be explained by a complex interplay of contradictory forces and relations of production and the social and ideological spheres of society. His notion that societies pass through an historical sequence of stages, concluding in communism, was derived from the writings of socialists such as Saint-Simon, Babeuf, Fourier, and Robert Owen. The genius and profundity of Marx's general thesis and vision was the grounding of these historical sequences on economic theory, which, given the social context, gave these incendiary ideas scientific stature and legitimacy. In the capitalist stage the organization of productive forces necessitated that people enter into relations with each other as capitalist or wage earner, "independently of their will," even though, historically, human beings established the organization of productive forces. Marx's theories of capitalism are embedded in his materialist conception of history. For Marx, if alienated labour was to be an agent for social change, the dialectically self-destructive nature of the capital-labour relation had to be scientifically explained, as did the corresponding forces of production and the mechanisms of their development. Marx's economics, in contrast to orthodox mainstream economics, cannot be separated from his philosophy, history, or sociology, particularly in that his economic theory is concerned with social relations, social structure, and agency rather than with the technical relations between commodities and prices. As such, Marx's economic writings are deeply textured and profoundly sociological.

Marx's critique of the economics of capitalist society is found in various works: *Wage-Labour and Capital* (1849); *The Grundrisse: Foundations of the Critique of Political Economy* (1857–58), which was only published in 1953; and the three volumes of *Capital* (*Das Kapital*), which constitute the centrepiece of his economic writing. As previously noted, only the first volume of *Capital* (1867) was published in his lifetime, and therefore he had no opportunity to edit the completed work, eliminate inconsistencies and repetitions, and clarify ambiguities. This chapter focuses in a simple way, at the risk of oversimplification, on Marx's analysis of the nature of capitalism. Its goal is to allow the reader to engage with the original texts, and to discover the complexity, subtlety, and the deeply social nature of Marx's economics. First of all, as we must, the chapter briefly examines Marx's methodology. We then proceed to discuss commodity production and Marx's notion of commodity fetishism. From this it is a rational next step to examine the logic of capitalist exploitation, Marx's labour theory of value, and, his most outstanding contribution, the theory of surplus value. Finally, we examine one of the most controversial areas of Marx's economics, his theories of capitalist cyclical crises.

Methodology

Marx's economic theory is closely interconnected to his theory of history in that it ultimately aims "to lay bare the economic law of motion of modern society."[4] His methodology can be found in "The Method of Political Economy" in *The Grundrisse* and the preface to the second German edition of *Capital*. The three volumes of *Capital* are challenging to read because of their dialectical structure and interdisciplinary nature. As Marx says in *Capital, Volume I*, "every beginning is difficult"[5] and there are several reasons that make his economic theory difficult. First, *Capital* is difficult to comprehend because of the "Hegelian cast" over the text.[6] As discussed in a previous chapter, in his early works, Marx had rejected the metaphysical abstractions of German philosophy. As Marx describes it in the afterword to *Capital*, his methodology is inarguably dialectic. He asserts that the study of capitalism as a system must start not with the directly observable, such as the population of a country or its markets, but with chosen abstractions and should probe empirical observations arising from the economic structures they represent. For Marx, a scientific economic theory is one that adopts the principle of totality, which involves an understanding of the relations of the most simple to the more complex, the part to the social whole.[7] The principle of totality explains why Marx begins *Capital* with an analysis of a commodity. A commodity is the most basic *part* of the society that must be related to the social *whole*, a totality. Marx's holistic methodology emphasizes the need to investigate the multiple and historically changing inner connections between productive forces and all other non-economic facets of society.

A second factor that makes *Capital* difficult is the level of abstraction and the scope of its analysis. On the first point, as we discussed in the proceeding chapter, Marx simplifies observable reality by using abstract models. For example, the notion of ideal capitalism is an abstract conception that does not actually exist, but is a methodological tool to permit analysis of infinite reality. *Capital* is also difficult because of the theoretical scope of Marx's analysis. He is highly critical of bourgeois economics, which he believed to be superficial and inadequate. He eschewed Adam Smith and David Ricardo's theory of value, which centres on price and the art of economizing, and he emphasized the need for political economy to distinguish between *appearance* and *essence* and to take nothing for granted. For Marx, the function of economic theory is to penetrate beneath the markets of society (appearance) to the social foundation on which the markets are based (essence).[8] Orthodox economists inevitably take for granted those features of capitalist society—such as private ownership of productive forces and social relations—that Marx believed were necessary to explain. In *Capital* Marx sets himself the task of explaining how, in a capitalist society, the core capital-labour relation and its inner dynamics is the engine propelling capitalist development and the structural contradictions that cause its implosion.

A third factor that makes *Capital* a challenge to understand is the use of irony, an observation rarely made by Marx's detractors.[9] Marx uses a vast array of empirical data—government statistics, parliamentary reports, and reports from factory and health inspectors—but he also draws upon literary fiction. To illustrate capitalist pathologies, *Capital* is littered with irony. For example, to expose employers' tendency to abdicate any responsibility for the human casualties of technological change, Marx turns to Bill Sykes's plea to the jury in Charles Dickens's *Oliver Twist*: "Gentlemen, no doubt the throat of this commercial traveller has been cut. But that is not my fault; it is the fault of the knife. Must we, for such a temporary inconvenience, abolish the use of the knife? ... If you abolish the knife—you hurl us back into the depths of barbarism."[10] There are echoes here of the contemporary debate on gun control. Marx is a great ironist, and British biographer Francis Wheen plausibly argues that more value can be derived from *Capital* if it is read, not as a straightforward text on bourgeois economics but, as a work of art, a "vast Gothic novel whose heroes are enslaved and consumed by the monster they created."[11]

Commodity Production

In any society people have to *produce* by their own labour things that satisfy their basic needs. In some form or other they also *distribute* among one another the products of their productive labour. The individual members of the society *consume* the distributed products according to their needs. In *Capital* Marx explains how these three activities occur in a capitalist society. For Marx, the basic element of a society is a single commodity, and its wealth is "an immense accumulation of commodities." Thus, his economic theory of the capitalist mode of production begins with an analysis of a *commodity*, defined as any "object outside us, a thing that by its properties satisfies human wants of same sort or another."[12] In Marx's theory the term *commoditization* refers to a fundamental feature of capitalist modernity: a highly complex interdependent system of commodity production for the purpose of exchange, through the market, as opposed to direct use by the producer.

Following Adam Smith, Marx states that every commodity has a twofold aspect: its utility or *use value* and its *exchange value*. The use value of a commodity is determined by its capacity to satisfy a human need, which cannot be quantified. Use values are specific, concrete, and ahistorical, in the sense that they exist in all societies. The exchange value of a commodity refers to the value a commodity has when offered in exchange for other commodities. The exchange has to satisfy certain properties, for example, quantity or weight. If x exchanges for y, then x is equivalent in exchange to y. For example, if a dairy farmer produces cheese, by virtue of its natural properties, part will be consumed to satisfy a need. Any surplus may be taken to a market and exchanged either by barter for another product that the farmer cannot produce (e.g., a scythe) or for money. Thus, the commodity (cheese) acquires another feature unrelated to its use value, namely exchange value. Exchange value refers to the way a quantity of one commodity, say a kilo of cheese, can be expressed in terms of another commodity, say a scythe. Every commodity has a use value, but every commodity does not have an exchange value, either because it's something freely available (e.g., air, sunshine) or it is not exchanged (e.g., something produced for personal consumption).

Marx saw the exchange value of a commodity as embodying a numerical equivalence relationship between commodities, which can be quantified. But although every commodity is characterized by its particular physical or natural properties that give it its use value, the question that Marx addressed is what is the determinant of a commodity's exchange value. This had been a prime object of study of classical economists Adam Smith and David Ricardo. Adam Smith, in *The Wealth of Nations* (1776), postulates that value is conferred on a commodity by the act of labour. Smith explained it this way:

> Every man is rich or poor according to the degree in which he can afford to enjoy the necessaries, conveniences, and amusements of human life. But after the division of labour has once thoroughly taken place, it is but a very small part of these with which a man's own labour can supply him. The far greater part of them he must derive from the labour of other people, and he must be rich or poor according to the quantity of that labour which he can command, or which he can afford to purchase. The value of any commodity, therefore, is equal to the quantity of labour which it enables him to purchase or command. Labour, therefore, is the real measure of the exchangeable value of all commodities.[13]

For both Smith and Ricardo, labour adds value to a commodity. While Marx's most basic model of capitalist production incorporates both Ricardo's distinction between use value and exchange value and also Smith's labour theory of value, Marx used the economic concepts to draw very different conclusions.

Based upon Smith and Ricardo's labour theory of value, it is inarguable, Marx says, that what creates the relationship of exchange is not a physical property derived from the use value but a historically specific social one; it is the amount of labour time embodied in the commodities of production. Thus, the property that all commodities have in common, that creates the relationship of exchange, is that they are the product of labour. Marx next claims that labour, like commodities, has also a dual character depending on whether it produces use value or exchange value.

Concrete labour is labour of a particular type and purpose that creates use value. *Abstract labour*, on the other hand, creates exchange value based upon the quantity of abstract labour. Under capitalism, labour is, at the same time, both concrete and abstract, and its product is both a use value and an exchange value. Marx believed that his account of the "twofold character of labour" was one of the best points in *Capital*.[14] Marx's abstract treatment of value does not ignore the importance of demand. Commodities do exchange above their value; the *social necessary labour time* to produce them takes into account both direct (living) labour inputs and indirect (dead) labour inputs: the social necessary labour time to produce machinery and extract raw materials, that is, the means of production. Marx, unlike bourgeois economists, recognizes that demand has a class dimension: "supply and demand presuppose the existence of different classes and sections of classes which divide the total revenue of a society and consume it among themselves as revenue, and, therefore, make up the demand created by revenue."[15] Further, market price for commodities will be modified by differing capital-labour ratios, scarcities, tastes, skills, and monopolies.[16]

The capitalist mode of production is characterized by the production of social use values, and the exchange of the products of concrete labour is expressed, in exchange, as abstract social necessary labour. If value were determined by actual abstract labour time it would mean that a commodity produced by a slow and incompetent worker would produce a more valuable commodity than an identical one produced in less time by a conscientious worker. This problem is avoided because of the concept of social necessary labour time, which means the average amount of time and level of skill and effort required for the production of the commodity in a particular industry.

Marx's labour theory of value embodies a social relationship that can be theoretically quantified by calculating the exchange value of a commodity in relation to the total amount of labour time expended to produce the commodity. What characterizes the capitalist mode of production is not just the exchange of commodities but the buying and selling of the worker's capacity to work, which Marx called labour power. For Marx, it is only historic abstract labour power that defines capitalism: "On the one hand all labour is, speaking physiologically, an expenditure of human labour-power, and in its character of identical abstract human labour, it creates and forms the value of commodities. On the other hand, all labour is the expenditure of human labour-power in a special form and with a definite aim, and in this, its character of concrete useful labour, it produces use-values."[17] Under capitalism, labour power becomes a commodity; the buyer is the capitalist; the seller is the worker. The price of labour power is the wage. As a commodity, labour power must have a use value: therefore, it is the creator of use values in the form of commodities and, as such, embodies abstract labour. In this process labour power is unique as a commodity because its use value creates specific values in commodity form, and hence, it's the creator of value for the capitalist. Although the worker creates value, the capitalist's ownership and control over the means of production ties the worker to the wage system. Thus, Marx's labour theory of value not only explains commodity production but also embodies the basic relations of production specific to capitalism. The social exchange of labour power is predicated upon the private ownership of the means of production, on the one hand, and the existence of a class of workers selling their labour power, on the other.

Capitalist Exchange Process

Having established that a commodity has a twofold nature—its use value and exchange value—and that the exchange value of a commodity is determined by the amount of labour time necessary for the production of a commodity, Marx provides a lengthy account of the genesis of money in the exchange process and how money becomes capital. Exchange relationships between commodities predate capitalism, which develops when labour power itself becomes a commodity and money is introduced into the exchange process. Money is the most abstract of commodities. It is a means of payment, a unit of account, and a store of wealth. As a means of payment, it avoids simple bartering and mediates the process of exchange by creating a set of equivalencies among intrinsically different physical commodities (e.g., food, sweatshirts, and fuel) and labour power.

Typically, under capitalism simple commodity exchange starts with an individual who owns some commodity (e.g., one tonne of corn) that needs to be exchanged for another. First, the commodity must be exchanged for money. Marx expressed this step by C–M, where C denotes commodity and M is money. Second, the money received is exchanged for the needed commodity (e.g., fertilizer), expressed as M–C. In order to purchase other commodities, certain commodities are sold for money, which is essentially a use value. This simple exchange process is represented by C–M–C, the circulation of commodities, and is shown in figure 5.1.

FIGURE 5.1 Simple commodity exchange: selling in order to buy

C ———————— **M** ———————— **C**

In simple commodity exchange, C denotes the two extremes of the circulation because each is in commodity form and each has the same value; however, they are *not* the same commodity. This simple commodity exchange can also illustrate the sale of the commodity of labour power, which is the wage labourer's only means for the consumption of goods and services. In this case, labour power (C) is exchanged for wages (M) and eventually wage commodities (C).

Marx had to show how it is possible for the capitalist to make a profit and accumulate capital. A capitalist starts, not with labour power, but money. With money the capitalist purchases particular types of commodities, raw materials, machinery, and tools, the means of production and labour power. A prerequisite for capitalist production is the willingness of workers to exercise their "freedom" of exchange and sell their labour power. Whereas Smith and Ricardo characterize this process as two equal parties pursuing their individual interests, Marx argues that the exchange is fundamentally asymmetrical because the capitalist owns the means of production and labour power is the only commodity that labour is able to sell. The capitalist organizes the productive forces and sells the resulting commodities, or outputs, for money. The capitalist's exchange process is represented by M–C–M_1, the general formula for capital shown in figure 5.2.

FIGURE 5.2 The capitalist exchange paradigm: buying in order to sell higher

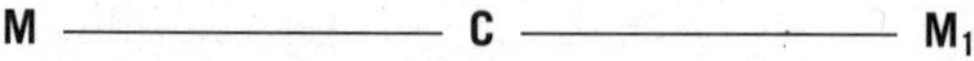

In contrast to simple commodity exchange, the M–C–M_1 circulation begins and ends with money, not commodities. The two extremes (M) are the same commodity (money), but they are *not* the same value. The industrial capitalist's motive of exchange is to expand value; so the money received at the end of the cycle (M_1) is greater than the money advanced at the start (M). Money used to generate more money (profit) is called *capital*, hence capitalism. The aim of the "circuit of capital" is to act as self-expanding value,that is, profit in the form of money.

Commodity Fetishism

Marx's theory of value calls attention to the social division of labour and the relationships of interdependence underlying commodity production, which are obscured by what he called fetishistic or reified commodities.

Marx identifies positive aspects of technical innovation. New technology, such as robots, *potentially* frees workers from dehumanizing labour and offers the opportunity for men and women to engage in creative labour, in which they exercise their unique human capacities.

The term *fetish* can be interpreted as an example of Marx's use of irony to comment on the "scientific" mindset embodied in modernity. "A commodity *appears*, at first sight, a very trivial thing," writes Marx, "Its analysis shows that it is, in reality, a very queer thing, abounding in metaphysical subtleties and theological niceties" [italics added].[18] Here Marx juxtaposes commodity production alongside a world of apparitions and social illusion, in which value exists essentially in commodities—inanimate objects—instead of being added through labour. In market (money) exchanges, the complex relationships underlying commodity production are not noticeable to consumers. They mistakenly believe that a commodity, such as an iPod, or iPhone, or MacBook Air, or a pair of Nudie denim jeans, has autonomous power and social status, while those who produce it are perceived as commodities and are treated as inanimate things.

Marx's notion of commodity fetishism is rooted in his account of alienation in the 1844 *Manuscripts*. Under pre-capitalist modes of production, the God illusion concealed and justified the lord-serf and master-slave relationships. In the imagination of primitive people, inanimate objects acquire superhuman qualities and become a fetish. Paralleling his critique of religion, Marx writes that capital appears as an object (money) while social relations take on an illusory or fetish form. Whereas in primitive social forms God is the human's own creation, in capitalist modernity people also create market relationships between commodities, concealing exploitative social relations, and this is justified by the doctrine of freedom of exchange. A look at the textual evidence speaks to the illusory form of capitalist exchange: "A commodity is therefore a mysterious thing, simply because in it the social character of men's labour appears to them as an objective character stamped upon the product of that labour, because the relations of the producers to the sum total of their own labour is presented to them as a social relation, existing not between themselves, but between the products of their labour. This is the reason why the products of labour become commodities, social things whose qualities are at the same time perceptible and imperceptible by the senses."[19] The link between Marx's notion of commodity fetishism and his critique of religious consciousness is made explicit in *Capital*:

> There is a definite social relation between men that assumes, in their eyes, the fantastic form of a relation between things. In order, therefore, to find an analogy, we must have recourse to the mist-enveloped regions of the religious world. In that world the productions of the human brain appear as independent beings endowed with life, and entering into relation both with one another and the human race. So it is in the world of commodities with the products of men's hands. This I call Fetishism which attaches itself to the products of labour, so soon as they are produced as commodities, and which is therefore inseparable from the production of commodities.[20]

Commodity fetishism describes the tendency for consumers and capitalists alike to display excessive devotion towards material "things," to believe that things have an independent existence and are endowed with extraordinary powers. Indeed, the premise of commodity fetishism is that relations between people have been substituted for relations between things. By being granted independence as a commodity, in the sense that it becomes endowed with the powers of human beings, things appear to exert control, and, as such, what happens to people depends upon the movement of markets, not the social relations of production characteristic to capitalism. For example, in the United States after the credit market meltdown began in August 2007, the loss of a person's life savings or home was typically blamed on an objective, natural thing—the credit market—rather than on the deranged logic of market fundamentalism and the imperative of maximizing shareholder value. Over the last several decades much of the developed and developing world has experienced the effects of market fundamentalism that underlay Thatcherism,

Reaganomics, and the so-called Washington Consensus.[21] The result has been an increase in commodification. Neo-liberal policies of privatization and deregularization, and the hollowing out of government, have had the effect of increasing the number of commodities acquiring an exchange value, including water supply, pensions, education, health care, radio and TV airwaves. These events can only be understood in relation to the needs of capital, which we turn to next.

Theory of Surplus Value and Exploitation

So far we have focused on Marx's economic analysis of the capitalist system of commodity production. To understand the development of a capitalist society, to expose Marx's "economic law of motion," we have to examine the process of extracting a surplus from labour power. This is Marx's second great law—referred to by Engels in his "Speech at the Graveside"—the theory of surplus value. It is the social theory of capitalist production. Importantly, this is the theory that explains the forces that propel the development of capitalism.

In figure 5.2, M_1 has a greater value than M. This means that in the movement C–M_1, extra value has been created. Marx called this extra value *surplus value*, the difference between the values of inputs and outputs. That productive labour creates surplus value is not controversial; what is contentious, however, is the premise behind Marx's theory that the source of profit on capital comes from the exploitation of labour. The thesis that capital exploits labour stems from a presupposition of the labour theory of value that labour power is the only commodity that produces surplus value. Marx's theory of surplus value explains the long-term future of capitalism. Marx foresaw a relative decline in workers' standard of living, the need for capitalists to continually transform the production process, and the tendency for capitalism as a whole to experience period crises.

Marx's theory of surplus value makes distinctions between *constant capital* and *variable capital* and between *necessary labour* and *surplus labour*, and it describes methods to increase surplus value. Constant capital refers to that part of capital that constitutes the means of production and does not, in the process of production, undergo any quantitative change of value. Variable capital, on the other hand, is "that part of capital, represented by labour power, [which] does, in the process of production, undergo an alteration of value. It both reproduces the equivalent of its own value, and it produces an excess, a surplus value, which may itself vary, may be more or less according to the circumstances."[22] The value of labour power is the cost of its purchase, which is the labour time necessary to produce the real wage, a subsistence basket of commodities (food, shelter, clothing) necessary for its maintenance. The value it creates in production is the quantity of labour time exercised in return for that wage. Under capitalism the contribution made by labour power to the value of output exceeds its cost. In *Wage-Labour and Capital* Marx writes: "The worker receives means of subsistence in exchange for his labour power, but the capitalist receives in exchange for his means of subsistence labour, the productive activity of the worker, the creative power whereby the worker not only replaces what he consumes but *gives to the accumulated labour a greater value than it previously possessed* ... [I]t is just this noble reproductive power that the worker surrenders to the capitalist in exchange for the means of subsistence received. He has, therefore, lost it for himself."[23] The system compels the worker to work longer than is sufficient to embody in the product the value of his or her labour power. The rate of surplus value can be quantified by dividing the working day of the wage labourer; it falls into two parts: socially necessary labour time and surplus labour time, as in figure 5.3.

FIGURE 5.3 The rate of surplus value

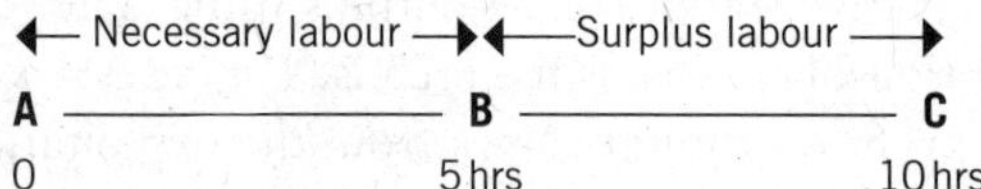

In figure 5.3, the line A to C represents a working day of ten hours. Suppose a worker works a ten-hour day, and that the socially necessary labour time to produce her wage is five hours. During the first five hours of the working day (A to B), the worker produces a value equivalent to the value of the means of subsistence necessary for the reproduction of her labour power. This is what Marx calls "necessary labour time" and the work spent during this time is *necessary labour*. The necessary labour time will vary considerably in different industries depending on the level of technology, the degree of human skills, and the cost of raw materials. The work undertaken during the second part of the working day, the line B to C, brings no advantage to the worker, and she works for "free" for the capitalist. As Marx explains, "During the second period of the labour process, that in which his labour is no longer necessary labour, the workman, it is true, labours, expends labour power; but his labour, being no longer necessary labour, he creates no value for himself. He creates surplus value which, for the capitalist, has all the charms of a creation out of nothing."[24] Thus, Marx calls this productive activity in the second period of the working day "surplus labour time" and the value produced in the second five hours is *surplus value*, which is appropriated by the capitalist.

For Marx, the appropriation of surplus value is the basis of profit, once other fixed and variable costs (e.g., rent and raw materials) have been deducted. The rate of surplus value, defined as the ratio of surplus labour time to the necessary labour time, is 5/5, which equals 1 or 100 per cent. This can be explained as follows:

$$\text{Rate of surplus value} = \frac{s}{v} \quad \frac{\text{surplus labour time}}{\text{necessary labour time}} = \frac{5}{5} = 100\%$$

The rate of surplus value expresses the degree of exploitation of the worker by the capitalist: "The rate of surplus value is therefore an exact expression for the degree of exploitation of labour power by capital, or of the labourer by the capitalist."[25] The rate of exploitation is $e = s / v$, where v, the necessary labour time, is called variable capital because it varies during the production, contributing more value to output than it costs as an output. For Marx, the appropriation of surplus value applied also to the pre-capitalist feudal modes of production, but it is only under capitalism that exploitation in production is veiled by the ideology of freedom of exchange. Thus, the surplus value ratio, like capital itself, embodies a particular class relation and a form of domination. The accumulation of surplus value depends directly on the total amount of labour the capitalist employs and on the rate of exploitation. For Marx, "capital is dead labour, that, vampire-like, only lives by sucking living labour, and lives the more, the more labour it sucks."[26]

As a system, capitalism imposes an imperative objective on capitalists or its agents (managers): the means of production must be operated for the purpose of valorization or profit maximizing. On the basis of existing technology, extending the length of the working day can increase the rate of surplus value. For example, in figure 5.3, if the capitalist extends the working day by two hours, from ten to twelve hours, the extension B–C of the line A–B represents an increase in the rate of surplus value: e is 7/5 or 140 per cent. Physiological and legal restrictions limit the capitalist's ability to increase absolute surplus value by extending the working day. The surplus value produced by lengthening the working day, Marx termed *absolute surplus value*.

The dynamic nature of capitalism itself generates the production of *relative* surplus value as the dominant method of increasing the rate of exploitation: e. New technology, by cheapening the labour costs, can reduce necessary labour time to produce commodities, *v.* If, for example, machinery reduces the necessary labour time from five to four hours each day, *e* would be 6/4 or 150 per cent. In figure 5.3, the line A to B would be shortened. The surplus value produced by the reduction of the necessary labour time, Marx termed *relative surplus value*. To increase the "productiveness of labour," Marx predicts that modes of production must be revolutionized. He writes, "When surplus value has to be produced by the conversion of necessary labour into surplus labour, it by no means suffices for capital to take over the labour process in the form under which it has been historically handed down, and then simply to prolong the duration of that process. The technical and social conditions of the process, and consequently the very mode of production must be revolutionized, before the productiveness of labour can be increased."[27]

In part 4 of *Capital, Volume I*, Marx details the many strategies for increasing relative surplus value. His analysis foreshadows the genesis of management in modern society. In the context of the increasing dominance of the factory system, Marx believed that a "directing authority" or management derives its essential features from large-scale bureaucratic organizations: "A single violin player is his own conductor; an orchestra requires a separate one."[28] Cooperation, therefore, between different categories of workers is "a necessary concomitant of all production on a large scale," writes Marx.[29] The production of relative surplus value is increased by the finer division of labour within workshops, which has the effect of giving the capitalist "undisputed authority" over the workers. [30] For Marx, however, machinery, the "instruments of labour" both symbolize modern industry and offer the most powerful means to increase relative surplus value "beyond all bounds set by human nature."[31] When controlled by capitalists, machinery cheapens commodities by increasing the pace of work, stimulating scientific innovation, and exponentially reducing the value of necessary labour time: "Machinery produces relative surplus value, not only by directly depreciating the value of labour power, … but also … by converting the labour employed by the owner of that machinery, into labour of a higher degree and greater efficacy, by raising the social value of the article produced above its individual value, and thus enabling the capitalist to replace the value of a day's labour power by a smaller portion of the value of a day's product."[32]

Marx continued his incisive critique of capitalism by describing the effects of machinery on workers. His chapter on "Machinery and Modern Industry" gives a detailed account of how machinery in the hands of capitalists causes "a more intensified labour"[33] and "endless drudgery," which "dominates and pumps dry, living labour power" and moulds workers' behaviour into "a barrack disciple"[34] as they are forced to comply with the uniform motion of the machinery. Maximizing control over workers is seen by Marx to derive from the fact that the wage-labour exchange secures only a *potential* labour power for the production of surplus value. He calls attention to a pronounced tendency for improvements in machinery to be labour saving and, somewhat less obvious, to substitute one type of worker for another, the less skilled for the more skilled, the young for adult, and the female for male, as the "special skill of each individual insignificant factory operative vanishes as an infinitesimal quantity before the science."[35] Marx predicts a permanent pool of unemployed workers, the "industrial reserve army" of labour, which would have the designed effect of downward adjustments in wage rates. It is false, however, to assume that Marx's analysis of machinery under capitalism was totally negative. In *Capital* he also identifies positive aspects of technical innovation: "Modern Industry, indeed, compels society, under penalty of death, to replace the detailed-worker of today, crippled by life-long repetition of one and the same trivial operation, and thus reduced to the mere fragment of a man, by the fully developed individual, fit for a variety of labours, ready to face any change of production, and to whom the different social functions he performs, are but so many modes of giving scope to his own natural and acquired powers."[36] This passage is one of the most expressive testimonials written to capitalism's achievements. It also speaks to Marx's notion that creative labour, in which men and women exercise their unique human capacities, defines what it is to be human and what the relationship is between people and paid work. Thus, technology *potentially* frees men and women from dehumanizing labour and offers the opportunity for labour to correspond to human essence.

Although, potentially, new productive technology offers enhancement in human experience and living standards, Marx's economic thesis predicts dire living conditions for the working class:

> To say that the worker has an interest in the rapid growth of capital is only to say that the more rapidly the worker increases the wealth of others, the richer will be the crumbs that fall to him, the greater is the number of workers that can be employed and called into existence, the more can the mass of slaves dependent on capital be increased. We have thus seen that: Even the *most favourable situation* for the working class, the *most rapid possible growth of capital*, however much it may improve the material existence of the worker, does not remove the antagonism between his interests and the interests of the bourgeoisie, the interests of the capitalists. *Profit and wages* remain as before in

> *inverse proportion*. If capital is growing rapidly, wages may rise; the profit of capital rises incomparably more rapidly.[37]

In other writings, such as the *Grundrisse*, Marx is less pessimistic about the effects of capitalism on the working class, but his analysis of capitalism in *Capital* speaks to the vulnerability of wage labour to capital. The relationship between the working class and the capitalist, even in the most favourable economic conditions, is one of contradiction. The capitalist has an interest in intensifying work and minimizing labour costs to maximize the production of relative surplus value. Whereas *Capital, Volume I*, analyzes production of surplus value inside the factory, *Volumes II and III* examine a whole series of capitalist phenomena, including crises, outside in the market.

Theories of Crises

Finding ways to produce relative surplus value makes capitalism highly dynamic, but the process generates three tendencies that are central to capitalist development: the accumulation of capital in fewer hands, the organization of labour into finer and more complex division of labour, and the creation of global markets as capital seeks new markets and cheaper labour. A central objective of Marx's economic theory was to demonstrate that, although capitalism was historically the most efficient mode of production, it was prone to chronic economic crises. In essence, Marx postulates that crises are inevitable for two reasons: insufficient demand and the falling rate of profit.

Inherent in Marx's theory of relative surplus value is a fundamental contradiction between production and consumption: on the one hand, the capitalist class is driven by the urge for wealth to increase the production of surplus value, which increases the supply of commodities that must be converted into money; on the other hand, accumulation is based on the fact that consumption by the producers of surplus value—the exploited workers—is restricted to basic necessities. In any society other than capitalism, the overproduction of commodities would be a celebration; extra commodities would mean increased individual consumption. However, for capitalism, private consumption is necessary, but not sufficient; consumption must realize a profit. In *Capital, Volume II*, Marx points to insufficient demand or under-consumption as a causal mechanism for economic crisis: one unsold "stream of commodities" entering the market causes commodity producers to compete with one another and to sell at lower prices. Thus, a crisis breaks out when insufficient consumption causes the supply of commodities to exceed consumer demand.[38] For example, when unsold automobiles build up on distributors' forecourts, autoworkers are laid off, and the economy enters a crisis until the unsold automobiles are purchased and the automobile manufacturer restarts production. This illustration is a breakdown of an individual capitalist producing a particular commodity, but the economy is a network of capitals that are intimately integrated with other circuits of capital. As consumption of a commodity (e.g., automobiles) falls, it triggers a decrease in investment for automobile machinery, which, in turn, causes a crisis among capitals producing the machines that build automobiles. It is this interconnected system of unplanned "commodity capital" (e.g., automobile manufactures) and "productive capital" (e.g., robot manufacturers supplying the automobile industry) that led Marx to refer to the anarchy of capitalist production. Economic crises break out extremely often, given the anarchy of capitalist production, fluctuations in market prices, the vagaries of the credit system (e.g., 2008 collapse of the U.S. housing market due to sub-prime mortgages), and technological change.

In *Capital, Volume III*, Marx synthesizes his analysis of the production surplus value and realization of profit into his contentious "law" of the tendency of the rate of profit to fall. While classical economists believed that the unavoidable tendency for the rate of profit to fall was a natural fact, Marx's treatment of the falling rate of profit was placed in the social context of capitalist relations of production. Mathematically, a theoretical demonstration of the falling rate of profit can be given, but Marx articulates this situation in a sociologically more interesting way as follows:

> Proceeding from the nature of the capitalist mode of production, it is thereby proved a logical necessity that in its development the general average rate of surplus value must express itself in a falling general rate of profit. Since the mass of the employed living labour is continually on the decline as compared to the mass of materialised labour set in motion by it, i.e., to the productivity consumed means of production, it follows that the portion of living labour, unpaid and congealed in surplus value, must also be continually on the decrease compared to the amount of value represented by the invested total capital. Since the ratio of the mass of surplus value to the value of the invested total capital forms the rate of profit, this rate must constantly fall.[39]

In essence, Marx's argument is that as more productive capital (machinery) is introduced into the production of surplus value less necessary labour time is needed to produce the same quantity of commodities. As a result, the costs of "constant capital" (c) increase relative to the "variable capital" (v). Following Marx, the rate of profit (r) is defined as the ratio of surplus value (s) to the total capital employed $[c + v]$: $r = s / [c + v]$. In words, since the cost of total capital employed is increasing in relation to the rate of exploitation, the rate of profit must inevitably fall. The "breakdowns" between capitals, and a general tendency for the rate of profit to fall, account for economic booms and recessions, which characterizes the capitalist business cycle.

For Marx, crises stem from the fundamental contradiction of capitalist production and consumption: unrestrained production without regard to corresponding levels of consumption. Marx writes, "The *real barrier* of capitalist production is *capital itself* ... This means—unconditional development of the productive forces of society—comes continually into conflict with the limited purpose, the self-expansion of the existing capital. The capitalist mode of production is, for this reason, a historical means of developing the material forces of production and creating an appropriate world-market and is, at the same time, a continual conflict between this its historic task and its own corresponding relations of social production."[40]

Marx's conception of crises is not simply an economic concept that goes along with the theory of value; it is a sociological theory, the centre of which is a particular mode of productive forces and hierarchical relations. Crises are highly probable because the anarchic nature of the capitalist mode of production is the social outcome of interactions among capitalists' individual economic actions; whereas a falling rate of profit is a social outcome that makes such economic actions inevitable.[41] While Marx believed that crises were endemic to capitalism, nowhere in his writings does he predict an inevitable apocalyptic economic collapse. Economic crises do, however, function as a force towards equilibrium by eliminating overcapacity, and they play a crucial role in fostering revolutionary consciousness and collective action.

Criticism

Critics of Marx's economic theories have been numerous and prolific, but space permits only a brief consideration of some major criticisms that have the most direct bearing on themes covered in this chapter. One set of criticisms relates to a main tenet of Marx's analysis of capitalism, his theory of value. The first major criticism is its inapplicability to the managing of an economy and, in particular, its inutility for the rational allocation of commodities and scarce resources in an economy. Marx's proposition that labour is the source of all value is "useless at best, harmful and misleading at its not infrequent worst."[42] Moreover, the limitation of the theory of value, critics argue, is glaringly apparent in the formation of prices because this theory ignores the key factor of relative scarcity, which is central to determining equilibrium prices in markets and the equilibrium rate of profit: the classical economic "invisible hand" analysis. There is textual evidence that explicitly repudiates this critique. Marx's theory of value is a model of commodity production that ignores the effect of all production costs apart from labour; it is "*not* meant as a general theory of relative prices."[43] Marx's dialectic method and theoretical approach necessitates an abstract model of commodity production in historical materialist terms; it is not a general theory that attempts to account for all the surface economic phenomena of capitalist society.

The second major criticism of Marx's economics is the doctrine of "progressive pauperization" of the proletariat. Marx forecast that, as capitalist modernity matured, there would be periodic recessions, the growth of colossal quasi-monopolistic corporations, and growing unemployment resulting from technological change. In this scenario the working class would experience increasing misery as living standards undergo long-time decline. The forecast is based on the premise that capitalists are impelled by a competitive imperative to increase the amount of capital invested in technology, as opposed to increasing the proportion paid to labour in wages. The received economic wisdom is that the ownership by the working classes of the ubiquitous automobile, satellite disk, flat-screen TV, etc., has proven Marx wrong. In retrospect, it's easy to see why his forecast has long since appeared incorrect: Marx underestimated the effects of the rise of liberal democracy. In the *Communist Manifesto*, progressive income tax and free universal education, for example, were listed as programs that the victorious proletariat would implement. In Western capitalist societies, at least, these programs and more are now regarded as basic to postmodern liberal democracies. Marx did not anticipate "varieties of capitalism"[44] and the rise of Keynesian[45] policies involving state-sponsored investment in the economy to create employment or "soft capitalism"[46] that reflects local realities, local cultures, and, ironically, the political clout of local social movements. The notion of diversity is illustrated by contrasting the capitalism practised in the Nordic states of Europe, Norway, Sweden, and Finland, with their varying degrees of national economic planning and welfare programs, with the more laissez-faire capitalism of the United States.

Marx's economic theory, arguably, did not adequately take into account the growth of political democracy in the Western world, but it's also important to understand that the orthodox economic critique is based on a misreading of Marx's *Capital*.[47] When Marx proclaims,

"Pauperism forms a condition of capitalist production, and the capitalist development of wealth. It enters into the *faux frais* of capitalist production; but capital knows how to throw these from its own shoulders on to those of the working class and the lower middle class,"[48] he is referring not to the impoverishment of the entire proletariat but to the "lowest sediment": the underclass of the unemployed, the widows, the addicts, the sick that capital is unwilling to pay for directly. After the Second World War most Western governments, through the creation of more or less generous social welfare programs, have met the incidental operational costs of capitalism. They have supplied education and training, infrastructure, health care and, increasingly, pollution management—costs that capital is all too happy to pass on to the working and middle classes. Periodically, for the capitalist system to work, the state (i.e., taxpayers) has to intervene directly in the economy. This was plainly demonstrated in 2008 when the British government rescued the financial institution Northern Rock, and the U.S. administration intervened to save mortgage giants Fannie Mae and Freddie Mac. In such cases the cost to the taxpayer can be huge. As *The Economist* acknowledged in July 2008, "The unpalatable truth is that by the time a financial crisis hits, the state often has to ... shoulder a large part of the losses."[49] That capital's profits are privatized, but risks and losses are socialized, would not have surprised Marx in the least.

For the last quarter-century that venerable legacy of post-war Keynesian-inspired governments has increasingly been characterized by free-market ideologues as a "nanny state,"[50] pampering the slothful, coddling the wicked, and successive governments have turned to neo-liberal policies to reduce the scope of state intervention and have dismantled many social welfare programs. The historical process of interventions by Western states from 1945 up to the late 1970s is essentially that of the fall and rise of laissez-faire or market fundamentalism: a shift from *Keynesianism*, the active intervention of the state to correct for market failures, to *market fundamentalism*, the belief that intervention is a distortion only likely to make capital pathologies worse.[51] The change in economic policy is closely related to the new political reality in Europe: the disintegration of the Soviet Union. The "mixed" economies, with state and private investment and social welfare programs characteristic of post-war European countries, emerged *because* of the threat of Soviet communism. In *The Shock Doctrine*, Naomi Klein argues persuasively that with this threat removed capital did not need to make major concessions in the face of powerful social movements, and thus, "capitalism stripped of its Keynesian appendages ... no longer has to work to keep us as customers, that can be as anti-social, anti-democratic and boorish as it wants."[52] Marx did forecast that as capitalism matured there would be a *relative* decline in wages, not an absolute decline: "It follows that in proportion as capital accumulates, the lot of the labourer, *be his payment high or low*, must grow worse [italics added]."[53] Thus, the fact that in 2008 top CEOs, such as Richard Branson's Virgin and Bill Gates's Microsoft and others, receive within the first ninety minutes of the first working day of each new year the average *yearly* income of a worker in full-time employment[54] makes Marx's provocative economic ideas still relevant and prescient.

A third major criticism relates to Marx's theories of capitalist crises. Marx's dialectical method commits him to foretell that certain social changes are historically inevitable. Much of his economic theory is an exposition of the mechanism that "inevitably" brings about economic crises. His model on the tendency for the rate of profit to fall has received much criticism. Critics have pointed out, for example, that if, as Marx contends, the rate of profit falls because of investment in productive forces, then presumably the decline should be avoided when capitalists disinvest or when stagnation in technical innovation sets in.[55] Furthermore, Marx neglects that those capitalists experiencing a fall in the rate of profit might adopt a business strategy that generates counter-tendencies that partly or completely offset it: for example, by entering a global market or by expanding consumption through easier access to credit. Also, it's glaringly apparent that globalization has undermined the international solidarity of the proletariat. While in the *Communist Manifesto* Marx and Engels urge all workers of "all countries to unite,"[56] in reality Canadian and U.S. automobile workers identify more closely with their aggrieved employers, as Japanese automobiles made by Japanese workers dominate the North America market. In the early twenty-first century, reality is much more complex than might have been expected by a writer who died over 126 years ago.

Conclusion

The two main pillars of Marx's analysis of capitalism are the labour theory of value and the theory of crises. In opposition to classical accounts of value, Marx's labour theory of value embodies a social theory of commodity production, which makes *Capital* "unrivaled" as a work of sociological theory.[57] The theory characterizes capitalism as a fundamentally exploitative system or "an act of robbery."[58] "The work of Marx taken as a whole," writes C. Wright Mills, "is a savage, sustained indictment of one alleged injustice: that the profit, the comfort, the luxury of one man is paid for by the loss, the misery, the denial of another."[59] *Capital* also explains the forces propelling the development of capitalism. The exploitation of labour is analyzed through the concept of surplus value. The subversive thesis that profit arises from the exploitation of labour was centrally important in Marx's economics because it provided the exploited with a moral and theoretical justification for taking collective action against capitalism. The central object of Marx's theories of crises was to demonstrate that the "anarchic" capitalist system, while historically the most efficient mode of production, was prone to periodic economic crises. These crises were inevitable because of insufficient demand causing over-capacity and incessant capital accumulation causing the rate of profit to fall. Nowhere in his writings does Marx predict an inevitable apocalyptic economic collapse.

In spite of the fact that Marx's economic theories contain omissions, ambiguity, and underestimate the chameleon nature of capitalism, we need to balance the criticisms of Marx's economics with its not inconsiderable achievements. Perhaps the main achievement of Marx's *Capital* is its pioneering contribution to the sociological analysis of technological change and management. Marx's work on the effects of machinery pioneered the sociological analysis of the effects of technological change, particularly what is known as labour process theory, which seeks to reveal the social and class interests behind technological change. It is this perspective which Harry Braverman in *Labor and Monopoly Capital* (1974) employed to account for employers' strategies to control and deskill workers through the application of new technology. In "post-Braverman" sociological studies of paid work, labour process concepts have been applied to clerical occupations and also to a variety of Japanese management strategies.[60] Marx's work also identifies the genesis of management as an outcome of the historical development of production and power relations. Critical sociological studies of management, which derive their theoretical perspective from Marx, conceptualize management as a control mechanism that advances and protects the economic and political interests of the ruling class. In opposition to contemporary orthodox accounts of management, in which its practices tend to be exercised without reference to the asymmetrical power relations in which they are embedded, Marx's analysis centres attention on the dominant imperative that management has to realize a satisfactory degree of control over antagonistic capital-labour relations necessary to secure the efficient extraction of surplus value (what is now called labour productivity), and levels of profitability that it secures.[61]

Another major achievement of Marx's economics is its correct prediction of the growth of corporations, or big business, and economic globalization. For Marx, the logical tendency of capitalism was the concentration and centralization of capital. The process of concentration refers to the amount of capital individual capitalists control. The process of centralization, on the other hand, refers to the merging of capital. The effect of both is to lead to giant business corporations that have substantial control over markets, capable of destroying many of their smaller competitors and dictating contracts with smaller producers that supply the conglomerate. The effect of the giant U.S. retailer Wal-Mart on small local retailers and their suppliers attests to this prediction. As Joel Bakan's *The Corporation* (2004) persuasively argues, an aggregate of capital is a "pathological institution" that relentlessly pursues, without exception, "its own self-interest, regardless of the often harmful consequences it might cause to others."[62] Marx never developed a comprehensive theory of imperialism and colonialism (where the imperialists actually settled in the colony), although in various places in *Capital* he explains that in its quest for profit monopoly capital seeks cheaper resources and expanding markets in underdeveloped colonial territories. Marx's economic concepts explaining the long-term tendency of monopoly capital constitute an indispensable intellectual element of critical globalization theory.

The postmodern economic globalization perspective predicts that international markets operate in accordance with universal principles and will result in a convergence of markets and national employment relations. For example, global capital imperatives will drive wages down, erode employment standards, and lead to the transfer of production from relatively expensive labour markets (e.g., North America) to less expensive ones (e.g., China and India). All these issues are part of a public consciousness towards globalization today, but that we can find these ideas in Marx's economic writings indicates a remarkable achievement in its time. Importantly, so much of human activity today—from politics to education, and health policy to culture—is "perceived principally through the prism of economics,"[63] but this would come as no surprise to those familiar with Marx's economic writings. And in the context of global market crises experienced in 1998 and 2009, and in the post-Kyoto ecology panic, it must be conceded that Marx's early realization of the effects of unfettered global expansion makes him in a certain sense more postmodern today than many of his intellectual detractors.

Notes

1 David McLellan, *Karl Marx: Selected Writings*, 2nd ed. (Oxford: Oxford University Press, 2000), 377.

2 Francis Wheen, "50 Greatest Books—*Das Kapital*," *The Globe and Mail* (March 1, 2008), D13.

3 Fred Lee, Professor at the University of Missouri, Kansas City, quoted in Tom Green, "Thought Control in Economics," *Adbuster, Journal of the Mental Environment* 16, no. 4 (July/August 2008): 49.

4 Robert C. Tucker, ed., *The Marx-Engels Reader*, 2nd ed. (New York: Norton, 1972), 297.

5 Ibid., 295.

6 McLellan, *Karl Marx*, 376.

7 Alan Swingewood, *A Short History of Sociological Thought* (New York: St. Martin's Press, 2000), 40.

8 See Allen W. Wood, *Karl Marx*, 2nd ed. (New York: Routledge, 2004).

9 See Francis Wheen, *Karl Marx* (London: Fourth Estate, 2000).

10 Ibid., 304.

11 Ibid., 305.

12 Tucker, *The Marx-Engels Reader*, 303.

13 Adam Smith, *The Wealth of Nations*, (1776; London: Penguin, 1997), 133.

14 Letter from Marx to Engels (August 24, 1867) in McLellan, *Karl Marx*, 564.

15 Karl Marx, *Capital, Volume III* (1894; London: Lawrence & Wishart, 1971), 194–5.

16 In addition to specific works cited, I have drawn from Ben Fine, *Marx's Capital* (London: Macmillan, 1975); B. Fine and L. Harris, *Rereading Capital*. (London: Macmillan, 1979); P. Sloan, *Marx and the Orthodox Economists* (Oxford: Blackwell, 1973).

17 Tucker, *The Marx-Engels Reader*, 312.

18 Ibid., 319.

19 Ibid., 320–1.

20 Ibid., 321.

21 See, for example, Joseph Stiglitz, "A Global Lesson in Market Failure," *The Globe and Mail* (July 8, 2008) A15.

22 Karl Marx, *Capital, Volume I* (1867; London: Lawrence & Wishart, 1970), 209.

23 Tucker, *The Marx-Engels Reader*, 209.

24 Marx, *Capital, Volume I*, 217.

25 Marx, *Capital, Volume I*, 218.

26 Tucker, *The Marx-Engels Reader*, 362–3.

27 Ibid., 379.

28 Ibid., 385.

29 Ibid., 388.

30 Ibid., 395.

31 Ibid., 404.

32 Ibid., 405.

33 Ibid., 407.

34 Ibid., 410.

35 Ibid., 409.

36 Ibid., 413–4.

37 Ibid., 210–1.

38 Karl Marx, *Capital, Volume II* (1885; London: Lawrence & Wishart, 1974), 78.

39 Karl Marx, *Capital, Volume III*, 213.

40 Ibid., 250.

41 Fine, *Marx's Capital*, 58.

42 Jon Elster, *Making Sense of Marx* (New York: Cambridge University Press, 1985) 120.

43 Wood, *Karl Marx*, 228.

44 See P. Hall and D. Soskice, *Varieties of Capitalism* (Oxford: Oxford University Press, 2001); Leslie Sklair, *Globalization: Capitalism and Its Alternatives* (New York: Oxford University Press, 2002).

45 The word *Keynesian* is derived from the economic theories of British economist John Maynard Keynes (1883–1946).

46 See Paul Heelas, "Work Ethics, Soft Capitalism and the 'Turn to Life,'" in *Cultural Economy*, eds. Paul du Gay and Michael Pryke (London: Sage, 2002), 78–96).

47 Wheen, *Karl Marx*, 300.

48 Tucker, *The Marx-Engels Reader*, 429.

49 Anonymous, "Twin Twisters," *The Economist* (July 19, 2008), 15.

50 Z. Bauman, *Work, Consumption and the New Poor,* 2nd ed. (Maidenhead: Open University Press, 2005), 113.

51 In economic terminology, this shift in policy is from Keynesianism (named after British economist John Maynard Keynes) to monetarism (closely associated with the U.S. economist Milton Friedman). A very readable account of the changes in government intervention is W. Keegan, *Mrs Thatcher's Economic Experiment*, (Harmondsworth: Penguin, 1984). One Marxist account is given by B. Jessop, *Theories of the Capitalist State*, (London: Martin Robertson, 1982). Another readable account is Bob Jessop, *Thatcherism: A Tale of Two Nations* (Cambridge: Polity Press, 1988).

52 Naomi Klein, *The Shock Doctrine* (Toronto: Alfred A. Knopf Canada, 2007), 303.

53 Tucker, *The Marx-Engels Reader*, 431.

54 Peter J. Nicholson, "The Curious Absence of Class Struggle," *The Globe and Mail* (January 5, 2008), A13.

55 Wood, *Karl Marx*, 157.

56 Tucker, *The Marx-Engels Reader*, 500.

57 Ken Morrison, *Marx, Durkheim, Weber,* 2nd ed. (London: Sage, 2006), 81.

58 Harry Schwartz, introduction in *Marx on Economics*, ed. Robert Freedman (London: Penguin, 1962), xv.

59 C. Wright Mill, *The Marxists*, (New York: Dell Publishing, 1962), 33.

60 See John Bratton, *Japanization at Work*, (London: Macmillan Press, 1992); T. Elger and C. Smith, *Global Japanization*? (London: Routledge, 1994).

61 See Mike Reed, *The Sociology of Management* (London: Harvester Wheatsheaf, 1989); David Knights and Hugh Willmott, eds., *Managing the Labour Process* (Aldershot: Gower, 1986).

62 Joel Bakan, *The Corporation*, (Toronto: Penguin, 2004), 1–2.

63 John Ralston Saul, *The Collapse of Globalism* (Toronto: Viking Canada, 2005), 18.

6. Emile Durkheim: The Division of Labour in Society

> Apart from Marx himself, there can be few social thinkers whose fate it has been to be so persistently misunderstood.
>
> —Anthony Giddens[1]

> More than any other social theorist of the first rank, Durkheim sought to contribute sociology as a distinct and autonomous science with its own theoretical protocols and professional infrastructure.
>
> —Alex Callinicos[2]

IN *THE DIVISION OF LABOUR IN SOCIETY,* Durkheim gives an analysis of the evolution of society from small-scale societies with little division of labour to complex, industrial, urban societies in which he identifies a breakdown in shared norms and values. The book is also a work of theory in which he explores the relationship between the individual and society and in which he argues that even the idea of individualism depends upon changes in the social structure. The moral and political problems that emerged from the evolution of large, complex societies included questions of how to reconcile individual freedom and social order and how to find forms of social organization that would produce both social solidarity and individual freedom. In discussing the idea of social solidarity, Durkheim variously refers to the ties, or social links, which bind the individual to the group and ensure social cohesion. He also refers to these ties as "social cement" because of attachments between individuals that could have an intense emotional hold over individuals.[3]

Life and Works

David Emile Durkheim was born in 1858 at Épinal, the regional capital of the Vosges in France. His father was Chief Rabbi in the region, but while still a schoolboy, Durkheim decided against following his father into the rabbinate. He was a clever pupil and obtained his baccalaureates in Letters in 1874 and in Sciences in 1875. He spent three years preparing for entry to L'École Normale Supérieure in Paris. During this period he turned to the study of morality, society, and sociology. He was influenced by one of his teachers, Renouvier, whose interest in the scientific study of morality, views on social cohesion based on the individual's dependence on others, preference for justice over utility, and advocacy of producers' associations and secular state education later became themes in Durkheim's work.[4] Durkheim also drew from Auguste Comte's work, particularly the idea that society could be studied scientifically and that the task was to establish exactly what the subject matter of sociology should be and to show how it could be used to diagnose social pathologies in order to provide a guide to future action.

After his *agrégation*—a prestigious competitive examination for the recruitment of secondary teachers in France—in 1882, Durkheim became a philosophy teacher, and during this period he began to focus on the ideas that were eventually to be his doctoral thesis, as well as the core of his first book, *The Division of Labour in Society*. He began to concentrate on the relations of the individual personality to social solidarity, and he came to see that the solution to the problem belonged to the new science of sociology.[5] At the time, sociology was mainly seen as being associated with Comte and was looked upon critically by philosophers in France.

Emile Durkheim was born in 1858 at Epinal, France. He is the theorist of social cohesion in which society is held together through shared values. Consequently, he became increasingly interested in religion and morality. He died in 1917.

In 1887 Durkheim took up a position at the University of Bordeaux and in the following fifteen years produced three major works: *The Division of Labour in Society*, *The Rules of Sociological Method*, and *Suicide*; he also established the first sociological periodical, *L'Année Sociologique*. In 1902 he moved to the Sorbonne, in Paris, and later became Professor of Education (only in 1913 was his chair renamed Science of Education and Sociology).[6] This appointment was met with considerable hostility, especially from the Catholic Right, who opposed giving the responsibility for teacher education to a secularist and advocate of the new, controversial discipline of sociology.[7] During this period Durkheim's main sociological concern was the study of religion and morality, which led to the publication of *The Elementary Forms of Religious Life* in 1912. His work on morality was never completed, and he died in 1917 at the age of fifty-nine. Durkheim's achievement was the founding of sociology as an academic discipline. His many publications attracted scholars to work with him and to help build a body of sociological work.

Marcel Mauss (1872–1950), Durkheim's nephew, was a central figure within a school of Durkheimian social thought who became an important figure in anthropology.

Intellectual Influences

Several intellectual influences shaped Durkheim's analysis of society and his conception of sociology. An important one was Auguste Comte's discussion of scientific methodology, or positivism, as outlined in *A Course in Positive Philosophy,* published in 1834. This methodology posits an alternative to the dominant, speculative philosophical doctrines of the eighteenth and nineteenth centuries, which it sought to replace with knowledge based upon observation.[8] As we discussed in chapter 2, Comte's Law of Three Stages depicts knowledge and human consciousness in three stages: the theological stage in which nature is understood in terms of the will of anthropomorphic gods; the metaphysical stage of knowledge based upon abstract, conceptual thought; and the final, positive stage based on scientific laws derived from the observation of facts. This evolutionary trajectory made speculative thought appear less developed. In addition, as Morrison points out, Comte developed a system for comparing and ranking different sciences in which he showed that the most developed sciences, such as physics and biology, were positivistic and, therefore, were more successful because of their use of scientific methods. In comparison, history, philosophy, and economics appeared less advanced, and this critique provided a receptive climate for the spread of positivism in France and England. Positivism advocates the extension of scientific method to the social sciences, including the abandonment of abstract analysis in favour of the search for law-like, causal regularities and the basing of knowledge on observation. Durkheim drew upon the influence of Comte in his attempt to establish sociology as a scientific discipline during his years at Bordeaux.[9]

A second influence on Durkheim's view of society was a philosophical perspective known as realism.[10] From this perspective, social realities exist in a world that is external and independent of people's perceptions. According to realists, this external reality exists in the structures or customs of society, and the structures can restrain people by influencing how they behave, for example if they feel obliged to conform. Thus, these external structures can be seen as material objects of study; they can be observed in order to see how they affect people's behaviour. These ideas will be discussed more fully in the following chapter.

A third influence on Durkheim was the perspective of individualism that was prominent towards the end of the nineteenth century.[11] The ideas of the Enlightenment and the political changes of the French Revolution raised the profile of the individual and increased individual political and legal rights. At the beginning of Durkheim's career there was a strong sense in France that individual rights were undermining collective obligations and authority. Any perspective that viewed society as simply an agglomeration of individuals undermined Durkheim's effort to establish a discipline of sociology based upon the idea that society is an objective and constraining material reality, external to the individual. Durkheim opposed the utilitarian doctrine that was influential in the second half of the nineteenth century. The views of John Stuart Mill and Jeremy Bentham, the main advocates of utilitarianism, put the freely acting individual at the centre of social life. Such individuals, it was argued, pursue their own interests, especially private economic gain, and relate to society only if required by their pursuit of private utility. Society, in this theory, is based just on rational individuals merely pursuing their private goals. In *The Division of Labour in Society* Durkheim emphasizes that social order cannot be based only on freely contracting individuals because there are social rules regarding which contracts are just and there are moral codes concerning the honouring of contacts.[12] In addition, individuals are not analytically separate from society, as they cannot exist outside a social framework. In *The Division of Labour in Society* Durkheim argues that, historically, society precedes the individual and that only under certain social structural conditions can the idea, or the reality, of individual autonomy, exist.

The Division of Labour in Society

A central concern in Durkheim's first book is the relationship between the individual and social solidarity. He notes that there are two apparently contradictory movements—as individuals became more autonomous they became more dependent upon society—and he proposes that this contradiction can be resolved by changes in social solidarity flowing from changes in the division of labour.[13] Although Adam Smith discussed division of labour in relation to the specialization of economic activities, Durkheim perceived it as a much broader process that affects political, administrative, judicial, and educational institutions, as well being present in the arts, philosophy, and sciences. Debates in the study of biology extended the principle of the division of labour to organisms, as well as to societies: "It may even be stated that an organism occupies the more exalted a place in the animal hierarchy the more specialized its functions are."[14] Thus, the division of labour is placed almost at the beginning of life and is considered a fundamental process within "the essential properties of organized matter," rather than a recent product of the intelligence and will of men. In these terms, the increasing division of labour appears to be a manifestation of a general process, and Durkheim contended that it was becoming "one of the fundamental bases of the social order."[15]

In his discussion of the functions of the division of labour, Durkheim gives a much greater significance to division of labour than does Adam Smith, who attributes it to the increase in production. Durkheim argues that the division of labour is the principal source of social solidarity, which "links those co-operating together at the present time" and provides "order, harmony and social solidarity."[16] Because social solidarity is a moral phenomenon that cannot be directly observed, Durkheim argues that an external index of social solidarity, such as a type of law, has to be noted. He identifies two types of law based upon the different sanctions attached to them. The first type is penal law, which has repressive sanctions involving loss or suffering for the person who has infringed such laws. The second type includes civil, commercial, procedural, administrative, and constitutional law and has restitutive sanctions which consist in "restoring the previous state of affairs" to their normal form.[17]

Durkheim argues that in small societies with little division of labour there is mechanical solidarity based upon likeness, and in such societies there is a strong *collective* or *common consciousness* made up of the "totality of beliefs and sentiments common to the average members of society," which "forms a determinate system with a life of its own."[18] This collective consciousness continues to exist irrespective of which particular individuals live in a society at a particular time. It is separate from individual conscience, though it requires this for its continued existence. Crime, then, refers to an act that offends the collective conscience. Durkheim states, "In other words, we must not say that an act offends the common consciousness because it is criminal, but that it is criminal because it offends that consciousness. We do not condemn it because it is a crime, but it is a crime because we condemn it."[19] In a society with a strong social likeness and a strong collective consciousness, offences against the collective consciousness are perceived as threats to social bonds—to something greater than the individuals, the very basis of the existence of society—and such a society calls forth vengeful, penal sanctions. This is because it is the society that "is harmed even when the harm done is to individuals, and it is the attack upon society that is repressed by punishment."[20] In societies of a mechanical nature, punishment of crime is repressive, and has a quasi-religious nature, because the crime offends a morality that "we vaguely feel is more or less outside and above us."[21] Revenge is extracted because crimes are against collective sentiments and are perceived as a threat to society. Penal laws reflect a type of social solidarity that is mechanical because it is based upon social likeness. People have a shared common consciousness and a shared psychic type and a collective existence. Penal law represents mechanical solidarity where members of society share common states of consciousness, and the more extensively the common conscience regulates social life, the "more also it creates ties that bind the individual to the group; the more, consequently, social cohesion derives completely from this cause."[22]

In Durkheim's view organic solidarity can be recognized when there are restitutive sanctions that are concerned with only a restoration of the normal situation rather than with punishment or disgrace. This is possible because repressive law is linked to the collective conscience, while restitutive law has feeble links with the collective conscience. Restitutive law is administered within specialized tribunals and systems of arbitration that are concerned with specific groups and specialized activities. Areas of law such as domestic law, contract law, procedural and administrative law, and constitutional law regulate the co-operation that derives from the division of labour. This body of co-operative law is restitutive and "exempt from the effects of the collective consciousness" because it governs specialized activities, ones that concern only a limited section of society, rather than being common to all. Without the central role of the collective conscience, these rules do not demand expiation and are concerned merely with regulating social relations.

The two forms of solidarity have different sanctions and types of law, and they also permit different degrees of personality or individuality. The form of solidarity that has little degree of division of labour and a strong collective consciousness can only be strong if the ideas shared by all members are more intensively experienced than ideas held by individuals. Durkheim explains the distinction: "The solidarity that derives from similarities is at its *maximum* when the collective consciousness completely envelops our total consciousness, coinciding with it at every point. At that moment our individuality is zero."[23] The individual does not exist in this type of society and, indeed, individuality is a function of a different type of social solidarity, one that assumes individual differences. There has to be an element of individual personality that is not touched by the collective conscience in order for people to pursue their special functions. In this case, individuality can flourish, but it does not undermine social cohesion:

> The more extensive this free area is, the stronger the cohesion that arises from this solidarity. Indeed, on the one hand each one of us depends more intimately upon society the more labour is divided up, and on the other, the activity of each one of us is correspondingly more specialised, the more personal it is. Doubtless, however circumscribed that activity may be, it is never completely original. Even in the exercise of our profession we conform to usages and practices that are common to us all in our corporation. Yet even in this case the burden that we bear is in a different way less heavy than when the whole of society bears down upon us, and this leaves much more room for the free play of our initiative. Here, then, the individuality of the whole grows at the same time as that of the parts. Society becomes more effective in moving in concert, at the same time as each of its elements has more movements that are peculiarly its own.[24]

Durkheim calls this form of social solidarity—due to the division of labour—organic, as it is analogous with the solidarity found in the organism of higher animals, where the biological unity is based upon the specialization of individual parts. So specialization produces interdependence and co-operation among people who depend upon one another's specialiality.

The basis of social order is not just socialization in the form of mechanical solidarity and division of labour in organic solidarity. The law has a role to play too. While the law appears in Durkheim's theory as an index of solidarity, in mechanical society it is a product of similar collective consciences, which, through the imposition of repressive measures, then "impose upon everybody uniform beliefs and practices."[25] The division of labour in advanced societies produces restitutive laws that regulate the divided functions. In addition, moral rules accompany each type of solidarity. Under mechanical solidarity there are extensive moral and religious rules that govern social activities. Where a highly developed restitutive law exists and does not touch closely upon the collective conscience, there is still a need for moral rules. One source of moral rules, Durkheim believed, is the development of an occupational morality for each profession. Such moral rules and ideas of justice force individuals, when entering into commercial relationships, to consider the ends of others, to make compromises, and to consider ends beyond their own. Also, outside the occupational sphere in domestic or social situations, people have to consider their obligations, and here, the state is increasingly "charged with reminding us of the sentiment of common solidarity."[26]

This stress on the moral nature of organic society shows how Durkheim rejects the idea that social order in advanced societies is based upon individuals pursuing their own interests through contractual relationships. He thus distances himself from utilitarian and laissez-faire nostrums. Durkheim argues that contracts cannot exist unless there is some socially derived moral force to ensure their regulation. He denies that a moral society could be replaced by one based upon the pursuit of individual economic interests. While co-operation has its moral basis, Durkheim sees the co-operative, interdependent society as one in which individual personality can become strong. Nevertheless, there is still a role for morality. Each profession has its occupational morality: among groups of workers or professionals, there are "opinions," and "usages and customs." And although they are not enforced legally, they command obedience, "which none can infringe without incurring the reprimand of the corporation."[27] People can choose their professions and features of their personal life, and while the rules and morals that are necessary to support organic solidarity limit individual initiative, they do not do so in the rigid way that the morality of mechanical solidarity does. The laws and morals of organic solidarity are not so repressive and are amenable to negotiation or change.

For Durkheim, there is an inverse relationship between the collective conscience and individuality. Initially, only tribal societies with mechanical solidarity existed, and because these were based upon identical groups or clans, they "comprise a system of homogenous segments similar to one another,"[28] which he called segmental societies. The structure of organic societies is different because they are made up of a system of different organs with specialized roles and they contain their own differentiated parts. Gradually, organic societies grew, and the existence of features of mechanical solidarity became more hidden; although, as Durkheim believed they never completely disappeared. The causes of this evolution need to be examined.

In Durkheim's reasoning, the expansion of the division of labour comes about as the social segments lose their individuality, become more permeable, and combine in new ways. Such changes enable new relationships to develop among individuals who were previously separated. Individuals come into greater contact with each other as the boundaries between segments are loosened. Division of labour expands as interaction and commerce grows between segments—a process that Durkheim calls increasing "moral density." This is a process in which territorial segregation between segments declines, no matter whether it's a society of nomads, hunters, shepherds, or agricultural villagers. A further development is the rise of cities that permit more intimate and intense contacts. Developments in communication and transportation also increase the moral density as they reduce the gaps between segments.

Moral density increases intra-social relations, and its effects are multiplied when the population grows, producing an increase in social volume. This dual pressure results in an increase in the division of labour because the "struggle for existence becomes more strenuous."[29] It enables people to avoid conflict by refining and specializing their tasks, and its benefits enable more people to be maintained and survive. As a sociologist, Durkheim had a different focus on the division of labour compared with an economist: "We see how different our view of the division of labour appears from that of the economists. For them it consists essentially in producing more. For us this greater productivity is merely a necessary consequence, a side effect of the phenomenon. If we specialise, it is not so as to produce more, but to enable us to live in the new conditions of existence created for us."[30]

Durkheim theorized that as society increases in volume the collective conscience becomes more abstract and cannot make specific demands upon personal conduct because the collective conscience must then influence a larger population spread over a greater space. As society's demands become less discrete and more universal, the collective conscience leaves greater space for individual variation. The collective conscience in segmental society is a traditional form of authority. One factor that breaks down this traditional constraint on individuality is the growth of the city, and as the city is based upon the migration of people into its ranks, the power of segmental society and its collective conscience erodes. The city dweller becomes cut off from authority figures. New ideas, fashions, and beliefs develop in this context where individuality and rationality gain more freedom to develop. Durkheim concludes, "As society spreads out and becomes denser, it envelops the individual less tightly, and in consequence can restrain less efficiently the divergent tendencies that appear."[31] In the urban context as moral density and volume increase, the individual is less watched and controlled, and this enables the individual to escape such controls. The individual becomes increasingly free of the collective conscience, permitting greater individuality. Therefore, the division of labour is a function of the social structure. A segmental society encloses the individual within tradition, and as structural changes weaken its grip, individuality and the division of labour can emerge.

Lukes points out that the content of the collective conscience changes in organic societies: since there are few collective beliefs that can take on the strength of religious character, the collective conscience becomes more rational and secular.[32] Durkheim gives an exception to this:

> There is indeed one area in which the common consciousness has grown stronger, becoming more clearly delineated, viz., in its view of the individual. As all the other beliefs and practices assume less and less religious a character, the individual becomes the object of a sort of religion. We carry on the worship of the dignity of the human person, which like all strong acts of worship, has already acquired its superstitions. If you like, therefore it is indeed a common faith ... It is indeed from society that it draws all this strength, but it is not to society that it binds us: it is to ourselves. Thus it does not constitute a truly social link.[33]

As we will discuss later, the place of human dignity in the collective consciousness had to be buttressed by notions of equality of opportunity, a work ethic, and social justice:

> If, on the other hand, we call to mind that the collective consciousness is increasingly reduced to the cult of the individual, we shall see that the characteristic of morality in organised societies as compared to segmentary societies, is that it possesses something more human, and consequently more rational about it. It does not cause our activity to depend upon ends that do not directly concern us. It does not make us the servants of some ideal powers completely different in nature from ourselves, powers who follow their own course without heeding the interests of men. It requires us only to be charitable and just towards our fellow-men, to fulfil our task well, to work towards a state where everyone is called to fulfil the function he performs best and will receive a just reward for his efforts.[34]

In Durkheim's view, organic society does have rules, but they are concerned with the functions of each organ of society. Different parts of the division of labour have their own rules, moralities, and laws, but they do not restrict the broader freedoms of the individual. These occupational rules only invoke a small number of consciences and do not require or invoke a collective conscience. His generally optimistic tone regarding the possibility of social cohesion within organic solidarity begins to change during his discussion of the moral nature of organic society and, especially, when he admits that there is "only reason to believe, as we shall see later more clearly, that in our present-day societies this morality has still not developed to the extent which from now onwards is necessary for them."[35]

This theme reoccurs in Durkheim's discussion of the origins of the division of labour when he states, "The division of labour can therefore only occur within the framework of an already existing society. By this we do not just simply mean that individuals must cling materially to one another, but moral ties must also exist between them. Firstly, material continuity alone gives rise to links of this kind, provided that it is lasting. Moreover, they are directly necessary. If the relationships beginning to be established during the period of uncertainty were not subject to any rule, if no power moderated the clash of individual interests, chaos would ensue from which no new order could emerge."[36]

The Abnormal Forms of the Division of Labour

Despite Durkheim's portrayal of the organic society as normal, in the last section of *The Division of Labour in Society*, he discusses some abnormal forms of the division of labour, which he represents as pathological states.

Anomie

The first example, called *anomie*, refers to industrial and commercial crises and bankruptcies that represent a lack of adjustment in the division of labour. Durkheim says that the number of bankruptcies in France rose by 70 per cent between the years 1845 and 1869. The struggle between capital and labour is an example of conflict, rather than solidarity, that proceeds from increases in the division of labour.[37] Durkheim describes an industrial history in which conflict increases with successive changes in the division of labour and the organization of work. For example, the medieval workshop is described as one of co-operation, equality, and regular interaction between the master and his workers. From the fifteenth century, he argues, a separation developed between workers and the masters, and each formed their own organizations, which would periodically come into conflict and engage in strikes and boycotts; however, the conflicts were not perpetual. From the seventeenth century, with the birth of large-scale industry, workers and employers became more separated, work became more specialized and regimented, revolts become more frequent, and, as Durkheim wrote, the "war has become increasingly more violent."[38]

The existence of periodic industrial crises and conflicts shows that organic solidarity has not been perfectly achieved. In Durkheim's analysis, this is not because of the decline of mechanical solidarity but because "all the conditions for the existence of the former [organic solidarity] have not been realized."[39] In particular, the regulation of different functions did not develop properly. There has to be a system of regulation, which in most instances predetermines the way in which specialized organizations relate to each other in order to facilitate co-operation and avoid constant conflict. This system of regulation is an extension of the division of labour. If specialized organs relate and interact together in a mutual way then these actions are repeated and become habits, which, in turn, may develop into rules of conduct. Mutually beneficial transactions among the functions of the division of labour lead to repetition or customary practices, and even become obligatory, but they are not the source of organic solidarity. This regulatory system grows out of, and helps, the division of labour to function.

Durkheim argued that the necessary regulation did not exist in, or was out of step with, the current stage of the division of labour, and, therefore, "this lack of regulation does not allow the functions to perform regularly and harmoniously."[40] Durkheim clearly believed that some form of regulation is necessary over and above the price mechanism that economists use as the device for regulating the relationship between supply and demand. The price mechanism cannot avoid periods of disruption and instability, and the greater the complexity of social organization the greater is the need for regulation. Where the division of labour does not produce solidarity in markets or the factory system it is because they are not regulated; this lack of regulation is what he calls anomie. The state of anomie cannot exist where specialized organs have been in regular contact over time because regulation is consolidated in this way. Anomie arises when contacts are rare, or infrequent, or too new, and so each situation is one of trial and error. Durkheim takes the example of economic markets. In the segmental or mechanical type of society, markets correspond to each segment. Producers are near their consumers and can easily calculate the needs of the local population. With organic solidarity the boundaries of these segments break down, and local markets expand so that they are national or even global in scale. Producers are no longer supplying a local and known market, and they cannot easily see the market's extent or limits. Production becomes unregulated, with a tendency for over- or under-estimations of demand and ensuing crises.

Assembly-line work showing the repetitive and socially isolated work described by Durkheim as anomic.

Anomie also exists in the industrial factory system, which developed to service large markets and caused changing relations between employers and employees. The introduction of machinery to replace manufacture, the regimented discipline of the factory, the separation of the workers from their families during the working day, and the separate life styles of the employers and employees all required new organization and regulation. The rapid pace of growth of the industrial system meant that "the conflicting interests have not had time to strike an equilibrium."[41] Like Marx, Durkheim analyzed the effects of machinery: another manifestation of anomie is the experience of specialized workers who tend machines and perform repetitive work. This work is often performed as a monotonous routine, without interest or understanding, and the worker "is no more than a lifeless cog, which an external force sets in motion and impels in the same direction and in the same fashion."[42] One solution to this debasement of workers would be to provide them with a general education; but once they are accustomed to a concern with art or literature, Durkheim argues, they would find being treated as a machine even more offensive. Unlike Marx, however, he regarded the experience of the denatured and isolated worker as a product of the rapid development of specialization at work, rather than an inherent product of the capitalist division of labour. In its normal development workers within the division of labour interact with their fellow workers in their different, but related, tasks. Durkheim explains:

> He is not therefore a machine who repeats movements the sense of which he does not perceive, but he knows that they are tending in a certain direction, towards a goal that he can conceive of more or less distinctly. He feels that he is of some use. For this he has no need to take in vast areas of the social horizon; it is enough for him to perceive enough of it understand that his actions have a goal beyond themselves. Thenceforth, however specialised, however uniform his activity may be, it is that of an intelligent being, for he knows that his activity has a meaning.[43]

Durkheim took up these issues again in his preface to the second edition of *The Division of Labour in Society*. Here, he portrays economic life as unregulated, chaotic, and anarchic, where no one knows what their roles and obligations are and where the great conflict and disorder exists. Those who defend market society, do so because they believe it supports individual liberty, but he argues that true liberty can only be realized when there is regulation by a superior moral force to prevent the abuse of physical or economic power.

For anomie in economic life to cease, there must be a group that can generate the rules that are needed. Durkheim thought that the state was not sufficiently involved in economic activities to be able to create adequate regulation, and so he believed that each professional and occupational group, drawn from all participants in each industry and organized into a single body, should carry out this task. In general terms, such bodies would have to be capable of morally regulating national and international markets; therefore, they would have to include all members of an occupation distributed over large territories. National assemblies of elected representatives of employers and employees would head the corporations. Corporations would fix levels of production; wages and salaries; the duties of agencies within the industry, both to each other and to the public; and they would be a source of employment law within each industry. Durkheim thought that such corporations would go beyond providing economic and moral regulation of economic life to fulfill other needs such as education, welfare, and the cultural needs of their members. They would establish a political organ between the individual and the state, especially because old sentiments towards local communities had weakened.

The Forced Division of Labour

A second abnormal division of labour is the forced division of labour; this point directs attention to structural inequalities and how these restrict people's opportunities and lead to oppression and, possibly, class conflict. Here, Durkheim entered the territory of class inequalities more usually associated with Marx, but instead of seeing such structural features as endemic to capitalism, he chose to see them as temporary features of the pathological state of the division of labour. The existence of classes, he thought, not only leads to the allocation of less rewarding and satisfying work to the lower classes but also can be the source of class conflict if people cease to be satisfied with restricted opportunities and if they believe that the restrictions can be removed. Since humans have different abilities and aptitudes—and if social solidarity is to develop with the division of labour—specialized tasks have to fit the individual's natural talents. The existence of classes and castes hamper the spontaneous allocation of work to those with the appropriate aptitudes and abilities.

The inheritance of occupational positions through family ties is not in accordance with a spontaneous allocation of work. The children of those who own businesses may not inherit the needed aptitudes and abilities, and allocation along hereditary lines restricts the opportunity of others who may possess the necessary talent. Similarly, the hereditary transmission of wealth may give advantage to some, particularly in ways that are discrepant with their personal qualities. Where the division of labour is spontaneous, "social inequalities express precisely natural inequalities," and perfect spontaneity requires "absolute equality in the external conditions of the struggle," even though this situation is never perfectly realized. In segmental societies the collective conscience may legitimate inequalities in the way work is allocated, but in organic solidarity contracts are central to social and economic life. In such contracts, where people exchange equivalent values, the contract must be just, not a product of inequality. External conditions must become level:

> Every form of superiority has repercussions on the way in which contracts are arrived at. If, therefore it does not depend upon the person of individuals and their services to society, it invalidates the moral conditions of the exchange. If one class in society is obliged, in order to live, to secure the acceptance by others of its services, whilst another class can do without them, because of the resources already at its disposal, resources that, however, are not necessarily the result of some social superiority, the latter group can lord it over the former. In other words, there can be no rich or poor by birth without there being unjust contracts.[44]
>
> Because the segmentary type is vanishing and the organised type developing, because organic solidarity is gradually substituting itself for the solidarity that arises from similarities, it is indispensable that external conditions should be evened out. The harmony between functions, and consequently in existence, is at this price. Just as ancient peoples had above all need of a common faith to live by, we have need of justice.[45]

In *Professional Ethics and Civil Morals*, Durkheim refers to the need to end the inheritance of wealth in order to prevent the forcing of unjust contracts upon the poor. The ending of inheritance within propertied families implies the handing over of wealth to the corporations who would become the new heirs.[46] Also, in the conclusion of the second preface to *The Division of Labour in Society*, he states his support for the socializing of production. His discussion of the need to allocate people to tasks that are commensurate with their natural abilities and aptitudes and his reference to equalizing the external conditions in which people enter the competition for work appear to point in the direction of a meritocracy, where social inequalities would reflect natural inequalities only. Such appeals for economic justice reflect the arguments of socialists in his time.[47] Durkheim's analysis of social, structural, and moral change built upon the contrast between two types of social solidarity. This led him to the conclusion that a new type of social solidarity was possible based upon new forms of rights and duties, ones in which there would be more individual freedom and choice of action. However, this increased liberty requires the existence of rules and justice to regulate the more complex, specialized society. The shattered old morality cannot be resuscitated as it no longer corresponds to new conditions. Durkheim's diagnosis points to the need for a new goal—the creation of a new moral code—which cannot be created in the study of a social theorist but would have to be created in cumulative responses to emerging social strains and conflicts.

Criticisms

Durkheim was well informed regarding the ideas of Marx and other socialists, and he gave a series of lectures in 1895 in which he discussed the socialist ideology and the social conditions that gave rise to socialist ideas.[48] Durkheim did not find the class character and conflictual nature of socialist ideas attractive, and he regarded socialist ideas as a reaction to the tensions produced by the decline of social regulation and the injustice produced by class divisions. It is not surprising that his theory based upon organic solidarity, rather than one based upon class conflict, would be criticized by Marxist sociologists for not referring to the structural contradiction between social classes. The contrast between mechanical solidarity in simple societies and organic solidarity in complex ones is fundamental to Durkheim's theoretical position, but it has been challenged by Hunt who argues that the anthropological evidence suggests that Durkheim overemphasized the role of repressive law in primitive societies and that, although his argument about the expansion of restitutive law is strong, there is evidence that the capitalist state has expanded some repressive laws, especially in relation to offences dealing with property.[49]

Conclusion

The Division of Labour in Society introduces several enduring themes in Durkheim's work. One of them is the idea of social evolution from simple, mechanical solidarity to a more complex organic one. The analysis of this evolution involves an analysis at the level of social structure, in which structural change, such as the increasing volume and moral density of society in its evolution from the segmental type, leads to changes in the collective consciousness as well as the differentiation of specialized organs of society. The idea of the freedom of the individual is also connected to this process of structural change.

Anomie is a key critical concept that Durkheim introduced in *The Division of Labour in Society*. It describes the breakdown of social regulation and the failure to regulate people's naturally limitless desires that result from rapid social change. Since the 1980s, when U.S. President Ronald Reagan, Britain's Prime Minister Margaret Thatcher, and Canada's Prime Minister Brian Mulroney furthered the influence of neo-liberal thinkers such as the economist Milton Friedman and the philosopher von Hayek, the discourse of free markets, individualism, and the laissez-faire state became popularized. This helped to usher in a less regulated, more market-oriented version of capitalism. One possible outcome of the *marketization* of society is that a lack of regulation (or anomie) could produce a situation that is conducive to corporate crime. In 2002, for instance, there was a wave of corporate accounting scandals that implicated top U.S. executives at Enron, Adelphia Communications, and WorldCom. President George W. Bush's rhetoric promised harsh punishment for corporate leaders who "cook the books" and violate public trust. Rather than being an application of the anomie theory, the president's implication was that corporate crime could be solved by removing a few "bad apples," that is, a minority of the corporate malefactors.[50] Another contemporary example of anomie occurred when community colleges in England and Wales were removed from the control of local governments and made into corporations capable of competing nationally (or even internationally) for students. A study documents a spate of scandals that occurred when many colleges embraced an entrepreneurial spirit by developing thousands of franchise agreements with private education providers. Many of these agreements were bogus, but the colleges claimed millions of pounds from the British government for non-existent courses and students.[51] Passas has applied anomie theory in a wide-ranging analysis of globalization and neo-liberalism in the developed world, where social inequalities have increased, and in the developing world, where traditional goals and constraints have weakened under the impact of Western consumerist goals. The country that has experienced the most extreme anomie, he says, is post-Soviet Russia, which underwent the transition from socialism to capitalism after the collapse of its command economy and it embarked on a rapid neo-liberal experiment: "In the 1990's, however, the rates of fraud, prostitution, drug trafficking and abuse, alcoholism, smuggling, white-collar crime, violence and corruption sky-rocketed."[52]

Notes

1 Anthony Giddens, *Capitalism and Modern Social Theory* (Cambridge: Cambridge University Press, 1971), p.ix.

2 Alex Callinicos, *Social Theory* (Cambridge: Polity Press, 1999), 124.

3 Ken Morrison, *Marx, Durkheim, Weber: Formations of Modern Social Thought*, 2nd ed. (London: Sage Publications, 2006), 160.

4 Steven Lukes, *Emile Durkheim: His Life and Work* (Harmondsworth: Penguin Books, 1973), 54–5.

5 Ibid., 67.

6 Ibid., 366.

7 Frank Parkin, *Durkheim* (Oxford: Oxford University Press, 1992), 5.

8 Ken Morrison, *Marx, Durkheim, Weber*, 150.

9 Ibid., 151.

10 Ibid., 152–3.

11 Ibid., 153.

12 Emile Durkheim, *The Division of Labour in Society* (New York: The Free Press, 1997), 162.

13 Ibid., xxx.

14 Ibid., 3.

15 Ibid., 3.

16 Ibid., 24.

17 Ibid., 29.

18 Ibid., 38.

19 Ibid., 40.

20 Ibid., 48.

21 Ibid., 56.

22 Ibid., 64.

23 Ibid., 84.

24 Ibid., 137.

25 Ibid., 172.

26 Ibid., 173.

27 Ibid., 172.

28 Ibid., 131.

29 Ibid., 208.

30 Ibid., 217.

31 Ibid., 238.

32 Steven Lukes, *Emile Durkheim*, 156.

33 Emile Durkheim, *The Division of Labour in Society*, 122.

34 Ibid., 338.

35 Ibid., 174.

36 Ibid., 218.

37 Ibid., 292.

38 Ibid., 293.

39 Ibid., 301.

40 Ibid., 303.

41 Ibid., 306.

42 Ibid., 306–7.

43 Ibid., 308.

44 Ibid., 319.

45 Ibid., 321.

46 Irving M. Zeitlin, *Ideology and the Development of Sociological Theory*, 7th ed. (New Jersey: Prentice Hall, 2001), 345.

47 Susan Stedman Jones, *Durkheim Reconsidered* (Cambridge: Polity Press, 2001), 51.

48 Irving M. Zeitlin, *Ideology and the Development of Sociological Theory*, 331.

49 Alan Hunt, *The Sociological Movement in Law* (London: Macmillan, 1978), 70–2.

50 John Bratton, Keith Grint, and Debra Nelson, *Organizational Leadership* (Carlsbad, CA: Southwestern Press, 2004), 35.

51 David Denham, "Marketization as a Context for Crime: The Scandals in Further Education in England and Wales," *Crime, Law and Social Change* 38 (December 2004): 373–88.

52 Nikos Passas, "Global Anomie, Dysnomie and Economic Crime: Hidden Consequences of Neoliberalism and Globalization in Russia and Around the World," *Social Justice* 27 (2000): 16–44.

7. Emile Durkheim: The Rules of Sociological Method and Le Suicide

Without denying the importance of his concern with "solidarity" and the conservation of societies, we have found good cause to support the view that there is an important strand of radical criticism in his work, backed by a secular reforming spirit.

—S. Fenton[1]

Émile Durkheim taught the modern world how to think about suicide. Before him, suicide seemed a matter of purely individual despair. Durkheim saw that suicide has a social dimension. People from different religions, classes and religious backgrounds destroy themselves in different proportions. Durkheim asked why this should be.

—R. Sennett[2]

THE DIVISION OF LABOUR IN SOCIETY and two other books that this chapter is devoted to represent Durkheim's endeavour to establish a scientific method of studying society, one that focuses on society as a distinct level of analysis. He was opposed to the utilitarians, such as John Stuart Mill and Jeremy Bentham, who believed that isolated individuals were free to enter into contracts in the pursuit of self-interest and, thus, owed nothing to society. In *The Division of Labour in Society* he argues that contracts cannot exist unless there are pre-existing rules and customs surrounding contracts that both enable and restrain contractual relationships. Durkheim argues that "collective life did not arise from individual life; on the contrary, it is the latter that emerged from the former."[3] He wanted to establish a subject matter for sociology, which he believed needed to concentrate on a level of reality that is external to the individual and which could be based upon techniques of observation. He distinguished between the study of the mind of individuals, psychology, and the study of facts that are external to individuals in order to challenge the idea that the individual is at the centre of society. He was critical of Tarde, who argued that society is no more than the transmission of acts from one person to another through imitation, and, therefore, he based society upon individual acts.[4] Durkheim was also opposed to early sociologists such as Comte and Spencer who, he thought, were still too wedded to speculative theories of evolution rather than to an objective analysis based upon the observation of social facts. A contemporary student might think that a book entitled *The Rules of Sociological Method* would contain a discussion of different ways of collecting information, such as surveys, questionnaires, or focus groups. Instead, it is a highly polemical work concerned with establishing the new discipline of sociology and challenging individualistic, psychological explanations and philosophical speculation.

The Rules of Sociological Method

Social Facts

In his second book, *The Rules of Sociological Method*, Durkheim tries to make the method he developed in *The Division of Labour in Society* more explicit. To begin with, Durkheim establishes that there are *social facts* that are external to individuals and which affect how people act: "When I fulfil my obligations as brother, husband, or citizen, when I execute my contracts, I perform duties which are defined, externally to myself and my acts, in law and in custom."[5] These social facts are external because individuals do not create them and only become aware of their existence through their education or socialization. Examples of social facts are the religious beliefs and practices that people hold, the language used to express thoughts, the system of currency, and professional practices; all of these function independently and exist independent of the individuals who live in a society at a particular time. He states: "Here, then, are ways of acting, thinking, and feeling that present the noteworthy property of existing outside the individual consciousness."[6]

In addition, Durkheim argues that these social facts possess a "coercive power" and impose themselves upon the individual. In many instances people consent and conform to the type of conduct expected of them and do not experience constraint unless they try to resist the social constraints when they become aware of their force. The law counters its violation with expiation or compensation for the harm done, and public attitude exercises a check on morality and administers less violent (though possibly more emotionally hurtful) punishments than does the law. The breaching of conventions such as dress codes or ways of speaking may lead to ridicule or ostracism. Durkheim writes, "Here, then, is a category of facts with very distinctive characteristics: it consists of ways of acting, thinking, and feeling, external to the individual, and endowed with a power of coercion, by reason of which they control him."[7] These social facts—which contain ways of acting and their representations—are not biological phenomena, nor are they psychological phenomena: they are outside individual consciences. Durkheim claims to have identified a new variety of phenomena to be called social because the source of social facts is not in the individual, "their substratum can be no other than society,"[8] and "these ways of thinking and acting constitute the proper domain of sociology."[9] In this view, people do not completely determine themselves: rather, "most of our ideas and tendencies come from without. How can they become a part of us except by imposing themselves upon us?"[10]

Social facts such as legal and moral rules, religion, and financial constraints suggest that they are derived from social institutions; however, people might experience feelings from *social currents*, such as the emotion that can develop in a crowd. Other social currents might be currents of opinion on religious, political, or artistic affairs. Another example given by Durkheim is the socialization and education of children: "All education is a continuous effort to impose on the child ways of seeing, feeling, and acting which he could not have arrived at spontaneously."[11] Social facts might be recognized by the way they are written down, communicated, or become a moral or legal rule. They take on collective dimensions as beliefs, tendencies, or practices, even though individual manifestations have their own features. Currents of opinion may impel certain groups to certain levels of marriage, birth rate, or suicide, which can be expressed in statistics, but the details of individual cases are concealed within the statistics.[12] The domain of sociology is the study of social facts, and "a social fact is every way of acting, fixed or not, capable of exercising on the individual an external constraint; or again, every way of acting which is general throughout a given society, while at the same time existing in its own right independent of its individual manifestations."[13]

The Observation of Social Facts

Durkheim's next step was to establish some rules for the observation of social facts, which he believed could be considered things. Something has the character of a thing if it can be subject to observation—it can be treated as data—and Durkheim (as was seen earlier) identified some specifically sociological facts. Social life is imbued with values, and although these cannot be directly observed, it is possible to scientifically study them because there is a "phenomenal reality" that expresses them. For instance, morality is expressed in the body of rules governing conduct. Social phenomena are distinct from the "consciously formed representations of them in the mind" and can be studied "objectively as external things."[14] These phenomena are objective because individuals cannot alter them with their will, and an understanding of them that reflects their nature has to be developed empirically. Laws are embodied in legal codes; statistical data is collected on social activities; fashions are preserved in clothing; and taste is developed in works of art: all of these take on an independent existence external to the consciousness of individuals. Later in the text, he refers to these social phenomena as "collective representations" that convey "the way in which the group conceives itself in relation to objects which affect it."[15] As Lukes says, Durkheim's sociology of knowledge and of religion involved a systematic study of collective representations.[16]

The Normal and the Pathological

Durkheim was able to find a justification for science to be a guide to practical action by making a distinction between normal and unhealthy societies: "Briefly, for societies as for individuals, health is good and desirable; disease, on the contrary, is bad and to be avoided. If, then, we can find an objective criterion, inherent in the facts themselves, which enables us to distinguish scientifically between health and morbidity in the various orders of social phenomena, science will be in a position to throw light on practical problems and still remain faithful to its own method."[17] He defines *health* as the "perfect adaptation of the organism to its environment" and *morbidity* as anything which "disturbs this adaptation." Since these arguments apply to living organisms, he thought they could be extended to societies; therefore, he needed criteria for assessing the health or morbidity of societies, that is, the "various degrees of completeness of this adaptation." [18] Normal states are social conditions that are generally found within societies—bearing in mind the stage of the society's development, just as the young adult stage will be different from that of an old person.[19] Morbid or pathological states are ones that depart from this normal state.

Durkheim applied his definition of normality to crime, which is commonly seen as a pathological condition. Although what is deemed to be crime varies between societies, he claims that all societies identify some acts as deserving of punishment. To say that the existence of crime is normal seems a startling conclusion. Durkheim does not say that crime is ever present because all societies contain wicked people, but he asserts that it is "a factor in public health, an integral part of all healthy societies."[20]

Crime is normal because all societies have it and also because it offends the collective conscience. Crime is functionally useful to society because punishment reinforces the values that a crime offends, and some criminals could be harbingers of a new and more progressive morality.[21]

Rules for the Explanation of Social Facts

In the fifth chapter of *The Rules of Sociological Method* Durkheim makes a distinction between the functions of a fact and the cause or origin of that fact. The demonstration that a fact is useful does not explain its origins. We may have a need for things but we cannot will them into existence. So again, Durkheim uses his discussion of social facts to stress their independent nature and force and to distinguish between individualistic and sociological explanations: "But since each one of them is a force, superior to that of the individual, and since it has a separate existence, it is not true that merely by willing to do so may one call them into being. No force can be engendered except by an antecedent force."[22] Causal and functional analyses are separate orders of analysis. However, they each give a fuller understanding of a social phenomenon because a fact may need to have a function for it to survive. Durkheim was critical of Comte and Spencer's discussions of society that were ultimately teleological and psychological. Rather than looking at society as based on individual psychology, Durkheim argued that society "exercises pressure on individual consciences"; it is an external impulse to which people submit. The pressure exerted by society is the "pressure which the totality exerts on the individual": the whole is greater than the sum of its parts. Furthermore, a system formed by the association of individuals is a reality with its own characteristics. The group gives people ways of thinking, feeling, and acting which are different from how they would be if they were isolated. "Collective representations, emotions and tendencies are caused not by certain states of the consciences of individuals but by the conditions in which the social group in its totality is placed." Sentiments are formed by the social group—by social organization rather than by the individual. For these reasons, sociological and psychological explanations are very different. Psychological states may be associated with social conditions, but rather than explaining social facts by psychological or innate human characteristics, sociologists explain these characteristics with reference to the preceding social facts. In other words, the sociologist is concerned with how the human milieu "exerts influence on the course of social phenomena." Durkheim refers to two aspects of the social milieu that affect social existence: the volume or size of a society and its dynamic density, that is, the number who share a common life; the fusion of social segments; and the intensification of social life so that the horizons of individual thought and action can be extended.[23]

Rules Relative to Establishing Sociological Proofs

Durkheim states that the only way to establish that a given social fact is the cause of another is to observe how one fact (the cause) varies in relation to another (its effect). In sociology these social facts cannot be artificially produced in an experimental situation, and so they must be observed as they occur in social situations by using the method of comparison, in what may be described as an indirect experiment. Because of the complexity of social phenomena, Durkheim argues that the methods of agreement and difference are not applicable, particularly as it may be impossible to isolate all but one of the causal variables. Consequently, he argues for the utility of the method of concomitant variations, a method that can test the variation or movement between two variables. From the analysis of observed data, a sociologist may be able to deduce how one of two phenomena may produce the other. Comparisons can then be made to test a theorized possible cause of a particular effect, and if the connection is verified through the comparison, the cause, it is said, can be proven. Durkheim suggested that throughout history there have been many variations in collective life and sociologists can draw upon the evidence of this. Some evidence is present in all societies, including crime, suicide, birth rate, marriage rate, and the practice of thrift; these are manifest in different forms according to a diverse social milieu, such as geographical location, profession, or religious faith. In the *The Rules of Sociological Method* Durkheim sets out an argument for a causal science of the social world to achieve an objective analysis by treating social facts as things.

Suicide

Suicide was perceived in the late nineteenth century as a growing social problem, and it served as a test of Durkheim's methodology and his concept of the field of sociology. Durkheim defines *suicide* as "the term applied to any case of death resulting directly or indirectly from a positive or negative act, carried out by the victim himself, which he was aware would produce this result."[24] Psychology concentrates on individual factors such as character, temperament, or features of the individual's life prior to suicide, but Durkheim emphasized the centrality of the suicide rate, which he argues is an objective social fact. He provides statistics for several countries and demonstrates that each tends to have a relatively stable suicide rate over a period of years, unless there is sudden social upheaval. Suicide rates are thus seen as social facts; each society has its own tendency to produce voluntary deaths, and it is the social causes of these rates that constitute the sociological study of suicide.[25]

Durkheim criticized explanations of suicide that are based on extra-social factors such as psychopathic or mental states, race, heredity, climate, and imitation. The elimination of individual and psychological explanations enabled him to develop his original theory regarding the connection between the total rate of suicide and different social contexts. He stressed that the focus should be on the general social state that produces suicides, rather than on suicidal motives, which are only the most apparent causes and are "merely the individual repercussions of a general state ... One might say that they indicate the individual's weak points, those through which the current, which comes from outside inviting him to destroy himself might most easily enter."[26] Only later in his thinking, does Durkheim consider how the general causes of suicide impact the individual in ways that produce suicidal acts.

Social Integration: Egoistic Suicide and Altruistic Suicide

Durkheim linked two types of suicide with the degree of social integration, by which he meant the feeling of attachment individuals have towards groups. He predicted that the suicide rate would vary inversely with the degree of social integration. When social groups have less of an integrative role, Durkheim argues, the individual's goals preponderate over communal ones, and the individual is more orientated to the pursuit of his or her private interests. This situation makes certain individuals susceptible to *egoistic* suicide, which originates from excessive individualism.[27] Egoism is a cause of suicide "because the link that attaches [an individual] to society has itself been relaxed,"[28] which makes life appear purposeless. In contrast, when people are strongly integrated they feel more constrained to fulfill their duties to society, and less inclined to evade them by taking their own life. Where people belong to a group they love, they feel less likely to let the group down, or if they have loyalties to group goals, they feel their own private troubles less.

Religion and egoistic suicide

Drawing upon statistics from various sources in a range of countries and regions, Durkheim showed that, without exception, Protestants were much more likely than Catholics to commit suicide: the difference is from 20 to 30 per cent and up to 300 per cent.[29] This difference cannot be explained by reference to religious beliefs because each religion condemns suicide. The significant difference, Durkheim insists, is related to the fact that Protestantism allows "a great deal more freedom of enquiry"[30] than Catholicism which, he says, is a more traditional, hierarchical system of authority in which believers accept a ready-made faith, in contrast to Protestantism, where individuals are more the authors of their faith. Protestantism, Durkheim asserts, allows more scope for individual judgment, which results in a less religious influence over people's lives and, thus, less social integration.

The family as protection against egoistic suicide

Durkheim reasoned that the family could produce greater social integration and have an effect similar to religion. The absolute figures he used show that unmarried persons were less likely to commit suicide, and this confirmed the common sense view that suicide is a way of escaping the burdens of life. An unmarried person could be seen to have an easier life, with fewer responsibilities. However, Durkheim points out that a more careful examination of the statistics shows that the reality is otherwise: the absolute figures for the unmarried include all persons under sixteen and this age group had a low rate of suicide. After adjusting the rate for age, Durkheim demonstrates that the suicide rate for married people was less than that of the unmarried. In France during the period 1889–91, for every million inhabitants the suicide rate for thirty- to forty-year-old unmarried men was 627, compared with 226 for the married men of that age; and the rate for forty- to fifty-year-old unmarried men was 975, compared with 340 for married men.

Durkheim argues that the lower suicide among married men was related to the structure of the domestic environment. The family can be regarded as containing two different environments: the conjugal family of husband and wife and the family that included husband and wife and their children. Quoting statistics from the French census of 1886, he demonstrates that the state of marriage had only a slight preservative effect on men aged forty to fifty, since married men without children commited suicide only a third less often than unmarried men.[31] Furthermore, he reasoned that it is not the conjugal family that had the greatest preservative power and that families with the most density (in terms of numerical size and frequency of interaction within families) had the lowest level of suicide. Thus, rather than increasing suicide by adding to the burdens of life, large families "are on the contrary, the daily bread without which one cannot survive."[32] Why does the family have this preservative value? Durkheim's answer is that larger domestic groups have greater integration because there is a more intense and continuous interaction between relatives.

Integration of the political system and suicide

Typically, Durkheim begins his discussion with reference to comments of contemporary authors, who believed that as political systems disintegrate suicide increases. He points out that, ever since the collection of suicide statistics in European states in the nineteenth century, the evidence contradicts this view. In France following the revolutions in 1830 and 1848, the drop in the number of suicides was about 10 per cent. As the revolution spread throughout Europe, suicide declined as much as 18 per cent in Denmark, Prussia, Bavaria, Saxony, and Austria. Revolutions in France produced a decrease in suicide in Paris, 13 per cent fewer in 1830 and 32 per cent fewer in 1832. Also, Durkheim refers to suicide statistics during political crises, election periods, and wars, in which a decline of up to 14 per cent is recorded. Durkheim concludes that social upheaval and popular wars, which stimulate collective sentiments, patriotism, and national sentiments, contribute to a stronger integration of society. Durkheim reasons that crises produce struggles, and "since these oblige men to cling together in order to confront a common danger, the individual thinks less of himself and more of the community,"[33] and this leads to a reduction in egotistic suicide.

Altruistic suicide

Durkheim believed that egoistic suicide was rare in tribal societies but that three types of altruistic suicide, produced by insufficient individuation, were widespread: obligatory, optional, and acute. To describe the obligatory form of altruistic suicide, performed as a duty, he gives examples of societies where death from old age or sickness was a disgrace and where old men would kill themselves to avoid dishonour. Such societies might reinforce these practices with the belief that those who take their own life enter a beautiful world, or that those who die of sickness or old age are condemned to a harsh and intolerable existence. In addition, some social customs expected women to kill themselves on the death of their husband, and in others, the followers and servants of chiefs were expected to take their own lives after the death of the chief.[34] This type of suicide was a product of a socially defined duty, backed by religious sanctions and the loss of honour. Durkheim's explanation of this type of suicide contains references to the lack of individuality, which was first expounded in his discussion of mechanical solidarity. For altruistic suicide to exist there has to be little concept of individual personality, and the individual has to be absorbed into a highly integrated group. In tribal societies the group was small and the individual was easily, collectively supervised, thus preventing the emergence of individual egos as a source of resistance to a collective demand for the cessation of life.

Durkheim refers to the second type of altruistic suicide as optional, such as that which might occur in societies of Polynesia or among aboriginal people of North America; this form of suicide was not expressly imposed by society, but it might be a culturally condoned act in defence of a person's honour, such as following an offence against someone, a marital quarrel, or a disappointment. Such acts, by which a person might avoid stigma or gain esteem, were enabled in cultures that place little emphasis on individual interests. The third type, which Durkheim calls acute altruistic suicide, refers to suicides where people take their own life "for the pleasure of sacrifice."[35] Some religions of India furnish examples of this type of martyrdom, including the practices of seeking death in sacred rivers, allowing oneself to be crushed under the chariot wheels of the idol Juggernaut, or throwing oneself from a cliff into sulphur mines. Altruistic suicide is a product of over-integration; this occurs when individuals have a goal beyond themselves and their own life is seen as an obstacle to achieving this goal. Egoism produces feelings of "incurable lassitude and dreary depression," but altruism is "derived from hope, because it comes from the fact that more beautiful prospects are glimpsed beyond this life."[36]

In contemporary society, as individual personalities become increasingly free from the collective identity, altruistic suicide becomes very rare. However, Durkheim identifies the army as a social context in which altruistic suicide was chronic. The statistics for several European countries and the United States that compare suicide rates in the military with those for civilians show a difference of between 25 and 900 per cent: Austria, United States, and Italy had the highest incidence of suicide among their soldiers. One explanation could be that most soldiers are bachelors, but Durkheim demonstrates that suicide among French soldiers was higher than for unmarried civilians. Another explanation is the hardship of military life, but Durkheim shows that the suicide rate was higher for the longer serving soldiers who had re-enlisted, and it was higher for officers, whose conditions were more comfortable. Thus, suicide was most associated with soldiers who chose a military career and who possessed the "acquired habits or natural predispositions that make up the military ethos."[37] Durkheim deduced that the explanation of such high suicide rates was the culture within the army, which lacks individualism, as soldiers have to follow and not question orders. This lack of individualism in the army makes it a unique institution of modern society and one that is similar to the high integration/low individualism of tribal societies: "The military mind is itself in certain respects a survival of primitive morality. Under the influence of this predisposition, the soldier kills himself at the slightest disappointment, for the most trivial reasons, for a refusal to grant leave, for a reprimand, for an unjust punishment, for a hitch in promotion, for a matter of honour, for a passing fit of jealousy or even quite simply, because other suicides have taken place before his eyes or to his knowledge."[38]

Social regulation: Anomic and Fatalistic Suicide

Anomic suicide

In addition to integrating individuals by developing their sentiments, society regulates and controls people. Durkheim developed two more types of suicide based upon the degree of regulation of the individual. Anomic suicide is related to a lack of regulation, wherein society begins to lose its ability to set adequate restraints upon individual desires. Durkheim discussed anomie in relation to economic crises, which he demonstrated leads to increases in suicide rate. He referred to a financial crisis in Vienna, 1873–04, that led to a 70 per cent increase in suicide. The same crisis induced a 45 per cent increase in suicide in Frankfurt-on-Main in 1874. A crash on the Paris Bourse in 1882 produced an increase of 11 per cent in the three months closest to the time of the crash. Bankruptcies also reflect the vagaries of economic life. The average increase in bankruptcies between 1845 and 1869 was 3.2 per cent; but it was 26 per cent in 1847; 37 per cent in 1854; and 20 per cent in 1861. Suicide increased on average in this period by 2 per cent per year, but in each of the years of high bankruptcies, it increased dramatically: 17 per cent in 1847; 8 per cent in 1854; and 9 per cent in 1861.[39]

Once again, Durkheim challenged a common sense explanation, this time by stating that suicide increases because poverty has increased and life has become more difficult. If suicide varies according to the level of poverty, the rate would be expected to decline in periods of prosperity. Durkheim provides statistical data relating to Italy during the 1870s and 1880s which indicate people were enjoying a period of economic growth, yet suicide rates increased annually in the 1870s from 29 per million during 1864–70 to 40.6 per million in 1877. Following German unification, there was commercial and industrial expansion, but suicides increased by 90 per cent between 1875 and 1886. To further enhance his claim that poverty does not stimulate higher suicide levels he cites the examples of poor countries, such as Ireland, Italy (Calabria) and Spain and poorer regions in France, as places with low suicide rates. Poverty, he concludes, appears to be a protection from suicide. He proposes that industrial and financial crises, no matter whether they produce more poverty or greater prosperity, increase the number of suicides because they disturb the social order.[40]

Durkheim's explanation of the suicidal impetus of social disturbances involved his views on human nature and social regulation. He asserted, "No living person can be happy or even live unless his needs are well adjusted to his means."[41] If a person's needs cannot be granted, then there is friction and dissatisfaction, which reduces the will to live. Durkheim reasoned that animals have material and instinctive needs, but once these are satisfied they do not ask for anything else. An animal's "power of reflection is not sufficiently developed to imagine other ends than those implicit in its physical nature."[42] It is much harder, however, to decide upon the limits to appetites, needs, and wants of human beings, and such limits are not to be found in human biological or psychological nature. In Durkheim's view, the attachment to life becomes weakened when the demands of life cannot be satisfied because they lead to insurmountable obstacles, or because the pursuit of one demand just leads to another one. Hence, Durkheim wrote, "For things to be otherwise, it is above all necessary that passions should be limited. Only then can they be harmonised with the faculties and then satisfied."[43] An external moral force that people feel is just, which they respect, and to which they can respond spontaneously must accomplish this. This moral power is society, which is superior to the individual. Society can create laws, set limits beyond which the passions cannot go, and it "alone can assess what prospect of reward should be offered to every kind of official in the common interest."[44]

Durkheim believed that there is usually awareness, in the moral consciousness, of the worth and lifestyle appropriate to different functions within the social hierarchy and that these set limits to ambitions and expectations. These relative limitations, though, are not static; they are subject to gradual change over time and as conditions change; they "make men content with their lot, while at the same time giving them moderate encouragement to improve it; and it is this average contentment that gives rise to feelings of calm, active happiness, to the pleasure at being and living which, for societies as for individuals, is a sign of health. Each person, at least in general, is then in harmony with his condition and wants only what he can legitimately wish for as the normal reward for his activity."[45]

This superior, moral, socially derived consciousness usually governs people's behaviour and normally overrides the demands and needs that are ultimately located within the nature of the human as a biological organism. When there are sudden social crises, this moral constraint may temporarily lose its effect, and lead to a sudden increase in suicide, because individual aspirations are stimulated. Whether these crises introduce poverty or prosperity, it takes time for the moral conscience to re-establish itself, and for a while people do not know what aspirations are just or unjust, what the limits are, and what demands and hopes are reasonable. In this period of anomie, passions are less disciplined. At times of upheaval such discipline is most needed because the relations within economic functions are shaken up and social conflict may arise as a result. According to Durkheim's theory, in this context the desire to live is weakened.

Economic crises can produce fluctuations in the suicide rate, but in Durkheim's vision, anomie is in a chronic state in the sphere of trade and industry. He argued that industrial relations became less regulated as traditional religion and the guilds lost their moral hold over the relations between employers and workers—the ability to explain and limit aspirations was lost. Markets had been extended beyond the local region, potential gains greatly increased, and expectations excited: "From top to bottom of the ladder, desires are aroused but have no definite idea on what to settle. Nothing can appease them, since the aim towards which they aspire is infinitely beyond anything they might attain."[46] The constant pursuit of new experiences, pleasures, and novelties led to a situation in which people had become disillusioned with a finally meaningless "endless pursuit" of new pleasures, sensations, and novelties. In modern industrial economies people who work in trade and industry are the least regulated by the old mechanisms of restraint, and these workers have a much higher suicide rate compared with those employed in agriculture—people who, Durkheim concludes, were still subject to some of the old forms of regulation.

Fatalistic suicide

Durkheim confines his comment on the fourth type of suicide—fatalistic suicide—to a footnote at the end of the chapter on anomic suicide, and he only includes it for the sake of theoretical completeness. This type is the opposite of anomie and refers to suicide emanating from excessive regulation among people whose futures are "pitilessly confined and whose passions are violently constrained by oppressive discipline."[47] Thinking it was of little contemporary significance, he gave very few examples and cited only the suicides of very young husbands and married women who are childless. Historically, the term could also be applied to the suicide of slaves, because of their excessive regulation. Pearce points out that Durkheim's formulation of fatalistic suicide is too cryptic and that the notion of over-constraint and repressive discipline could be extended to the phenomenon of the forced division of labour,[48] as discussed in the previous chapter. Inheritance and privilege influence how people are recruited or excluded from positions in the division of labour. If this inequality in the allocation of people to work is seen as unjust, and if it were perceived as an unalterable constraint, then, in Pearce's view, it could produce potentially suicidal conditions. Durkheim believed that the rapid increase in suicide in the most industrially advanced parts of Europe was due to the rapid transformation of the social structure, which had destroyed old social institutions without putting anything in their place. He reasoned that established religions, the family, and the state were not able to provide sufficient influence over individuals, resulting in the increase in egoistic and anomic suicides. The social structure had changed in ways that reduced the ability of society to inculcate a collective morality and adequate restraint over individual desires. He returned to the idea of occupational associations,[49] which he believed could exist between the individual and state as a new source of regulation and morality.

Criticisms

Durkheim referred to social or collective forces that give each society a "suicidal propensity." Society's "moral constitution ... determines at any moment the number of voluntary deaths" and each society has a collective force, "which drives men to kill themselves."[50] The suicide rate in this sociological theory does not result from individual inclinations or temperament; rather it is the other way around. Each society possesses currents of egoism, altruism, and anomie, each with a corresponding mental state of "languid melancholy, active renunciation, or exasperated lassitude." These societal-wide tendencies "penetrating the minds of individuals make them decide to kill themselves."[51] Durkheim was convinced that suicide rates, which remain stable unless there is a sudden change in the social environment, demonstrate that society has a influence on behaviour that is distinct from psychology and that it is possible to study social regularities, such as suicide rates, scientifically. According to Durkheim, the reason why some individuals succumb to suicidal currents (apart from insanity)[52] is because "the mental constitution of the former, such as nature and events have made it, offers less resistance to the suicidal current."[53] Despite his argument that approaches to understanding suicide based upon individual motive or psychological analyses of individuals could not explain the consistency of suicide rates between countries and social groups, his admission that the individual's mental constitution leads some to succumb to suicidal pressures opens up the role of individual psychology in the explanation of why particular individuals take their own life. This might be seen as a weakness of his positivistic, sociological approach, but Parkin points out that Durkheim was concerned with differential suicide rates, not with predicting which individuals would be at risk.[54] In this regard Durkheim's sociology shares similarities with studies of collective behaviour, such as correlations between social class and educational achievement, which do not predict which individuals will succeed educationally, or correlations with etiological studies of disease, which relate lifestyle factors with ill health but cannot say who will contract the disease and who will not.

As will be seen in the later discussion of Weber, sociology is divided according to those who believe that sociology can copy the method of the natural sciences, which is positivism, and those who argue that human action is meaningful and that a proper understanding of action requires an interpretive approach that considers people's meanings and motives. Durkheim was consistent in his advocacy of the study of social facts (i.e., social constraints which regulate collective life) as described in *The Rules of Sociological Method,* but he made assumptions about the meaning of suicide to people, which he inferred from their situations in the currents of egoism/altruism and anomie/fatalism, rather than based upon qualitative research of actual motives. Lukes criticizes Durkheim for not including people's subjective perceptions and for making a rigid distinction between external (social) and internal (subjective) factors.[55] Durkheim was aware of the problem, but explicitly dismissed approaches based upon motive as lacking the ability to explain variations in suicide rates. Also his formulation of collective representations as material representations of social values puts him outside of the interpretivist tradition in sociology; however, he could be criticized for smuggling meaning back into his explanation of suicide through his assumptions of the meanings people hold in particular social milieus.

Douglas raises the issue of motives in the context of the decision-making processes of officials such as police, doctors, and coroners who decide, often when the evidence is far from conclusive, whether or not a death was a product of suicidal motives.[56] These decisions involve a reconstruction of the events leading to death and a weighing of circumstances and possible reasons for a motive of suicide. These deliberations open up the possibility of subjective judgment at the base of the official statistics, which are the "facts" that Durkheim relies upon in his analysis. Although he was aware of these problems, he dismisses deliberations on the motives for suicide by officials as liable to error and not actually relevant to understanding the deeper causes of suicide. Douglas raises some serious issues concerning how suicide statistics are socially constructed. For instance, in Catholic societies officials may be reluctant to identify a death as suicide because of its social stigma and its implications for the deceased's salvation in the eyes of the church. Such deliberations would seriously compromise the statistics, quoted by Durkheim, that show lower suicide rates amongst Catholics, who he deemed to be protected by their higher levels of social integration. Douglas also argues that suicide statistics are a product of negotiation: Articulate, high-status people may be able to influence the designation of the type of death by the coroner's court in a way that minimizes the total of recorded suicides in these groups. Under Douglas's critique it appears that Durkheim's theory is based on questionable and possibly fictitious statistics. However, in his summary of this debate Parkin points out that Durkheim found that higher educated groups were more likely to commit suicide: a finding which would not occur if Douglas's argument is correct. Douglas throws doubt on Durkheim's theory, but Parkin argues that there is insufficient evidence to establish that social groups do systematically organize themselves in a way to influence the courts.[57]

The resurgence of feminism in the 1960s stimulated the teaching of undergraduate and post-graduate courses on women's studies, as well as research and theorizing on women in society. So far in these chapters, our selection of topics from Durkheim's work has been governed by their relevance to the analysis of capitalist society—hence the discussion of economic anomie and the forced division of labour. However, in the Introduction, we referred to the impact of capitalist modernity on the experience of women, and so it is necessary to discuss Durkheim's treatment of women within his sociology. Sydie, in a trenchant critique, argues that Durkheim's "analysis of sex roles is coloured by [his] understanding of natural dichotomies between the sexes. This belief in the invariable significance of biological difference means that the hierarchies of power in society, which relegate women collectively to a subordinate status to men, are taken as givens that do not require sociological analysis."[58]

Men are most likely to be affected by economic anomie, but women, who in the division of labour were more likely to be confined to family and domestic roles, suffered negatively within marriage and the family. Sydie points out how Durkheim was struck by figures which showed that suicide rates varied according to the regulation of marital relations—with married women tending to commit suicide more often than single women and married men where there is no divorce—and that marriage "does her less service than it does man."[59] When divorce was permitted, men were more prone to suicide due to "conjugal anomie," and they were less protected from suicide when compared to married men in societies that did not tolerate divorce. To explain why husbands and wives react differently to the marital situation, Durkheim resorted to a combination of assumptions about their different biological and intellectual capacities. He argued that marriage regulates sexual relations, but these are not just instinctive; rather they have accumulated aesthetic and moral characteristics that are not regulated organically: "This is the function of marriage. It regulates all this life of the passions, and monogamous marriage more strictly than any other. By obliging the man to attach himself to only one woman, and always the same, it supplies a rigorously defined object for the need to love, and closes its horizon."[60] So the husband has to limit his desires and "find happiness in his situation," and also his wife is duty-bound "not to fail him," providing him with pleasures which are not only "circumscribed" but also "assured and this certainty constitutes his mental bedrock."[61] In contrast, the bachelor may become prey to sexual anomie because he has no restriction on his aspirations, and his life opens up "endless new experiments raising hopes that are dashed and leaving behind them a feeling of weariness and disenchantment."[62] When divorce is allowed the regulatory powers of marriage are weaker, as the "calm and tranquillity that made the husband strong are reduced"[63] and the commitment to the restraints of marriage are less heeded, since marriage is not guaranteed.

In Durkheim's opinion, men need indissoluble marriage and women benefit from less severe marital bonds because "the sexual needs of a woman are less intellectual in character, because, in general, her intellectual life is less developed."[64] Thus, biology makes her sexual needs more restrained, and so she does not require such a strict social regulation as monogamous marriage. Durkheim's analysis of the different functions of marriage for men and women, and the opposing interests between men and women, which lead to more suicides for men, if divorce is allowed, and more for women, if it is prohibited, produces a sociological impasse. He appears to prefer a solution that favours and protects men until women take up a more equal participation in social life. Yet, his views about the trends in the division of labour, the greater public participation of men, which makes them more intellectual and less organically governed than women, and the psychological differences between the sexes mean that efforts to reduce the differences between men and women will take a long time to work out and cannot be resolved by imminent legal changes alone. In answer to those who demanded that women be granted equal rights with men, Durkheim cautioned, "They are too inclined to forget that the work of centuries cannot be abolished in an instant; and that ... such legal equality cannot be legitimate as long as there is such flagrant psychological inequality."[65] Thus, Sydie argues: "Durkheim's account of the roles and functions of the sexes based on the idea of the "natural" and therefore unchangeable dualities of physiology and psychology is no more than a continuation of a tradition in western social theory. However, it is particularly interesting that Durkheim's sociological imagination deserted him when it came to dealing with the prejudices of his time regarding the capacities and roles of the sexes."[66]

Although Durkheim failed to transcend assumptions of his day about gender differences, there are features of his work which could be of interest to feminist sociologists, including his emphasis on the importance of social integration and individualism, which opens up the comparison of the socialization of boys and men with girls and women and the preparedness of the latter to make sacrifices for others at the expense of their own individualism.

Conclusion

Durkheim powerfully states the case for the analysis of an objective structure of society that pre-exists individuals and continues beyond their lifetimes. Of course, individuals act and develop meanings within this structure, and many of these meanings help to maintain the social structure over time. However, much of contemporary sociological theory revolves around the articulation of the ways in which structure influences human behaviour, and around the degree of meaningful action or agency that can exist and would allow individuals, as Giddens puts it, "to make a difference in the world."[67] The idea of a dichotomy between structure and agency is a key idea in contemporary sociological theory, and Durkheim's influence is still felt in these debates: But is Durkheim's sociology still relevant in the analysis of contemporary society?

As was seen in the discussion of anomic suicide, Durkheim believes that in stable economies there exist collective beliefs concerning the appropriate rewards that different *functions* or social classes—as we would say today—should expect for their labour. In neo-liberal capitalism there has been a rapid widening of the gap between the rich and the poor in terms of income and wealth. The extremely high incomes of the wealthiest in the population, and the lack of a consensus about what are reasonable incomes and disparities in wealth, can be seen in Durkheimian terms as evidence of chronic anomie. Since the 1980s in the United States, Canada, and Great Britain, income differentials have widened. Dunn refers to official Canadian statistics to show how the income gap in Canada has widened between 1973 and 1996.[68] In 1973 the richest 10 per cent of income earners received 21 times more than the bottom 10 per cent, and in 1996 the top 10 per cent earned 314 times more than the bottom 10 per cent of income earners.

The lack of a moral consensus concerning the growing gap between the incomes of the wealthiest and the poorest members of society has been revealed in comments and articles in British newspapers about salaries and bonuses of lawyers and financiers in the City of London and the directors of large companies. In 2006–07 some lawyers at the top City firms earned more than £2 million each, and their overall income rose by 13 per cent.[69] In 2006, boardroom pay, including large increases to basic salaries, large cash bonuses, and payments from share schemes increased by 37 per cent. The average total pay for a chief executive was £2,875,000, and the ratio between boardroom pay and employees widened from 93.1 in 2005 to 98.1 in 2006. The highest paid full-time director was Bob Diamond, chief of the investment-banking arm of Barclays Bank, who earned £23 million. Giles Thorley, head of the Punch Taverns pub group was the third highest paid director, with an income of £11 million. Thorley is the director whose salary is the highest in relation to his employees, equaling the total salaries of 1,147 of his employees. Part-time chairmen of top companies, who generally only work several days per week, receive average annual earnings of £311,000.[70] Sir Ronald Cohen, one of Britain's richest men, warned in the summer of 2007 that "the gap between rich and poor could lead to riots"[71] and the General Secretary of the Trades Union Congress, Brendan Barber, commented: "It is impossible to believe that top directors have become so much more productive than the rest of their staff over the past year. This growing gap is not just morally offensive but hits workforce morale, feeds through into house price inflation, and threatens social cohesion. Britain's boardrooms are slowly losing touch with reality."[72]

A study by social geographers in Britain documents the clustering of poverty and low wealth in urban areas and the concentration of wealth in the southeast of England, which suggests a negative effect on social cohesion.[73] A study of public attitudes towards inequality indicates that 73 per cent of respondents thought that the gap between those with high and low incomes was too large and that those on higher incomes are greatly overpaid.[74] There is evidence that social inequality may have an impact on psychosocial welfare and health[75] and that the high level of inequality may lead to a sense of fatalism and disengagement from the political process.[76] Inequalities in income and opportunity, which produce a wealthy section of society that can buy private health, education, and second homes and can live in exclusive areas, raise issues for social solidarity and social justice akin to those discussed by Durkheim as forms of anomie.

Notes

1 Steve Fenton, *Durkheim and Modern Sociology* (Cambridge: Cambridge University Press, 1984), 3.

2 Richard Sennett, Introduction to *On Suicide*, Emile Durkheim (London: Penguin Books Ltd., 2006), xi.

3 Emile Durkheim, *The Division of Labour in Society* (New York: The Free Press, 1997), 220.

4 Ken Morrison, *Marx, Durkheim, Weber: Formations of Modern Social Thought*, 2nd ed. (London: Sage Publications, 2006), 186.

5 Emile Durkheim, *The Rules of Sociological Method* (New York: The Free Press, 1938), 1.

6 Ibid., 2.

7 Ibid., 3.

8 Ibid.

9 Ibid., 4.

10 Ibid.

11 Ibid., 6.

12 Ibid., 7–8.

13 Ibid., 13.

14 Ibid., 28.

15 Emile Durkheim, *The Rules of Sociological Method* (New York: The Free Press, 1901), xliv.

16 Steven Lukes, *Emile Durkheim His Life and Work: A Historical and Critical Study* (London: Penguin Books Ltd., 1975), 6.

17 Durkheim, *The Rules of Sociological Method*, 49.

18 Ibid., 50.

19 Ibid., 55–7.

20 Ibid., 67.

21 Ibid., 67–71.

22 Ibid., 90.

23 Ibid., 114–5.

24 Emile Durkheim, *On Suicide* (London: Penguin Books Ltd., 2006), 19.

25 Ibid., 25–7.

26 Ibid., 154–5.

27 Ibid., 225.

28 Ibid., 231.

29 Ibid., 160.

30 Ibid., 163.

31 Ibid., 197.

32 Ibid., 214.

33 Ibid., 223.

34 Ibid., 234–5.

35 Ibid., 240–1.

36 Ibid., 244.

37 Ibid., 253.

38 Ibid., 259.

39 Ibid., 263.

40 Ibid., 263–7.

41 Ibid., 269.

42 Ibid.

43 Ibid., 271.

44 Ibid., 272.

45 Ibid., 273–4.

46 Ibid., 280–2.

47 Ibid., 305.

48 Frank Pearce, *The Radical Durkheim* (London: Unwin Hyman, 1989).

49 Durkheim, *On Suicide*, 436.

50 Ibid., 331.

51 Ibid., 332.

52 Ibid., 358.

53 Ibid., 359.

54 Frank Parkin, *Durkheim* (Oxford: Oxford University Press, 1992), 25.

55 Lukes, *Emile Durkheim: His Life and Work*, 222.

56 Jack D. Douglas, *The Social Meanings of Suicide* (Princeton New Jersey: Princeton University Press, 1967).

57 Parkin, *Durkheim*, 23.

58 Rosalind A. Sydie, *Natural Women, Cultured Men: A Feminist Perspective on Sociological Theory* (Milton Keynes: Open University Press, 1987) 49.

59 Ibid., 28.

60 Durkheim, *On Suicide*, 299.

61 Ibid., 299.

62 Ibid.

63 Ibid., 300.

64 Ibid., 301.

65 Ibid., 431.

66 Sydie, *Natural Women, Cultured Men*, 41.

67 Anthony Giddens, as cited in Derek Layder, *Understanding Social Theory* (London: Sage Publications, 1994), 5.

68 J. R. Dunn, "Are Widening Income Inequalities Making Canada Less Healthy?" The Health Determinants Partnership Making Connections Project 2002. Available at: www.opha.on.ca/resources/incomeinequalities/incomeinequalities.pdf (accessed September 26, 2007).

69 T. Macalister, "Top City Lawyers Taking Home More than £2m," *The Guardian* (August 23, 2007), 28.

70 J. Finch, "The Boardroom Bonanza," *The Guardian* (August 29, 2007), 1.

71 A. Seager, "City Bonuses Hit Record High with £14bn Payout," *The Guardian* (August 28, 2007), 1.

72 Finch, "Boardroom Bonanza," 1.

73 D. Dorling, J. Rigby, B.Wheeler, D. Ballas, B.Thomas, E. Fahmy, E. Gordon, and R. Lupton, *Poverty, Wealth and Place in Britain 1968 to 2005* (York: Joseph Rowntree Foundation, 2007). Available at: www.jrf.org.uk/ bookshop/ ebooks/2019-poverty-wealth-place.pdf (accessed September 26, 2007).

74 M. Orton and K. Rowlingson, *Public Attitudes to Economic Inequality* (York: Joseph Rowntree Foundation, 2007) x. Available at: www.jrf.org.uk/bookshop/ ebooks/2080-attitudes-economic-inequality.pdf (accessed September 26, 2007).

75 R.Wilkinson, *Mind the Gap: Hierarchies, Health and Human Evolution* (London: Routledge, 2005), cited in Orton and Rowlingson, *Public Attitudes*, 3.

76 R. Lister, "The Real Egalitarianism? Social Justice 'After Blair,'" in *After Blair*, ed. G. Hassan (London: Lawrence and Wishart, 2007).

8. Emile Durkheim: Religion and Education

> The collective effervescence of ritual life reintegrated individuals into the group. Thus religion was a form of social glue.
>
> —Turner[1]

THE ELEMENTARY FORMS OF RELIGIOUS LIFE is widely regarded as Durkheim's most important work. In it he demonstrates his evolutionary approach to the study of society by choosing to study religion in its most simple form. In his analysis of the totemic religion of Australian tribes he explains how religion is based upon the awareness of a force that genuinely exists and is a source of moral authority, although his scientific explanation goes behind the appearance of things in the eyes of believers. The work is also a theory of knowledge, as religion is seen as the first way in which human beings articulate their understanding of the world.

It has already been pointed out that Durkheim was employed at Bordeaux and Paris to lecture, primarily to trainee school teachers, and that his employment as an educationalist enabled him gradually—and against much opposition—to introduce sociology as an academic discipline within higher education. Two courses of lectures on education were published shortly after his death, and a third on the evolution of secondary education was first published in 1938. These lectures show how he regarded education as a source of morality and how he explained the evolution of education as a reflection of social structural conditions.

The Elementary Forms of Religious Life

Durkheim wished to carry out a scientific analysis of religion; so he chose to study the religion of the simplest society in order to understand man's religious nature, which he believed is an essential and permanent aspect of human culture. He argued that an institution such as religion couldn't rest on an error or a lie; otherwise it would flounder on the resistance to it of social reality. Primitive religions, he argues, "are rooted in reality and are an expression of it."[2] The reasons that individuals give to explain their beliefs are most likely to be mistaken, and so it is the task of the scientist to "reach beneath the symbol to the reality it embodies and which gives it its true meaning."[3] The study of the religion of Australian tribes, he argues, enables the scientist to study the features of a religion in its most essential aspects, and relate these features to the tribe's social conditions, in the absence of the complexities that develop with the evolution of religion.

Durkheim's study of religion is more than a study of the social basis of religion: he declares early in his work that religion is the original source of theories of the nature of the world and is thus the basis of science and philosophy. Furthermore, he argues that religion has shaped forms of knowledge and that basic categories of thought such as notions of time, space, genus, cause, substance, and personality—without which it would be impossible to have shared reasoning—have their basis in primitive religious beliefs. A central part of Durkheim's argument is that religious representations are collective representations that are created when the assembled group participates in rituals, which create and reinforce certain mental states. Similarly, the categories of thought that are created in religious beliefs and ceremonies are social things. Durkheim takes a position on the nature of knowledge that differs from the two opposing doctrines of *apriorism* and *empiricism*. The first views the basic categories as logical and independent of the human mind and human experience; the second views them as subjective and dependent upon the personal experience of the individual. A problem with apriorism is that categories of reason appear to have a reality of their own based upon the power of reason, the basis of which remains unaccounted for. The problem with empiricism is that if knowledge is based upon individual experience then the idea of reason itself, as a form of impersonal rationality, is jettisoned. Durkheim believed that he found a solution which took into account the objections to each position, and he regarded categories of thought as products of the meeting of many minds over space and generations. Thus, individual experiences contribute to the intellectuality of the group. From the experience of the collectivity, then, an agreement emerges concerning what can be logically accepted: "This is the authority of society colouring certain ways of thinking that are the indispensable conditions of all common action."[4] A discussion of Durkheim's sociology of knowledge will be taken up again after a discussion of his sociology of religion.

The Definition of Religion

In his definition of religion Durkheim states that religious phenomenon can be divided into beliefs and rites and that all religious beliefs classify the representations of material or ideal things that people devise. He presents two comprehensive, but opposing, categories—the *sacred* and the *profane*.[5] The first refers to beliefs about spirits, myths, legends, the nature of sacred things and their powers; even a rock, a tree, or a vegetable can be imbued with a sacred character. Rites, also part of the sacred, are actions that are fixed, such as words or formulaic ways of speaking that relate to sacred beliefs and which may be said by consecrated persons. Everything else belongs to the category of the profane. The sacred and the profane are conceived as two separate worlds, with nothing in common, and may even be seen in the human mind as antagonistic. Hence, they cannot intermingle and boundaries have to be set to demarcate when people may move between the two. Mankind and its gods have a mutual dependency, according to Durkheim: just as a man depends upon his gods, the gods depend upon people performing rites in their honour, such as offerings or sacrifices; otherwise the gods would die.[6]

Durkheim defines *religion* as "a unified system of beliefs and practices relative to sacred things, that is to say, things set apart and surrounded by prohibitions—beliefs and practices that unite its adherents in a single moral community called a church."[7]

The identification of religion's communal nature enabled Durkheim to distinguish between magic and religion. The former contains beliefs and rites as well, and it calls upon similar forces as religion. The difference lies in the collective nature of religious beliefs, which, as Durkheim stressed, are held by a collective group of people who profess the same beliefs and practice their religious rites. Magic is different. There might be a collection of magicians who share beliefs, but they do not share them with a wider community of worshippers. The magician has a clientele, not a church, and does not have a continuous relationship with a body of worshippers.

Two existing theories of religion, *animism* and *naturism*, come under a detailed critique. The first refers to the origins of religion as being located in the experience of dreams, which leads to the religious experience of spirits, the soul, demons, and deities with a human-like consciousness and superior powers.[8] The latter locates the experience of the "great cosmic forces" of nature as the source of an inexhaustible force.[9] Durkheim's critique of each of these theories amounts to the same kind of refutation. He argued that each was based upon the notion of hallucination, but each would have been seen for what it was and could not have convinced people throughout the centuries. Prayers, chants, and feast days could rarely appear to produce the desired control over nature and protect people, or produce the desired results. The all too frequent failure of these rituals would have persuaded people that their beliefs were false. Therefore, Durkheim asserts that all beliefs in religion and myth "must have some objective foundation," despite being "mistaken about the true nature of things."[10] Something else must have given man a sense of an "infinite power outside him to which he is subject"[11] and this idea figures in Durkheim's theory of people's sense of the divine.

Totemic Beliefs

Durkheim's study draws mainly on research by anthropologists who had described and analyzed tribal societies in central and northern Australia. Durkheim divides his study into religious beliefs and rites, and although these are interdependent, he begins by outlining the totemic beliefs of Australian tribes. Their society is based on tribes that have two exogamous groups called *phratries*, and each of these phratries contains several clans. Clans constitute a basic element of collective life, and although they are not related by blood, "they regard each other as part of the same family."[12] They bear the same name and they respect mutual obligations, as recognized among kin, including vengeance, mourning, and the avoidance of intermarriage. The name of each clan is its own totem, which usually is a plant or an animal with which the clan believes it has a special relationship. Usually individuals receive their clan names from the mother, who lives in the territory of the father, who, according to rules of exogamy, is of a different clan.

Durkheim describes tribal life as akin to a federation of clans in which each clan has its totem. The worship of the clan totem is the most frequent level of religious experience among the Australian aboriginal people and the one that Durkheim particularly focuses on. Each phratry and tribe also has its totem, and entire tribes sometimes meet to carry out totemic ceremonies such as initiation rites. He describes how totemism is a religious system of the whole tribe.[13] Each clan has a name, such as crow or white cockatoo, which Durkheim describes as an emblem, coat of arms, or a flag. Images of the totem are reproduced on things owned by the clan, such as weapons, and even on the bodies of men during religious ceremonies. A totem is the name of the clan, but its use in religious ceremonies demonstrates how it is also a sacred thing. Each totem group has a collection of sacred pieces of wood or polished stone called *churingas*, which feature in their sacred rites and which have engraved drawings that represent the group's totem. Some of the wooden ones, usually referred to as bullroarers, have holes pierced in them, and with the use of a thong they can be swung rapidly in the air to make a loud noise during ceremonies. The *churingas* are the most sacred possession of the clan, and profane persons such as women and uninitiated young men are not allowed to touch or see them. Where they are stored between ceremonies (perhaps in a small cave), is kept hidden, and the uninitiated are not allowed near this sacred place. The *churingas* are believed to possess special qualities: touching them can cure wounds and illnesses. They can confer power on the totemic species and ensure its successful reproduction, and they can give men strength and weaken their enemies. They are not just useful to individuals, rather the "collective fate of the whole clan depends upon them."[14] The stone or wood *churingas* are similar to many other objects, except they are painted or carved with the emblem of the totem, and this is what makes them sacred.

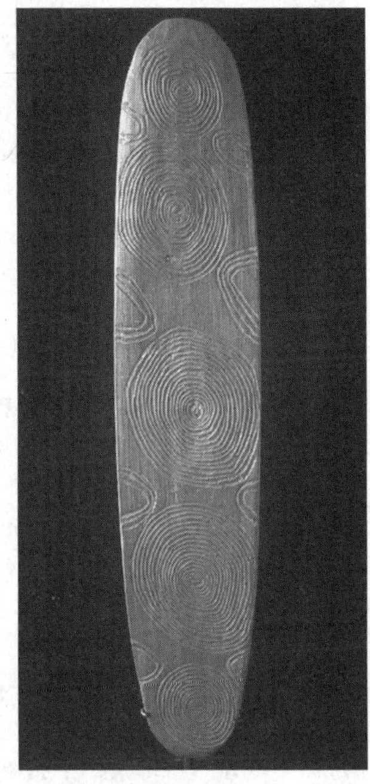

A *churinga*.

The animals or plants that are related to the totem of a clan are also sacred. Restrictions surrounding the *churingas* are much greater than those related to access to the totemic animal or plant that commonly exists in the profane world. From this Durkheim concludes that the images of the totemic being are more sacred than the totemic objects.[15] In fact, he identifies a hierarchy of sacredness: first the emblem of the totem, then the totem, and then each member of the clan are invested with a sacred nature. The Australian, Durkheim explains, believed that he was both a man and also an animal or plant of his totemic species. Although this may be hard for others to understand, Durkheim says this belief was made more plausible for the clan member through myths that relate to the common origins of the clan member and the totemic being. The emblem of the totem, the totemic species, and the clan members share elements of sacredness; however, men have more sacred dignity than women and the uninitiated young members of the clan, and old men have the greatest religious nature. Nevertheless, totemism is not the worshipping of animals or plants; both men and their totemic beings are seen as sharing a degree of sacredness. Totemism is a shared religion of "a kind of anonymous and impersonal force that is found in each of these beings though identical with none."[16]

This anonymous and impersonal force is independent of particular individuals and it pre-exists and survives them. While individuals die and are succeeded by new generations, this force remains constant. It is, Durkheim states, "an impersonal god, without a name, without a history, immanent in the world, diffused throughout a multitude of things."[17] The Australian, in Durkheim's view, is not aware of this force in an abstract way but sees it as a material thing, as an animal or plant; though the basis of the cult is an energy that is diffused throughout the universe. Each clan within the tribe has a notion of these forces as belonging to their totem. These forces, which have a physical aspect upon which life is seen to depend, also have a moral aspect that obliges a person to behave in particular ways towards other members of the clan, or to perform certain rites. In addition, in common with other religions, the ritual practices of totemism give man more confidence in his dealings with the world.

The Origins of Totemic Beliefs

The totem is the symbol of the god and the symbol of the clan. So Durkheim reasoned that the god of the clan, the totemic principle, must be the clan itself, "transfigured and imagined in the physical form of the plant or animal species that serve as totems."[18] In order to explain how this came about, Durkheim describes how life in the Australian clan alternated between two different phases. For most of the time the population was scattered in small groups of hunters and gatherers providing for their needs. At agreed-upon times people would congregate in particular places where the entire tribe or clan would meet for periods of several days, or weeks, to participate in religious ceremonies. This lifestyle offered a stark contrast between a mundane existence, which was the profane part of their life, compared with their sacred rituals, where the proximity of individuals generated a stimulating environment and a state of high exaltation. Durkheim, quoting anthropological studies, describes the excitement and tumult created during the whirling of bullroarers, the chanting and rhythmic dancing often enhanced by the illumination from fires, and the subsequent collective effervescence and unleashing of passions. In these circumstances individuals would feel that they had entered into relations with extraordinary powers. In the Australian context religious activity was concentrated in these periods of collective effervescence where, Durkheim believed, the religious idea was born: "Therefore it is in these effervescent social settings, and from this very effervescence, that the religious idea seems to be born. And this origin seems confirmed by the fact that in Australia, strictly religious activity is almost entirely concentrated in the times when these assemblies are held."[19]

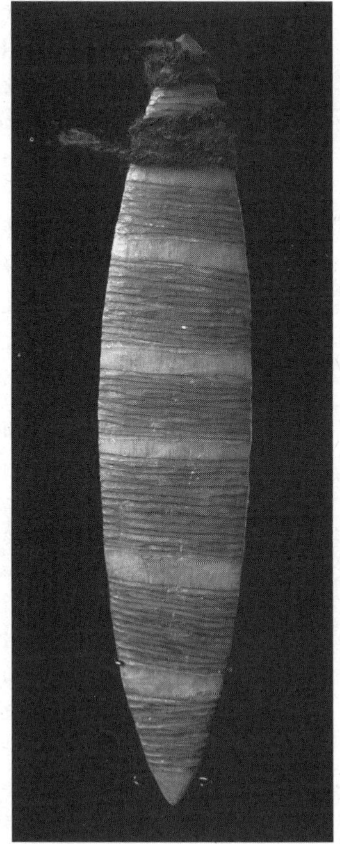

A bullroarer.

When the clan meets it "awakens in its members the idea of external forces that dominate and exalt them," but the clan is "too complex a reality for such rudimentary minds to picture clearly its concrete unity."[20] The native does not see that the group has generated these feelings or that the group is capable of generating new energies with the power to transform people. Furthermore, these new sensations are experienced at a time when the emblem of the group is everywhere—on the *churingas* and painted on the bodies of the assembled clan members. Later, when people see the totem's emblem again, their memories of that state of heightened emotions are revived. When people congregate, and the emblem is everywhere during these gatherings, mysterious forces are generated, which the native Australian believes emanate from the clan's emblem. The totem is seen to be the source of actions that benefit or harm the clan, and so the clan must take action to influence this force by performing rites addressed to this foremost of sacred things. Because of the resemblance between the clan's emblem and the animal or plant from which the clan takes its name, the actual animal or plant takes on sacred qualities, and it ranks above man in the sacred hierarchy. Although the religious force of the totem appears to be external, it can only be realized through the active participation of clan members; they come to imagine that the totem is imminent in them and that they too have a religious character, though to a lesser degree.

Being in opposition to animism and naturism, Durkheim rejects the notion that religion is based upon physical or biological sensations and, therefore, is no more than a hallucination. In a key passage, he states that "the worshipper is not deluding himself when he believes in a higher moral power from which he derives his best self: that power exists, and it is society."[21] The exalted experience of the clan member is real and is "really the product of forces external and superior to the individual." It is a mistake to believe that this heightened vitality is a product of the power derived from a plant or an animal, but "there is a concrete and living reality."[22] For Durkheim, the main purpose of religion is to provide a system of thought which enables individuals to imagine the society to which they belong and their relationship with it. In particular, it refers to "an eternal truth that something exists outside us that is greater than we are, and with which we commune ... god is merely the symbolic expression of society."[23] Rather than the act of worship strengthening the ties of the worshipper and his god, they strengthen the ties between the individual and society because "god is merely the symbolic expression of society."[24]

Totemic Rites

Durkheim identified negative and positive rites. The *negative rites* comprise various prohibitions on behaviour, which serve to preserve the separation between the sacred and profane. Prohibitions on profane behaviour and the suffering of privations make the individual feel more elevated and on a level with sacred and moral forces. The *positive rites* refer to bilateral relations between man and the totemic forces. Durkheim draws heavily from the writing of anthropologists who described a ceremony of the Arunta tribe, referred to as the *intichiuma*, which appeared to be a widespread practice among other tribes as well. Among the Arunta, this ceremony starts at the beginning of the rainy season, which brings forth a sudden appearance of vegetation. The first phase of the ceremony is concerned with the preservation of the prosperity of the animal or plant species that is the clan's totem. Members of the tribe believe that their ancestors had left rocks in the places where they had disappeared into the ground. These imperishable rocks are seen as a source of life for the totemic species; to ensure the reproduction of the totemic species and allow people to continue to draw upon their powers, they must be visited annually. The ceremony of the Witchetty Grub clan, for instance, involves all the men of the tribe walking solemnly around the sacred site, stopping at rocks that are thought to represent the grub, and striking the rocks to displace some dust that is regarded as the seeds of its life. The dust is dispersed by men who wave tree branches in the belief that they are maintaining the abundant reproduction of the grub that the clan both protects and depends upon.[25]

In a second phase of the *intichiuma*, there is a strict prohibition against the eating of the totem animal for a period of time. In the Witchetty Grub clan, the grubs are gathered, cooked, and crushed into a powder, some of which the chief and the elders consume in a solemn ceremony. Durkheim believed that this type of ceremony, which took similar forms in other tribes, contains the essence of the institution of sacrifice that can be found in many more advanced religions.[26] Consuming the sacred totem enables clan members to incorporate its sacred principle within themselves, but because the sacred principle's powers gradually erode it must be replenished periodically.

In the first phase of the *intichiuma*, men of the clan assist in the fecundity of the totemic species to ensure that it survives. In the second phase they borrow from the species "the forces necessary to sustain and restore his spiritual being. So, we can say that it is man who makes his gods, or at least makes them endure, but at the same time it is through them that he endures."[27] Thus, the celebrations of the totemic cult bring about the renewal of belief in the gods, and they bring "internal and moral renewal" in the participants. Ritual life is circular, and so is social life as the individual takes from society his personality, culture, language, science, arts, and morality—all of what makes him civilized. If the individual's idea of society dies and social beliefs and traditions cease to be held, then the society will die. So rites possess an efficacy, though not the one perceived by the participants. They enable the creation and perpetuation of the gods, and a moral entity that is society, making individuals and society feel stronger. Common beliefs are strengthened, and the individual soul "is regenerated, too, by immersing itself once more in the wellspring of its life; subsequently, it feels stronger, more in control of itself."[28]

Sociology of Knowledge

The sociology of knowledge is intricately woven into Durkheim's sociology of religion. Religion, he argues was always a cosmology as well as theory of the divine, and thus philosophy and science grew out of religion. In addition, he argues that basic categories of understanding—ideas of time, space, genus, number, cause, substance, and personality—which are the basis of all thought, originated in religion.[29] Religious rituals are collective assemblies that produce collective representations about the relationship between man and his god(s), and, therefore, ideas about time or space, for instance, come from the collective thought of religion. Durkheim puts forward a sociological approach to knowledge that does not rely on the idea that categories are a priori in the human mind or a product of individual experience.

Durkheim argues that religions give a total representation of the world, and within Australian totemism, all things within the universe are part of the tribe and all men and objects are allocated between the clans. Those things that are allocated to an individual's clan, whether animate or inanimate, "are parts of the body of which he is a part."[30] Durkheim gives a number of examples: for instance, the Mount Gambier tribe is divided into two phratries, the Kunmite and the Kroki, and each of these has five clans. Everything in nature belongs to one or another of these clans, and so everything in nature is classified under ten totem-like species, under their own genera. While men and women may be identified with crows or white cockatoos, natural phenomena are also divided into their respective totems: rain, thunder, lightening, clouds, hail, and winter, for example, are also part of the crow totem. The way in which the notions of genus, or class, are formed was modelled on social organization: "Because men formed groups, they were able to group things; they classified things simply by placing them in groups they had already formed ... the social groups they belong to are themselves interdependent, and through their union form an organic whole—the tribe. The unity of these first logical systems merely reproduces the unity of society."[31] Durkheim uses this example to demonstrate that the notion of category can be a product of social organization. Initially, it could have been based on each phratry having opposing dichotomies—a white cockatoo in one phratry and a black cockatoo in the other. Where one clan is linked to the sun, the other is related to the moon and stars. Categorization could also be based on similarities: the black cockatoo is linked with the moon, and the sun with the white cockatoo. Durkheim writes, "Of course, we cannot always understand the obscure psychology that presides over many of these affinities and distinctions. But the preceding examples suffice to demonstrate that a certain intuition of similarities and differences evident in things has played a role in creating these classifications."[32] In Durkheim's view, the classification of categories, a genus, is a tool of thought, invented by people, which comes from society, not from some a priori existence outside us. "Society has provided the canvas on which logical thought has operated."[33] This canvas consists of a religion in which humans and natural phenomenon are linked. This system of religious thought enabled people to think that there are internal connections between things and that these can be categorized according to opposition and agreement; therefore, Durkheim insists, religion contains the basic elements of scientific thought.

Durkheim argues that the idea of a vague, anonymous force that influences men's minds and material objects was, in totemic religion, the earliest form of a later secular version found in the natural sciences.[34] Religion and science are, Durkheim insists, concerned with nature, man, and society: "Religion endeavours to translate these realities into an intelligible language that is no different in kind from the language employed by science; both involve connecting things to one another, establishing internal relations between them, classifying them, and systematizing them."[35] If religion is based on society and science originates in religion then, ultimately, knowledge is based in society, whether this reflects the way that space is divided up between social groups or how time is defined socially to enable people to meet to perform rites or participate in feasts. Similarly, Durkheim relates concepts—the material of logical thought—to society, because in order for people to communicate, concepts must be shared: thus, they are collective representations of the community. They represent social ways of thinking, which contain general and permanent properties, and combine the collective wisdom and knowledge, accumulated over centuries, with what personal experience can teach. Systems of concepts, derived in this way from society, help people to think impersonally in ways that surpass their own experiences.[36]

Durkheim provides a critique of theories that assume that religious experience is grounded in hallucinations, based on psychological perceptions or on the experience of nature, and that for religion to persist there has to be some form of underlying reality, which he identifies as society. This argument supports his own version of sociological rationalism, but, to those who believe, it must appear little different to the view that religion is based upon hallucination. Durkheim's belief that society is a moral phenomenon buttresses his view that society needs some kind of religion or system of unifying beliefs: "No society can exist that does not feel the need at regular intervals to sustain and reaffirm the collective feelings and ideas that constitute its unity and personality."[37]

This reaffirmation of morals is based on meetings or assemblies in which individuals come into close contact and reaffirm their common feelings. According to Durkheim's analysis, humanity is now in a period of transition, and it is hard to imagine what future ceremonies will be like: "The ancient gods grow old or die, and others are not yet born."[38] New cults cannot be created; they have to emerge from life. There will be new experiences of collective effervescence and new formulae will grow to serve humanity for a time; however, in an age when science is dominant, religion will have to accept its findings. As science slowly accrues knowledge, there is still a place for religion to "run ahead of science and develop theories about living and acting."[39]

Sociology of Education

During his years in Bordeaux and Paris, Durkheim was primarily employed as an educationalist, and while his regular lectures on education to trainee teachers may have interrupted his sociological work, they provided him with opportunities to reiterate many of his favourite themes, such as the relationship between man and society, his theory of evolution, and his views on social solidarity. Durkheim referred to a crisis in secondary education that had been felt since the second half of the eighteenth century. Economic and moral changes in society meant that the old educational ideals were inadequate; in the Middle Ages the goal was the creation of dialecticians, and after the Renaissance it was the creation of humanists. However, he argued that there was no clear notion of what conception of man should be created through secondary education in late nineteenth and early twentieth-century France.[40] Durkheim supported secular state education, and these too were matters of political contention.

Durkheim points out that an historic perspective on education shows that different periods have different educational organizational objectives, because education is shaped by custom, religion, political and economic organization, and the existing state of science. Education is the system of interaction between adults and youth in which a society attempts to create an "ideal of man" in terms of certain physical, intellectual, and moral states that each person is expected to possess. In addition, as society becomes more complex, education has to provide attributes that enable more specialized roles to be carried out. Education is a form of socialization of each new generation of asocial and egoistic beings, making people into social beings by exposing them to religious, moral, national, and other collective beliefs to enable them to lead a social life. It is a short step from this position to see education as the instrument through which society "represents the best in us" by making children into men.[41]

In the course he taught on moral education, Durkheim's task was to provide a conception of secular moral education for state elementary schools, which he regarded as the guardians of French national character. He argued that morality is not beyond scientific analysis; to accept that it is would mean accepting that something is essentially irrational. In a period in which people were becoming more rationalistic and individualistic, religion was thought to be losing its force. It had become, Durkheim believed, necessary to separate morality from religion; though in the process, new moral tendencies and demands for justice would emerge. The role of the teacher, he argued, was to help the new generation become conscious of the new ideal and also to "excite in them a desire to add a few lines of their own."[42] Durkheim regarded the first task as the determination of the basic elements of morality, that is, the fundamental mental states which could be adapted to particular circumstances, rather than teaching children a list of virtues. He believed that moral rules are a subtype of rules that are obeyed, not because of tradition or personal benefit but because they are outside the person and they prescribe ways of acting that people cannot alter: an authority backs those rules and demands their respect. Obedience is a duty that is derived from a spirit of discipline. This is the first element of morality. The idea of discipline is a basic component of morality in Durkheim's argument because, drawing on his theory of human nature, he believed that there have to be constraints upon people's passions to prevent egoism and anomie. For Durkheim, discipline is a key factor in education. Convinced that it is necessary for children's appetites to be restricted, he believed these could be defined in ways that lead to happiness and moral health so that children can have realizable goals that are compatible with their abilities. This is not a static view of human aspiration. Durkheim argues that with historical change, human nature changes and so do the boundaries of people's realizable expectations.

Durkheim further argues that moral acts are always in pursuit of impersonal ends, and once theological ideas are ruled out, the only superior entity is society. Therefore, moral authority comes from the social groups to which people are members, but the group itself is superior because it outlives the individual members. Thus, "we are moral beings only to the extent that we are social beings."[43] Durkheim refers to how society is superior to the individual, in that individuals owe so much to society—language, culture, and personality—and they are prepared to see society as the source of authority. Attachment to groups is the second element of morality. He states, "When our conscience speaks it is society speaking within us."[44]

The third element of morality in Durkheim's theory is autonomy or self-determination. The scientific knowledge of the natural world enables us to know how the external world works, and, because we have understanding of this, we accept its constraints and know we have no alternative. As Durkheim states, "We liberate ourselves through our understanding." If people understand the nature of moral rules and scientifically investigate the reasons for their existence in society, they can make rational decisions. As he puts it, "Now we are able to check on the extent to which the moral order is founded in the nature of things—that is in the nature of society—which is to say to what extent it is what it ought to be. In the degree that we see it as such, we can freely conform to it... Thus, on condition of having adequate knowledge of moral precepts, of their causes and of their functions, we are in a position to conform to them, but consciously and knowing why. Such conformity has nothing of constraint about it."[45] Durkheim concedes that the science of morality is less developed than the natural sciences but he believed that if people knew the reasons for moral imperatives they would obey voluntarily and desire this because they would know why the moral rules exist. Science can empower people to know and influence things that exert a control over them. A third dimension of morality is this "enlightened assent."

A meeting of doctors at the University of Paris. From a medieval manuscript "Chants royaux." Bibliothèque National Paris. Many features of modern universities, such as their division into faculties and a hierarchy of degrees from bachelor to doctor, were described in Durkheim's historical analysis of the medieval university in Paris in his lectures on the evolution of secondary education in France.

The role of a teacher in a modern secular morality is to help the child understand the rules he should abide by and to make him "understand his country and his times, to make him feel his responsibilities, to initiate him into life and thus to prepare him to take his part in the collective tasks awaiting him."[46]

After discussing the elements of morality, Durkheim turned his attention to educational psychology and the development of morality in the child. The school is a socializing agency between the family and the wider society; school rules and the social life of the classroom provide an introduction to the spirit of discipline in the child. The teacher should impress upon the child the general nature of these rules by which he too is constrained. The infraction of such rules should be punished by blame and by making it clear that others disapprove of this behaviour.[47] Consequently, he was opposed to corporal punishment in schools because contemporary morality is one of moral individualism based on freedom and human dignity: "One of the chief aims of moral education is to inspire in the child a feeling for the dignity of man. Corporal punishment is a continual offence to this sentiment."[48]

Attachment to the group is a second dimension of morality, and in this respect Durkheim identifies the school environment as one in which the child may experience a collective life that is more intense than the quieter life within the family, and where his participation in collective life enhances his being. Class life should not be sober but have a joyful aspect—which appears rather like a less intense version of the experience of some of the rites described in simple religions—and the teacher is encouraged to stimulate a sense of class identity or spirit.[49] The third level of morality in Durkheim's schema is autonomy or self-determinism within a moral system that requires people to evaluate their moral choices.

Durkheim drew upon the elementary introduction of natural sciences into the school to give the child a sense of the complexity of things and the role of experimental sciences.[50] In order to make moral choices people need to be aware of social reality, and in view of the lack of development within the social sciences, Durkheim identified historical knowledge as being capable of making pupils aware of social forces that move in their direction and also shape other people's experiences.[51]

In the course of his lectures in 1902, Durkheim gave a structural and historical analysis of the development of secondary education in France from the early middle ages. Because the Christian church had a mission to shape the man, schools grew up as moral communities attached to cathedrals and gradually became the secondary schools and universities. The church was the link between the Roman and Germanic societies, and it initiated people into "the only culture which then existed, namely classical culture."[52] However, because there was a tension between Christianity and the classical culture that was the product of pagan Greco-Roman culture, Durkheim discussed how the classical education selected features from that culture. He argued that in the early middle ages, the stress was on grammatical formalism, which was followed by a dialectical formalism. Changes in social class and educational philosophy in the sixteenth century ushered in a preference for the study of classical literature as the best way to mould pupils' minds. The closing of the wealth gap between the leisured classes and the nobility made the former desire to imitate the politeness of aristocratic society. Durkheim has been criticized for neglecting the relationship between social class and education, but in this regard he does describe the educational philosophy of the humanists as an ideology based on the values of aristocratic and leisured classes, which neglected the educational needs of masses of people "for whom education should have raised their intellectual and moral standards and improved their material condition."[53]

Conclusion

This chapter has provided a summary of Durkheim's ideas on religion, knowledge, and education. There have been criticisms of his ideas on religion from anthropologists who argue not only that there were societies simpler than the Australian natives which did not have a totem but also that Durkheim did not discuss the negative effects of religion on society.[54] The discussion of this key part of his work shows that Durkheim provides a perspective that relates consciousness to the structural organization of society: the tribe is the basis of totemism, or social organization is basic to categories of thought and education.

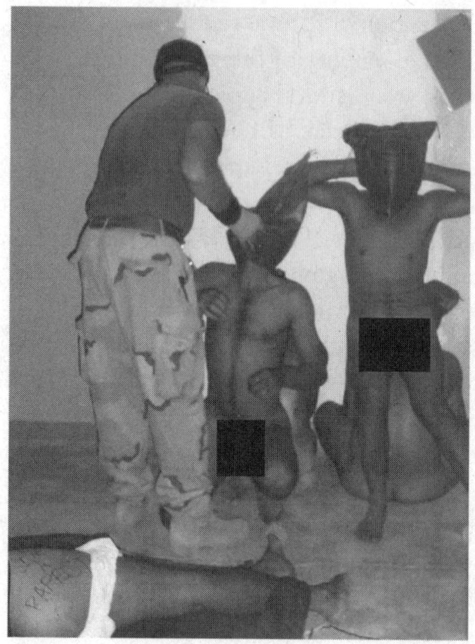

A lack of rules relating to the treatment of prisoners in Iraq has been seen as a sign of anomie in a contemporary war situation.

Durkheim insists that religious beliefs are not based upon some kind of hallucination; however, to argue that religious experience is a product of the membership of society seems to be not much different to those who have a faith. As Rosati puts it, "Durkheim's approach highlights how the believer, worshipping a transcendental and superior being that he identifies with god or with some mysterious force, is both right and wrong. He is wrong insofar as the content of what he represents to the mind through religious belief is not what he imagines it to be (God or another extra-social force); he is right in that the content is something that is transcendent and superior to him, namely society."[55]

Religion has social causes in Durkheim's theory, and all life has a material context, but religion is not just a product of the brain or economic conditions. Rather, Durkheim stresses how the collective consciousness "must be produced by a *sui generis* synthesis of particular consciousnesses" which have "the effect of unlocking a whole world of feelings, ideas and images that once born, obey their own laws."[56] Durkheim's analysis of religious beliefs and rites suggests that collective representations and the experience of a collective effervescence have a powerful role as a basis of feelings and beliefs. As explained above, Durkheim thought that the old religions had lost their powers, but he was aware that any new religion—even one based upon the cult of the individual—and human dignity require some kind of assembly of the community to reinforce those beliefs. Thus, Durkheim's sociology presents possible new insights into the study of culture; social bonding and regulation; the reworking of social solidarity; and, as his discussion of corporations shows, the role of civil society in maintaining social solidarity.[57]

In modern terminology the cult of the individual, which was discussed in chapter 6 and above, would be referred to as a discourse of human rights. Joas points out that Durkheim was the first person to discuss, during the political upheavals of the Dreyfus scandal, how the *human person* had become the most sacred object in society:[58]

> This human person, the definition of which is like the touchstone which distinguishes good from evil, is considered sacred in the ritual sense of the word. It partakes of the transcendent majesty that churches of all time lend to their gods; it is conceived of as being invested with that mysterious property which creates a void about sacred things, which removes them from vulgar contacts and withdraws them from common circulation. And the respect which is given it comes precisely from this source. Whoever makes an attempt on a man's life, on a man's liberty, on a man's honour, inspires in us a feeling of horror analogous in every way to that which the believer experiences when he sees his idol profaned.[59]

Because offences against the individual offend this new collective conscience, Joas discusses the impact on criminal and civil law and the changes in eighteenth-century penal policy. It is possible to see that the sacralization of the person has its roots in Judeo-Christian traditions, but Durkheim regards these religious roots as no longer important. Individuals may become increasingly included in political and legal rights but, as Joas states, the rights are not universally upheld because there are counter forces, even in the West.

The concept of anomie provides a critical concept for the exposure of irrational and unjust features of contemporary society. The previous chapters have shown how this concept can be used to explain corporate crime and the malaise of neo-liberal market societies. Anomie has also been effectively used to explain the systematic abuse of human rights and torture at Abu Ghraib prison in Iraq. U.S. government reports and the analysis of testimony given at the courts martial, held at Fort Hood, Texas, relating to the abuse at Abu Ghraib show that anomie—defined by Durkheim as *dérèglement* (derangement)—i.e., a "rule that is a lack of rule"—was ubiquitous at a range of levels within the U.S. government and the U.S. army. Low-ranking soldiers were blamed for the torture and abuse, although chaotic and inconsistent views about interrogation techniques and prisoners' rights prevailed at all levels of command, internationally, nationally, and locally.[60]

Notes

1 Bryan S. Turner, *Classical Sociology* (London: Sage, 1999), 196.

2 Emile Durkheim, *The Elementary Forms of the Religious Life* (Oxford: Oxford University Press, 2001), 4.

3 Ibid., 4.

4 Ibid., 19.
5 Ibid., 36.
6 Ibid., 38.
7 Ibid., 46.
8 Ibid., 47.
9 Ibid., 66.
10 Ibid., 70–2.
11 Ibid., 74.
12 Ibid., 88.
13 Ibid., 119–20.
14 Ibid., 98.
15 Ibid., 104.
16 Ibid., 140.
17 Ibid., 141.
18 Ibid., 154.
19 Ibid., 164.
20 Ibid.
21 Ibid., 170.
22 Ibid.
23 Ibid., 171.
24 Ibid.
25 Ibid., 247.
26 Ibid., 248.
27 Ibid., 253.
28 Ibid., 259.
29 Ibid., 11.
30 Ibid., 109.
31 Ibid., 112.
32 Ibid., 113.
33 Ibid., 115.
34 Ibid., 151, 168.
35 Ibid., 324.
36 Ibid., 330.
37 Ibid., 322.
38 Ibid., 322.
39 Ibid., 326.
40 Emile Durkheim, *Education and Sociology* (New York: The Free Press, 1956), 141.
41 Ibid., 72–76.
42 Emile Durkheim, *Moral Education* (New York: Dover Publications Inc., 2002), 14.
43 Ibid., 64.
44 Ibid., 90.
45 Ibid., 117.

46 Ibid., 124.

47 Ibid., 180–2.

48 Ibid., 183.

49 Ibid., 241.

50 Ibid., 260–1.

51 Ibid., 275.

52 Emile Durkheim, *The Evolution of Educational Thought* (London: Routledge & Kegan Paul, 1977), 25.

53 Ibid., 206.

54 Kenneth Thompson, *Emile Durkheim* (London: Tavistock Publications Ltd., 1982).

55 Massimo Rosati, "Inhabiting No-Man's Land: Durkheim and Modernity," *Journal of Classical Sociology* 8 (May 2008): 241.

56 Durkheim, *The Elementary Forms of the Religious Life*, 319.

57 Kenneth Thompson, Introduction to *Durkheim Today,* ed. W.S.F. Pickering (Oxford: Berghahn Books, 2002).

58 Hans Joas,"Punishment and Respect: The Sacralization of the Person and its Endangerment," *Journal of Classical Sociology* 8 (May 2008): 169–75.

59 Emile Durkheim, "Individualism and Intellectuals," in *Emile Durkheim on Morality and Society,* ed. R. Bellah (Chicago: University of Chicago Press, 1973), 43–75, quoted in Joas, "Punishment and Respect," 170.

60 Stjepan G. Mestrovic and Ronald Lorenzo, "Durkheim's Concept of *Anomie* and the Abuse at Abu Ghraib," *Journal of Classical Sociology* 8 (May 2008): 179–85.

9. Max Weber: Methodology

> One way to appreciate Max Weber's extraordinary achievement as a methodologist ... is to understand him historically, in relation to his own intellectual field. Seen in that way, Weber perfectly typifies the clarifying critic who restates, rationalizes, and thus partly transcends the assumptions of his own culture.
>
> —Fritz Ringer[1]

SO FAR WE HAVE EXAMINED how classical social theory understands society in terms of materiality, through the works of Marx and Engels, and morality, through the works of Durkheim. Like Marx and Durkheim, Weber is widely recognized for his substantive analysis of Western capitalism and modern forms of life. In Weber's writings, as is the case with Durkheim, the subject matter of sociology, method of human inquiry, and relationship to other disciplines is accorded significant attention. For Weber, a society is constituted through rationally calculated and goal-directed human action, and wholesale rationalization comes to dominate Western culture and institutions. Weber is also recognized as a pillar of sociological thought, but his identity as a sociologist is a complex topic. Although he engaged with sociologists and was a co-founder of the German Sociological Society, Weber conceived of himself first and foremost as a political economist, as is evident from his texts. Whereas Durkheim's work was influenced by Comteian positivism and his early studies were rather abstract and philosophical, by contrast, Weber employs the notion of interpretive understanding, *Verstehen*, in his discussion of methodology, and his early works are meticulous historical studies. Among Anglo-Saxon scholars, Max Weber's role as a founding figure of sociology has alternated since the 1980s between "in doubt" to "resurrection."[2] More recently, Weber along with Georg Simmel have been considered the most contemporary of the sociological canon, even representing the first signs of postmodernism.[3] And others posit that "Weber is one of the sources of our culture."[4] His *Methodology of the Social Sciences* and his later work on methodology, which this chapter will focus on, for example Durkheim's *Rules*, are highly polemical works that still inform modern sociology. They discuss analytical procedures and provide sociologists with an appreciation of the central unresolved problem of values and objectivity in social research. Weber's *Methodology* was heavily influenced by his intellectual heritage and written in response to his immediate circumstances; therefore, a contextual understanding of his work is necessary. This chapter examines the intellectual genealogy that shaped Weber's methodology and his key pronouncements on method.

His Life and Works

Max Weber was born on April 21, 1864, in Erfurt, a small city in the southeastern region of Germany. Shortly after his birth the Weber family moved to Berlin. Weber's parents were polar opposites. His mother Helene Fallenstein Weber was a devout Calvinist, a woman of culture and piety who led an ascetic life, and it was her austere Puritanism that came ultimately to shape Max Weber's personal ethics.[5] His father was a lawyer and politician who led a hedonistic lifestyle, in contrast to his wife. He was also allegedly a stereotypical Victorian: a disciplinarian to his children, arrogant and insensitive to his wife. The dissonance between his father's values and lifestyle and that of his mother's orientation to life negatively affected Weber's psychological development and shaped his intellectual direction. The family home attracted local artists, intellectuals, and business and political elites that would have exposed the young Weber to the educated "chattering class." After taking his *Abitur* and completing high school, Weber entered the University of Heidelberg and chose to study law, his father's profession. He also chose to follow his father's social life: drinking and partying a lot and studying a little. After a twelve months stint in the military he returned to his parents' home and resumed his academic studies at the University of Berlin, later in Göttingen. As a student Weber was financially dependent on his father, a situation he progressively grew to resent. And in the eight years living with his parents, he gravitated towards his mother's values and orientation to life, while his antipathy to his father increased. Young Weber became a disciplined and conscientious student. In 1889 he completed his doctorial dissertation on medieval trading companies, and in 1891 he presented his post-doctorial thesis (*Habilitationsschrift*) on Roman agrarian history. This formally qualified him for an academic university position, and he was appointed as a lecturer in law at the University of Berlin. In 1892 he married Marianne Schnitger, a scholarly interlocutor who supported her husband's academic career. After teaching economics at the University of Freiburg, in 1896, Weber accepted an appointment as professor at the University of Heidelberg, at the age of thirty-two. His contemporaries considered him very young to be appointed professor at such a prestigious German university.

It was at the University of Heidelberg that Weber suffered a nervous breakdown in 1898, and he resigned from the University. His mental illness occurred soon after the death of his father. It is a matter of conjecture whether quarrelling with Weber senior caused the mental illness. Shortly before his father's death, Max had a violent argument with him, which culminated in his ordering his father from the house. Father and son were never to speak to each other again. On hearing of his father's unexpected death, Max Weber was consumed by guilt and remorse. Unable to concentrate on his academic life, he travelled widely, especially around southern Europe. It was not until 1903, at the age of thirty-nine, that he was able to resume his academic career, which provided him with extended sabbaticals. In 1904, while travelling in the United States, he delivered his first lecture in more than six years. It is reported that he was enamoured of the U.S. democratic processes and by the pace and mayhem of life in the large cities. Travelling around the United States appeared to have a cathartic effect on Weber, for on returning to Germany, he produced some of his most important work on methodology and religion and capitalism. As did Emile Durkheim, Weber contributed to the development of the nascent discipline of sociology, which

Max Weber was born in Erfurt, Germany, in 1864. In 1892 he married Marianne Schnitger, an academic. Weber's circle of friends included the philosopher Georg Lukács, as well as the sociologists Robert Michels and Georg Simmel. Weber died of pneumonia 1920, at the age of fifty-six.

included his helping to establish the German Sociology Society. In 1903 he also accepted a position as associate editor of the prestigious Archive for the Social Science and Social Policy (*Archiv für Sozialwissenschaft und Sozialpolitik)*. His circle of friends included philosopher Georg Lukács, as well as sociologists Robert Michels and Georg Simmel.

Weber wrote more than ten books and numerous scholarly papers on a range of topics, including *The Methodology of the Social Sciences* in 1904 and his best-known work *The Protestant Ethic and the Spirit of Capitalism* during 1904 and 1905. He taught himself Russian and became proficient enough in reading contemporary Russian sources to write an article on the 1905 Russian Revolution. The First World War interrupted his scholarly productivity. Too old for active service, much to his regret, he worked as a hospital administrator for a short period before serving on an obscure government commission to examine tariff-related problems. After 1916 most of his time was devoted to writing about his lifelong interests: religion, political economy, and society. Shortly thereafter he published his important studies of world religions: *The Religion of China: Confucianism and Taoism* (1916); *The Religion of India: The Sociology of Hinduism and Buddhism* (1916); and *The Sociology of Religion* (1921). After the war he became politically active, joined the newly formed German Democratic Party (*Deutsche Demokratische Partie*) and was shortlisted as the party's candidate for a Frankfurt constituency. He failed to get the nomination and was apparently deeply disappointed by the decision.[6] For sociology, at least, his rejection was all to the good because Weber was able to continue working on his major project, the three volumes of *Economy and Society* (published posthumously in 1921). A sociological treatise, it has become an integral part of the sociological imagination.[7] Weber's publications are clearly many, diverse, complex, and possess a fragmentary character, which has had the effect of generating a variety of interpretations of his work.[8]

Weber's personality was full of paradoxes. On the one hand, he cultivated a puritan lifestyle but, on the other hand, he himself gave no sign he was a believer.[9] Though an academic mandarin, he craved to be a man of action and wrote, "I am not really a scholar; scientific activity is for me primarily an occupation for the leisure hours ... The feeling of being active in a practical way is entirely indispensable to me, and I hope that the pedagogic side of the teaching profession will satisfy this craving."[10] This contradiction of Weber's personality is summed up by Reinhard Bendix: "He continuously engaged in the simultaneous effort to be a man of science with the strenuous vigour more common in a man of action, and to be a man of action with all the ethical rigor and personal detachment more common in a man of science."[11] Though Weber is now recognized as a member of the sociological canon, his work contains paradoxes and ambiguity that have generated multiple and conflicting interpretations. Though he did not have a conception of society as a social system, he famously warned about the "iron cage" of industrial capitalism. His methodological ideas are ambiguous, and grappling with them has been characterized as "handling a bar of wet soap."[12] Weber died of pneumonia on June 14, 1920, at the age of fifty-six.

Intellectual Influences

Max Weber's social theories were shaped by the specific historical context of his time and several intellectual sources. An appreciation of these contexts is necessary in understanding Weber's substantive ideas on the methodology of the social sciences and his analysis of the origins and nature of modernity. Weber was writing during a period of profound political and intellectual uncertainty, and his sociology is hollow once divorced from the political context in which it is embedded.[13] As a member of the German educated middle class, Weber's political and cultural values reflect his commitment to nationalism, the problem of the economic retardation of Germany, and the country's position in global politics. In his inaugural address at the University of Freiburg in 1895, Weber emphasized the need for a strong, united Germany. He declared, "The object of our work in social policy is not to make the world happy, but to unify socially a nation surrounded by economic progress."[14] Following Bismarck's resignation in 1890, debates on the weakness of the German middle classes, the stifling effect of state bureaucracy, the leadership vacuum, and the perceived external threat of Britain, Russia, and the United States fashioned Weber's theories on bureaucracy, leadership, and class structure.[15]

The influence of Marx's ideas on Weber's intellectual apparatus has been the topic of considerable debate and scholarship. It was the American sociologist Talcott Parsons, in *The Structure of Social Action* (1937), who first introduced Weber's work to Anglo-Saxon sociologists. From Parson's reconstruction of Weber, it became common parlance that Weber intended *The Protestant Ethic and the Spirit of Capitalism* and *Economy and Society* as a "refutation" of Marx's thesis on capitalism. It is not difficult to support this incorrect view when, for example, Weber makes reference to "naïve historical materialism."[16] In Marx's conception of history, the change in the economic base had come first—from feudalism to capitalism—followed by changes in the superstructure, such as religious beliefs. In identifying the influence of religious ideas on the development of capitalism, Weber's analysis in *The Protestant Ethic* appears to reverse the base-structure assumption of Marx. Weber

Weber argued that sociologists can understand, or *Verstehen,* social action by penetrating to the subjective meanings those humans themselves attach to their own behaviours. This contemporary photograph shows a homeless person spending the night in the public space of the metropolis. Weber's methods suggest that researchers cannot understand the homeless, for example, unless they examine how the homeless themselves view and explain their situation.

explicitly denies this interpretation: "We have no intention of defending any such foolishly doctrinaire thesis as that the 'capitalist spirit' ... let alone capitalism itself, *could only* arise as a result of certain influences of the Reformation."[17] Weber calls Marx a "great thinker,"[18] and acknowledges the importance of economic conditions of society. One study of Marx and Weber shows that, despite very different political standpoints, their social theory shares a central interest in the dehumanizing effect of industrial capitalism.[19] Thus, both classical theorists reveal a convergence in their critique of capitalism, and there are substantive affinities between Marx and Weber.[20] Marx's theory of alienation and Weber's concepts of rationalization and disenchantment, as in the iron cage, for example, exhibit significant similarities.[21]

The hypothesis of the "debate with the ghost of Marx," as an intellectual milieu for understanding Weber's work, has been replaced by the thesis that the German philosopher Friedrich Nietzsche (1844–1900) was a decisive intellectual influence on Max Weber.[22] Nietzsche is acknowledged as the principal philosopher responsible for the dethronement of Enlightenment reason and the celebration of the irrational. According to Nietzsche, people must understand that the social world is replete with ambiguity, absurdity, cruelty, injustice, and unconscious impulses and strivings dominate human behaviour, not rational principles. As a late-modern philosopher, Nietzsche believed there exist no absolute moral standards whose truth can be demonstrated by reflective reason: nothing is true. Christianity, said Nietzsche, smothered human's true essence, the spark of life. In proclaiming that "God is dead" and Christian morality is defunct, Nietzsche believed that traditional moral values had lost their authority and binding power in late-capitalist societies. His writings are riven with contradictions that inspire multiple interpretations, controversy, and conjecture.[23]

Nietzsche's philosophy shaped the development of Weber's sociology in several important ways. Like Nietzsche, Weber emphasizes the primacy of power in social life. In *Economy and Society,* Weber writes, "Domination in the most general sense is one of the most important elements of social action."[24] Furthermore, Nietzsche's views on the loss of authority of traditional moral values, with his "God is dead" and his criticism of absolutist notions of truth, profoundly influenced Weber's ideas about the ability of the social sciences ever to establish, unambiguously, the "truth" in the social world. A legacy of Nietzsche's philosophy was that truth exists only from a particular standpoint or perspective. Thus truth is always contingent. There are no meta-narratives. Weber's critical observations on the moral basis of intellectual inquiry and his pessimistic analysis of modern bureaucracy's capacity to eliminate "love, hatred, and all purely personal, irrational, and emotional elements"[25] can be traced back to Nietzsche.

In addition to Marx and Nietzsche, a third intellectual force influencing Weber's encyclopedic writings is neo-Kantianism, particularly the works of Wilhelm Dilthey (1833–1911), Wilhelm Windelband (1848–1915), and Heinrick Rickert (1863–1936).[26] In the 1880s the natural sciences, with their positivist thinking, were pre-eminent in discovering truths about the natural world, and this raised questions about the intellectual authority of the philosophical sciences. The dispute about the relationship between the natural sciences (*Naturwissenschaften*) and human sciences (*Geisteswissenschaften*) initiated what is known as the *Methodenstreit* debate. The German neo-Kantian movement was an expression of dissatisfaction with the dominance of positivist thinking and the crisis in philosophical sciences. In education, realistic, or modern, schools challenged the pre-eminence of classical studies, while utilitarian, or technical, schools gained strength. Among German mandarins, there was widespread revulsion against positivism, it was considered "a kind of intellectual acid, a potentially disastrous dissolvent of holistic concepts, traditional beliefs, and socially integrative certainties."[27] The neo-Kantian movement aimed to secure the intellectual authority of the humanities and social sciences. The triumvirate Dilthey-Windelband-Rickert addressed two central issues: subject matter and theory of knowledge. According to Dilthey, the natural sciences and the social sciences studied different objects. He also challenged the secular sobriety of French positivism and instead emphasized humanity's creative and meaningful commonality, which was unmasked by hermeneutics approaches, a process of understanding, interpretation, and explanation. In Dilthey's words: "Everything in which the mind has objectified itself contains something held in common between I and thou. Every square planted with trees, every room in which seats are arranged, is intelligible to us from our infancy because human planning, arranging and valuing—common to all of us—have assigned a place to every square and every object in the room."[28] Dilthey's hermeneutics work to understand social life has been described variously as a declaration of war against positivism,[29] or as a declaration of independence on behalf of humanities.[30] He never abandoned his conviction that empathy is an element in interpretation, but in a 1907 essay on descriptive psychology, Dilthey developed the concept of *Verstehen* to capture human meanings from social experience. Georg Simmel articulated aspects of Dilthey's *Verstehen* as early as 1892. Like Dilthey, Simmel emphasized the relationship between inner movements of the soul and their outward manifestations. This point is important, because Simmel influenced Weber more directly than Dilthey.[31]

By contrast, Wilhelm Windelband held that the subject matter of the human sciences seeks fully to describe a single event in its "unique actuality" at a particular location in time. He argued that, methodologically, the natural sciences pursue nomothetic knowledge (*Gesetz*) in the form of universal laws, and the human sciences strive for ideographic knowledge (*Gestalt*) of single patterns or actions. The younger Rickert refined Windelband ideas. Heinrick Rickert believed that the principal distinction between the natural and human sciences was between the respective methods. For Rickert, the natural sciences generalize, the human sciences individualize. He also conceived human cultures as systems of values. Facts, argued Rickert, are constituted out of experience and given form by cognitive activity, which connotes selection and judgment. Rickert's belief was "first we judge and then we know."[32] While the natural sciences explain phenomena in terms of causal arguments, the human sciences are concerned with understanding the significance and importance of cultural phenomena. Thus, both physics and anthropology are sciences but they require different methods of inquiry. Whereas physics can be studied within the framework of laws and causes, in anthropology the emphasis is with hermeneutics and the problem of how to *Verstehen*, understand, interpret, and make judgments about the meaning of ritual acts and customs, with reference to values, which are embedded in the cultural context of the researcher.

Weber and the *Methodenstreit*

While the genealogy of Weber's methodological essays is complex,[33] Nietzsche's philosophy and the neo-Kantian view of concept formation undoubtedly influenced Weber's writings on the methodology of social research. Weber's contribution to the *Methodenstreit* debate was his integration of two divergent positions.[34] Weber agreed with the anti-positivists that the application of general laws to study social reality in its totality is problematic. However, Weber argued that rational scientific methods should be applied to the human sciences and should not be exclusively reserved for the natural sciences. Whatever the object under investigation, scientific criteria are always the aspiration; the specificity of the human sciences, the motives and values that guide human inquiry, necessitate special consideration.[35] The problem of values, normative judgments and empirical knowledge, or truth, is addressed in *The Methodology of the Social Sciences*. Weber distinguishes between value freedom and value relevance. He recognizes that in the initial research stage, personal and cultural values cannot be exorcized and, consequently, what is selected for investigation mirrors the researcher's values. However, Weber insists that social science be value-free in the analysis stage. Weber writes, "An *attitude of moral indifference* has no connection with *scientific* 'objectivity.'"[36]

For Weber, objectivity involves a moral commitment to the pursuit of knowledge, that is, truth. While sociologists recognize the value of knowledge from "one-sided points of view," objectivity in research and scholarship demands "the insistence on the rigorous distinction between empirical knowledge and value-judgements."[37] For many years Weber's position on objectivity has been widely misinterpreted to mean value freedom (*Wertfreiheit*), implying a simple objectivity that requires researchers to free themselves of all values in the course of their research. Weber intended the term *objectivity* to mean that researchers have an obligation to be aware of the ideologies and values that dominate their own perspectives and observations, and to strive to go beyond their own individual views. The meaning of Weber's distinction between value freedom and value relevance is found in the following quotation:

> The problems of the social sciences are selected by the value-relevance of the phenomena treated ... The expression 'relevance of values' refers simply to the philosophical interpretation of that specifically scientific 'interest which determines the selection of a given subject-matter and the problems of an empirical analysis ... Together with historical experience, cultural (i.e.,

> evaluative) interests give purely empirical scientific work its direction …
>
> Without the investigator's evaluative ideas, there would be no principle of selection of subject-matter and no meaningful knowledge of the concrete reality. Just as without the investigator's conviction regarding the significance of particular cultural facts, every attempt to analyze concrete reality is absolutely meaningless, so the direction of his personal belief, the refraction of values in the prism of his mind, gives direction to his work.[38]

Thus, Weber emphasizes that human inquiry involves moral choices, and the implication is that sociologists need to explain the moral choices that they make.[39] Like Rickert, Weber conceived culture as a value concept. This quote is typical of his argument: "The *significance* of a configuration of cultural phenomena and the basis of this significance cannot … be derived and rendered intelligible by a system of analytical laws ... since the significance of cultural events presupposes a value-orientation towards these events."[40] The social scientist must abstract sufficiently unambiguous conceptualizations from the infinite complexity of social reality. But what is the criterion by which a segment of social life is selected for investigation? Weber, influenced by Rickert, formulates what he believes to be the decisive feature of social sciences methodology, the principle of *value orientation*. Social sciences analyze segments of social action in terms of their *significance*; but importantly, these are only the segments that have become significant to the scientist because of their value relevance. In Weber's words:

> Only a small portion of existing concrete reality is coloured by our value-conditioned interest and it alone is significant to us. It is significant because it reveals relationships which are important to us due to their connection with our values. Only because and to the extent that this is the case is it worthwhile for us to know it in its individual features … The focus of attention on reality under the *guidance of values* which lend it significance and the selection and ordering of the phenomena … is entirely different from the analysis of reality in terms of laws and general concepts. [italics added] [41]

Weber argues that, given the infinite variety of empirical reality, only a chaos of judgment would result from any serious attempt to analyze segments of social reality "without presuppositions." For instance, a Canadian researcher investigating the social barriers facing young women entering higher education may assume there is a potential connection between social class and university access. On the other hand, a social scientist is likely to have a different presupposition if the same study is conducted in Turkey, a predominantly Muslim country. Weber's position is clear: What is deemed meaningful is a cultural construct. As Weber states, "A chaos of 'existential judgements' about countless individual events would be the only result of a serious attempt to analyze reality 'without presuppositions.' And even this result is only seemingly possible, since every single perception discloses on closer examination an infinite number of constituent perceptions, which can never be exhaustively expressed in a judgement. Order is brought into this chaos only on the condition that in every case only a *part* of concrete reality is interesting and *significant* to us, because only it is related to the *cultural values* with which we approach reality."[42]

For Weber, as for Rickert, in the human sciences judgments of relevance and meaning will be developed with reference to cultural values. Further, where the uniqueness of a social phenomenon is concerned, causality is not a matter of abstract general laws, but of specific, concrete, causal relationships. For Weber, an objective analysis of social reality that proceeds according to the ideal of laws is meaningless.[43] Weber's preoccupation with such topics as ethical neutrality in teaching and objectivity in social inquiry was driven by practical circumstances around academic freedom in Germany's universities and from Nietzsche's critique of absolutist notions of truth behind Enlightenment. Weber accepted Nietzsche's argument that truth is always contingent upon the perspectives of the inquiring scholar. If God is dead, the "freedom" of a social science means that there is no grounding by which any one perspective could have legitimacy over other perspectives. Weber's deliberations on the problem of objectivity in the social sciences, and particularly the problem of understanding human action, was an attempt to address these problems.[44]

Definition of Sociology and Methodologies

The *Methodenstreit* controversy underpins Weberian sociology. In *Economy and Society*, Weber refers to the science of society as interpretive sociology (*Verstehend* Soziologie), and he defines sociology as "a science concerning itself with the interpretative understanding of social action and thereby with a causal explanation of its course and consequence."[45] Sociology is concerned with investigating social action, which includes both the failure to act and a passive acquiescence that may be oriented to the past, present, or future behaviour of others. However, not every kind of human action is social action. This is where Weber makes a distinction between behaviour and action. Behaviour is an observable act or movement that humans do without attaching a meaning to it. For example, if a person coughs or faints, the act can be understood as the result of a physical cause rather than meaningful action.

Social Action

Sociology investigates meaningful social action or reaction, whether meaning is attributed to actions of a single individual, those prevailing on the average within a particular group, or those attributed to a hypothetically constructed, typical actor.[46] His well-known definition of *social action* states: "The acting individual attaches a subjective meaning to his behaviour—be it overt or covert, omission or acquiescence. Action is 'social' insofar as its subjective meaning takes account of the behaviour of others and is thereby oriented in its course."[47] Weber's definition makes a distinction in that sociology is concerned only with meaningful *social* action that is affected by or oriented towards others. The example Weber uses to show this distinction is an accident between two cyclists. The collision may be looked at as a natural event, a result of a causal chain of physical events: Although the cyclists are engaged in meaningful action, neither intended the collision to occur. On the other hand, if an altercation or an apology follows the collision, this would constitute meaningful social action in which each is directing her or his action towards the other. Weber also insists that actions conditioned by crowd psychology or the imitation of the action of others do not constitute social action. Weber's theorizing of human action is significantly different to that of Marx or Durkheim. For Marx, economic forces, of which people often have little or no understanding and to which they do not attribute a subjective meaning, constantly affect human action. For Durkheim, the notion of social consciousness implies that meaning itself is socially constructed: people are socialized into ways of thinking. Weber's meaningful social action might be described as norm-following, and by definition, *norms* reflect or embody a culture's values and are always backed by sanctions of one kind or another: Norms are cultural constructs.

Weber identifies four types of social action: traditional, affectual, value-rational, and instrumentally rational. *Traditional action* is rooted in a body of cultural beliefs, customary habits of thought, and practices, which produce almost automatic action following habitual stimuli, as for example, with showering, eating, walking, or a priest following church doctrine. The great mass of everyday action approaches this type of action and is on a borderline between pre-social (non-reflective) and social (meaningful). *Affective* or *emotional action* is designed to capture diverse emotional states of individuals by means of empathy. Such empathy is easier, writes Weber, "the more we ourselves are susceptible to such emotional reactions as anxiety, anger, ambition, envy, jealousy, love, enthusiasm, pride, vengefulness, loyalty, devotion, and appetites of all sorts, and to the 'irrational' conduct which grows out of them."[48] This type of action is also on the borderline of what can be considered meaningfully oriented action, for it is not primarily goal directed. An example might be an individual leaping with joy during a religious service.

Value-rational action (*Wertrational*) is anchored in a conscious belief in the ultimate value of some substantive goal (e.g., salvation) by calculated—rational—means (e.g., ascetic lifestyle). Examples of value-rational action are those of individuals who, regardless of personal cost, put their convictions into practice to do what seems to them to be required by a religious call, personal loyalty, duty, or the importance of some cause. An example would be Martin Luther King, Jr., who strove for racial equality in the United States in the 1960s, but who advocated non-violent means of achieving the movement's goal. *Instrumentally rational action* (*Zweckrational*) takes into account the ends, the means, and the secondary outcomes; in which case the goals themselves have been rationally chosen. This type of action is the most rational and, in Weber's words, is determined by "expectations as to the behaviour of objects in the environment and of other human beings; these expectations are used as 'conditions' or 'means' for the attainment of the actor's own rationally pursued and calculated ends."[49] Instrumentally rational action involves calculated consideration of alternative means to the end, of the relations of the end to the secondary consequences, and of the relative importance of different possible ends. Weber's typology is an abstraction, and actual social action, as in the case of ascetic Protestant sects in *The Protestant Ethic*, is likely to involve all four—that is, non-rational (traditional and affective types) and rational (value and instrumental types)—in different degrees.[50]

The significance of Weber's interest in legal philosophy is seldom factored into his methodological writings. In German civil law cases the problem facing legal experts is that they must attribute effects to causes in particular circumstances, and thus engage in the doctrine of singular causal analysis. For example, in assessing the role of negligence in an accident, legal opinion compares the sequence of events or actions that actually occurred with what could have been expected if normal caution or action had prevailed. According to Weber, sociology is concerned with causal explanation of social action, and his suggested method relies heavily upon the doctrine of singular causal analysis.[51] In *The Logic of the Cultural Sciences* essay, Weber examines the methodological foundations of singular causal claims. He writes, "For the meaning of history as *a science of reality* can only be that it treats particular elements of reality not merely as heuristic *instruments* but as *objects* of knowledge, and particular causal connections not as premises of knowledge but as *real* causal factors."[52] The social scientist has to exclude the reproduction of the totality of concrete conditions in order to conceptually isolate complex antecedent conditions that more or less favour the outcome to be explained. Therefore, to achieve adequate causation, the *judgements of possibility*—that is, propositions regarding what *would* happen in the event of the exclusion of certain conditions—are "a matter of isolation and generalization" and involve "the continuous reference to empirical rules' [*Erfahrungsregeln*]."[53] Weber's writes, "The 'knowledge' on which such a judgement of 'significance' rest is … on the one hand, knowledge of certain 'facts,' ('ontological knowledge'), 'belonging' to the 'historical situation' … and on the other, knowledge of certain known empirical rules, particularly those relating to the ways in which human beings are prone to react in a given situation ('nomological knowledge')."[54] Weber's formulation of the causal explanation of varieties of social action is a representation of causal relationships that deals in *trajectories* of actions and in the divergences between trajectories and outcomes. Weber's creative reformulation and application of singular causal analysis set him apart from other participants in the *Methodenstreit* debate.

Understanding Social Action

According to Weber's definition, sociology concerns itself with the subjective meaning of social action. But what does Weber mean by the term *subjective*? How do sociologists truly grasp meaningful social action? Developing the work of hermeneutic philosopher Wilhelm Dilthey, Weber argues that social scientists can understand, *Verstehen*, types of social action by penetrating to those subjective meanings that humans attach to their own actions and to the action of others. Whereas the natural sciences examine the *outer states* of the natural world, the human sciences are concerned with the interpretation of the subjective *inner states* of actors. All interpretations of meaning, argues Weber, "strive for clarity and verifiable accuracy of insight and comprehension."[55] However, since social actions range from the highly rational to the highly emotional, the basis for accuracy in understanding may be rational, emotional, empathic, or artistically appreciative. Accordingly, Weber is amenable to using two types of understanding: direct and explanatory. Table 9.1 indicates the relationship Weber sees between the types of understanding and the types of evidence. He focuses primarily on explanatory (rational) understanding. Types I and II represent *direct understanding*, which involves comprehending the meaning of an action by virtue of the physical or symbolic characteristic of the act, such as observing that certain facial or body movements indicate anger, boredom, and so forth. These are understandings in which the directly observable evidence is sufficient to establish an interpretation, such as why someone moves their hand away from a hot stove or chops wood for winter fuel.

TABLE 9.1 Types of understanding and evidence[56]

TYPE OF UNDERSTANDING	TYPE OF EVIDENCE	
	Intuitive	Rational
Direct	I	II
Explanatory	III	IV

Weber's own example of direct understanding is the Pythagorean theorem in reasoning and the proposition $2 \times 2 = 4$. Types III and IV represent *explanatory understanding*, which entails comprehending the meaningful connection between an action and the likely reasons and motives underlying that act. For example, chopping wood may be part of a fitness routine for a person in a sedentary occupation or it may be a therapeutic exercise if a person is angry after a quarrel with his or her boss. For Weber, the fact that an interpretation cannot be derived directly from the action observed and empathized with suggests that, for valid knowledge of individual subjective motives, some method is required that involves assessing interpretative hypotheses as causes. Weber writes that the method of explanatory understanding is "not normative correctness, but rather, on the one hand, the conventional habits of the investigator ... in thinking in a particular way, and on the other, as the situation requires, his capacity to 'feel himself' empathically into a mode of thought which deviates from his own and which is normatively 'false' according to his own habits of thought."[57] Explanatory understanding requires the investigator to engage in a mode of thought that is sensitive to the context in which the researched and the researcher are located. For example, if we were informed that there is a statistical correlation between the numbers of students attending university and the polar bear population, we would regard the causal relationship as meaningless. On the other hand, if we were informed that there is a correlation between the numbers of students attending university and family income, we would likely consider the causal connection plausible. Why? Because we are members of the society that generated the data, we have experience of tuition fees, and we can follow the likely motives and reasoning underlying the social action. Explanatory understanding differs from direct understanding in that it requires more intellectual effort to understand, it strives to understand social action within a context on the basis of the relevant facts and experience, and it involves judgment. For Weber, interpretive sociology accomplishes something that is never attainable in the natural sciences: the capacity to confer intelligibility on social action of the component individuals.

Ideal Type as a Logical Construct

Weber's methodology is primarily about conceptualization and the challenge of generating meaningful selections from an infinite and multifarious reality. In order to strive for scientific precision on the meaning of social phenomena, and to arrive at a *causal explanation* of the observed reality, Weber developed his *ideal type*, defined as "one-sided emphasis and intensification of one or several aspects of a given event."[58] The concept is borrowed from neoclassical economic theory. In empirical research, the ideal type has only one function: "Its function is the comparison with empirical reality in order to establish its divergences or similarities, to describe them with the *most unambiguously intelligible concepts*, and to understand and explain them causally."[59] An ideal type is not a description of reality, neither is it an average of something, nor a normative exemplar to be achieved: ideal types are logical hypothetical constructs. Weber's conception of the ideal type is central to his method because it simplifies the multiple complexes of social reality: "An ideal type is formed by the one-sided *accentuation* of one or more points of view and by the synthesis of a great many diffuse, discrete, more or less present and occasionally absent *concrete individual* phenomena, which are arranged according to those one-sidedly emphasized viewpoints into a unified *analytical* construct [*Gedankenbild*]. In its conceptual purity, this mental construct [*Gedankenbild*] cannot be found empirically anywhere in reality. It is a *utopia*."[60] The more precisely an ideal type is constructed, that is, the more abstract it is, the better it can perform its function in formulating terminology and potentially useful hypotheses. Ideal types are indispensable as cognitive *means* to the extent that they lead to knowledge of concrete social phenomena in their interrelatedness, their causes, and their significance.[61] Ideal types also possess substantial heuristic as well as expository value. In that they are constructed to project a hypothetical *progression* of observable action that *could* be explained in terms of understandable motives, ideal types are an integral part of Weber's triadic model of singular causal analysis. In the analysis of *real* social action, ideal-type projections become the basis for the causal ascription of deviations from the rationally understandable progression of actions. A diagrammatic representation of ideal-type analysis is shown in figure 9.1.

FIGURE 9.1 Weber's ideal-type analysis of social phenomena[62]

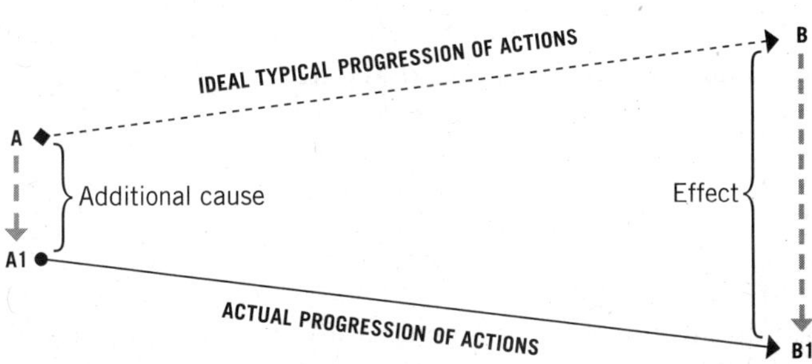

The line A–B represents the external progression of rational actions that would have occurred if the individual had acted as specified in the ideal type. The line A1–B1 is the actual progression of actions observed by the investigator. The positing of the ideal type allows the investigator to compare A1–B1 with A–B and thus "quantify" the deviation B–B1 that must be causally attributed to the difference between A, the "motives" hypothetically ascribed to the ideal, typical individual, and A1, the "motivation" of the actual individual or individuals studied. For example, in a pure ideal-type form, bureaucracy has certain traits, such as specialized tasks, continuity, formal procedures and rules, clarity, strict subordination, unified control, appointed positions on the basis of technical qualifications, and defined hierarchy. Weber's ideal type of bureaucracy is compared with the observed conduct or processes of a bureaucratic organization.

One problem facing the investigator is, how do we know we have constructed an ideal-type conception of the social phenomena we wish to study? Weber's criterion for evaluating the usefulness of an ideal type is matter-of-fact. Weber notes in the canonical text, "*Theory*-construction can never be decided *a priori*. There is only one criterion, namely, that of success in revealing concrete cultural phenomena in their interdependence, their causal conditions and their *significance*. The construction of abstract ideal-types recommends itself not as an end but as a *means*."[63] Examples of what Weber means by ideal-type constructs include Marx's capitalist modes of production, Durkheim's mechanical and organic solidarity, Ferdinand Tönnies's *Gemeinschaft* and *Gesellschaft* as well as

Weber's own typology of social action. Ideal types can also be constructed for developmental stages, such as feudalism, or historical particularities, such as the industrial city. As Weber posits, "all specifically Marxian 'laws' and developmental constructs—insofar as they are theoretically sound—are ideal types."[64] For Weber, the construction of ideal types has three main functions in social theorizing: they help to conceptualize the multifarious mosaic that is social life in modernity; they help to formulate empirical research questions and *suggest* potential causal relationships; and they underscore the active role of the researcher in the interpretation of social action.

Criticism

There have been several criticisms of Weber's methodology.[65] The first criticism questions the fact-value dichotomy and the notion of value neutrality. Weber's position is criticized on the grounds that since human science operates within a moral universe, it is naïve to believe that it can avoid moral judgment of its data; moreover, in conditions of "irrational power politics" (e.g., fascism), so-called impartiality may be an abdication of responsibility. The second criticism relates to Weber's ideal types, which, critics argue, are located in the context of asymmetrical power relations. For feminists, a critical issue is the relationship of women to the process of power. Weber's key methodological tool occurs in the context of a "natural inequality" between the sexes. While Weber posits that all knowledge of social reality is always knowledge from particular standpoints, when he actually applies his concept of power to forms of domination, it is obvious that he regards the access to power and domination by men as natural and inevitable. A contemporary iconoclastic feminist affirms that the "ideal type patriarchy assumes that the domination of women is a 'natural' phenomenon."[66] The third criticism is that Weber's conception of instrumental rational social action is limited to a relationship between means and ends, with each step leading on to the next in a linear fashion, until the desired end is achieved. Critics consider this conception of rationality as one that is more concerned with domination: the control and exploitation of the natural world.[67]

The fourth criticism relates to Weber's approach to understanding, *Verstehen*. While *Verstehen* calls for the investigator to be perceptive of meaningful connections between actions and context, it creates only causal hypotheses, which do not constitute knowledge per se, however plausible an interpretation may appear. In other words, the validity of the relationship needs to be established empirically. Another critique relates to relativism, which is raised by the notion of interpretation. For Weber, the meaning of any social action is deeply embedded in its cultural context. This argument appears to be relatively clear, but if meaning is specific to local, how is any *general* knowledge of society as such possible? If, for example, the strategies of multinational companies have to be interpreted within the context of national spaces and values, can there be a universally relevant sociology of work? Finally, Weber's notorious typology has been critiqued because it poses problems of validation, which Weber attempted to resolve with judgments of plausibility and empirical evidence. As others have pointed out, how does the researcher know that the central traits of a social phenomenon have been thoroughly abstracted from reality? And, once abstracted, how much deviation from the ideal type is scientifically acceptable before the researcher must conclude that it bears too little resemblance to social reality to be useful? Although ideal type was central to his sociological work, Weber was never able to provide a satisfactory definition of the ideal-type rational social action. His quest for objective social science and his extreme form of constructivism, critics argue, reflects his "ontological insecurity," which is rooted in his pessimistic view of humans in modernity.

Conclusion

Max Weber made an immense contribution to social research discourse. Neo-Kantian thinkers such as Nietzsche, Dilthey, Simmel, Windelband, and Rickert heavily influenced his writings. Weber extended the *Methodenstreit* debate in several important ways by emphasizing that the subject matter of the social sciences was made up of individuals whose social action was based on values; that in both natural and social sciences, facts never speak for themselves, they require interpretation; and that research methods are always shaped by the researcher's cultural values and ideologies. Weber's value-freedom/value-relevance dichotomy, as well as his use of singular causal analysis, his theory of social action, the application of *Verstehen* as a distinct mode of understanding, and the nature and the purpose of ideal-type constructs are central concepts and procedures in his methodology. Weber laid the foundations for the furtherance of testable procedures in social research. Weber's essays, charting the boundary between judgments and epistemological neutrality, have been given canonical status in most introductory social research methods texts.[68]

What emerges from Weber's work on social inquiry is that historical understanding is always interpretative and his methods foreshadow postmodernist thinking, in particular the multiple challenges to metanarratives. Moreover, his methodological legacy still provides researchers with concepts and practices, and a deep appreciation of the problem of values and meaning in research. Weber's status as a classical sociologist affirms his own argument that science does not stand outside ideology. Talcott Parsons misinterpreted Weber's *Protestant Ethic* and the methodological *Essays* as a refutation of Marx's thesis on capitalism and as a support for "value-free" research. And the context that shaped this theoretical interpretation of Weber's work was global politics that eventuated in the Cold War. While the central metaphor for much of modern human inquiry is the crystal—with its infinite variety of shapes, patterns, colours, and transmutations—rather than the ideal type, Weber's work is a vivid reminder that the interpretive process of social phenomena involves a complex interaction among the conceptual world of the researcher, the situational constraints, and the reality of the people and culture they seek to understand. It's a reflection of his legacy that within the matrix of contemporary uncertainty his ideas remain remarkably relevant in epistemology considerations, and his insights on the complexity of interpretive understanding still resonate with social scientists today.

Notes

1 Fritz Ringer, *Max Weber's Methodology* (Cambridge, MA: Harvard University Press, 1997), 168.

2 Keith Tribe, ed., *Reading Weber* (London: Routledge 1989); B.S. Turner *For Weber* (London: Sage, 1996).

3 Ian Craib, *Classical Sociological Theory* (Oxford: Oxford University Press, 1997), 43.

4 Stephen Turner, ed., *The Cambridge Companion to Weber* (New York: Cambridge University Press, 2000), 1.

5 Reinhard Bendix, *Max Weber: An Intellectual Portrait* (New York: Anchor Books, 1962), 1.

6 Marianne Weber, *Max Weber: A Biography* (New York: Wiley, 1975).

7 Guenther Roth, introduction to Max Weber's *Economy and Society*, eds. Guenther Roth and Claus Wittich (Berkeley, CA: University of California Press, 1968).

8 Bryan S. Turner, *For Weber* (London: Sage, 1996).

9 Sven Eliaeson, *Max Weber's Methodologies* (Cambridge: Polity Press, 2002), 3.

10 Bendix, *Max Weber*, 4–5.

11 Ibid., 6.

12 Eliaeson, *Max Weber's Methodologies*, 126.

13 Turner, *For Weber*, 74.

14 Quoted in Anthony Giddens, *Capitalism and Modern Social Theory* (Cambridge: Cambridge University Press, 1971), 190–1.

15 Turner, *For Weber.*

16 Max Weber, *The Protestant Ethic and the Spirit of Capitalism* (New York: Penguin, 2002), 13.

17 Ibid., 36.

18 Max Weber, *The Methodology of the Social Sciences*, trans., E. Shils and H. Finch (Glencoe, Il: Free Press, 1949), 103.

19 Karl Löwith, *Max Weber and Karl Marx* (London: George Allen & Unwin, 1982), translated from "Max Weber and Karl Marx," *Archiv für Sozialwissenschaft und Sozialpolitik* Vol. 66 (1932): 53–99 and 175–214, and cited in B.S. Turner, *Classical Sociology*, (London: Sage, 1999), 51–55.

20 I.M. Zeitlin, *Ideology and the Development of Sociological Theory*, 7th ed. (Upper Saddle River, NJ: Prentice-Hall, 2001), 196.

21 B.S. Turner, *Classical Sociology* (London: Sage, 1999).

22 In addition to primary sources, this section draws from Alex Callinicos, *Social Theory: A Historical Introduction* (Cambridge: Polity Press, 2007); Turner, *Classical Sociology*.

23 See John Ralston Saul, *Voltaire's Bastards* (Toronto: Penguin, 1993); also J. Lavin, *Nietzsche*, (New York: Scribner, 1971), who argues that all the fascist theories can find some support in Nietzsche's philosophy.

24 Max Weber, *Economy and Society* (1921; Berkeley, CA: University of California Press, 1978), 941.

25 Ibid., 975.

26 This section draws from Ringer, *Max Weber's Methodology*; Eliaeson, *Max Weber's Methodologies*; and Ken Morrison, *Marx, Durkheim, Weber* (London: Sage, 2006); Callinicos, *Social Theory*; and Turner, *Classical Sociology*.

27 Ringer, *Max Weber's Methodology*, 22.

28 W. Dilthey, "Awareness, Reality: Time," in *The Hermeneutic Reader*, ed. K. Mueller-Vollmer (Oxford: Blackwell, 1985), and quoted in L. Ray, *Theorizing Classical Sociology* (Buckingham: Open University Press, 1999), 118.

29 Morrison, *Marx, Durkheim and Weber*, 332.

30 Ray, *Theorizing Classical Sociology*, 125.

31 Ringer, *Max Weber's Methodology*, 29.

32 Morrison, *Marx, Durkheim and Weber*, 336.

33 Anthony Giddens, *Capitalism and Modern Social Theory* (Cambridge: Cambridge University Press, 1971), 133.

34 Ringer, *Max Weber's Methodology*.

35 Eliaeson, *Max Weber's Methodologies*, 18.

36 Weber, *Methodology of the Social Sciences*, 60.

37 Ibid., 49.

38 Ibid., 20–1, 82.

39 Ian Craib, *Classical Social Theory* (Oxford: Oxford University Press, 1997), 52.

40 Weber, *Methodology of the Social Sciences*, 76.

41 Ibid., 76.

42 Ibid., 78.

43 Ibid., 80.

44 Turner, *Classical Sociology*, 61.

45 Weber, *Economy and Society*, 4.

46 Ringer, *Max Weber's Methodology*, 101.

47 Weber, *Economy and Society*, 4.

48 Ibid., 6.

49 Ibid., 24.

50 Turner, *Classical Sociology.*

51 Ringer, *Max Weber's Methodology.*

52 Weber, *Methodology of the Social Sciences*, 135.

53 Ibid., 173.

54 Ibid., 174.

55 Weber, *Economy and Society*, 5.

56 Adapted from Eliaeson, *Max Weber's Methodologies*, 42.

57 Weber, *Methodology of the Social Sciences*, 41.

58 M. S. Zouboulakis, "From Mill to Weber: The Meaning of the Concept of Economic Rationality," *European Journal of Economic Thought* 8, no. 1 (2001): 30.

59 Ibid., 34.

60 Weber, *Methodology of the Social Sciences*, 90.

61 Ringer, *Max Weber's Methodology*, 112.

62 Adapted from Ringer, *Max Weber's Methodology*, 115.

63 Weber, *Methodology of the Social Sciences*, 92.

64 Ibid., 103.

65 These criticisms are largely drawn from Turner, *Classical Sociology*; Anthony Giddens, *The Consequences of Modernity* (Cambridge: Polity Press, 1990); Eliaeson, *Max Weber's Methodologies*; and Ringer, *Max Weber's Methodology.*

66 R.A. Sydie, *Natural Women, Cultured Men*, (Vancouver: University of British Columbia Press, 1994), 84.

67 See Turner, *Classical Sociology.*

68 See, for example, Allan Bryman and James Teevan, *Social Research Methods* (Don Mills, Ontario: Oxford University Press, 2005).

10. Max Weber: Capitalism and Society

To understand modernity is to understand Weber.

—Bryan S. Turner[1]

Weber's work is like a gigantic quarry with many shiny stones to pick up—many concepts and hypotheses to extend, elaborate and transcend.

—Sven Eliaeson[2]

Weber's writings could provide a starting-point both for the root-and-branch critique of capitalism developed by the Frankfurt School and for the functional sociology of Talcott Parsons.

—Alex Callinicos[3]

AS WE EXPLAINED IN THE preceding chapter, Weber's sociological studies are thoroughly grounded in his methodology. Though there have been several forays into Weber's writings with the purpose of discovering a principle of thematic unity, scholars widely acknowledge that it is difficult to impose a single, unifying, theme over his work. The quest for an organizing theme has been complicated by problems connected to the transmission of his ideas through translation, publication, and fragmentation.[4] Much contemporary Anglo-Saxon Weberian scholarship argues that Weber's theory of modernity centres on the primacy of rationality and the process of rationalization. Weber used the term rationalization to describe a set of interrelated social processes by which nature, individuals, culture, and institutions have been systematically transformed by rational human action. It is important to note that, like his writings on social methodology, Weber's critique of capitalism was fashioned from many intellectual sources. A number of translated texts have tended to be identified as constituting the core of Weber's sociological writings. Prominent among these are his best-known and influential work *The Protestant Ethic and the Spirit of Capitalism* and the assortment of manuscripts posthumously published under the title *Economy and Society.* His writings are ambiguous, fragmented, and full of paradoxes. Though he did not have a conception of society as a social system, he famously warned about the iron cage of industrial capitalism. Reinhart Bendix notes the paradoxes of his scholarly work: "His lifetime study [the development of rationalism] revealed not only the complexity of its antecedents, but the precariousness of its achievements."[5] Also, his triumph, rational calculability, and its concomitant bureaucratization were not necessarily to be applauded because they created the "disenchantment" of the world. The aim of this chapter is to elucidate the core elements of Weber's sociology that have been most analyzed by English-speaking sociologists, including his study of the complex connections between capitalism and religious beliefs, social class, status and power, and domination and bureaucracy. In so doing, we shall identify some major differences between Marx and Weber.

Rationalization Thesis

An overarching theme in Weber's social theory is the concept of rationalization. The term appears repeatedly in *The Protestant Ethic* and in *Economy and Society*, but the most extensive treatment of the concept appears in his *Sociology of Religion.*[6] Whether the rationalization thesis is Weber's pivotal theoretical core or whether it is one of several crucial concepts he used to analyze modern life is a matter of protracted debate.[7] Attempts to explain or reject Weber's rationalization thesis are not helped by the ambiguity and inconsistency in his technical use of the term. However, no complete understanding of Weber's sociology is possible without examining this important concept. Weber sees a systematic process of rationalization underlying Western industrial capitalism. The term is complex and multi-faceted, but at the risk of oversimplification, *rationalization* describes a constellation of ubiquitous interrelated processes that systematically transformed Western European societies by a long-run tendency to bring order and perfection to what in its "natural" state is less ordered, and imperfect. The following passage by a Weber scholar offers a lucid picture of Weberian rationalization:

> Weber's rationalization is ... the product of scientific specialization and technical differentiation peculiar to Western

> culture ... sometimes associated with the notion of intellectualization. It might be defined as the *organization of life through a division and coordination of activities on the basis of an exact study of men's relations with each other, with their tools and their environment, for the purpose of achieving greater efficiency and productivity.* Hence it is a purely practical development brought about by man's technological genius.
>
> Weber also described rationalization as a striving for perfection ... as an ingenious refinement of the conduct of life and the attainment of increasing mastery over the external world ... he analyzed its evolution in all major branches of human activity—religion, law, art, science, politics, and economics—while being careful not to go beyond the limits of what is objectively ascertainable.[8]

The essence of the concept consists of three facets: secularization, calculability, and rational action. The process of rationalization involved the decline of magical interpretations and explanations of the world, the authority of the Church, the erosion of the social status of the clergy, and the general secularization of the modern world. The tsunami of rational calculation in all spheres of life has created the phenomenon that Weber identified as the *disenchantment* or *de-enchantment* of modernity. What he meant by these terms is a process by which enchantment becomes expunged from everyday life through a progressive loss of faith in the invisible but enchanted shapers of the human theatre provided by folk beliefs as well as by organized religions.[9] The regimented forms of thought and social action had, for Weber, virtually replaced religion as the unquestioned, motivating creed across much of Western civilization.[10] Within the legal system, rationalization involves the decline and erosion of ad hoc legal decision-making in favour of law making, such that "in both substantive and procedural matters, only unambiguous general characteristics of the facts of the case are taken into account."[11] In the political sphere, rationalization is associated with the decline of traditional domination and the rise of legal-rational systems of authority. The rationalization in the sphere of human labour involves the explicit, systematic design of paid work from the point of view of calculability, efficiency, predictability, and profitability. The notion of timed labour epitomizes rationalization and modernity. A contemporary of Weber explained modern factory work and the need to calculate tasks precisely: "The idea [is] that man must have every second necessary but not a single unnecessary second."[12] In social terms, generally, rationalization involves the extension of scientific rationality to the conduct of social life itself, including modern systems of surveillance and the rise of bureaucratic forms of administration.

Weber's rationalization thesis is closely interlinked with his notion of rationality, which occupies a central place in *Economy and Society.* Rational action is differentiated from other forms of social action. The former involves submitting social action to constant calculative scrutiny by weighing up the means and ends prior to action, which produces a continuous drive towards change. In his writings, Weber identifies four types of rationality: practical, theoretical, formal, and substantive.[13] *Practical rationality* assumes no external mystical causes affecting the outcome of human actions and sees reality in terms of what is given. *Theoretical or technical rationality* involves a cognitive effort to master the world through causality, and logical deduction and induction. This type of rationality allows individuals to understand the meaning of life by means of abstract concepts and conceptual reasoning. *Formal rationality* refers to the application of technically appropriate modes of calculation (means) that go into decisions to ensure consistency of outcome and efficiency in attaining specific goals (ends). *Substantive rationality* refers to the degree to which human action is guided or shaped by a value system regardless of the outcome of the action. Accordingly, where formal rationality involves a practical orientation of social action in relation to goals or ends, substantive rationality involves an orientation to values.

Religion and Capitalism

Marx, Durkheim, and Weber studied religion, and in their respective conceptions of religion, they are in some ways compatible. Marx believed that religion has ideological implications that serve to justify social inequality. Durkheim emphasizes the role of religion in supporting social cohesion. Weber's study of the "economic ethics" of major world religions examines the link between religion and cultural development. These studies form the context of what is a very complex argument concerning the significance of Western rationality. Weber notes, "To the natural uncertainties and resistances facing every innovator, religion adds powerful impediments of its own. The sacred is the uniquely unalterable."[14] His study of Chinese religion identifies the importance of the ancestor as an impediment to rationalism. Weber's study of Hinduism and Buddhism refers to a "magical garden" from which rationality could not develop.[15] Weber emphasizes the affinities between Judaism and Puritanism.[16] In Western Europe some sects of Protestantism did prove to be amenable to rational capitalism, to be alterable, which brings us to Weber's classic work on the Protestant ethic.

In *The Protestant Ethic*, Weber aims to discern the significance of ascetic Protestantism—in relation to other formative elements of culture—to the growth of modern capitalism in the West and to illustrate the process by which ideas become a force for social change.

> The task before us is to indicate the significance of ascetic rationalism for the content of the *ethic* of the *social* economy, that is, for the type of organization and the functions of social communities, from the conventicle to the state. Then its relationship to humanist rationalism and its ideals and cultural influences, to the development of philosophical and scientific empiricism, and to technological development and the arts must be analyzed ... It must be shown in what way Protestant asceticism itself was influenced in its growth and character by the totality of the culture, and especially economic conditions of society.[17]

As we have seen, Weber asserts that a high degree of formal rationality characterizes capitalism as a modern phenomenon and that the process of rationalization effects all dimensions of social life. Weber's thesis, in brief, proposes that a new attitude to work and the pursuit of wealth, in which work becomes a means of demonstrating godliness, was linked to the rise of Calvinism and that this cultural shift was associated with the rise of *rational* capitalism. Weber's investigation begins by focusing on significant cultural differences between European Protestants and Catholics. Comparing the two denominations, he posits that Catholic school students, unlike Protestant, were averse to studying commerce, which, he argues, helps explain "the low participation rate of Catholics in capitalist business life."[18] Further, Protestant skilled workers tended to migrate to the new factories where they formed the "upper echelons of skilled workers and management," whereas Catholic journeymen showed a "greater inclination to remain in craft work."[19] Weber held that "the choice of occupation and future career has undoubtedly been determined by the *distinct mental characteristics* which have been instilled in them."[20]

John Calvin (1509–1564). Weber argues that Calvin's ascetic vision of Protestantism was one of the principal wellsprings of the capitalist "spirit," which was an important factor influencing the growth of industrial capitalism.

A surface-level comparison of Protestantism and Catholicism might conclude that the latter induces its followers to an ascetic lifestyle, and, on the other hand, by secularizing every dimension of life Protestantism must induce in its followers a hedonistic lifestyle. To illustrate this perception Weber cites a popular adage: "Protestants like to eat well, while Catholics want to sleep well."[21] Weber held that, on the contrary, this is not the case. The English, Dutch, and American Puritans were characterized by "the very opposite of enjoyment of life," argues Weber.[22] Indeed, Weber contends that Protestants had an "inner affinity" towards an ascetic lifestyle that made them especially receptive to the rational capitalist culture.

To support his elusive principal thesis—the ideal type—Weber extensively quotes Benjamin Franklin, who, although no Calvinist, personified the new capitalist ethos. Franklin, an eighteenth-century version of contemporary management guru Tom Peters (*In Search of Excellence*), is important to Weber's thesis because his writings emphasized the link between religiosity and entrepreneurship.[23] Franklin enumerates what Weber regards as the ideal-type "spirit" of capitalism:

> Remember, *time is money*. He that can earn ten shillings a day by his labour, and goes abroad, or sits idle, one half of that day, though he spends but sixpence during his diversion or idleness, ought not to reckon *that* the only expense; he has really spent, or rather thrown away, five shillings besides.
>
> Remember, that *credit is money*. If a man lets his money lie in my hands after it is due, he gives me the interest, or so much as I can make of it during that time.
>
> Remember, that money is the *prolific, generating nature*. Money can beget money, and its offspring can beget more, and so on.
>
> Remember this saying, *the good paymaster* is lord of another man's purse. He that is known to pay punctually and exactly to the time he promises, may at any time, and on any occasion, raise all the money his friends can spare. This is sometimes of great use.
>
> The most trifling actions that affect a man's credit are to be regarded. The sound of your hammer at five in the morning, or eight at night, heard by the creditor, makes him easy six months longer, but if he sees you at a billiard table, or hears your voice at the tavern, when you should be at work, he sends for his money the next day ... It shows, besides, that you are mindful of what you owe; it makes you appear a careful as well as an *honest* man, and that still increases your *credit*.[24]

For Weber, the importance of Franklin's mantra is the notion that the individual has a *duty* to accumulate wealth, which is assumed to be an end in itself. Franklin also acknowledged that this spirit is more than a case of purely "egocentric maxims"; the actions constitute a religious conviction and search for salvation. In Benjamin Franklin's words:

> The "*summum bonum*" (great good) of this 'ethic' is the *making of money* and yet more money, coupled with a strict avoidance of all uninhibited enjoyment. Indeed, it is so completely devoid of all eudaemonistic, let alone hedonist, motives, so much purely thought of as an end *in itself* that it appears as something wholly transcendent and irrational, beyond the 'happiness' or the 'benefit' of the *individual.* The aim of a man's life is indeed money making, but this is no longer merely the means to the end of satisfying the material needs of life. This reversal of what we might call the 'natural' state of affairs is a definite leitmotiv of capitalism, although it will always be alien to anyone who is untouched by capitalist aura.[25]

Whereas Marx understood the same phenomenon in terms of the subordination of use-value to exchange-value, capital accumulation, and a change in the relations of production, Weber understood it as resulting from a change in ethical orientation towards the world.[26]

Weber explains that Calvinism as such did not foster the capitalist spirit; rather it was Calvin's followers and the doctrine of predestination that infused the social ethic of capitalist culture. But Catholics, according to Weber, believed they could secure their place in heaven through, among other things, good works on behalf of the poor or by performing acts of faith on earth. For example, the premodern Christian interpretation of the sermon, "It is easier for a camel to go through the eye of a needle than for a rich man to enter the kingdom of God,"[27] made the renunciation of wealth for the sake of the poor a primary condition of avoiding being "cast into hell." On the other hand, Weber asserted that Calvinism had developed a set of beliefs around the concept of predestination that broke the hold of tradition. Followers of Calvinism came to believe that their predestined future left them with no means of knowing or altering their ultimate destination. This uncertainty led anxious Calvinists to search for signs from God that they were among the "elect" to have a place in heaven. Wealth was taken as a manifestation of being among God's elect, thereby encouraging believers to apply themselves rationally to acquire wealth through their ascetic lifestyles. Thus, Protestant preaching stressed that followers had "a duty to *regard* themselves as elect, and to dismiss any doubts as a temptation from the devil ... The exhortation of the apostle to 'make one's own calling sure' was interpreted as a duty to strive for the subjective certainty of one's election and justification in daily struggle ... And ... *tireless labour in a calling* was urged as the best possible means of *attaining* this self-assurance. This and this alone would drive away religious doubt and give assurance to one's state of grace."[28]

According to Weber, this led to the emergence of what he calls an "ethic of inner conviction" (*Gesinnungsethik*) in which the external observance of holy law is displaced by a more dynamic and intense cultivation of an inner religious state.[29] Herein lies the ultimate source of ascetic Protestantism's social-transforming potency: "Wherever the power of the Puritan philosophy of life extended, it always benefited the tendency toward a middle-class [*bürgerlich*], economically *rational* conduct of life, of which it was the most significant and only consistent support. This is, of course, far more important than merely encouraging the formation of capital. *It stood at the cradle of modern 'economic man'* [italics added]."[30] Weber recognized that asceticism provided a religious legitimacy for the exploitation of human labour. A look at the textual evidence supports this point of view: "Protestant asceticism ... did add tremendous depth to the view and created the psychological *drive* for this norm to achieve its effect by interpreting such work as a *calling*, and as the *sole* means of making sure of one's state of grace. It also legalized the exploitation of this characteristic willingness to work by interpreting the employer's moneymaking as a 'calling' too."[31] Protestant asceticism transformed the world when it "moved out of the monastic cells and into working life, and began to dominate inner worldly morality," writes Weber. And in a prophetical observation he speculates that "this mighty cosmos determines ... the style of life not only of those directly involved in business but every individual who is born into this mechanism, and may well continue to do so until *the day that the last ton of fossil fuel is consumed*" [italics added].[32] While Weber did not believe Calvinism was *the* cause of the transformation of society, he did believe rational capitalism, in part, grew from Calvinism. In contrast to Marx, Weber argues that the growth of Western capitalism cannot be explained through wholly material and structural forces: it was embedded in the process of rationalization. The Protestant ethic thesis is often incorrectly interpreted as a refutation of Marx, but as we explained in chapter 9, this debate has become passé, archaic, and discredited. Weber's thesis of an increasing rationalization in all dimensions of social life informs his theories of social class and power, domination, and bureaucracies.

Social Class and Status

In his writings on social class, Weber finds much common ground with Marx. Weber agrees with Marx that industrial capitalism is predicated on a reservoir of formally free labour. There must be a sufficient pool of individuals who are in a state of extreme economic dependence and compelled to sell their labour power to employers. Weber writes, "The development of capitalism is impossible, if such a propertyless stratum is absent, a class compelled to sell its labour services to live."[33] In his theory of social class, it is clear that Weber builds upon the analysis developed by Marx. In *Economy and Society*, Weber explicitly makes reference to Marx: "The unfinished last part of Karl Marx's *Capital* apparently was intended to deal with the issue of class unity in the face of skill differentials."[34] Weber and Marx both regard society as characterized by conflicts over resources and power. Sounding distinctly Marxist, Weber argues that the ownership of property constitutes "positively privileged property class"[35] and the factor that produces class derives from the "relative control" within "a given economic order."[36] In an oft-quoted passage, Weber identifies three conditions for a class to exist: "We may speak of a class when (1) a number of people have in common a specific causal component of their life chances, insofar as (2) this component is represented exclusively by economic interests in the possession of goods and opportunities for income, and (3) is represented under the conditions of the commodity or labour markets. This is the 'class situation.'"[37] Thus, Weber sees a class emerging when a large number of people share similar life chances in the commodity or labour markets. By *life chances* he means the ability to gain access to scarce and valued goods and services such as property, education, and training. The ownership of property confers power on the property classes. For Weber, as for Marx, social class in a modern capitalist society is more complex than a simple two-class model of capitalist and proletariat. Although Marx in his later work refers to "three big classes," he also recognizes the existence of a "middle and intermediate strata."[38] Weber also identifies a variety of social classes: "The working class as a whole—the more so, the more automated the work process becomes, the petty bourgeoisie, the propertyless intelligentsia and specialists (technicians, various kinds of white-collar employees, civil servants—possibly with considerable social differences depending on the cost of their training), the classes privileged through property and education."[39]

In their 1848 *Manifesto*, Marx and Engels predicted that the petty bourgeoisie would "decay and finally disappear"[40] and "sink" into the working class in the face of modern industry. Over a quarter-century after the death of Marx, Weber noted the enduring presence of the petty bourgeoisie. He also witnessed the unprecedented growth of the new middle class: technicians, supervisors, and civil servants. Weber's class analysis closely overlaps with his theory that rationalization comes to dominate the modern world. As an economic process, rationalization is associated with mass production and highly specialized division of labour. This process is vividly demonstrated by 1914–18 trench warfare, which, according to Weber, "means the world-wide triumph of this form [rationalization] of life."[41] Trench warfare battles of 1914–18 were battles of materials (*Materialschlacht*). During the battle of Jena in 1806 Napoleon expended less than 1,500 rounds of artillery to defeat the Prussians. In 1914 France planned for 10–12,000 shells of artillery *a day*; by 1918 production had reached 200,000 shells a day.[42] The mass slaughter of human lives on the Western Front required mass production of hitherto inconceivable quantities of military products, which, in turn, accelerated rationalization, specialization, and bureaucratic modes of control essential for mobilization of resources. This rationalization of war caused a burgeoning of white-collar technicians, managers, and civil servants.

For Marx, the class stratum is determined according to people's common relationship to the means of production, the means by which a large-scale grouping of people gain a livelihood. For Weber, by contrast, the organizational theorist, it was apparent that property ownership, together with differences in training, education, and the possession of marketable skills are the chief bases of class differences: "Class situation and 'class' refer only to the same (or similar) interests which an individual shares with others. In principle, the controls over consumer goods, means of production, assets, resources and skills each constitute a *particular* class situation. A *uniform* class situation prevails only when completely unskilled and propertyless persons are dependent on irregular employment. Mobility among, and stability of, class positions differs greatly; hence the unity of a social class is highly variable."[43] Here Weber's view of social class emphasizes that skill may constitute a form of property. Thus, Weber distinguishes between *property classes*, who are

For Weber, the access that people have to societal resources, such as education, is crucial in determining people's life chances. This photograph of "ragged children" with their teacher was taken in the 1890s in England. Notice that the children are not wearing shoes, and contrast this image with that of "public" (private) boarding schools for children of the Victorian social elite.

typically "rentiers" receiving income from the ownership of land, mines, factories; *commercial classes,* who are typically "entrepreneurs" offering services on the market, such as bankers and financiers; and *professionals*, who are typically lawyers and physicians. These social classes are "positively privileged." In contrast, paupers and unskilled who have neither property nor specialized skills constitute the "negatively privileged."

For Marx, social class and class-consciousness is inextricably bound up with class struggle. Here Weber differs sharply from Marx, recognizing that Marx's notions of a "class for itself" and class solidarity did not resonate among the new white-collar managers, intelligentsia, and government mandarins. Whereas Marx refers to the spectre of class antagonisms and class struggles, Weber emphasizes that social conflict and demands for radical changes to the economic system need not occur simply because of the differentiation of classes. The following passage explains his argument:

> The mere differentiation of property classes is not "dynamic", that is, it need not result in class struggles and revolutions. The strongly privileged class of slave owners may co-exist with the much less privileged peasants or even the declassed, frequently without any class antagonism and sometimes in solidarity (against the unfree). However, the juxtaposition of property classes *may* lead to revolutionary conflict between landowners and the declassed or creditors and debtors. These struggles need not focus on a change of the economic system, but may aim primarily at a redistribution of wealth. In this case we can speak of "property revolution" [*Besitzklassenrevolutionen*].[44]

As an example of the absence of class conflict, Weber cites the relationship of the "poor white trash" to the plantation owners in the southern United States. The former were, he argues, "far more anti-Negro than the plantation owners, who were often imbued with patriarchal sentiments."[45] Weber believed that his multiple-class model of class meant that there is no simple relationship between class position and class-consciousness. Importantly, the mere differentiation of class is not dynamic, as conceived by Marx. For Weber, class constitutes a vital objective factor in the formation of consciousness, affecting "life chances" in the market, in a variety of ways; but importantly, economic and class interests are not automatically transposed to "solidaristic" class consciousness.[46]

Weber recognized that class is not purely an economic and market phenomenon. Alongside the objective aspect of social class is a subjective aspect whereby individuals are located hierarchically in society by virtue of status (*Stände*). In Weber's theory, *status situation* refers to differences between social groups in terms of social esteem, or prestige, or honour. In modern society, argues Weber, status came to be expressed through people's style of life. Symbols of status, including formal education, manner of speech, apparel and occupation, all have the effect of shaping an individual's social status in the eyes of others sharing the same culture. Weber defines the notion of status as follows: "In contrast to the purely economically determined 'class situation', we wish to designate as a *status situation* every typical component of life of men that is determined by a specific, positive or negative, social estimation of *honour*."[47]

In practice, suggests Weber, class and status tend to correspond, but he is adamant that this need not necessarily be the case. In multicultural societies a disjuncture between class and status positions may occur in the ethnic status. For instance, a wealthy Asian entrepreneur may well not be situated in the same subjective or status hierarchy as a member of the majority population who, in pure economic terms, has an identical class position. Weber explains the disjuncture between class and status as follows: "Status *may* rest on class position of a distinct or ambiguous kind. However, it is not solely determined by it: Money and an entrepreneurial position are not in themselves status qualifications ... the lack of property is not in itself a status disqualification ... The class position of an officer, a civil servant or a student may vary greatly according to their wealth and yet not lead to a different status since upbringing and education create a common style of life."[48] For Weber, status may vary independently of class position. The term *genteel poverty*[49] refers to the conferment of high status to an individual with little or no economic wealth. A *status group* refers to a plurality of individuals who are socially distinct and exclusive in terms of consumption patterns and lifestyle, and as such, asserts Weber, "the status group comes closest to the social class."[50] He further explains, "With some over-simplification, one might thus say that classes are stratified according to their relations to the production and acquisition of goods; whereas status groups are stratified according to the principles of their *consumption* of goods as represented by special styles of life."[51]

There is a dynamic dimension to social stratification that results from struggles between different classes and status groups in production and markets. Power constitutes an expression of the distribution of interests within society and is an integral dimension of social stratification. Power may be valued for the economic rewards it confers but also for the social status it bestows on itself. For Weber, classes, status groups, and political parties, which represent interests determined either through class or status positions, are "phenomena of the distribution of power within a community."[52] Weber's writings on the complex interplay of class, status, and party offer a foundation for analyzing social stratification. They have had a considerable influence on American sociology, where status and social mobility is central to the "American dream"[53] and where status forms part of the structural functionalist theory of social stratification.

Power, Domination, and Bureaucracy

Bendix explains that Weber, in his sociology of religion gives greater weight to ideology and interests than to the theme of power (*Macht*) and domination (*Herrschaft*), which has also been translated as "authority." This emphasis is reversed in his sociology of politics.[54] At the centre of Weber's political sociology are his theories of power, domination, and the state. He does not define *power* in terms of class economic interests, but in terms of social action as "the chance of a man or a number of men to realize their own will in a social action even against the resistance of others who are participating in the action."[55] He emphasizes that, in this general sense, power is an aspect of virtually all social relationships. Men can exercise power in the family unit, at social events, in public discourse, and in the market. However, the underlying premise of his analysis is that power per se is an insufficient basis for ordering social action. Weber defines *domination* as "the probability that certain specific commands (or all commands) will be obeyed by a given group of persons."[56] Domination, according to Weber, can be legitimate and illegitimate (coercion). Weber was primarily interested in legitimate forms of domination or power, or what he called legitimate authority that allocates the right to command and the duty to obey. He argues that every form of rule attempts to establish and cultivate the belief in its legitimate authority. The starting point for his theories is his three types of legitimate domination: traditional, charismatic, and legal-rational. These typologies are related to Weber's social action, and they are also ideal types as discussed in chapter 9.

Traditional domination is based on the sanction of immemorial traditions and the belief in the legitimacy of those who exercise authority. The pure form of traditional domination is *patriarchy*, literally translated as "rule of the father," which describes domination by male heads of household. Weber suggests that the feudal system of monarch, nobles, and serfs is a form of patriarchal domination. The patrimonial authority will be based on personal loyalty and obligation to the ruler: "The obedience is owed to the *person* of the chief who occupies the traditional sanctioned position of authority and who is (within its sphere) bound by tradition."[57] In such regimes the exercise of power is highly personalized and discretionary in a variety of ways, for instance, by eating at the ruler's table, by rights of land use in return for services, and by fiefs.[58]

Charismatic domination is based on devotion to the exceptional sanctity, heroism, or exemplary character of an individual person, whose authority will typically be theocratic. The English word *charisma* derives from the Greek *kharisma*, meaning "favour" or "grace." Weber defines the term charisma as "a certain quality of an individual personality by virtue of which he is considered extraordinary and treated as endowed with supernatural, superhuman, or at least specially exceptional powers or qualities. These are such as are not accessible to the ordinary person, but are regarded as of divine origin or as exemplary, and on the basis of them the individual concerned is treated as a 'leader.'"[59] Weber believes that charisma involves four related elements: an individual of exceptional powers or qualities, a social crisis, a radical solution to the crisis offered by the individual, and devoted followers. Ancient and modern history offers many examples of charismatic power. Thus, presumably, the disciples obeyed Jesus Christ because he possessed charisma; leaders such as Mahatma Gandhi in India and Ayatollah Khomeini in Iran were also charismatic. Weber posits that charismatic power, unlike traditional domination, is a powerful force for social change, which abandons traditional rules: "Charismatic belief revolutionizes men 'from within' and shapes material and social conditions according to its revolutionary will," writes Weber.[60]

Winston Churchill and, more recently, Margaret Thatcher provide alternative examples of charismatic domination. Based on Marx's analysis of Napoleon Bonaparte's coup, Durkheim's notion of collective effervescence, and Weber's insistence that charismatic leaders emerge only during periods of a crisis or "moments of distress"[61] an alternative understanding of charismatic power emerges as a quality conferred on a "supernatural" leader by virtue of particular situations and crises, rather than as a quality of individual traits.[62] Thus, in 1940 following the evacuation of the British Expeditionary Force at Dunkirk, the British Prime Minister Winston Churchill demonstrated charisma. In the United States, writes the Canadian historian Margaret Macmillan, "the cult of Winston Churchill" evokes his stirring speeches—"Britain shall never surrender"[63]—in his stand against appeasement with the charismatic, demonic Adolf Hitler. But Churchill's charisma melted away like fresh snow in late spring. In 1945 the Labour Party in the general election defeated Churchill's conservative government. In Britain, Churchill is also remembered as a politician who had his share of failures and his controversial views: as architect of the disastrous Gallipoli campaign in 1915; for his rabid anti-union views, for example when he advocated a "shoot them down" policy towards strikers during the labour unrest of 1910–14;[64] for his strongly imperialist position; and for his notorious comment about Mahatma Gandhi, "this malignant subversive fanatic."[65] In the 1980s it appeared that Margaret Thatcher also possessed charismatic powers during the Malvinas (Falklands) War with Argentina, and this view was later reinforced, for some, with her government's victory in the coal miners' strike of March 1984 to March 1985. A twist in Weber's thinking is his argument that the influence of a situation may lie not in the presence of a moment of crisis but in its *absence*. The absence of crisis, uncertainty, and fear, argues British academic Keith Grint, may generate a need on the part of some people for an exciting alternative to the routine boredom of everyday life.[66] Importantly, charismatic power is conferred upon a leader by his or her followers, but it can also be retracted. Weber devotes time to discussing how charismatic power, in its pure form, is foreign to the routines of everyday life and involves the "routinization of charisma."[67] Once a crisis has passed, charismatic leaders must transform themselves back into everyday life, but in so doing, their power or qualities begin to fade. Charisma will, therefore, tend to develop into either traditional or legal-rational domination.

Joan of Arc (1412–1430) is a national heroine of France. She led the French army to several major victories during the Hundred Years' War. She is a good example of Weber's charismatic authority.

Legal-rational domination refers to "a belief in the legality of enacted rules and the right of those elevated to authority under such rules to issue commands (legal authority)."[68] In modern democratic political systems, obedience is owed to the legally established impersonal laws. The *pure* type of legal-rational domination rests on the acceptance of the validity of several mutually interdependent ideas: the legal norms are established by agreement or by imposition on grounds of expediency or value-rationality or both; every body of law is part of a consistent system of abstract rules; the leader is subject to the same body of law; the followers obey in their capacity as a member of a community, organization, or state; and followers obey only what is the law.[69]

Legal-rational domination may take several structural forms, but generations of sociology students have come to know this type of power through Weber's ideal-type bureaucracy. For Weber, bureaucratic administrations are "the purest type of exercise of legal authority."[70] Under a formal legal system, a bureaucracy is both a *form* of domination and a way of describing the *location* of domination. A bureaucracy is governed by the following key principles: official conduct is bound by written *rules*; it is structured in a clearly defined *hierarchy* in which lower offices are controlled by higher ones; each office holder has a clearly defined sphere of *competence*; each member is appointed, not elected, on the basis of technical *qualifications*, and promotion is based on seniority or merit as deemed by the judgment of superiors; members are compensated by fixed *salaries* in money; and *ownership* of the means of production or service is separate from the office holder. As we noted in the preceding chapter, a bureaucracy is an example of an ideal type, and Weber depicts bureaucratic administrations in such terms:

> The purely bureaucratic type of administrative organizations is ... capable of attaining the highest degree of efficiency and is in this sense formally the most rational known means of exercising authority over human beings. It is superior to any other in precision, in stability, in the stringency of its discipline, and in its reliability. It thus makes possible a particularly high degree of calculability of results for the heads of the organization and for those acting in relation to it. It is finally superior both in intensive efficiency and in the scope of its operations, and is formally capable of application to all kinds of administrative tasks.[71]

The increasing spread of bureaucracy in modern capitalist societies may be explained by the systematic rationalization of economic and social life. As Weber observes, "The decisive reason for the advance of bureaucratic organization has always been its purely *technical* superiority over any other form of organization. The fully developed bureaucratic apparatus compares with other organizations exactly as does the machine with the non-mechanical modes of production. Precision, speed, unambiguity, knowledge of the files, continuity, discretion, unity, strict subordination, reduction of friction and of material and personal costs—these are raised to the optimum point in the strictly bureaucratic administration, and especially in its monocratic form."[72]

Weber viewed the power exercised through modern bureaucracies with some apprehension and he discusses at length the potential negative aspects of bureaucracies. He states that the more perfectly bureaucracy is developed, "the more it is dehumanized,"[73] as it "reduces every worker to a cog in this [bureaucratic] machine and, seeing himself in this light, he will merely ask how to transform himself from a little into a somewhat bigger cog."[74] He believed that once such bureaucratic structures are established, the calculus of self-interest within the system of legal-rational domination "is practically indestructible."[75] The individual bureaucrat cannot squirm out of the specialized activity and is only a small cog in the total organizational machine. The masses, for their part, cannot abolish the bureaucratic apparatus once it exists, for it is predicated upon an attitude set on habitual, expert, knowledge and expertise, and thus the idea of dismantling this apparatus becomes more utopian. Bureaucratic regimes were a threat to individual initiative because of the irresistible force of "rational discipline," which amounts to nothing less than consistently rationalized, methodically prepared, and exact execution of the received order. Mired in with bureaucratic regimes, personal autonomy and creativity is suspended, and, argues Weber, the mandarin is unswervingly and exclusively set for carrying out commands. Likely under the influence of Nietzsche, Weber assigns substantial weight to charismatic leaders as an antidote to the anti-democratic ethos of bureaucracies.[76] And Weber's writings reveal a symmetry in his thinking if his pure types of domination are placed alongside his typology of social action: traditional action/traditional authority; affectual action/charismatic authority; and instrument-rational/legal rational authority.[77]

A feature of modernity is bureaucratic organizations. Weber's "'ideal-type" bureaucracy has an hierarchical structure of authority in which specialized members fulfill specialized responsibilities according to codified rules. An ideal type is a model of a social phenomenon that extracts its essential elements if it existed in impossibly "pure" form.

Criticism

Almost every aspect of the Weber's Protestant asceticism thesis has been subject to criticism by economic historians and sociologists.[78] Weber was well-informed regarding Marx's materialist conception of history, and he believed that Marx's major analytical concepts were "extraordinarily fruitful." Weber seems to repudiate the importance of economic processes and assigns primacy to ideologies in governing human action. This interpretation leads to the criticism that Weber illegitimately replaced Marx's materialist thesis with an idealistic one. Weber explicitly denies this: "It cannot be our purpose," writes Weber, "to replace a one-sided 'materialist' causal interpretation of culture and history with an equally one-sided spiritual one."[79] This has not stopped Marxist sociologists criticizing Weber for his apparently subjectivist and individualist perspective to social change.[80]

A second criticism is that Weber neglected the fact that capitalism predates Calvinism. Evidence that capitalism took shape well before the 1780s, and before the influence of Calvinism began, is part of a postmodernist debate that disputes whether or not the British Industrial Revolution occurred, or if it is in fact a myth. The British historian Eric Hobsbawm, who wrote *On History*, comments: "It has become fashionable ... to deny that objective reality is accessible ... I believe that without the distinction between what is and what is not so, there can be no history."[81] Weber's account of the connection between Calvinism and capitalism does not obviate the pre-existence of capitalism in the early-modern period. By 1850, however, there was abundant evidence of rational capitalism on an unprecedented scale that counts as an Industrial Revolution and, for Weber, Calvinism did *not* cause capitalism, but it did help shape the qualitative formation and the quantitative growth of the social revolution. Weber's account of the trajectory of modernity is Eurocentric and excludes most women and non-whites from the "community of moderns."[82]

A third criticism of Weber is that he viewed charismatic leaders purely positively and disregarded despotism.[83] As we have pointed out Weber assigned considerable weight to the role of "superhuman" individuals in history. He believed that charisma could be an antidote to the inexorable advance of bureaucracy. Weber was personally committed to authoritarian citizenship, and his view of German politics is definitely elitist, which sits somewhat uncomfortably with his commitment to Western liberal tradition.[84] While Weber considered the unrestrained will of the German working classes and their demands for equality posed a threat to Western liberal democracy, by contrast, he "regarded as comparatively negligible the danger that the rule of the *Führer*, legitimized through personal plebiscite, could turn into a dictatorial (or even fascist) regime."[85] Undoubtedly, Weber's theory of charismatic political leaders reveals the pending threat to liberal democracy from the rise of German fascism in the 1930s, headed by the charismatic in demonic form, Adolf Hitler. Given that Weber was well aware of the political weakness of the German middle class, it is incomprehensible "why he failed to anticipate the possibility of an anti-liberal fusion of the charismatic and bureaucratic principles."[86]

A fourth criticism of Weber's analysis of capitalism is linked to his deterministic iron cage thesis, particularly its incessant pessimism. While Weber and Marx's views are grounded in a similar philosophical anthropology, Weber, as we have seen, was pessimistic about the effects of domination on human liberation and the likelihood of escape from the iron cage. Weber never recognized the human agency to exploit *inherent* potential within capitalism and to shape alternatives. Marx, on the other hand, was optimistic about the opportunity for liberation. The difference in their views has been summed up succinctly: "Marx proposes a therapy while Weber has only a diagnosis to offer."[87] These contrasting views of Weber and Marx might help us to understand why Marx, not Weber, still has a following in the liberation movement. The reappraisal of Weber's work, however, points to the possibility of taking advantage of "rusting iron cages" and the potential for "breaking vicious circles" within the dynamics of late modernity.[88]

Conclusion

Along with the controversy over "value freedom" in research, the *Protestant Ethic* debate has been one of the longest-standing disputes in modern sociology.[89] According to Weber, ascetic Protestantism accelerated the process of rationalization and this, in turn, affected the trajectory of modernity. In contrast to Marx, Weber's narrative of development avers that the development of Western capitalism cannot be explained through wholly material and structural forces: it was embedded in the interconnected process of rationalization. The concept of "elective affinity" (*Wahlverwandtschaft*) is an analytical tool used by Weber for interpreting human history.[90] According to Weber, there is an elective affinity between ascetic Protestantism and the capitalist spirit. Similarly, there is an active relationship or elective affinity between rational capitalism and rationally designed bureaucracies.

Weber's thesis on rationalization informs his theories of social class, politics, and bureaucracies. Weber believed that class divisions derive not only from control of the means of production and property but also from access to resources such as training and education, which affect an individual's position in the labour market and, in turn, strongly influences overall life chances. Weber and Marx's approaches have been combined into an influential theory of class by the American sociologist Erik Olin Wright[91] At the centre of Weber's political sociology are his theories of power, domination, and the state. He focuses on legitimate forms of power or what he calls legitimate authority, which allocates the right to command and the duty to obey. For Weber, bureaucracies are the purest form of legal-rational authority.[92]

In *The Protestant Ethic*, Weber pessimistically warns of the tendency of people in the modern world to experience an iron cage. His stark image of modernity is that of individual autonomy being suffocated by the pervasive process of rationalization in all spheres of modern life. Informed by nineteenth-century scholars, such as Alexis de Tocqueville, and by his intellectual contemporary Simmel, the iron cage, metaphor features prominently in his analysis of bureaucracy and is one of the most influential metaphors among the general critiques of modernity. The process of rationalization is unremittingly paradoxical. In Weber's words, "No machinery in the world functions so precisely as this apparatus of men and, moreover, so cheaply ... Rational calculation ... reduces every worker to a cog in this [bureaucratic] machine and, seeing himself in this light, he will merely ask how to transform himself from a little into a somewhat bigger cog ... an attitude you find, just as in the Egyptian *papyri*, increasingly among our civil servants and especially their successors, our students. The passion for bureaucratization drives us to despair."[93]

Weber's dire warnings of creeping rationalization in all dimensions of Western culture have inspired artists and sociologists alike. In literature, Huxley's *Brave New World*, George Orwell's *1984*, and Margaret Atwood's *Handmaid's Tale* are examples of popular expressions of ubiquitous bureaucratization. In the early twenty-first century Weber's theories are relevant and continue to inform sociologists. For example, George Ritzer was inspired by Weber's work to formulate the "McDonaldization" of local and global social relations.[94] Arguably, McDonaldization exemplifies global capitalism, postmodern superficiality, and a world in which "the sincere express of emotion and affect have been all but eliminated."[95] Weber's rationalization and bureaucratization theories also resonate with Naomi Klein's notion of "McMilitary," specifically, the danger to civil liberties that results from the outsourcing of massive state surveillance by increasingly authoritarian regimes, and is fully justified by the War on Terror.[96] Finally, contemporary sociologists draw on Weber's ideas to make the argument that ecological problems cannot be understood without making the ideological connections between Christianity, Western rationalism, and environmental domination. The work of Ulrich Beck and others, for example, represent a renaissance of Weberian historical sociology.[97] This intellectual genre recognizably draws upon the tradition founded by Weber in arguing that global capitalism and contemporary social change are caused by the interaction of several irreducibly distinct forms of power and domination.[98]

Notes

1 Bryan S. Turner, *Max Weber: From History to Modernity* (London: Routledge, 1992), vii.

2 S. Eliaeson, *Max Weber's Methodologies* (Cambridge: Polity Press, 2002), 3.

3 Alex Callinicos, *Social Theory*, 2nd ed. (Cambridge: Polity Press, 2007), 178.

4 K. Tribe, *Reading Weber* (London: Routledge, 1989); B.S. Turner, *For Weber* (London: Sage, 1996).

5 R. Bendix, *Max Weber: An Intellectual Portrait* (New York: Anchor Books, 1962), 9.

6 Max Weber, *Sociology of Religion* (Boston: Beacon Press, 1963).

7 The thesis that rationality and rationalization is the key to Weber's work is associated with Reinhard Bendix's early work, *Max Weber: An Intellectual Portrait* (New York: Anchor Books, 1962), and F. Tenbruck "The Problem of Thematic Unity in the Works of Max Weber," *British Journal of Sociology* 31, no. 3 (1980): 316–51. For an alternative reading of Weber, see Wilhelm Hennis, "Max Weber's Central Question," *Economy and Society* 12, no. 2 (1983): 136–80, and for an extended discussion on the merits of the argument see Turner, *Max Weber.*

8 Julien Freund, *The Sociology of Max Weber*, trans. M. Ilford (New York: Random House, 1968), 18, and quoted by A. Sica, "Rationalization and Culture," in *The Cambridge Companion to Weber*, ed. Stephen. Turner (Cambridge: Cambridge University Press, 2000), 48.

9 Stewart R. Clegg, "Max Weber and Contemporary Sociology of Organizations," in eds. L.J. Ray and M. Reed, *Organizing Modernity* (London: Routledge, 1994), 46–80.

10 Sica, "'Rationalization and Culture," 42–58.

11 Max Weber, *Economy and Society*, vol. 2, (Berkeley, CA: University of California Press, 1978), 656–7.

12 Henry Ford, quoted in H. Beynon *Working for Ford* (Harmondsworth: Penguin, 1984), 33.

13 Ken Morrison, *Marx, Durkheim, Weber* (London: Sage, 2006), 285.

14 Max Weber, *Economy and Society*, vol. 1, eds. G. Roth and C. Wittich, (Berkeley, CA: University of California Press, 1978), 406.

15 Ian Craib, *Classical Social Theory* (Oxford: Oxford University Press, 1997).

16 J. Love, "Max Weber's Ancient Judaism," in *The Cambridge Companion to Weber*, Stephen Turner, 200–20.

17 Max Weber, *The Protestant Ethic and the Spirit of Capitalism* (New York: Penguin, 2002), 121–22.

18 Ibid., 3.

19 Ibid., 4.

20 Ibid.

21 Ibid., 5.

22 Ibid.

23 I. M. Zeitlin, *Ideology and the Development of Sociological Theory* (Upper Saddle River, NJ: Prentice-Hall, 2001).

24 Max Weber, *The Protestant Ethic*, 9–10.

25 Ibid., 12.

26 Ian Craib, *Classical Social Theory*, 251.

27 See the Bible: Matthew 19: 23–24; Mark 10: 24–25; and Luke 18: 24–25; and the teachings of Saint John the Baptist.

28 Max Weber, *The Protestant Ethic*, 77–8.

29 J. Love, "Max Weber's Ancient Judaism," 199.

30 Max Weber, *The Protestant Ethic*, 117.

31 Ibid., 119.

32 Ibid., 120–1.

33 Max Weber, *General Economic History*, trans. F. H. Knight (1927; New York: Dover, 2003), 277.

34 Max Weber, *Economy and Society*, vol. 1, 305.

35 Ibid., 303.

36 Ibid., 302.

37 Weber, *Economy and Society*, vol. 2, 927.

38 Robert Tucker, ed., *The Marx-Engels Reader* (New York: Norton & Company, 1978), 441.

39 Weber, *Economy and Society*, vol. 1, 305.

40 Tucker, *The Marx-Engels Reader*, 482.

41 Weber, *Economy and Society*, vol. 2, 1400.

42 E. J. Hobsbawm, *The Age of Extremes, 1914–1991*, (London: Abacus, 1995), 45.

43 Weber, *Economy and Society*, vol. 1, 302.

44 Ibid., 303–4.

45 Ibid., 304.

46 Alan Swingewood, *A Short History of Sociological Thought* (New York: St. Marin's Press, 2000).

47 Weber, *Economy and Society*, vol. 2, 932.

48 Weber *Economy and Society*, vol. 1, 306.

49 The term is used by Anthony Giddens, *Sociology* (Cambridge: Polity Press, 2009).

50 Weber, *Economy and Society*, vol. 1, 306–7.

51 Weber, *Economy and Society*, vol. 2, 937.

52 Ibid., 937.

53 For an interesting perspective on the so-called American Dream as it applies to the sociology of work, see David E. Guest, "Human Resource Management and the American Dream," *Journal of Management Studies* 27, no. 4 (1990): 377–97.

54 R. Bendix, *Max Weber: An Intellectual Portrait* (New York: Anchor Books, 1962), 290.

55 Weber, *Economy and Society*, vol. 2, 926.

56 Weber, *Economy and Society*, vol. 1, 212.

57 Ibid., 216.

58 Ibid., 235–41.

59 Ibid., 241.

60 Weber, *Economy and Society*, vol. 2, 1116.

61 Ibid., 1111.

62 Craib, *Classical Social Theory.*

63 Margaret Macmillan, *The Uses and Abuses of History* (Toronto: Penguin, 2008).

64 Alan Hutt, *British Trade Unionism* (London: Lawrence & Wishart, 1975), 60.

65 A. Herman, *Gandhi and Churchill* (New York: Random House, 2008), 359.

66 J. Bratton, K. Grint and D. Nelson, *Organizational Leadership* (Mason, OH: Southwestern, 2005).

67 Weber, *Economy and Society*, vol. 1, 246–54.

68 Ibid., 215.

69 Ibid., 217–20.

70 Ibid., 220.

71 Ibid., 223.

72 Weber, *Economy and Society*, vol. 2, 973.

73 Ibid., 975.

74 Weber, *Economy and Society* vol. 1, lix.

75 Weber, *Economy and Society*, vol. 2, 987.

76 Zeitlin, *Ideology and the Development of Sociological Theory.*

77 Ray, *Theorizing Classical Sociology.*

78 Ibid.

79 Weber, *The Protestant Ethic*, 122.

80 See "Weber and Late Capitalism," in B.S. Turner, *For Weber* (London: Sage, 1996), 352–68.

81 E.J. Hobsbawm, *On History,* (London: Weidenfeld & Nicholson, 1997), viii.

82 L. Ray and M. Reed, eds., *Organizing Modernity* (London: Routledge, 1994).

83 Zeitlin, *Ideology and the Development of Sociological Theory.*

84 See Ray and Reed, *Organizing Modernity*; Callinicos, *Social Theory.*

85 W. Mommsen, *The Political and Social Theory of Max Weber* (Cambridge: Polity Press, 1989), 34, and quoted in Zeitlin, *Ideology and the Development of Sociological Theory*, 238.

86 Zeitlin, *Ideology and the Development of Sociological Theory*, 238.

87 Turner, *Classical Sociology*, 52.

88 Ray and Reed, *Organizing Modernity.*

89 Ibid.

90 Callinicos, *Social Theory*, 163.

91 See E.O. Wright, *Classes* (London: Verso, 1985); E.O. Wright, *Class Counts: Comparative Studies in Class Analysis* (Cambridge: Cambridge University Press, 1997).

92 See Paul du Gay, *In Praise of Bureaucracy* (London: Sage, 2000) for an alternative view of the conventional critique of bureaucracy.

93 Weber, *Economy and Society*, vol. 1, lix.

94 See G. Ritzer, *The McDonalization of Society* (Thousand Oaks, CA: Pine Forge Press, 2000).

95 Ibid., 186–7.

96 See Naomi Klein, "Shock Therapy in the U.S.A.," in *The Shock Doctrine* (Toronto: Alfred A. Knopf Canada, 2007), 341–69.

97 Callinicos, *Social Theory.*

98 See U. Beck, *What Is Globalization?* (Cambridge: Polity Press,1999); U. Beck, "Living Your Own Life in a Runaway World: Individualism, Globalization and Politics," in *On the Edge: Living with Global Capitalism*, eds. Will Hutton and Anthony Giddens (London: Jonathan Cape, 2000), 164–74; Anthony Giddens, *The Consequences of Modernity* (Cambridge: Polity Press, 1990); and M. Rustin "Incomplete Modernity: Ulrich Beck's Risk Society," *Radical Philosophy* 67 (1994) 3–12.

PART III

EXPANDING THE CANON

11. Georg Simmel on Modernity

> The deepest problems of modern life derive from the claim of the individual to preserve the autonomy and individuality of his existence in the face of overwhelming social forces, of historical heritage, of external culture, and of the technique of life.
>
> —Georg Simmel[1]

> Behind Simmel's whole work there stands not the ethical but the aesthetic ideal.
>
> —R. Goldscheid

THIS CHAPTER EXTENDS THE CLASSICAL sociological canon of understanding society based on the notions of materiality, morality, and rationality (see figure 0.1) to an approach that aims to make the social intelligible, in terms of cultural dynamics, through the writings of Georg Simmel. In the writings of Emile Durkheim and Max Weber the subject matter of sociology is explicitly addressed. In the case of Georg Simmel, sociology represents only one of his several fields of intellectual interest. Indeed, Simmel seeks to understand modernity, particularly life in the large city or metropolis, from a perspective that is more philosophical than sociological.

Born in Berlin, Simmel was an intellectual contemporary of highly recognized thinkers, including his colleague Ferdinand Tönnies (1855–1936) and George Herbert Mead (1863–1931). Simmel regarded society as a myriad web of complex interactions and social relations between individuals. As a social theorist, he is attentive to the seemingly unimportant nuances of everyday urban life, such as linguistic practices, human interaction in small groups, and the cultural implications of body language. An unorthodox sociologist, David Frisby, posits that "no sociologist before him had sought to capture the modes of experiencing modern life nor the fleeting moments of interaction. Simmel's sociological texts are richly populated with fortuitous fragments of reality, with seemingly superficial phenomena, with a myriad of social vignettes."[2] Stemming from his interest in Kant, Simmel was interested in how human beings impose forms on the world of experience and make sense of the world, and how modernity impacts on the possibilities of human self-actualization.[3] In the late twentieth century, Simmel was described as the "first sociologist of modernity,"[4] ironically, just as some of his ideas led others to label him as a precursor of postmodern sociology.[5] His sociology is diverse, multi-faceted, and cross-disciplinary. In this chapter we will review some of his central concepts and, in particular, his work on the geometry of social life, social forms types, the metropolis, money, and alienation.

His Life and Works

Georg Simmel was born in 1858 near the centre of the vibrant city of Berlin. Although both of Simmel's parents were baptized Christians, their origins were Jewish, and he experienced anti-Semitism. After his father's death, a wealthy businessman adopted him and left him a substantial inheritance; so his academic earnings were relatively unimportant to him. He completed his doctoral studies in philosophy at the University of Berlin. His analysis of modernity was unorthodox, and he was considered an outsider in the academy, not gaining a full-time professorship until 1914 at the University of Strasbourg. Simmel died of cancer in 1918. In addition to the openly expressed anti-Semitism, Simmel's slow progress in the academy was partly due to his unconventional approach to academic work and his disregard of academic etiquette.[6] He had an undocumented way of writing and a showman's style of lecturing,[7] and he has been described as an "unsystematic theorist."[8] Many of his topics seemed unimportant relative to the grand sweep of historical-comparative research favoured in German university circles. Few of his contemporaries agreed with him that "perhaps the most neglected of all the great vital issues has been love."[9] Louis Coser, who owed a great deal to Simmel, described him as "an intellectual coquette, engaged in a high form of literary play, which is primarily intended not to instruct or enlighten but to exercise that seductive charm and fascination he describes in the essay on flirtation."[10] Despite this, or even because of this, Simmel attained international recognition as a brilliant scholar, and his lectures were popular with students and the cultural elites of Berlin. He stood at the intersection of many intellectual circles, addressed himself to a variety of audiences, and enjoyed the freedom of belonging to many groups but being held by none. His home was a regular meeting place for a select society of artists, writers, and intellectuals, including the anti-modernist poet Stefan George, the sociologist Max Weber, and Weber's Marianne.[11]

Simmel produced more than thirty books, innumerable scholarly papers, and newspaper opinion pieces. These include *On Social Differentiation* (1890), *The Philosophy of Money* (1900), the essay "The Metropolis and Mental Life" (1902–03), *Sociology* (1908), and *Fundamental Questions of Sociology* (1917). His topics include the tragedy of culture, public policies, and the position of women in society. Much of his work is focused on formal sociology, a kind of spatial geometry of social relations that emphasizes social distance and also a kind of mathematical treatment of the effect of number on social forms. He writes about social types that emerge in interaction, such as the stranger, the adventurer, the renegade, the man in the middle, and the pauper. The most influential of his writings are *The Philosophy of Money*, and the closely related essay "The Metropolis." All of his works deal with the struggle of individual subjectivity—the individual personality—to integrate, master, and transcend the objective and objectifying culture of modern society.

Intellectual Influences

Georg Simmel was born in the city of Berlin, Germany, in 1858. His analysis of modernity was unorthodox, and he was considered an "outsider" in the academy and described as an "unsystematic theorist." Simmel produced more than thirty books. He died of cancer in 1918.

Simmel studied with leading scholars in the fields of science, music, history, psychology, and philosophy. His writings particularly reflect the paradigms of the philosophers Kant, Hegel, and Nietzsche. Neo-Kantianism influenced his conception of the human mind as active, rather than as a passive object. Simmel goes beyond Kant in searching for specifically *sociological* meanings and for sociological first principles or *apriorities*.[12] In Simmel's terms, the fundamental social *apriority* is the life force. The social is emergent when human beings respond to the demands of their inner life force. He writes, "Neither hunger nor love ... as they are given immediately and in their strict sense, signify socialization. On the contrary, they constitute it only when they shape the isolated side-by-sideness of the individuals into definite forms of with-and-for-one-another, which belong under the general concept reciprocity."[13]

He also developed a micro-sociological version of Hegel's dialectic. For Simmel, dialectical change occurs as social phenomena or thoughts develop until what is *other* in them is revealed. At this point, the other challenges its origin until a new synthesis is produced, which will, in turn, be transcended. This dialectic, unlike Hegel or Marx's, allows for many sources of interaction and an indeterminate outcome. In this, it is more like chaos theory, or the postmodern ideas of Michel Foucault, rather than like the theories of Marx, Weber, or Durkheim. Another important intellectual influence on Simmel's social theory is the German philosopher Friedrich Nietzsche. Like Nietzsche, Simmel celebrates the ambiguity and diversity of human life and acknowledges the limits of rationality on society and human behaviour. By showing that an aesthetic sensibility and a fluid, erratic, self are primary features of urban life, Simmel extends Nietzsche's arguments and offers a far more nuanced theory of modernity. Like Weber, Tönnies, Marx, and Durkheim, Simmel recognizes the emergence of the division of labour, its accompanying economic and social differentiation, and the development of secondary relationships such as those found in bureaucracies. While Weber discusses the "dead hand" of bureaucracy and Marx sees capitalism as leading to alienation and revolution, Simmel goes beyond Marx's idea of the fetishism of economic commodities into an examination of broader cultural objectification (a fetishism of objective culture). He resists the Marxist idea of a final utopian synthesis. All of Simmel's work is related in some manner to the dialectical tension between the individual and the group. For Simmel this outlined the dimensions of the human struggle for freedom, individuality, and spirituality.

Simmel's Method and Sociology

According to Simmel's unique view of sociology, the discipline "contains no subject matter not already treated in one of the existing sciences." Sociology "only proposes a new *way* for all of them"—a way that involves a process of abstraction similar to induction. He argues, "Sociology rests its whole right of existence as a separate science upon this abstraction of the forms of society, just as mathematics rests upon an abstraction of the mere spatial forms from material things ... The subject-matter of sociology is, therefore, the forms or ways in which human beings exist beside, for, and with each other."[14] Simmel isolates two dimensions of sociological investigation: the longitudinal and the cross-sectional. The first dimension, he writes, "follows the longitudinal direction of a particular evolution." In second place, it provides "a cross-sectional view of such evolutions, which ... lays bare by induction that which is common to them all, the social forms, as such."[15] The central task is to isolate social forms from the on-rush of impressions and details. His conception of society is strongly influenced by his fears of "solidification," or "ossification," or "cultural alienation."[16]

Simmel's unsystematic sociological methodology is akin to induction theorizing. He would present each object (form, content, type) in terms of its social element, then assess this in a kind of sociological deconstruction that removed distracting details and left only the elements of form: inside-outside, superordination-subordination, and boundary-bridge. His style of abstracting many facets rooted in social reciprocities meant that his audience was constantly surprised and amazed. It is not an easy methodology to practice or to teach. In this, Simmel's approach contrasts with the proto-sociologists of the day. He was not a paradigm builder, in the way of August Comte, or a theorist with a grand narrative that envisioned revolution, in the way of Marx. He was not interested, as were historians, in the minute description of the contents and order of unique events. And although he felt that sociology was to be distinguished by its practice rather than its content, he was not a sociological methodologist. His one quantitative empirical study, very early in his career, involved a survey of yodelers.[17] In contrast to Durkheim, he regarded statistics as "purely parallel phenomena," rather than evidence of social facts. Simmel writes, "We ... confuse statistical similarities and synchronisms of a purely individual nature, with those which can be referred back to the real principle of society [which is] the reciprocity of cause."[18] Simmel's disorderly approach to theorizing the social can be seen as an attempt to safeguard his autonomy: "For Simmel, any method imposed on a member by a scientific community binds that member and restricts his ability to articulate his individuality."[19]

Simmel's thinking was both vitalistic and dialectical. *Vitalism* in this context holds that when something exists, it becomes self-emergent. The acorn contains within it the oak tree. Human beings contain within them the potential for sociality. Even apparently inanimate objects, such as a ruined building, may transcend nature while submitting to nature. He observes that the ruin of a building is "the realization of a tendency inherent in the deepest layer of existence of the destroyed."[20] Thus, for Simmel, the environment, including nature, art, and existing social forms, is not passive and inert, and not simply "constructed" by human action. It has a latent potential to develop according to forces within it. In his time, theory was divided about whether society was real and organic (sociological realism) or, conversely, an unreal abstraction (sociological nominalism), since only individuals are real. Both Marx and Durkheim believed that society is real and exists *sui generis*: the view of society as an emergent level of reality that is analytically independent from individuals and, therefore, subject to processes that can be understood only with reference to other social forces. Simmel argued that neither society nor the individual could constitute itself. Each requires the other for *sociation* to occur. Society is neither an organism, as claimed by Comte, Durkheim, and Spenser, nor a (ideal) mental construction; it has a real existence in the web of reciprocal effects (interactions) among people and between people and their environment.

Central to Simmel's sociological work are four core concepts: form, reciprocity (*Wechselwirkung*), distance, and dualism. The concept of *form* refers to those aspects of human life that compel individuals into associations (sociation) with each other: people's needs, drives, and goals. The most concrete forms are social relationships; the most abstract is society itself. For Simmel, society is emergent when individuals, prompted by life-force drives or wants, engage in reciprocal interaction. In Simmel's words, "This interaction always arises on the basis of certain drives or for the sake of certain purposes. Erotic, religious or merely associative impulses; and purposes of defense, attack, play, gain, aid or instruction—These and countless others cause man to live with other men, to act for them, with them, against them and thus to correlate his condition with theirs."[21]Social relationships always contain the capacity for creativity, innovation, and change. Simmel writes, "Sociation is the form (realized in innumerably different ways) in which individuals grow together into unity and within which their interests are realized. And it is on the basis of their interests ... that individuals form such unities."[22] Simmel's second core concept is *reciprocity*, which is often translated as interaction, but is more accurately translated as "reciprocal effects." With this concept Simmel recognizes that each social phenomenon has meaning only through its relationships with others. Reciprocal effects can be ephemeral and relatively inconsequential, or they can be longer lasting and give rise to social forms. For Simmel, society is neither an organism—*sociological realism*—nor an idea—*sociological idealism*. Society has an empirically real existence in the web of reciprocal ideas and reciprocal effects. Thus, he states, "Our situations develop themselves upon the basis of a reciprocal knowledge of each other, and this knowledge upon the basis of actual situations ... [This is] one of the points at which reality and idea make their mysterious unity empirically perceptible."[23] The third concept, *distance*, means that the properties of form and meanings are relative to the distances between individuals or things. Finally, modernity can be understood by the concept of *dualism*, which might involve conflicts between opposite categories. These four core concepts serve to connect the disparate nature of Simmel's analyses of modernity.

FIGURE 11.1 Incremental effects of group size on relationships

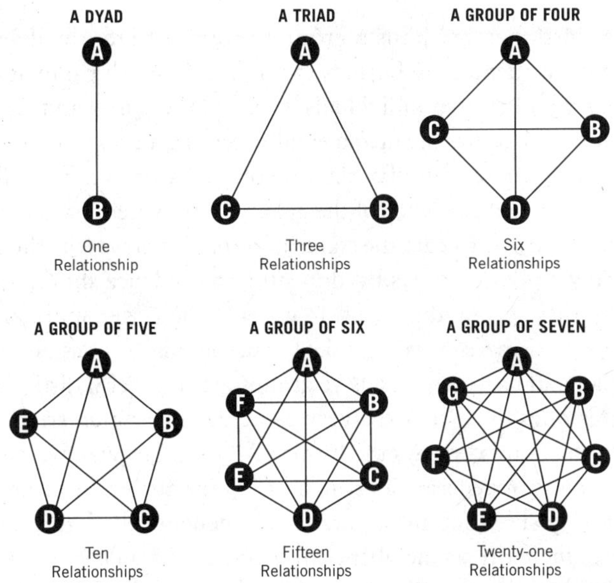

For Simmel, the size of a group influences how group members interact with one another. Adding to the group alters the group dynamics, since the increased number of relationships results in different configurations of interactions. While two individuals form a single relationship, a group of five has ten relationships.

Social Geometry and Group Size

Simmel described sociology as the geometry of social life. Geometry, he argued, "has the advantage of having at its disposal extremely simple structures into which it can resolve the more complicated figures." Thus it "can construe the whole range of possible formations from a relatively few fundamental definitions."[24] Simmel was particularly interested in the effects of increasing or decreasing numbers on the structure of social groups: "A group of a certain extent and beyond a certain stage in its increase of numbers must develop for its maintenance certain forms and organization which it did not previously need ... on the other hand, more restricted groups manifest qualities and reciprocal activities which, in the case of their numerical extension, inevitably disappear."[25]

The dyad, a relationship of two; the triad, a relationship among three; and the mass, a relationship among many, are examples of forms in which group size affects the organization of the group and the kind of relationships that are possible within it. The romantic relationship, or best-friend relationship, is typically a dyad.[26] Each member experiences reciprocal effects with one other person only. The dyad might appear to be a cohesive form to outsiders, but the relationship evaporates if one person leaves.

When a third member joins a group to form a triad, the dynamics change: one new member (C) brings two new relationships: in addition to the interaction between individuals A and B, there is A and C, and B and C. Figure 11.1 shows the incremental effect of group size on relationships. The third person can play the role of mediator in any conflict to protect the continued existence of the group, be outvoted, or manipulate the other two in order to gain the status of *tertius gaudens* (the third who enjoys).[27] Any reader who has lived in student residence should be able to recognize these group dynamics. In general, the larger, more broadly based groups are less easily extinguished than the smaller ones. As Simmel states, "Small and narrowly exclusive groups are in general distinguished from greater ones in … that the very same destiny which strengthens and renews the latter destroys the former. A disastrous war, which ruins a petty state, may regenerate a great state."[28] Simmel's treatment of the effects of group size contains a paradox. In general, the larger the size of the group, the more its members can become dissimilar to each other, and more independence and intellectual development can take place. This does not happen, however, when the form is that of the crowd or the mass. Here, the larger the group, the lower the intellectual and moral level of those who compose it; they share only what they have in common, and a cool intelligence is not what men hold in common. Thus, Simmel argues that the individual in the crowd is swallowed up rather than made free or responsible: "It is one of the most instructive, purely sociological phenomena: that individuals feel the surrounding 'voice' of the mass as an external force that takes them in, irrespective of their own individual being and will. And yet this mass consists, in the end, of such individuals. Their basic mutual influence unfolds a dynamic through which their size appears as something objective that hides each individual contribution. In fact, he is carried away in that he is carried away."[29]

Sociation and Conflict

The basic problem of sociology, Simmel believed, was to identify pure forms of sociation. Some interactions occur frequently enough that, when we ignore what is unique about them, we can understand them as relatively stable configurations of forms and types. Each of these can be analyzed in order to reveal the common element of sociation. Here we can only select a few of Simmel's topics, such as the adventure and social conflict, in order to demonstrate his procedures.

The adventure can involve physical activity, such as a hike, or mental activity, such as the investigation of a topic, or it can be the emotional adventure of love. Adventure originates in a bounded set of experiences that are discontinuous with the structure and motives of daily existence. Adventure carries an attractive danger and risk. Love can be a kind of adventure, but only for men, because women's love "usually falls into other categories."[30] The adventure exists only for youth, as "the adventure does not belong to the life-style of old age." Simmel argues that adventure is not defined by extreme experience, but by its "experiential tension."

> That one has faced mortal danger or conquered a woman for a short span of happiness; that unknown factors with which one has waged a gamble have brought surprising gain or loss; that physically or psychologically disguised, one has ventured into spheres of life from which one returns home as if from a strange world—none of these are necessarily adventure. They become adventure only by virtue of a certain experiential tension ... Only when a stream flowing between the minutest externalities of life and the central source of strength drags them into itself; when the peculiar color, ardor, and rhythm of the life-process become decisive and, as it were, transform its substance—only then does an event change from mere experience to adventure.[31]

Conflict, for Simmel, is a "lack of harmony" within a relationship. It may stem from such dissociating elements as hatred, envy, want, and desire, but it happens in ongoing relationships, not when people are indifferent to each other. When conflict breaks out, Simmel says, "It is in reality the way to remove the dualism and to arrive at some form of unity, even if through the annihilation of one of the parties."[32] Simmel observes, as Durkheim does, that conflict serves a purpose in the stabilization of group forms. He states that "a group which was entirely centripetal and harmonious—that is, 'unification' merely—is not only impossible empirically, but it would also display no essential life-process and no stable structure. As the cosmos requires '*Liebe and Hass*,' attraction and repulsion, in order to have a form, society likewise requires some quantitative relation of harmony and disharmony, association and dissociation, liking and disliking, in order to attain a definite formation."[33]

Simmel also notes that conflict within a group may increase its solidarity and bring out its strengths: Throwing one member out, or finding an external enemy, strengthens the bond that the remaining members have to the idea of the group. He argues that when this happens "each party must hate in its opponent, not its opponent merely, but at the same time the enemy of its higher sociological unity."[34]

Simmel held unorthodox views on war. "A disastrous war," he writes, "which ruins a petty state, may regenerate a great state."[35] As we noted in chapter 1, the narrative of Western Europe and classical sociological theory is intimately connected to colonialism, because rival European states occupied far-flung overseas territories.[36] Colonialism encouraged a new type of aggressive nationalism that helped to pave the way for further industrialization, rationality, the enthronement of bureaucracy, and increasing decision-making by "experts." Military nationalism also shaped the public and intellectual discourse, much as the War on Terror in recent contemporary society has given rise to a debate on national identity. The prospect of war in Simmel's time produced calls for patriotism and nationalism. His writings about the First World War embrace the German soul and express intense support for the conflict that he believed would encourage the development of the German idea against the rational state of France and the materialism of America. Simmel felt that war, as conflict, would increase social cohesion, and, simultaneously, it would make choices more meaningful than the endless round of empty amusements characteristic of modernity.[37] The war was supposed to uproot cynicism, *mammonism* (materialism) and indifference.[38] War, he wrote, would "till the soil of Europe," reversing its descent into decadence, and encouraging new growth.[39] As early as 1915, however, Simmel showed awareness of the darker side of military conflict. He writes, "Europe stands in the act of committing suicide, and America sees in that the opportunity for itself, to put itself at the tip of world happenings."[40] His war writings seem inconsistent with much of his previous intellectuality. They are consistent, however, with his constant attempt to find ways to create expanded areas of subjective self-fulfillment and freedom in a world that encourages only the most superficial forms of individuality.

Social Types

In his essays on social types—miser, spendthrift, adventurer, and stranger—Simmel describes the new personality types that he thinks embody particularly significant things about metropolitan life.[41] He is not interested in why individuals become a miser or a stranger, but what characterizes them as recurrently constituted social types. The sociological significance of the stranger, the topic of his most well-known essay on social types, lies in the fact that in some way or other they are excluded from society. The notion of the stranger is often taken as a metaphor for Simmel himself and his exclusion from the academy. He describes the position of the stranger in the following passage:

> If wandering is the liberation from every given point in space, and thus the conceptional opposite to fixation at such a point, the sociological form of the "stranger" presents the unity, as it were, of these two characteristics. This phenomenon too, however, reveals that spatial relations are only the condition, on the one hand, and the symbol, on the other, of human relations. The stranger is thus being discussed here, not in the sense often touched upon in the past, as the wanderer who comes today and goes tomorrow, but rather as the person who comes today and stays tomorrow. He is, so to speak, the *potential* wanderer: although he has not moved on, he has not quite overcome the freedom of coming and going. He is fixed within a particular spatial group, or within a group whose boundaries are similar to spatial boundaries. But his position in this group is determined, essentially, by the fact that he has not belonged to it from the beginning, that he imports qualities into it, which do not and cannot stem from the group itself. [42]

The stranger may choose to be more conformist than others in the group, or she and he may express their differences in independent action. The stranger can be the objective mediator in conflicts. Simmel's stranger is "freer practically and theoretically; he surveys conditions with less prejudice; his criteria for them are more general and more objective ideals; he is not tied down in his action by habit, piety, and precedent."[43] The stranger may also be an easy scapegoat when the group is looking for someone to blame. Thus, Simmel writes that the stranger's freedom contains "many dangerous possibilities."[44]

The Metropolis, Money, and Alienation

In his most influential essay "Metropolis and Mental Life," and his book *The Philosophy of Money,* Simmel provides a very different perspective on social relationships. "Metropolis" was originally part of a lecture series connected with the opening of the Dresden Cities Exhibition of 1903.[45] He was expected to lecture on the positive cultural influence of the city. Instead, he argued that the excessive specialization and translation of everything into monetary terms, although a natural feature of modernity, led to a dominance of "objective spirit" and culture over "subjective spirit" and personality.[46] The new metropolis put humans under siege. All that was unique, whole, and deep about human personality was flattened and made meaningless. Simmel observed that "from one angle, life is made infinitely more easy in the sense that stimulations, interests, and the taking up of time and attention, present themselves from all sides and carry it [life] in a stream, which scarcely requires any individual efforts for its ongoing. But from another angle, life is composed more and more of these impersonal cultural elements and existing goods and values which seek to suppress particular personal interests and incomparabilities."[47] For Simmel, the primary characteristic of urban life is one of "intensification of emotional life" in "deep contrast to the slower, more habitual, more smoothly flowing rhythm of the sensory-mental phase of small town and rural existence."[48] The urban individual, he argues, protects her or his inner core by developing intellectuality, reserve, and a blasé attitude.[49] Intellectuality is developed as urban individuals react with their head instead of their heart, that is, with "that part which is furthest from the depths of the personality."[50] Reserve, "with its overtone of concealed aversion," establishes a kind of personal freedom.[51] A blasé attitude emerges from the city's "boundless pursuit of pleasure,"[52] which

Simmel argues that culture grows increasingly beyond the capacity of individuals to absorb and transcend, forcing them to give up more and more of their uniqueness, identity, and spiritual freedom. Is this image an example of cultural imperialism?

makes one blasé "because it agitates the nerves to their strongest reactivity for such a long time that they finally cease to react at all ... An incapacity thus emerges to react to new sensations with the appropriate energy.[53] It is not just the overstimulation but also the city's extreme specialization that makes the metropolis a place of superficial relationships. The division of labour demands from the individual an ever more specialized, one-sided accomplishment[54] and threatens to eliminate the subjective sense of personal uniqueness.

The problems of metropolitan life are intimately intertwined with the omnipresence of money in modern society. When money replaces barter, it reduces everything (including individuals) to what it has in common: its exchange value. Simmel sees money as "the frightful leveller" that "expresses all qualitative differences of things in terms of *how much*?"[55] He writes, "To the extent that money, with its colourlessness and indifferent quality, can become a common denominator of all values ... it hollows out the core of things, their peculiarities and specific values and their uniqueness and incomparability in a way which is beyond repair."[56] In *The Philosophy of Money*, Simmel offers a far-ranging analysis of the social and psychological meanings of money in modernity. Like Marx in *Capital*, Simmel begins his analysis with a discussion of value and money. Unlike Marx, his primary focus is exchange value. He explicitly rejects Marx's labour theory of value. Simmel argues that money provides a standard for all exchanges and that economic value is the objectification of subjective value, which occurs through the act of exchange: "The technical form of economic transactions produces a realm of values that is more or less completely detached from the subjective-personal substructure. Although the individual buys because he values and wants to consume an object, his demand is expressed effectively only by an object in exchange. Thus the subjective process ... changes to an objective, supra-personal relationship between objects."[57] Despite his apparent differences with Marx's economics, scholars suggest that there is a multitude of parallels between Marx's theories in *Capital* and Simmel's theories concerning the relativism of money, as found in *The Philosophy of Money*.[58]

Simmel's most insightful observation concerns the effect of the cash nexus on individual personality.

> Only the combination and fusion of several traits in one focal point forms a personality which then in its turn imparts to each individual trait a personal-subjective quality. It is not that it is this *or* that trait that makes a unique personality of man, but that he is this *and* that trait. The enigmatic unity of the soul cannot be grasped by the cognitive process directly, but only when

> it is broken down into a multitude of strands, the re-synthesis of which signifies the unique personality.
>
> Such a personality is almost completely destroyed under the conditions of a money economy. The delivery man, the money lender, the worker, upon whom we are dependent, do not operate as personalities because they enter into a relationship only by virtue of a single activity such as the delivery of goods, the lending of money, and because their qualities, which alone would give them a personality, are missing ... The general tendency, however, undoubtedly moves in the direction of making the individual more and more dependent upon the achievements of people, but less and less dependent upon the personalities that lie behind them.[59]

According to Simmel, money is the exact measure of material achievements; it increases the number of relationships between people and enhances individual freedom but is "very inadequate for the particular and the personal."[60]

Simmel's notion of alienation naturally invites comparisons with Marx's *Capital* and Durkheim's *Division of Labour in Society.* Simmel argues that the objectification of culture affects people's relationship to objects. Specialization and the cash nexus exorcises from objects everything connected with spirituality and special, personal significance. In a passage that parallels some of Marx's early writing on product alienation, Simmel writes:

> The process of objectification of culture that, based on specialization, brings about a growing estrangement between the subject and its products ultimately invades even the more intimate aspects of our daily life. During the first decades of the nineteenth century, furniture and objects that surrounded us for use and pleasure were of relative simplicity and durability and were in accord with the needs of the lower as well as of the upper strata. This resulted in people's attachment as they grew up to the objects of their surroundings, an attachment that already appears to the younger generation today as an eccentricity on the part of their grandparents.[61]

The growing estrangement between people and objects is caused, Simmel argues, by the sheer quantity of objects coming onto the market, which makes it difficult for individuals to form a personal relationship with them. Frequent changes in fashion, Simmel also argues, discourages personal relationships with objects, even when people find, for instance, their old chair or shoes more comfortable. These tendencies thus lead to "the strangest eccentricities" carried on simply in order to be different.[62] According to Simmel, the metropolis is the centre of two human tragedies that he elaborates in his later work.[63] The most overwhelming is the *tragedy of modern culture* in which humans create an objective culture that overwhelms them. Culture grows increasingly beyond the capacity of individuals to absorb and transcend it, forcing them to give up more and more of their uniqueness and spiritual freedom. Simmel's observations about objective culture might be interpreted as part of the process that Weber saw as rationalization.[64] The other tragedy, discussed above, is the *sociological tragedy*: in which individuals become part of the mass and their distinctive individualities are crushed.[65] Unlike Marx, however, Simmel does not posit a vision of communism to overcome these tragedies but echoes Weber's fatalism as to people's ability to avoid the iron cage of repressive bureaucratic rationality. Cultural objectification, Simmel argues, is simply a fact of life, part of the general human fate, and "it is not our task to complain or condone but only to understand.[66]

Gender and Culture

The more critical assessments of Georg Simmel's work expose his paradoxical thinking towards gender relationships in society. On the one hand, he championed the right of women to enter the professions such as medicine where sensitivity, intuition, empathy, and other feminine characteristics can be useful.[67] But on the other hand, he believed that specialization is more congruent with the "nature" of the male than the female. Further, he states that objective culture, including art, culture, and social structures, was made by men and is suited to the essential character of men.[68] The absorption of the objective culture, according to Simmel, was not compatible with women's mode of being. Women, he claims, are situated in subjectivity, relatively ahistorical and passive, more holistic in their totality than men. Women exist in being, while men exist in becoming.[69] According to Simmel, woman's greatest cultural achievement is the home, in which the distinction between objective culture and subjective experience does not exist.[70] He shared the commonly received opinion that women are in danger of becoming masculinized rather than humanized when they participate in objective culture. This meant that women do not suffer from the tragedy of (male) culture. The tragedy of women, he wrote, is that they "live in a world of otherness." Viewing themselves through the lens of the male culture, they come to see themselves as valued only as "means for the man, for the home, for the child."[71]

Like other gender writers of his time, Simmel saw a parallel between the position of slave and the position of women, but he, unlike later feminist writers, did not treat this as a social problem.

> It is one of the privileges of the master that he does not always need to think about the fact that he is a master. The position of the slave, on the other hand, ensures that he will never forget his status. There is no doubt that the woman loses a conscious sense of her being as a female much more rarely than holds true for the man and his being as a male. There are innumerable occasions on which the man appears to think in a purely objective fashion without his masculinity concurrently occupying any place in his perceptions. On the other hand, it seems as if woman never loses the feeling—which may be more or less clear or obscure—that she is a woman. This forms the subterranean ground of her life that never entirely disappears. All the contents of her life transpire on its basis.[72]

Although many other male classical sociologists engaged in discussion of "the woman question,"[73] Simmel was the only one who clearly expressed the idea that it was a male view that was developing, rather than an objective view of the female. Women were being viewed through a masculine lens, not a neutral lens, when they were studied.

Criticisms

Despite the breadth of his subject matter and scholarly publications, his choice of apparently lightweight topics earned him charges of excess playfulness and dilettantism. He was much criticized, even by those, such as Max Weber, who liked him and by those, such as Emile Durkheim, who published some of his writings. Weber and Durkheim felt that Simmel's work was inconsistent, and scattered.[74] While Simmel wrote about sociology as a special way of knowing, rather than as a field of study, in practice he felt that any specific method imposed by a scientific community would be transcended. Individual social scientists would express themselves by developing their own style and structure as they interacted with other social scientists and social science as a whole. He did not even attempt to make his work a paradigm for the discipline. His idea of forms was a search for commonalities across borders of time and place in ways that can be insightful and provocative. However, the idea can also be criticized as running the risk of finding universal subjective commonalities that may not actually be there. We do not know that participants in a medieval battle understood their objective circumstances and agency in the same way as participants in recent conflicts. The similar appearance may be just that, similar but not the same. Compared to earlier classical sociology, Simmel's four core concepts of form, reciprocity, distance, and dualism eclipse economic processes as symbolic cultural trends.[75]

Simmel's veneration of female qualities and his championship of women's liberation was avant-garde at the time. He shares with early feminists the conviction that women are essentially different from men. His interpretation tends to treat the nature of the women in his day as stemming from ontological difference, rather than being a response, to a large degree, to the pressure of objective culture, as it is for men. His idea that women cannot participate in the creation of culture without denying their essence will find few feminist supporters in contemporary sociology. Even those who cannot embrace his philosophically based theories of *dialectical vitalism*, however, recognize the brilliance of his insights into the intersection of objective culture and individual freedom in society.

Conclusion

Compared to the more systematic structural sociology that was encouraged in the academy of his time, Simmel's work represents a less conventional theoretical reaction to modernity. His sociology shifted the focus away from an exclusive concern with macro-issues, such as the domination of capital, specialization, and centralized tendencies, towards individualism, differentiation, and seemingly superficial moments of micro-social interaction. Importantly, his work has not only influenced the sociology of culture, including the culture of modernity, but also has had an affect upon cultural production itself.[76] His thoughts on the social conditions of spiritual growth, and the nature of individual soul, spirit, and inner life remain outside the boundaries of contemporary sociology. Although he was not as intensely, or centrally, involved in the building of sociology as Durkheim and Weber, Simmel was a co-founder, along with Weber and Tönnies, of the German Society for Sociology and a co-editor and contributor to the *American Journal of Sociology*. He published in Durkheim's *Sociological Yearbook* (*L'Année Sociologique*) and was a member of the Institut Internationale de Sociologie. His ideas have been refracted into the evolving paradigms of the Chicago School theory, interaction theory, functionalism, conflict theory, and early postmodernism. Translations of his early work appeared in the *American Journal of Sociology*. He remained stubbornly unique among sociologists, despite the criticisms and rebuffs of the academic world, and in his teaching challenged students to transcend the barriers of existing ideas and systems and to develop themselves while developing sociological insights. In 1918 he wrote, "I know that I shall die without intellectual heirs, and that is as it should be. My legacy will be, as it were, in cash, distributed to many heirs, each transforming his part into use conformed to *his* nature: a use which will reveal no longer its indebtedness to its heritage."[77]

In the early twentieth century, Simmel's contribution to social theory did not live up to Albion Small's early assessment that post-Simmelism might eventually be "a pillar in the ultimate sociology." His unstructured style of writing and the disorderliness of his method was too great a hurdle for the orthodox academically orientated professional sociology that emerged in the decades following his death. For the most part, those who have made use of Simmel's ideas have done so in their own terms. Robert Merton wrote that he had learned most from two sociologists, Emile Durkheim and Georg Simmel. But Merton's great strength was in the systematization of middle-level functionalism. George Ritzer has described Merton's extension of Simmel's ideas as "a creative misunderstanding." In Europe, Simmel's ideas travelled through the work of Marxists, such as Lukács, and the conflict theorist Habermas. In the United States they were absorbed into the work of Chicago School sociologists, particularly Robert Park and George Mend. In the late twentieth century, much more favourable assessments of his work were published, notably by David Frisby, and scholars began writing that Simmel's social theorizing goes beyond postmodernism.[78] Inarguably, his fluid view of society and the individual in society was, and is, much more in tune with postmodern theories of deconstruction and chaos.

Notes

1 Georg Simmel, "Metropolis and Mental Life" in *Georg Simmel: On Individuality and Social Forms,* ed. Donald Levine (Chicago: University of Chicago, 1971) 324; also www.gsz.hu-berlin.de/dokumente/georg_simmel-the_metropolis_and_mental_life.pdf (accessed February 15, 2008).

2 David Frisby, *Sociological Impressionism: Reassessment of Georg Simmel's Social Theory* (London: Heinemann, 1981), 103.

3 Alex Callinicos, *Social Theory*, 2nd ed. (Cambridge: Polity Press, 2007), 183.

4 David Frisby, *Georg Simmel* (London: Routledge, 2002), xxxiv.

5 D. Weinstein and M.A. Weinstein, *Postmodern(ized) Simmel* (London: Routledge, 1993).

6 Frisby, *Georg Simmel*, 27.

7 Albert Salomon, "Georg Simmel Reconsidered," in *Georg Simmel and the American Prospect*, trans. and ed. Gary D. Jaworski (Albany: Suny Press, 1997), 93.

8 Janet Stewart, "Georg Simmel at the Lectern," *Body and Society* 5, no. 4 (1999): 1–16.

9 Georg Simmel, "On Individuality and Social Forms in Education," in *Masters of Sociological Thought: Ideas in Historical and Social Context*, with introduction by Lewis Coser, (New York: Harcourt Brace Jovanovich, 1971), 235.

10 Georg Simmel, "On Women, Sexuality and Love," trans. and introduction by Guy Oakes (New Haven: Yale University Press, 1984), 56.

11 Coser, *Masters of Sociological Thought*, 196.

12 David Frisby, ed., *Georg Simmel: Critical Assessments* (London: Routledge, 1994), 361; George Psathas, *Phenomenological Sociology: Theory and Research*, (Lanham, MD: University Press of America, 1989); Georg Simmel, "How Is Society Possible?" in *Essays in Sociology, Philosophy and Aesthetics*, ed. K.H. Wolff (New York: Harper Torchbooks, 1959), 337–56.

13 Georg Simmel, "The Problem Areas of Sociology," in *The Sociology of Georg Simmel*, ed. K.H. Wolff (New York: Free Press, 1950), 16–25.

14 Georg Simmel, "Persistence of Social Groups," *The American Journal of Sociology* 3, no. 5 (March 1898): 662–98.

15 Georg Simmel, "The Problem of Sociology," *The American Journal of Sociology* 15, no. 3 (November 1908): 418–34.

16 Ian Craib, *Classical Sociological Theory* (Oxford: Oxford University Press, 1997).

17 "Fragen über das Jodeln" (Questions about Yodelling) *Jahrbuch des Schweizer Alpenclub* 14. Jg. Bern 1878–1879.

18 Simmel, "The Problem Areas of Sociology," 16–25.

19 Charles Axelrod, "Toward an Appreciation of Simmel's Fragmentary Style," in *Formal Sociology*, ed. L. Ray (Aldershot: Edward Elgar, 1991), and quoted in Craib, *Classical Social Theory*, 55.

20 Wolff, *Essays in Sociology, Philosophy and Aesthetics*, 263.

21 Simmel, "The Problem Areas of Sociology," 16–25.

22 Donald Levine, ed., *Georg Simmel: Individuality and Social Forms* (Chicago: Chicago University Press, 1971), and quoted in Craib, *Classical Social Theory*, 56.

23 Georg Simmel, "Types of Social Relationships by Degrees of Reciprocal Knowledge of the Participants," in *Sociology of Georg Simmel*, ed. Wolff, 318.

24 Wolff, *Essays in Sociology, Philosophy and Aesthetics*, 321.

25 Georg Simmel, "The Number of Members as Determining the Sociological Form of the Group: I," *American Journal of Sociology* 8 (1902), 41.

26 Ibid., 41.

27 Bart Nooteboom, "Fragment: Simmel's Treatise on the Triad (1908)", *Journal of Institutional Economics* 2, no. 3 (2006): 365–83.

28 Simmel, "Number of Members," 40.

29 Georg Simmel, *Grundfragen der Soziologie Individuum und Gesellschaft* (1917), passage translated by Linda Deutschmann, http://socio.ch/sim/grundfragen/grund_2.htm.

30 Georg Simmel, "The Adventure," in *Georg Simmel, 1858–1918: A Collection of Essays, with Translations and a Bibliography*, ed. K.H. Wolff (Ohio State University Press, 1959), 251.

31 Ibid., 253.

32 Georg Simmel, "The Sociology of Conflict," *American Journal of Sociology* 9 (1903): 798. Available at: www.brocku.ca/MeadProject/Simmel/Simmel_1904a.html (accessed on February 15, 2008).

33 Ibid., 799.

34 Ibid., 798.

35 Simmel, "The Number of Members," 40.

36 K.H. Tucker, *Classical Social Theory*, (Malden, Mass: Blackwell, 2002), 31.

37 Patrick Watier, "The War Writings of Georg Simmel," *Theory, Culture and Society* 8 (1991): 219–33.

38 Ibid., 220.

39 Georg Simmel, "The European Idea," trans. Linda Deutschmann. Available at: http://socio.ch/sim/verschiedeness/1915/europa_amerika.htm (accessed on February 15, 2008).

40 Georg Simmel, "Europa und Amerika: eine weltgeschichtliche Betrachtung," first published in *Das Berliner Tagblatt* (July 1915) trans. Austin Harrington, as introduction to Georg Simmel's essay "Europe and America in World History" in *European Journal of Social Theory*, 8 no. 1 (2005): 63–72.

41 "Georg Simmel on Individuality and Social Forms," in *Georg Simmel*, ed. David Levine, 137–144.

42 Georg Simmel, "The Stranger." Available at: http://condor.depaul.edu/~dweinste/intro/stranger.htm (accessed on February15, 2008); Wolff, *Georg Simmel*, 402.

43 Ibid.

44 Ibid.

45 David Frisby, ed., *Georg Simmel: The Philosophy of Money*, 3rd ed., trans. Tom Bottomore and David Frisby (London: Routledge, 2004), xxvi.

46 Simmel, "Metropolis and Mental Life" in *George Simmel on Individuality and Social Forms* [Die Großstädte und das Geistesleben, 1903], trans. and ed. Levine (Frankfurt: Suhrkamp, 2006); "Metropolis and Mental Life" adapted by D. Weinstein from K.H. Wolff, trans., *The Sociology of Georg Simmel* (New York: Free Press, 1950) 409–24; also www.gsz.hu-berlin.de/dokumente/georg_simmel-the_metropolis_and_mental_life.pdf; socio.ch/sim/english/index.htm; www.bolender.com/Dr.%20Ron/SOC3073%20Sociology%20of%20Community/Class%20Sessions/Class%20Session%20Two/Simmel%20Metropolis%20and%20Mental%20Life.htm (accessed February 15, 2008).

47 Simmel, "Metropolis," in *Georg Simmel*, Levine, 338.

48 Ibid., 325.

49 Ibid., 326, 329, 332.

50 Ibid., 326.

51 Ibid., 332.

52 Ibid., 329.

53 Ibid. Simmel notes that one does not expect a person who is stupid or intellectually dead to become blasé.

54 Ibid., 336–7.

55 Ibid., 330.

56 Ibid.

57 Simmel, *The Philosophy of Money*, ed. Frisby, 79.

58 Ibid., 11.

59 Ibid., 296.

60 Ibid., 303.

61 Ibid., 459–60.

62 Simmel, "Metropolis," 336.

63 Georg Simmel, "The Concept and Tragedy of Culture" ["Begriff und Tragödie der Kulltur"] in *Georg Simmel: The Conflict in Modern Culture and Other Essays,* trans. with introduction by Peter Etzkorn (New York, Teachers College Press, 1968), 24.

64 Craib, *Classical Social Theory*, 157.

65 Simmel, "Number of Members," 1–46.

66 Simmel, "Metropolis" in *Georg Simmel*, Levine, 339.

67 Georg Simmel, "*On Women, Sexuality and Love*," trans. Guy Oakes (New Haven: Yale University Press, 1984), 76–7.

68 Ibid., 70–1, 105–6.

69 Ibid., 88, 93.

70 Ibid., 70, 90–4, 97–8.

71 Lewis Coser, "Simmel's Neglected Contributions to the Sociology of Women," *Culture and Society* 2, no. 4 (Summer 1977): 873–4.

72 Georg Simmel, "*On Women, Sexuality and Love,*" 103.

73 Terry R. Kandal, *The Woman Question in Classical Sociological Theory* (Miami: Florida International University Press, 1988).

74 See Lewis Coser, *Georg Simmel* (Englewood Cliffs, NJ: Prentice-Hall, 1965), 48; also Levine, *Georg Simmel*, who calls Simmels method "unacceptable" but refers to his mode of presentation as "simply brilliant."

75 Ray, *Theorizing Classical Sociology.*

76 Frisby, *Georg Simmel: The Philosophy of Money,* xv.

77 Nachgelassenes Tagebuch (Diary) *Logos* 7 (1919), 121, quoted in Coser, *Georg Simmel*, 24.

78 Craib, *Classical Social Theory*, 17.

12. Gender and Social Theory

Theory without experience is nothing but a phrase, experience without theory but a prejudice. —Germaine De Staël[1]

The transformation of labour and the processes of urbanization wrought by the Industrial Revolution fundamentally changed gender relations and discourse about the public roles of men and women.
—Timm and Sanborn

THE INTELLECTUAL LEGACY OF ENLIGHTENMENT ideology is a masculine vision of the process of human history and of social life. This is despite the fact that women wrote and published philosophy in the eighteenth century. In the process of European industrialization, new specialized occupations and new ways of doing paid work had a profound impact on public attitudes towards gender roles, on everyday relationships, and on patterns of family life. Feminist writers have focused on the canonical writers' acceptance of the "natural" differences between the sexes based on the reproductive capacity of women and on their justification for hierarchical relations of female subordination. Moreover, the iconic founders of sociology were gender-blind in that they constructed the social through a masculine prism. This notable deficiency means that the traditional members of the sociological canon offer an inadequate framework for understanding many important aspects of modernity. We have seen throughout this text that Marx, Durkheim, and Weber largely neglect the gender dimension of the process of modernity. In Marx and Engels's

German Ideology, the anatomy of civil society is to be found in political economy. Productive labour in the material world mediates people and nature. But his account of the labour process both conceptually and empirically obscures the way that gender roles, patterns of family life, and conceptions of sexuality are socially constructed. Likewise, Durkheim's *Division of Labour in Society* offers a dichotomized, hierarchical perspective of the sexes,[2] and in *Le Suicide* Durkheim reiterates the typical assumptions of the age in respect to female biology and psychology. A critical issue for feminists in Weber's *Methodology of the Social Sciences* is the use of ideal types in his account that examines the relationship of women to the process of power. Weber's analysis of social life occurs in the context of "natural inequality" between the sexes, and he regards the access of power and domination by men as natural.[3] Simmel also proposed an understanding of women that promotes women's primary value as holistic homemakers, whose potential integration in the fields of education and medicine might provide a brake on the overwhelming masculine tragedy of culture. This did not augur well for women's freedom and equality.

It is our objective in this chapter to expand the traditional canon by reviewing the work of a small group of early feminist thinkers and sociologists in England and the United States. We explore the genesis of feminist social theory through the work of four of the best-known early women social theorists: Mary Wollstonecraft, Harriet Martineau, Jane Addams, and Charlotte Perkins Gilman. Had there been more space, we would have included many others, especially those who provide a standpoint based also in their experience of racial inequality.[4] As did the founding fathers, the "founding mothers" engaged with issues of materiality, morality, and rationality. Moreover, they challenged the rationality and morality of capitalism that does not give *all* human beings an equal opportunity to develop their inner potential and to take part in social progress.

Mary Wollstonecraft (1759–1797)

A product of European Enlightenment, Mary Wollstonecraft was one of the earliest bourgeois feminist thinkers who managed to publish her thoughts on the organization of society. She lived long before social science had a distinct existence but believed that the Enlightenment values of equality, rationality, and freedom ought not be restricted by gender or race. While these ideas found expression among elements of the educated elite, Wollstonecraft articulated her ideas in a particularly forceful way. She is recognized as a feminist contributor to the early development of a rational, empirically based sociological theory.

Wollstonecraft's Life and Works

Mary Wollstonecraft was born in London, England, in 1759. A product of European Enlightenment, she was one of the earliest feminist thinkers to publish her thoughts on the differences between Enlightenment thought and rhetorics and social realities. She died in 1797 while giving birth to her second daughter.

Mary Wollstonecraft was born in London, England, in 1759. Her father inherited wealth but handled it badly; so Wollstonecraft had to support herself. At first she attempted to live from professions considered suitable for women: governess, lady's companion, and principal of a small school. In 1787 she found her lifetime mentor, the publisher Joseph Johnson. In 1793 she moved to France where she observed at first-hand the turmoil and bloodshed of the French Revolution. Although appalled by the violence, she criticized those such as Edmund Burke who rejected the revolution on the basis of sentiment about the past.[5] In the context of eighteenth-century England, it's not surprising that Wollstonecraft was largely home-educated. A number of intellectual influences informed her feminist analysis of society. She had access to the writings of Mary Astell (1666–1731), described as the first English feminist.[6] She was also aware of the aspirations of the English working-class movement known as the Levellers, who campaigned for the equality of women and universal suffrage in the seventeenth century.[7] Another possible source of inspiration was her involvement in a group of Unitarian Rational Dissenters who believed, among other things, in the perfectibility of the conditions of life through applied conscience and reason, as opposed to hierarchy and tradition. Her major work, *A Vindication of the Rights of Woman* published in 1792, was widely and internationally read, translated, and publicly discussed in her time. She died in 1797 while giving birth to her second daughter.

Gender Equality

Theorizing about society is intimately connected with European Enlightenment and the birth of modernity. As we discussed in chapter 2, the Enlightenment movement was not a unified body of thinking, but was internally fractured and riddled by contradictions. The eighteenth-century public debate on women's emancipation and rights is an example of its intellectual silences and anomalies. Mary Wollstonecraft's *Vindication* is a product of this debate. The book is a rebuttal to Edmund Burke's *Reflections on the French Revolution* and to the views of Rousseau. However, it was Burke's notion that women's beauty is to be attributed to their "littleness and weakness," that Wollstonecraft found particularly abhorrent. In her view, women are not actually equal to men, but they deserve social equality with men and should be given the education necessary to compete on an equal basis.

> Should experience prove that they [women] cannot attain the same degree of strength of mind, perseverance, and fortitude, let their virtues be the same in kind, though they may vainly struggle for the same degree; and the superiority of man will be equally clear, if not clearer; and truth, as it is a simple principle, which admits of no modification, would be common to both. Nay, the order of society as it is at present regulated would not be inverted, for woman would then only have the rank that reason assigned her, and arts could not be practised to bring the balance even, much less to turn it.[8]

For Wollstonecraft, women's isolation in domestic activities and their socially engendered need to be physically attractive to men spoil them for full partnership in the making of a new world: "Strength of body and mind are sacrificed to libertine notions of beauty, to the desire of establishing themselves—the only way women can rise in the world—by marriage. And this desire making mere animals of them, when they marry they act as such children may be expected to act: they dress; they paint, and nickname God's creatures.—Surely these weak beings are only fit for a seraglio!—Can they be expected to govern a family with judgment, or take care of the poor babes whom they bring into the world?"[9] A look at the textual evidence shows that Mary Wollstonecraft never questioned the assumption that motherhood is a natural condition for women, or that some professions are unsuitable for them. "Women might certainly ... be physicians as well as nurses," she writes. "And midwifery, decency seems to allot to them ... They might also study politics ... Business of various kinds, they might likewise pursue, if they were educated in a more orderly manner, which might save many from common and legal prostitution. Women would not then marry for a support, as men accept of places under Government, and neglect the implied duties; nor would an attempt to earn their own subsistence, a most laudable one! sink them almost to the level of those poor abandoned creatures who live by prostitution."[10] Wollstonecraft's arguments largely focus on the family and education. An example of this is her response to Jean-Jacques Rousseau's instructive

Mary Wollstonecraft argued that young women should be given the education necessary to compete on an equal basis to men. This photograph taken around 1910 of working-class girls in a London school shows the slow pace of equality in education. For a working-class girl, training on how to wash clothes was part of the school curriculum to prepare her for the role of housewife or maid to the rich.

tale, *Emile*.[11] In book five of *Emile*, Rousseau describes how "Sophy, or Woman" is to be educated so that the hero, Emile, will be a family man without sacrificing his right to freedom. Sophy needs only the education, mainly sexual, that will keep her husband in a state of mind such that he wants to be at home. Wollstonecraft rejects sexuality as the basis for marriage and argues that women's education should give them as much knowledge of the world as men. She writes, "'Educate women like men,' says Rousseau, 'and the more they resemble our sex the less power will they, have over us.' This is the very point I aim at. I do not wish them to have power over men; but over themselves."[12]

Wollstonecraft argues that women deserve social equality with men, but in her analysis she connects the oppression of white women and black slaves.[13] In likening woman's historical subjugated position to that of slaves, she writes, "When, therefore, I call women slaves, I mean in a political and civil sense."[14] Thus she posits that if rationality is essentially human, it is irrational not to apply it to both women and slaves.

Harriet Martineau (1802–1876)

Harriet Martineau was a beneficiary of Enlightenment thinking, and she believed that the study of society ought to be methodologically rigorous. She agreed that the new American republic demonstrated that people had

Harriet Martineau was born in Norwich, England, in 1802. Despite the threat of violence and social exclusion, she was a fervent abolitionist and became prominent among anti-slavery circles. She died in 1876 at Ambleside, England.

the ability to govern themselves and that the Declaration of Independence embodied the principles of universal justice, but she also recognized that class split apart the society of the American republic. Further, like Alex de Tocqueville, she recognized that slavery and democracy contradict each other, similar to the exclusion of women from the democratic process. And like Wollstonecraft, she identified certain parallels between the status of white women and the status of black women slaves. Although she recognized Wollstonecraft's pioneering influence, Martineau did not agree with Wollstonecraft's way of approaching the woman question. She writes, "Every allowance must be made for Mary Wollstonecraft herself, from the constitution and singular environment which determined her course: but I have never regarded her as a safe example, nor as a successful champion of Woman and her Rights."[15] A strong-minded, cigar-smoking, unmarried, and outspoken woman, Martineau did not escape criticism in her own right.

Martineau's Life and Works

Harriet Martineau was born into an upper middle class Unitarian family in Norwich, England. Her father was owner of an import house and a member of an elite intellectual circle. Her mother was literate but lacking in formal education. Martineau loved to write but when callers came, she had to hide her writing, which was considered unsuitable for a woman.[16] By 1828 her family faced extreme financial difficulties when the family business dissolved. Showing an attitude that took her through life, she writes. "Being thrown, while there was yet time, on our own resources, we have worked hard and usefully, won friends, reputation and influence, seen the world abundantly ... and truly lived instead of vegetated."[17]

By 1829 she had made a precarious transition to a writing career. When her hearing loss became severe, she required a trumpet hearing aid. By 1834, however, she was financially secure, and she had become a regular participant in a London literary circle, which included Charles Dickens, William Wordsworth, Charlotte Bronte, and Charles Darwin. From 1834 to 1836 Martineau travelled through the United States, practising sociological observation. A fervent abolitionist, she became prominent among anti-slavery circles, despite the threat of violence and social exclusion that was aimed at women abolitionists of the time.[18] Martineau's first publications were in the Unitarian periodical *Monthly Repository.* One of these, "On Female Education" published in 1822, was a protest against the injustice of the exclusion of women from higher education.[19] Her reputation was established by her series of *Illustrations of Political Economy.*[20] These popular booklets explain the principles of political economy in a simplified form. Her engaging writing style carried on into her sociological works, such as *How to Observe Morals and Manners* (1838),[21] *Society in America* (1836),[22] and *Retrospect of Western Travels* (1838).[23] In 1855 she became desperately ill,[24] after which she did not leave her home. She died on 27 June 1876 at Ambleside, England.

Intellectual Influences

Harriet Martineau was profoundly influenced by Unitarian ideas and values during her youth. The Unitarians favoured rational democratic individualism and human responsibility for social conditions. This doctrine included *necessarianism*, which held that "all the workings of the universe are governed by laws which cannot be broken by human will." These ideas helped her to develop the idea that the identifying of universal laws and adjusting social life to them would bring progress.[25] Another of her major influences was the utilitarian belief of Jeremy Bentham that the purpose of life is to increase the amount of happiness in the world.[26] For Martineau, policies that enhanced happiness were deemed progressive. An example of this can be found in her explanation that higher forms of charity are those that alleviate and prevent the most unhappiness.

> The lowest order of charity is that which is satisfied with relieving the immediate pressure of distress in individual cases. A higher is that which makes provision on a large scale for the relief of such distress; as when a nation passes on from common alms giving to a general provision for the destitute. A higher still is when such provision is made in the way of anticipation, or for distant objects; as when the civilization of savages, the freeing of slaves, the treatment of the insane, or the education of the blind and deaf mutes is undertaken. The highest charity of all is that which aims at the prevention rather than the alleviation of evil. [27]

Morality, Slavery, and Politics

In Martineau's *Morals and Manners,* morals are widely shared values that are demonstrated through texts such as the Declaration of

Independence, songs, and writings that everyone knows, and gravestone epitaphs. Manners are actual practices. Manners can be empty formulae for courtesy, or can be deeply rooted customs. Wide differences between morals and manners, and areas of great unhappiness, are *anomalies* that require action. Slavery and the oppression of women are anomalies in a society that claims equality in the pursuit of happiness, and inequality of wealth is an anomaly in a republic of equals. Fear of public opinion is an anomaly in a nation that values freedom of expression.[28] Published in 1838, *How to Observe Morals and Manners* is the first systematic methodology and theory treatise in sociology. It outlines the mechanics of unbiased data gathering, corroboration, and the practice of theorizing based in concrete observations. In this, Martineau envisions the reader as a traveller, who should use informed "sympathetic understanding" as a research tool.[29] She understands that in every observation there are at least two sides, the observer and the observed, and that "the mind of the observer, the instrument by which the work is done, is as essential as the material to be wrought."[30]

Martineau's traveller searches for what is representative in the way that people talk (discourses), the way that they act (practices), and the records of these thoughts and activities (things). *Things* are the most important of these. The number and kind of suicides, and the number and kind of criminals are things that reveal the ideas and problems of the time. She observes that "in England almost all the offences are against property, and are so multitudinous as to warrant a stranger's conclusion that the distribution of property among us must be extremely faulty, the oppression of certain classes by others very severe, and our political morals very low."[31]

Martineau's *Society in America* reflects her method of comparing stated morals to actual practices. The American Declaration of Independence, which embodied John Locke's theory of natural rights, declared that government derives its power from the consent of the governed and that it is the duty of a government to protect the rights of its citizens. What so appalled Martineau was the advocacy by some leading democracy writers, such as Thomas Jefferson, for dominant masculine suppositions, the "political non-existence of women,"[32] and the exclusion of slaves from full citizenship in representative democracy. Thus, she holds up the American documents that claim government gets its legitimacy from the consent of the governed, and compares them with the actual condition of women (and slaves) in American society. Women were granted indulgence, not enfranchisement. She would later describe this method as flawed by "the American theory that I had taken for my standpoint."[33] The topic needed to be treated in a more concrete way, she said.[34] By this, she meant that social change should be found among the people themselves rather than the ideologies of government. It is on this basis that she criticized what she called the "Wollstonecraft crowd" who agitated for legal reforms.[35]

Martineau's later works show the continuation of her interest in social theory. *Eastern Life Present and Past* (1848), a study of the evolution of religion, was received mainly as a travel book about the near East.[36] Reviewers expressed shock at her position that religion is both socially constructed and outdated. Her best-known contribution to the development of sociology is her edited translation of Auguste Comte's six-volume *Cours de Philosophie Positive* into *The Positive Philosophy* (1853), a version Comte so approved that he translated it back into French and substituted it for his original edition.[37] The years between the 1850s and her death saw a prodigious output of her newspaper columns and articles on contemporary women's issues including education, discriminatory laws, and two historical texts, *History of the Peace: Being a History of England from 1816 to 1854* (1864), and *History of England, AD 1800 to 1815* (1865), and extensive political lobbying on social issues.

Jane Addams (1860–1935)

Jane Addams has been described as the most important female sociologist of the twentieth century.[38] In her time, she was best known as an activist for social justice and peace. She helped to create hundreds of co-operative ventures that improved the lives of immigrants, youths, blacks, and labourers. Her proudest achievements were Hull-House and the Women's International League for Peace and Freedom. Addams taught at the University of Chicago and received honorary degrees from thirteen universities, as well as the Nobel Prize for Peace in 1931.

Addams's Life and Works

Jane Addams was born on September 6, 1860 into an upper middle-class Quaker family in Cedarville, Illinois. Her father was a decorated soldier, bank and railway director, and member of the state legislature. Her mother's early death meant that she was raised, at first, by her eldest sister and later by her stepmother. Her father was a trustee of Rockford Female Seminary, a place where women were encouraged to get the same education as men but also taught that women had the supreme duty of preserving the religion, morality, and culture of Western civilization. While Addams did not personally experience the threat of poverty, her social activism made her aware of the advantages of class.[39] In 1888, when visiting a London university, she was impressed that male university students worked to help the poor. Addams believed

Jane Addams was born into a Quaker family in Cedarville, Illinois, in 1860. Her social activism made her aware of the privileges of social class and influenced her sociological work. With friends she founded Hull-House, a refuge for single women. She died of cancer in 1935.

that American women could do this kind of work. She writes, "We have in America a fast-growing number of cultivated young people who have no recognized outlet for their active faculties. They hear constantly of the great social maladjustment, but no way is provided for them to change it, and their uselessness hangs about them heavily."[40]

In 1889 Addams, with Ellen Gates Starr and other friends, founded Hull-House, a settlement for women. Most of the residents of Hull-House were single women. Hull-House came to have a radical reputation. According to Addams, its residents "differed widely in social beliefs, from the girl direct from the country who looked upon all social unrest as mere anarchy, to the resident [Florence Kelly], who had become a socialist when a student in Zurich, and who had long before translated from the German, Engels' 'Conditions of the Working Class in England.'"[41] Along with amenities such as art and music, Hull-House provided a public kitchen, a gymnasium, public bath, a labour museum, and adult education courses. It was also a meeting place for many different organizations and a place from which extensive public interest investigations were undertaken. Addams provides an example of how women social activists working from Hull-House engaged with the community:

> At a meeting of working girls held at Hull-House during a strike in a large shoe factory, the discussions made it clear that the strikers who had been most easily frightened, and therefore first to capitulate, were naturally those girls who were paying board and were afraid of being put out if they fell too far behind. ... one of them exclaimed: Wouldn't it be fine if we had a boarding club of our own, and then we could stand by each other in a time like this? ...We read aloud together Beatrice Potter's little book on Cooperation, and discussed all the difficulties and fascinations of such an undertaking, and on the first of May, 1891, two comfortable apartments near Hull-House were rented and furnished.[42]

Her contribution to sociology and sociological theory grew directly out of her social activism. Her most important publications are *Democracy and Social Ethics* (1902–07), *Newer Ideals of Peace* (1907), *Twenty Years at Hull-House* (1910), *The Long Road of Woman's Memory* (1916), *Peace and Bread in Times of War* (1922), and *The Second Twenty Years at Hull-House* (1930). In 1915 Addams participated in the formation of the Woman's Peace Party, attended the International Women's conference at The Hague, and became the head of a commission selected to seek an end to the First World War.[43] This put her at odds with the patriotic hawk sentiments of the time. The Daughters of the American Revolution expelled her and kept a dossier on her along with many others suspected of disloyalty.[44] She was castigated for her involvement with foreigners at home and abroad. Addams was investigated by the FBI[45] and placed on the Senate Judiciary Committee's traitor list in 1919. Despite this, she became a co-winner of the Nobel Peace Prize in 1931. She died of cancer on May 21, 1935.

Intellectual Influences

As a child, Jane Addams absorbed the family's Quaker religion along with the individual moral heroism of Ruskin[46] and Carlyle.[47] Later she tempered individualism with an egalitarian solidarity, similar to socialism, which she partially attributed to Leo Tolstoy.[48] She was exposed to the positivism of Auguste Comte during her first trip to Europe. She wrote, "I was enormously interested in the Positivists during these European years."[49] Addams contributed to the African-American sociologist W.E.B. DuBois's *Crisis* [50] and read British social reformer Charles Booth's work on mapping social data in order to influence public policy.[51] She influenced, and was influenced by, many women and men, including Herbert Spencer and academics such as John Dewey and George Herbert Mead who visited and gave lectures at Hull-House.[52]

The Hull-House Social Science Club was just one of the places in which ideas were exchanged. The University of Chicago, founded in 1892, established the first independent department of sociology, and was the first American university to admit female students. Addams was a member of a group of university women, referred to as the "Chicago women's school," who engaged in social activism and social research. Students were often sent into the streets to observe, record, and theorize about the life that they saw. Women still faced resistance from male professors even when they made extensive use of their ideas and data. Resistance to women was coupled with resistance to activist agitators, and combined to result in the increasing exclusion of women from sociology at the university. Women were channeled into social work, leaving sociology as a male profession.[53]

Social Ethics

Through her social activism Jane Addams developed a complex theory of gender inequality that demonstrates the value of experiences of *bifurcation consciousness*, that is, the awareness of a disjuncture between one's own lived experience and the formal narratives of life. She believed that "truth emerged through life experience." Jane Addams is best known for her writings on social ethics and is central to her sociological theory. In *Democracy and Social Ethics* she defines *social ethics* as the practice of rules of right relationship that produce and sustain in people an orientation to action based on "concern for the welfare of the community."[54] An example of social ethics is in her chapter on political reform, which begins with a description of her battles with a corrupt ward alderman. She uses "sympathetic understanding," to discover how this man remains popular: the common people of the ward see him as visible, sympathetic, and connected to their everyday lives. In this, she says, a corrupt politician could accomplish more (if he wished to) than any number of social reformers.

In *The Spirit of Youth and the City Streets* (1909), Addams argues that the city should take responsibility for the health and safety of the young people who migrate to the city for paid work. If the city did not provide for healthful recreation, then commercialism would provide vicious forms that degrade youth.[55] While some of Addams's work shows the influence of socialist ideas, she was not attached to labels or political orthodoxy. Her description of the happy young worker who is educated to understand her role in production does not indicate opposition to industrial capitalism as such. Thus, she writes: "If a child goes into a sewing factory with knowledge of the work she is doing in relation to the finished product, if she is informed concerning the material she is manipulating and the processes to which it is subjected; if she understands the design she is elaborating in its historic relation to art and decoration, her daily life is lifted from drudgery to one of self-conscious activity, and her pleasure and intelligence is registered in her product." In *A New Conscience and an Ancient Evil* (1912) she provides examples of white slavery (prostitution) and related city vices from the Hull-House records: "Our civilization becomes permanently tainted with the vicious practices designed to accelerate the demoralization of unwilling victims in order to make them commercially valuable. Moreover, a girl thus rendered more useful to her owner, will thereafter fail to touch either the chivalry of men or the tenderness of women because good men and women have become convinced of her innate degeneracy, a word we have learned to use with the unction formerly placed upon original sin. The very revolt of society against such girls is used by their owners as a protection to the business."[56]

For Addams, city government involves both business and public housekeeping. In *Women and Public Housekeeping* Addams argues for the inclusion of women in city government.[57] Women need political influence to combat urban problems that threatened their families, she writes: "Unsanitary housing, poisonous sewage, contaminated water, infant mortality, the spread of contagion, adulterated food, impure milk, smoke-laden air, ill-ventilated factories, dangerous occupations, juvenile crime, unwholesome crowding, prostitution, and drunkenness are the enemies which the modern city must face and overcome would it survive."[58]

Jane Addams's social activism for peace grew as World War I approached.[59] Peace is "not merely the absence of war, but the nurture of human life."[60] She writes, "You'd very likely forget that the real object of the State is to nurture and protect life, and out of sheer vainglory you would be voting away huge sums of money for battleships ... Every time a gun is fired in a battleship it expends, or rather explodes, seventeen hundred dollars, as much as a college education costs many a country boy, and yet you would be firing off these guns as mere salutes ... simply because you so enjoy the sound of shooting."[61] Her dissenting voice on peace was drowned out by the Second World War and, subsequently, by the Cold War which followed it. The men in the department of sociology at the University of Chicago—the Chicago School—wanted to shake off the social reform aspects of the discipline, and along with it much of the sociological theory of Jane Addams. As was true for Harriet Martineau, it remained to later observers to resurrect her memory and to uncover the path of her contribution to sociological theory and practice.

Charlotte Perkins Stetson Gilman (1860–1935)

Charlotte Anna Perkins was born July 3, 1860 in Hartford, Connecticut. Through her father, Frederick Beecher Perkins, she was related to the reform-minded Beecher family, including Isabella Beecher Hooker, a famous suffragist, and Catharine Beecher, a writer and supporter of women's education.[62] Her father was a librarian, and her mother was a cultivated, musically gifted woman. Her father abandoned the family in 1859. The family became "charity relatives" who had to move often to get ahead of their unpaid bills.[63] To finance her education at the Rhode Island School of Design during the years 1878 to 1883, Perkins painted advertisements and gave drawing lessons. In 1884 she married fellow artist Charles Walter Stetson. Their daughter Katharine was born a year

Charlotte Perkins Stetson Gilman was born in Hartford, Connecticut, in 1860. Like Friedrich Engels, she believed that the nuclear family and home was a site of women's oppression. Suffering from terminal breast cancer, she committed suicide in 1935.

later. She experienced "severe and continuous nervous breakdown leading to melancholia—and beyond."[64] In 1887 her condition worsened, and she decided that it was "better for that dear child to have separated parents than a lunatic mother"[65]; she left Stetson and moved to California. Her mental breakdown is vividly portrayed in *The Yellow Wall-Paper* (1992). In California she became involved with politics, found emotional support with women, and developed a reputation as a writer and public speaker. In 1896 she was invited to Hull-House. Her main contributions to social theory are found in *Women and Economics: The Economic Relation Between Men and Women as a Factor in Social Evolution* (1898),[66] subsequently published in nine editions and translated into seven languages; *The Home: Its Work and Influence* (1903), also published in nine editions and translated into seven languages; *Human Work* (1904) and *The Man-Made World* (1911). In 1902 Perkins married Houghton Gilman, a New York lawyer, who supported her writing and speaking career. A year after her husband's death, and suffering with terminal breast cancer, she ended her own life on August 17, 1935.[67]

Gilman's Intellectual Influences

Perkins Gilman's writing reflects a unique intertwining of Marx, Engels, Darwinism, Durkheim, eugenics, Fabian socialism, the Social Gospel, Lester Ward's gynaeco-centric (woman-centred) theory, Bellamy Nationalism, populism, progressivism and, of course, feminism. Like Marx, she believes human labour defines what it means to be human, and social power is based on the male control of economic resources. Like Engels she believes that the nuclear family and home is a site of women's oppression. Like Durkheim, she draws on the work of Herbert Spencer and adopts biological imagery to analyze the organization of society. More problematically, her interpretation of Social Darwinism informs her racist views on African-Americans,[68] and underlies her many calls to improve the race by reforming social institutions. Eugenics, both positive and negative, underlies her call for women to choose partners who are most suited to breed fit children, and her recommendation that defective criminals be sterilized. Her views on race and eugenics buttress the overt racism that was ubiquitous in the Anglo-American society of the early twentieth century. Aspects of Fabian socialism and Social Gospel also merge as she imagines that Christianity evolved into a socialist form, shorn of its patriarchal trappings. Perkins Gilman saw herself as a sociologist, and was influenced by sociologists. Among these, Lester Ward was particularly important. Ward's theory of androcentric society, she writes, was "the most important that has been offered the world since the Theory of Evolution; and without exception the most important that has ever been put forward concerning women.[69] She was also influenced by Jane Addams and the women of Hull-House, although she found their immersion in the lives of immigrants and the poor to be distasteful.

Work, Gender and Family

Perkins Gilman emphasizes the centrality of human labour and women's subordination in the economic process. In her most scholarly work, *Women and Economics*, she presents her feminist analysis of capitalism. The following tour de force contains the most succinct statement of her thought:

> The general course of life shows the inexorable effect of conditions upon humanity. Of these conditions we share with other living things ... the material universe ... What we do, as well as what is done to us, makes us what we are. But beyond these forces, we come under the effect of a third set of conditions peculiar to our human status; namely, social conditions. In the organic interchanges, which constitute social life, we are affected to a degree beyond what is found even among the most gregarious of animals. This third factor, the social environment, is of enormous force as a modifier of human life. Throughout all these environing conditions ... economic necessities are most marked in their influence ... Under all the influence of this later and wider life, all the reactive effect of social institutions, the individual is still inexorably modified by his means of livelihood ... the daily processes of supplying economic needs... In view of these facts, attention is now called to certain marked and peculiar economic conditions affecting the human race, and unparalleled in organic life. We are the only animal species in which the female depends on the male for food, the only animal species in which sex-relation is also an economic relation. With us an entire sex lives in relation of economic dependence upon the other sex, and the economic relation is combined with the sex-relation.[70]

On the importance of human labour, she writes: "To do and to make not only gives deep pleasure, but it is indispensable to healthy growth."[71] This is a partial echo of Marx, except that for Perkins Gilman a change in women's economic relationship would transform their social status and enable them to fulfill their creative potential. The social status of women in society is through the paid work of their men, rather than their own labour.

Perkins Gilman is best known for her critique of the nuclear family, and Engels and Durkheim influenced her thinking. Like Engels, she puts the nuclear family at the centre of women's subordination and exploitation. In *The Origins of the Family, Private Property, and the State* (1884), Friedrich Engels wrote: "The modern individual family is based on the open or disguised domestic enslavement of the woman; and modern society is a mass composed solely of individual families as its molecules."[72] Although Engels's analysis has been criticized for its "one-sided economic determinism," it appears to have shaped Perkins Gilman thought on the issue. Applying Durkheimian concepts to unpaid domestic labour and child care, Perkins Gilman argues that the specialization of labour is the basis of female emancipation and human progress. She argues that most women are essentially unskilled, unpaid labourers. Traditional housekeeping practices based on custom produce inefficient households. She argues that specialized occupations and training exist for cooking, cleaning, child care, and health care, and therefore, housekeeping should be professionalized too: "done by trained specialists with proper organization and mechanical conveniences, we could release the labor power of 80 percent of our women."[73] She also advocates community child care. In other words, Perkins Gilman argues for the family to be socialized.[74]

Charlotte Perkins Gilman is best known for her critique of the nuclear family, which, she argues, is the centre of women's subordination and exploitation. Taken during Gilman's lifetime, this photograph shows a British coal miner washing after a shift and his wife pouring warm water in a metal bath. The life of a miner's wife was hard: unremitting housework, childbearing, and providing for husbands and children on subsistence wage took a physical toll.

Her journal *The Forerunner* (1909–18) was used to propagate her views on racial progress through increased procreative fitness. For Perkins Gilman, the ideal marriage, in accordance with the laws of evolution, occurs when a woman who has developed herself mentally and physically chooses a male who will be the best father for her child. When men do most of the choosing, she notes, they tend to select women who are weak and good looking rather than racially fit to produce and raise children.[75] In lines that echo Wollstonecraft's discussion of excessive sex differentiation, Perkins Gilman argues "our civilized feminine delicacy" should be seen as less delicate when recognized as an expression of sexuality in excess." She writes, "The degree of feebleness and clumsiness common to women, the comparative inability to stand, walk, run, jump, climb, and perform other race-functions common to both sexes, is an excessive sex-distinction; and the ensuing transmission of this relative feebleness to their children, boys and girls alike, retards human development."[76]

Like Wollstonecraft, Perkins Gilman believed that women should be educated to take their place as leaders in society. A really feminine society, she argued, would accord women "freedom and knowledge; the knowledge which is power.[77] She expressed many of her ideas by inventing parallel worlds that satirically exposed social problems.[78] In the first of these, *Moving the Mountain* (1911), the narrator is a male who has come back to the United States after being lost in Tibet for thirty years. He finds a society in which men and women work just two hours a day. Meals are ordered from a specialized kitchen instead of made at home. Child care is shared. Women are not willing to marry sexually promiscuous, abusive, or drunken men, and so that vice has been wiped out. When asked how this wonderful change came about, he is repeatedly told that this is due to a change in women's consciousness: "the women woke up."[79] As with Martineau and Addams, Perkins Gilman endeavoured to reach the public with accessible materials that would challenge existing social practices.

Criticism

Throughout the twentieth century, successive generations of feminist thinkers have incorporated, developed, and extended the ideas of the early classical feminists. Classical feminist social theory, however, may have been subject to some of the weaknesses of "malestream" classical sociological theory. The first weakness is that, in their concern to reveal the social sources of women's subordination, the early feminists tended to neglect the effect of class inequality. Mary Wollstonecraft, for instance, had little to say on the economic exploitation of women or their subordination in general. Carole Pateman has argued that, in a society in which men monopolize paid work and women lack economic independence, the call for gender equality in education leads to what has been called "Wollstonecraft's dilemma."[80] That is, equality enables women to be treated and valued equally only to the extent that they can behave like men. This, of course, ignores the ways in which women's domestic responsibilities restrict their ability to compete for employment and how patriarchal strategies have historically excluded women from certain occupations,[81] which leaves women dependent on the goodwill of men to "snap their chains."[82] The classical "liberal" feminist theorists have also been criticized for their uncritical acceptance of an inherently male model of rationality and their portrayal of women's subordination as universal, when in reality their perspective reflects middle-class, white, Anglo-American women's experiences of subordination. This has led some critics to call early feminist thought "a bourgeois, white movement."[83] More specifically, Jane Addams has been criticized for her belief that evolution would be progressive if social policies strengthened the fitness of all. And a major criticism of Perkins Gilman's work is its ethnocentricity, elitism, and racism.[84] Second, the early feminists' analysis of man-made obstacles facing women does not take into account agency, that is, the creative potential of all members of society, irrespective of class, gender, or race, to understand, learn, adapt, and transform their social context. The early feminists viewed the individual as constituted by society and emphasized Enlightenment-inspired individual freedom and choice. This perspective leads to a third criticism, that they underplayed the effects of power relationships and social structures in capitalist societies, which limit choice and, importantly, perpetuate inequality.[85] Postmodernists are familiar with the notion that some voices are more equal than others, particularly those in positions of power. If we want to know, then, why female contributions have been written out of histories of classical sociological theory, we should examine not the content of the theory but the politics of class and gender and the resources with which the theory is disseminated. By this account, it's unsurprising that early feminist thought was erased from popular consciousness for many decades.

Conclusion

Our selection of pioneering works by early feminists thinkers extends the classical sociological canon, and challenges the theorizing and research of modernity that neglects gender relations. Theoretically, one of the most important corollaries of feminist sociological theorizing on modernity is its power to question the adequacy of perspectives that neglect exploitation, inequality, conflicts, and contradictions that cannot be readily subsumed under class. These early feminist theorists develop a sophisticated analysis of the nature of society and the interplay between gender relations and power. Mary Wollstonecraft, applying Enlightenment principles, emphasizes that the historical subjugation of women is connected to male desire for social power. Harriet Martineau highlights contradictions in the American Declaration of Independence, demonstrating how gender and race inequality in education have resulted in the exclusion of women and African-Americans from participating in the most significance spheres of economic, political, and cultural life. Through her social activism Jane Addams develops a complex theory of gender inequality, demonstrating the value of lived experiences of "bifurcation consciousness," that is, the awareness of a disjuncture between one's own lived experience and formal narratives of life. Perkins Gilman challenges the romantic view of the nuclear family, explaining how it obscures the oppression of women. Early feminist thought has helped successive generations of feminist thinkers to critically examine the position of women in modernity.

It is arguable that our choice of Wollstonecraft, Martineau, Addams, and Perkins Gilman simply maintains a bias that has already begun. Certainly there are many other founding mothers of social theory.[86] There are also the contributions of men, such as Friedrich Engels's *Origins of the Family*. In making our selection, we are conscious of the fact that we have omitted the issue of race, and the contribution of African-American sociologist W.E.B. Du Bois (1868–1963) to sociological theory. In *The Philadelphia Negro* (1899) and *The Souls of Black Folk* (1903), Du Bois discusses the interplay of race and class, power and knowledge, gender and cultural identity, and colonialism and how dominant voices hide marginalized ones.[87] While Marx adopted Hegel's master-slave dialectic to explain his concept of class-consciousness and class struggle as a motive force for social change, Du Bois adopts Hegel's analysis of the labour of servitude to interpret the distinctive life experience of African-Americans. There is little doubt, however, that the female writers discussed in this chapter helped to develop the structural perspective on social problems and had impact on the overall development of sociological theory in a critical, often pragmatic, way. It is also possible that their marginalization from mainstream sociology restricted that impact. Over the last two decades, many of these feminist thinkers have been rediscovered, and their role as sociologically informed public intellectuals and applied sociologists has become a recognized model in the field.[88]

Notes

1 Germaine De Staël, *Circonstances actuelles*, ed. Lucia Omacini (Geneva: Droz, 1979), 32.

2 See R.A. Sydie, *Natural Women, Cultured Men* (Vancouver: University of British Columbia Press, 1994), 13.

3 Ibid., 54.

4 Among others, Mary Astell, Ida B. Wells, Anna Julia Cooper, Mary McLeod Bethune, Rosa Parks, Daisy Bates, Septima Clark, Ella Baker, Nellie McClung, Marianne Weber, and Beatrice Potter Webb.

5 Mary Wollstonecraft, *Vindication of the Rights of Man*, ed. Miriam Brody (London: Penguin, 2004).

6 Valerie Bryson, *Feminist Political Theory* (Basingstoke: Palgrave, 2003), 9.

7 See Tony Benn, "The Levellers and the English Democratic Tradition," in *Tony Benn: Arguments for Socialism*, ed. Chris Mullin (London: Jonathan Cape, 1979), 29–39.

8 Wollstonecraft, *Vindication of the Rights of Woman*, 48.

9 Ibid., 15.

10 Ibid., 183.

11 Jean-Jaques Rousseau, "Sophy, or Woman," *Emile*, Bk. 5, trans. B. Foxely. Available at: www.gutenberg.org/dirs/etext04/emile10.txt.

12 Wollstonecraft, *Vindication of the Rights of Woman*, 81.

13 Moira Ferguson, *Colonialism and Gender Relations from Mary Wollstonecraft to Jamaica Kincaid* (New York: Columbia University Press, 1993), 22.

14 Wollstonecraft, *Vindication of the Rights of Woman*, 167, and quoted by Moira Ferguson, *Colonialism and Gender Relations*, 22.

15 *Harriet Martineau's Autobiography*, ed. Maria Weston Chapman, 3 vols. (1877; Boston: James R. Osgood & Company, 2007), 305.

16 Ibid., 99.

17 Ibid., 126.

18 Ibid..

19 Ibid., 113.

20 Harriet Martineau, *Illustrations of Political Economy*, 3rd ed., 9 vols. (London: Charles Fox, 1832). Available at: http://oll.libertyfund.org/title/1686 (accessed on March 22, 2008).

21 Harriet Martineau, *How to Observe Morals and Manners* (1838; New Brunswick, NJ: Transaction Books, 1989). Available at: http://ia301227.us.archive.org/2/items/howtoobservemora00martuoft/howtoobservemora00martuoft.pdf.

22 Harriet Martineau, *Society in America,* ed. S.M. Lipset (1837; Garden City, NY: Doubleday Anchor 1962). Available at: http://xroads.virginia.edu/~hyper/detoc/fem/martineau.htm.

23 Harriet Martineau, *Retrospect of Western Travel*, 3 vols. (London: Saunders and Otley, 1838). Available at: http://oll.libertyfund.org/title/1876 (accessed on March 22, 2008).

24 *Martineau's Autobiography,* vol. 2, 457–8.

25 Ibid., 127.

26 Jeremy Bentham, *The Works of Jeremy Bentham,* 11 vols., published under the Superintendence of his Executor, John Bowring (Edinburgh: William Tait, 1843), Section 8: "The greatest happiness of the greatest number requires—that such original draught, being the work of a single hand, be known to be so. Hand, known to be but one." Available at: http://oll.libertyfund.org/title/1925/116886 (accessed March 22, 2008).

27 Martineau, *How to Observe Morals and Manners,* 214.

28 Martineau, *Society in America*, vol. 2, 155–86.

29 Martineau, *How to Observe Morals and Manners*, 13.

30 Ibid., 11.

31 Ibid., 129.

32 Martineau, *Society in America,* 205, 406; http://xroads.virginia.edu/~hyper/detoc/fem/martineau.htm.

33 www.indiana.edu/~letrs/vwwp/martineau/martineau1.html.

34 *Martineau's Autobiography,* vol. 2.

35 *Martineau's Autobiography,* vol. 2, 305.

36 *Harriet Martineau, Eastern Life: Present and Past* (New York: Kessinger Publishing Company, 2007).

37 Patricia M. Lengermann and Gillian Niebrugge, "Early Women Sociologists and Classical Sociological Theory: 1830–1930," in *Classical Sociological Theory*, 5th ed., ed. G. Ritzer (New York: McGraw-Hill, 2008), 301.

38 Susan Hoecker-Drysdale, *Harriet Martineau: First Woman Sociologist* (Oxford: D Berg, 1992); Alice Rossi, "The First Woman Sociologist: Harriet Martineau (1802–1876)," in *The Feminist Papers: From Adams to de Beauvoir*, ed. A.S. Rossi (New York: Bantam Deegan, 1973), 118–24; Mary Jo Deegan, *Jane Addams and the Men of the Chicago School, 1892–1918* (New Brunswick, NJ: Transaction Books, 1988), 37.

39 Jane Addams, *Twenty Years at Hull-House* (New York: Macmillan, 1910), 150; www.gutenberg.org/etext/1325; http://digital.library.upenn.edu/women/addams/hullhouse/hullhouse.html; www.us.archive.org.

40 Addams, *Twenty Years at Hull-House,* 120.

41 Ibid., 196.

42 Ibid., 136.

43 Jane Addams, E.G. Balch and A. Hamilton, *Women at the Hague: The International Congress of Women and Its Results* (1915; Urbana, IL: University of Illinois Press, 2003).

44 D.A.R. Dossier: Jane Addams; http://womhist.alexanderstreet.com/milit/doc11.htm.

45 FBI records.

46 Dinah Birch, *Ruskin and the Dawn of the Modern* (Oxford: Oxford University Press, 1999); Julian Symons, *Thomas Carlyle: The Life and Ideas of a Prophet* (Oxford: Oxford University Press, 1952).

47 Carlyle's *Heroes and Hero-Worship* is available at www.fullbooks.com/Heroes-and-Hero-Worship2.html (accessed February 2008).

48 Addams, *Twenty Years at Hull-House*, 191–5.

49 Ibid., 82.

50 Mary Jo Deegan "W.E.B. Du Bois and the Women of Hull-House, 1895–1899," *The American Sociologist* 19, no. 4 (1988).

51 Charles Booth, *Life and Labour of the People in London*, 17 vols. (London: Macmillan, 1902–3); see also www.csiss.org/classics/content/45.

52 Herbert Spencer, *The Study of Sociology* (London: Henry S. King, 1873). Available at: http://oll.libertyfund.org/title/1335 (accessed on March 22, 2008).

53 Mary Jo Deegan, *Jane Addams and the Men of the Chicago School.*

54 Jane Addams, *Democracy and Social Ethics* (New York: Macmillan, 1902–07), 226, and quoted by Lengerman and Niebrugge, "Early Women Sociologists," 313. Available at: www.gutenberg.org/etext/15487. Jane Addams, *Democracy and Social Ethics* (New York: Macmillan, 1902–7).

55 Jane Addams, *The Spirit of Youth and the City Streets* (1909; Urbana, IL: University of Illinois Press, 1972). Available at: www.gutenberg.org/etext/16221. Addams, *The Spirit of Youth and the City Streets*, 6.

56 Jane Addams, *A New Conscience and an Ancient Evil* (Urbana, IL: University of Illinois Press, 2002), chap. 2). Available at: www.archive.org "Jane Addams."

57 Jane Addams, "Women and Public Housekeeping" (1913). Available at: http://etext.lib.virginia.edu/.

58 Ashley Montagu, ed., *Jane Addams: A Centennial Reader* (New York: Macmillan, 1960), 114.

59 Jane Addams, *Newer Ideals of Peace,* Citizen's Library Series (New York: Macmillan, 1907); Jane Addams, *Peace and Bread in Time of War* (1922; Urbana, IL: University of Illinois Press, 2002).

60 Jane Addams, *The Second Twenty Years at Hull-House* (New York: Macmillan, 1930) 35.

61 http://nationalhumanitiescenter.org/pds/gilded/power/text12/addams.pdf; Jane Addams, "If Men Were Seeking the Elective Franchise," in *Jane Addams and the Dream of American Democracy,* ed. Jean Bethke Elshtain (1913; New York: Basic Books, 2002).

62 Jane Addams, *A Treatise on Domestic Economy for the Use of Young Ladies at Home and at School* (New York: Harper, 1834). Available at: www.gutenberg.org/etext/21829.

63 Charlotte Perkins Gilman, *The Living of Charlotte Perkins Gilman: An Autobiography* (1935; New York: Harper & Row, 1975), 8–9.

64 Charlotte Perkins Gilman, "Why I Wrote the Yellow Wallpaper," *The Forerunner* (October 1913): 19–20. Available at: http://people.virginia.edu/~sfr/enam312/cpghp.htm (accessed September 11, 2008).

65 Gilman, *The Living of Charlotte Perkins Gilman*, 97.

66 http://digital.library.upenn.edu/women/gilman/economics/economics.html.

67 Denise D. Knight, "The Dying of Charlotte Perkins Gilman," *American Transcendental Quarterly* 6, no. 1 (1999).

68 Kenneth H. Tucker, *Classical Social Theory* (Malden, MA: Blackwell, 2002), 240.

69 Charlotte Perkins Gilman, *The Forerunner*, vol. 1 (1909–10). Available at: www.fullbooks.com/The-Forerunner-Volume-1-1909-1910-2.html (accessed September 11, 2008).

70 Charlotte Perkins Gilman, *Women and Economics: The Economic Relation Between Men and Women as a Factor in Social Evolution* (1898; New York: Harper & Row, 1966), 1–5.

71 Gilman, *Women and Economics*, 157.

72 Tucker, *The Marx-Engels Reader*, 744.

73 Gilman, *The Living of Charlotte Perkins Gilman*, 127.

74 Tucker, *Classical Social Theory,* 247.

75 Gilman, *Forerunner.*

76 Ibid.

77 Ibid., 9.

78 Minna Doskow, ed., *Charlotte Perkins Gilman's Utopian Novels: Moving the Mountain, Herland and With Her in Ourland* (Madison & Teaneck: Fairleigh Dickinson University Press, 1999).

79 Doskow, *Charlotte Perkins Gilman's Utopian Novels*. Available at: www.gutenberg.org/etext/32; www.deepleafproductions.com/utopialibrary/authors/CharlottePerkinsGilman.htm, 46, 65, 76, 101, 130, 175.

80 See C. Pateman, "The Patriarchal Welfare State," in *Democracy and the Welfare State*, ed. A. Gutmann (Princeton University Press 1988), and cited in Valerie Bryson, *Feminist Political Theory* (Basingstoke: Palgrave, 2003), 18.

81 See D. Knights and H. Willmott, eds., *Gender and the Labour Process* (Aldershot: Gower 1986).

82 Wollstonecraft, *Vindication of the Rights of Woman*, 263, and quoted in Bryson, *Feminist Political Theory*, 18.

83 R. Putman Tong, *Feminist Thought* (Boulder, Col: Westview Press, 1998), 43.

84 Alys Eve Weinbaum, "Writing Feminist Genealogy: Charlotte Perkins Gilman, Racial Nationalism, and the Reproduction of Maternalist Feminism," *Feminist Studies* 27, no. 2: 201–19.

85 See, for example, R.W. Connell, *Gender and Power* (Cambridge: Polity Press, 1987).

86 Mary Jo Deegan, ed., *Women in Sociology: A Bio-Bibliographical Sourcebook* (New York: Greenwood, 1991).

87 Tucker, *Classical Social Theory.*

88 American Sociological Association Task Force, 2005: www.msu.edu/~perlstad/History_Applied_Sociology_H_Perlstadt_Jun_05.pdf. American Sociological Association Task Force on Institutionalizing Public Sociologies, *Public Sociology and the Roots of American Sociology: Re-Establishing Our Connections to the Public,* Interim Report and Recommendations submitted to the ASA Council (July 2005). Available at: http://pubsoc.wisc.edu/e107_files/public/tfreport090105.doc.

PART IV

WHAT RELEVANCE NOW?

Epilogue

> Capitalist class … create their own contradictions, throw up opposing classes, provoke class struggles, set in train economic, political, and cultural changes. History, far being at an end, has hardly begun!
>
> —Leslie Sklair

THE PURPOSE OF THIS EPILOGUE is to review the main points of the book, to highlight some differences and similarities of ideas among the founding intellectuals, and to draw some general conclusions about the continuing relevance of classical sociological theory for explaining resurgent local cultures in the context of global capitalism. As dramatized in director Robert Zemikis's 1985 film, *Back to the Future,* the present and the future depend on the route taken in the past. Where sociology is going in the future depends upon its past and how sociologists have intellectually travelled from the past to the present. The preceding chapters have attempted to show that the ideas of eminent classical social thinkers have shaped the present world and our understanding of it. Marx, Durkheim, Weber, and Simmel, Wollstonecraft, Martineau, Addams, and Perkins Gilman were without doubt sociological thinkers. But they were also storytellers. As Noah Richler observes, stories provoke public discourse and play a role in societal conflicts. Stories reflect the world back to us, constituting the framework around which we build our system of morality and truths.[1] What these social thinkers have given us in their eminent works, ranging from *A Vindication of the Rights of Woman*, *Capital,* *The Division of Labour in Society* to Weber's *The Spirit of Capitalism* or Simmel's *Metropolis*, is a series of grand narratives on modernity, each as distinctive and insightful as any to be found in the celebrated novels of their age.

The classical legacy may be summarized by a series of concepts—*materiality, morality, rationality, culture,* and *gender*—that can be used to examine modern society.[2] We believe these ideas will continue to shape social theory and research, just as they continue to exert profound influence on intellectual inquiry, public consciousness, and human agency in the context of global capitalism. In the context of globalized capitalism, therefore, the ideas of the classical theorists should become part of the mental fixtures of every educated citizen because their thoughts continue to exert so profound an influence on intellectual inquiry, public consciousness, and human agency.

The Social and Intellectual Context

In part 1 of *Capitalism and Classical Sociological Theory,* we explored the social and intellectual context in which the classical theorists formulated their ideas. Just as one cannot interpret the Catholic Bible or the Koran without reference to the text's cultural context, so too, we believe, the classical works cannot be understood without reference to the turbulent social, economic, and intellectual context in which they emerged. The Introduction provided an account of how classical sociological theory is a response to, and is shaped by, the way that processes of industrialization, urbanization, and democratization of late-eighteenth- and nineteenth-century Western European societies impacted on the lives and thinking of early sociologists. As we explained, compared to the eighteenth century, Europe in 1914 was a qualitatively different world in several important respects. There were at least three significant aspects to the colossal technological and social transformations that occurred between the 1870s and the early 1900s. First, Western economies were no longer predominantly agriculture based. The factory system pioneered by Britain had migrated to the mainland of Europe and elsewhere, most notably to North America. In 1848, Britain was the superpower and the workshop of the world but in 1914 the superpowers included France, Germany, and the United States. Paradoxically, the industrial capitalism that owed its triumph to science and technology also engineered the mass-produced weapons of war that slaughtered millions in the trench warfare of 1914–18. Second, we observed that traditional norms and patterns of human social relationships were transformed by the unprecedented development of cities where wage labour increasingly took place. When compared with the socially integrated and regulated life of small communities, modern societies were dominated by unconnected individuals pursuing self-interest in an anarchy of competition. The third transformation discussed was democratization and the creation of mass national social movements that challenged despotism, capitalism, and historic inequality. By 1914 the trade unions had become firmly established as instruments of working-class self-defence and emancipation. The theorists highlighted in this text took various intellectual paths to uncover and explain the processes of social transformations and to identify the key characteristics of modernity, as contrasted with pre-industrial society.

One of the major themes running through this book has been to stress the continuities as well as the discontinuities across time. We have emphasized that the development of social theory has built upon the ideas of earlier philosophers and public intellectuals and that these have to be contextualized adequately if we are to appreciate their relevance. Thus, we can only really appreciate Marx's critique of consciousness if we know what debates on religion took place in his lifetime. The Enlightenment movement was not a unified body of thinking but was internally fractured and riddled by contradictions. The inconsistencies of the Enlightenment debate on slavery and women's rights provide examples of these contradictions. The public engagement between rationalist, secular, Enlightenment ideology and the conservative philosophical reaction has left a legacy in the form of classical propositions about the nature of society. The dominant propositions of classical social theory concern the organic nature of society, with its internal laws of unity and development. Classical theory posits that society creates the individual and individuals have no existence outside of a social context; society is composed of relationships and institutions; and society's institutions and customs are positively functional in that they either fulfill human needs directly or indirectly by serving other essential institutions. These ideas about society profoundly influenced and shaped the classical canon, as we detailed in chapter 2.

The Classical Triumvirate

In part 2 of *Capitalism and Classical Sociological Theory*, we examined the original classical triumvirate: Marx, Durkheim, and Weber. We began our journey into the canon with Karl Marx's contribution to social theory. At the centre of Marx's social theorizing is the primacy of capitalist production and the way this shaped the political and social life of the society. In chapter 3, we sketched Marx's biography before examining his philosophy and dialectic method. His philosophical concepts are not entirely original, but his use of them had profound impact. Marx's critique of idealism envisions society in materialist terms. For Marx, society is created by purposive praxis, and it is material conditions that determine human consciousness. Durkheim, in contrast to Marx, believes society is self-creating, exists over and above the individual, and wields an immense power. Also in contrast to Marx, Weber believes that society is the fragile outcome of human interaction, and that change in the realm of ideas is at least as important as change in the processes of economic production. Marx's multi-faceted conception of alienation in its political, religious, philosophical, and economic forms have had a lasting effect on the work of later sociologists and social philosophers. As we have noted, Marx's critique of consciousness is worthy of our attention for more than historical reasons. In contemporary debates on religion, multiculturalism, and the public discourse on Christianity and Islam, Marx's philosophical concepts continue to be insightful and suggestive, and they remain a fertile source for social theorizing. Turning to Marx's methodology, we argued for the continued significance of Marx's dialectic. The dialectic, which helps us to understand connections between disparate processes and events, allows us to think creatively about the apparent contradictions that lie at the heart of globalization and diversification in late-modern society. The dialectic can, for example, help us to conceptualize the intensified conflict over the Earth's shrinking reserves of natural resources and the rise of a more effective opposition to the economic sources of global climate change.

Marx's conception of history provides a series of interrelated structural concepts through which to interpret the development of the past and to expose contradictory social phenomena in the present, as illustrated in chapter 4. For Marx, humanity is essentially self-created through productive labour, which itself is social. Different social forms throughout the centuries are to be explained by the complex interplay of changing productive factors and the social and ideological spheres of society. Society is not a stable constellation of essential factors, but a socially constituted structure with interconnected, contradictory tendencies and movements. Certain laws characterize human history, but it is people who ultimately build a society through their labour or praxis, and change it. These ideas encourage sociologists to see the present society in historical-materialist terms. They underlie C. Wright Mill's notion of the sociological imagination, which requires us to relate personal troubles to the history of the social transformations that typically lie behind them.[3]

Significantly, we suggested that Marx's ideas on ideology are highly relevant in modern sociology as a means to analyze the nexus between the realm of ideas and those of economics. This is illustrated in the work of Canadian writer Naomi Klein, *The Shock Doctrine*. Klein shows that, in the 1970s, the dominant classes in Chile and Argentina used orthodox economic ideas propagated by the late U.S. economist Milton Friedman to legitimate their political and economic dominance. Klein describes the ascendancy of the ideology of U.S. global laissez-faire capitalism:

> Since the fall of Communism, free markets and free people have been packaged as a single ideology that claims to be humanity's best and only defence against repeating a history filled with mass graves, killing fields and torture chambers. Yet in the Southern Cone [South America], the first place where the contemporary religion of unfettered free markets ... was applied in the real world, it did not bring democracy; it was predicated on the overthrow of democracy in country after country. And it did not bring peace but required the systematic murder of tens of thousands and the torture of between 100,000 and 150,000 people.[4]

The import, and subsequent prominence, of laissez-faire capitalist ideologies into Chile, Argentina, in the 1970s and into Poland and Russia in the 1990s illustrate the crucial difference between Marx and Durkheim. Marx interprets industrial society as essentially divided against itself, whereas Durkheim interprets society as possessing an essential unity. The most recent history of neo-liberal economic policies demonstrates that market fundamentalism can survive only if social movements and democracy are suppressed.[5] For Marx, it follows that ideas and belief systems can serve to strengthen the position of a dominant social class, whereas, for Durkheim, they serve the whole of society.

In chapter 5 we examined Marx's theories of value and economic crises, which form the twin pillars of his critique of capitalism. The labour theory of value characterizes capitalism as a fundamentally exploitative system. There are two parts to the exchange value of labour power: an absolute minimum sufficient to enable the worker to subsist, and an extra amount that depends on the balance of social forces in the society. Over the last twenty-five years, in both in North America and Britain, it has become socially acceptable for the income gap between rich and poor to widen, with minimum wage rates close to subsistence level, and extremely high salaries at the top of the income pyramid. In Canada, for example, 99 per cent of Canadians working full-time throughout 2008 earned an average of $38,998. But by 10:33 a.m. on January 2, 2008, the top 100 chief executive officers of public companies in Canada had already been paid that amount. On average, the top 100 CEOs make over 218 times more than the average of weekly employment earnings of Canadians working full-time for a full year.[6] Statistics also show that in *real* terms—after subtracting inflation to keep the purchasing power of the dollar roughly constant—the earned median income in Canada was the same in 2004 as in 1982, and that between 1975 and 2005 the median family income in the United States increased by only 28 per cent, compared to 160 per cent for the top 1 per cent of the U.S. income pyramid.[7] Globally, capitalism has widened the gap between the world's rich and poor. Although the matter of global inequality is extraordinary complex, the statistics are truly breathtaking. In 2004 the world had 587 billionaires with a combined wealth of $1.9 trillion. Meanwhile, at the other end of the spectrum, about 2.7 billion people, or more than 50 per cent of the developing world's population, lived on less than $2 a day.[8] Inequality is the essence of Marx's theory of exploitation; it is not primarily the result of the behaviour of greedy or unethical employers; neither is it the result, as President George W. Bush said, in 2002, after the collapse of WorldCom and Enron, the nefarious behaviour of a few "bad apples"; but it is an innate feature of the capital-labour relationship itself—the buying and selling of labour power. The capitalist who refuses to engage in the exploitation of workers will most likely lose out to competitors who close their eyes to such issues. The system preserves those who accept the primacy of the profit motive, and makes losers of those who do not. The only way to step out of the system is to change it.

As we explained, *Capital* has made an immense contribution to the sociological analysis of technological change and management. Marx's pioneering work on the effects of machinery has morphed into what is known as labour process theory, which seeks to expose the social and class interests behind technological change. And critical sociological studies of management conceptualize management as a control mechanism that advances and protects the economic and political interests of the ruling dominant class. Marx's analysis centres attention on the dominant imperative that management must realize a satisfactory degree of control over antagonistic capital-labour relations that is necessary to secure the efficient extraction of profit in the form of surplus value.

Another major achievement of Marx's economics was the correct prediction of the growth of multinational companies and global markets. For Marx, the logical tendency of capitalism is the concentration and centralization of capital and the predictable effect of corporate control over markets, which had the capability of destroying smaller competitors. We cited the giant U.S. retailer, Wal-Mart, as an example of this tendency. Contemporary wisdom predicts that multinational corporations operate in accordance with universal principles that will result in a convergence of markets and business practices. Thus globalized capitalism will drive wages down and erode employment standards and lead to the transfer of production from relatively expensive labour markets (e.g., North America) to less expensive ones (e.g., China and India). We can also predict in a post-SUV economy the transfer of production to societies with weak carbon emission controls, as well as the transfer of pollution from environmentally regulated societies (e.g., European Union) to less regulated ones (e.g., China and India). With regard to contemporary debates on globalization and global warming, we have tried to show that Marx's economic theory is an insightful social theory that still resonates in the global capitalism era.

In chapters 6, 7, and 8 we covered the contribution of Emile Durkheim to social theory. Durkheim theorized that industrial societies, with their complex division of labour and their diverse and conflicting interests, constitute a moral entity held together by shared norms and values. The discussion of *The Division of Labour in Society* in chapter 6 showed how Durkheim presents a theory of social evolution that contains interplay between structural or material factors such as population size and interaction and cultural ideas. However, his analysis centres on the importance of culture and morality because the division of labour presupposes a prior morality and the development of a culture of anomie results from rapid social change that prevents new habits and moral values from becoming embedded in organic society. A concern with moral regulation is the central theme of Durkheim's major studies on suicide, religion, and education (discussed in chapters 7 and 8). Durkheim identified anomic and egoistic suicides as the main currents of suicide in organic societies due to a lack of regulation and integration. The role of collective representations in primitive religion and their contribution to social solidarity are themes in his study of religion. In studies of the division of labour, suicide, and religion he refers to the implications of his analysis by pointing to the need for the development of a new morality that matches new social arrangements. Durkheim's work on education is a continuation of this theme. He regarded the educational system as a reflection of society rather than an agency to change it. He thought that there was a crisis in education in the France of his day because there was a crisis in his society's moral system. Consequently, he was concerned that schools should be institutions capable of socializing children into a secular morality that was "like so many moulds with limiting boundaries, into which we must pour our behaviour."[9] Nevertheless, he thought that the teacher should make pupils aware of new demands for justice so that each generation could adjust morality in line with its times.

In each of his major studies Durkheim makes brief references to human nature and the individual's need for social regulation. In his discussion of education his portrayal of children as egoistical and asocial[10] reflects his general view of man as a bundle of desires that need to be channelled for the sake of social order.[11] This image of man is conservative, but he does not draw the conclusion that conservatives might try to argue for the re-establishment of traditional controls. Rather, he argues for the need for a new morality that would enable people to live in modern societies where they could develop their talents to their full potential, within a set of values that respected the individual.

Durkheim's nephew Marcel Mauss stated, "Durkheim was profoundly opposed to all wars of class or nation. He desired change only for the benefit of society and not of one of its parts—even if the latter had numbers and force."[12] Durkheim sympathized with the reformist socialism of Jaurès, but he was not an active political animal (the exception being his involvement in the Dreyfus case which polarized French society). Durkheim is sometimes interpreted as being influenced by a conservative reaction to social change,[13] but this is to neglect his more radical views on property ownership, his anti-clericalism, and his commitment to state secular education. Instead of political action, Durkheim preferred scientific, objective analysis of social problems as the basis of social change. For Durkheim, it was the absence of collectively held moral beliefs that lay at the root of social malaise in French society. However, as Turner argues, Durkheim's sociology of morality is not a conservative theory; rather, it is a "socialist response to the negative impact of an anarchic economy on moral life."[14]

If Durkheim thought that the free market of his day was anarchic and prone to anomie, then his theory has been given a new relevance by the neo-liberal advocacy of minimal interference in markets, free trade between countries, and individualism—anomie has become globalized. In their discussion of globalization, Hutton and Giddens refer to the worldwide communications revolution—especially the Internet—international financial markets, the collapse of Soviet communism in 1989, an aggressive capitalism, and a political leadership that sees no alternative as the major contributing factors to a situation where changes in how we work and live are ubiquitous.[15] As early as 1991, Mestrovic[16] and Eldridge[17] discussed the unleashing of greed as leading to financial disaster and business scandals as symptoms of contemporary anomie. During the course of writing this book a crisis occurred within the financial sector in the United States that can be interpreted as a product of anomie. In the pursuit of profits and performance-related bonuses, financial institutions in the United States sold mortgages to thousands of low-paid workers who had little prospect of maintaining their mortgage commitments, leading to enormous numbers of defaults and repossessions. As many banks in other countries had loaned money to finance these mortgages, this led to a widespread distrust between banks, and the unwillingness of the banks to lend to each other, producing an unprecedented liquidity crisis in the financial system. The crisis unfolding on Wall Street, as we write, has caused the collapse of Northern Rock bank in Britain and the investment banks Bears Stearn, Lehman Brothers, and Merrill Lynch; the nationalization of mortgage institutions Fannie Mae and Freddie Mac; and the government rescue of American International Group (AIG) in the United States. In addition, the idea of greed in a situation of anomie has become institutionalized and is illustrated by the encouragement of low-income Americans to acquire unaffordable mortgages. While both of the 2008 U.S. presidential candidates, Barack Obama and John McCain, promised greater regulation of the finance industry and to rein in "self-interest, greed, irresponsibility and corruption," others have argued that the root cause of the crisis is the value system at work on Wall Street: the disjunction of economics and morality.[18] As this drama plays out, the U.S. Federal Bureau of Investigation (FBI) has announced an investigation to determine whether the collapsed financial institutions concealed the extent of their deepening financial problems from regulators and investors. The historic bankruptcies on Wall Street not only threaten a global recession[19] but also they seem to suggest that the age of laissez-faire finance and of neo-classical orthodoxy, which held that markets are cyclically stable and self-correcting, may be coming to a close.

Max Weber's work on methodology in social science research still informs epistemological considerations today, as we explained in chapter 9. We began that chapter with a review of his life and works and a discussion of the intellectual currents shaping Weber's methodological ideas. Weber was a prolific writer, but the biographical sketch we provided helps explain the reasons for his modest academic accomplishments in his lifetime. His profound psychological breakdown shortened his academic career; the war disrupted his scholarly work; and much of his works were published posthumously, many not translated into English until the 1950s. Weber's methodological writings were strongly influenced by neo-Kantian thinkers such as Nietzsche, Dilthey, Windelband, and Rickert. We explained that Weber developed the *Methodenstreit* debate in several important ways by emphasizing that in both natural and social sciences, facts never speak for themselves—they require interpretation—and that research methods are always shaped by the researcher's cultural values and politics: research methods cannot be separated from ideology. Weber's value-freedom/value-relevance dichotomy, as well as his use of singular causal analysis, his theory of social action, the application of *Verstehen* as a distinct mode of understanding, and the nature and purpose of ideal-type constructs were examined. We explained that these concepts differentiate Weber from Marx. For Marx, economic forces of which people have little knowledge and to which they do not attribute subjective meaning can affect human action. For Weber, meaningful social action embodies rational principles by adhering either to formal rules or to specific means-ends calculations. Thus, any meaningful human action is rule-following and is therefore social. Central to Weber's discussion of social action is the notion of *Verstehen* or "interpretative understanding." According to Weber, social phenomena are identified not by their external characteristics but by social inquiry that captures humans' inner states through interpretative understanding. Weber's essays, charting the boundary between values, judgments, and epistemological neutrality, have been given canonical status in most introductory social research methods texts.[20] What emerges from Weber's work on social inquiry is that historical understanding is always interpretative and, therefore, there is no one way of understanding capitalist modernity, but multiple histories are relevant to the writer's values and interests. For Weber, human history flows along multiple paths and follows the logic of unintended consequences. Thus, his contribution to social research methods foreshadows post-modernist thinking, in particular the challenges to a universal human history and of meta-narratives.

Finally, we emphasized that Weber's rich and complex approach to human inquiry remains relevant to sociology today. In their introduction to the 2000 edition of the *Handbook of Qualitative Research*, Denzin and Lincoln aver that "the social sciences and the humanities become sites for critical conversations about democracy, race, gender, class, nation, freedom, and community."[21] At the same time they emphasize that "the interpretive *bricoleur* understands that research is an interactive process shaped by his or her personal history, biography, gender, social class, race, and ethnicity, and by those of the people in the setting. The political *bricoleur* knows that science is power, for all research findings have political implications. There is no value-free science ... The product of the interpretive *bricoleur's* labour is a complex, quilt-like bricolage, a reflexive collage or montage—a set of fluid, interconnected images and representations. This interpretive structure is like a quilt, a performance text, a sequence of representations connecting the parts to the whole."[22] Though the rational, non-empathetic character of Weber's *Verstehen* would put him at odds with many qualitative researchers, it is a reflection of his legacy that within the matrix of contemporary uncertainty his ideas about the research process being shaped by personal biography, the interconnectedness of parts, and the complexity of interpretive understanding remain remarkably relevant and still resonate with social scientists, more than eighty years after his death.

In chapter 10, we examined Weber's well-known thesis on ascetic Protestantism and capitalism and substantive areas of his sociology: social class, power, and bureaucracy. We discussed how difficult it is to impose a single overarching theme onto Weber's writings but suggested, as others have, that his conception of rationalization is a unifying theme. We examined his classic work on ascetic Protestantism and explained that, in contrast to Marx, Weber's narrative of societal development avers that the growth of Western capitalism cannot be explained through wholly material and structural forces. Moreover, it is embedded in the interconnected process of rationalization. We explained that Weber's thesis on rationalization informs his theories of social class, politics, and bureaucracies. While Weber rejected Marx's analysis of the capitalist mode of production as a system with structured internal contradictions and class struggle, his theory of social class reflects Marx's thinking: the absence of property constitutes basic class divisions, and unambiguous economic interest is a factor producing class. As we explained, Weber departs from Marx in emphasizing that the level of skill embodied in labour power may be a form of property that produces class differentiation, and thus a social class situation is ultimately a market situation. For Weber, access to resources such as training and education affect an individual's position in the labour market and, in turn, strongly influences overall *life chances*. To illustrate the continued relevance of Weber's work, we pointed out that Erik Olin Wright has combined the approaches of both Weber and Marx to formulate an influential theory of social class.[23]

We also explained that pivotal to Weber's political sociology are his theories of power, domination, and the state. Weber's account of the political process is "resolutely elitist."[24] The modern state is necessarily based on domination and coercion, and bureaucracies are the purest form of legal-rational authority, according to Weber. We discussed Weber's pessimistic image of modern society for individual liberty and stressed that his iron cage metaphor is one of the most influential metaphors in general critiques of modernity. In Weber's own words:

> It is as if in politics ... we were deliberately to become men who need "order" and nothing but order, who become nervous and cowardly if for one moment this order wavers, and helpless if they are torn away from their total incorporation in it. That the world should know no men but these: it is in such an evolution that we are already caught up, and the great question is therefore not how we can promote and hasten it, but what can we be opposite to this machinery in order to keep a portion of mankind

> free from this parcelling-out of the soul, from this supreme mastery of the bureaucratic way of life.[25]

Finally, we noted that Weber's rationalization thesis has inspired authors and filmmakers and continues to inform sociologists in the early twenty-first century. Perhaps the main strength of Weber's sociology is its continued relevance in debates on the environment and globalization. Contemporary sociologists draw on Weber's ideas to make the argument that ecological problems cannot be understood without making the ideological connections between Christianity, Western rationalism, and environmental domination. The work of social theorists Ulrich Beck, Anthony Giddens, Michael Mann, and W.G. Runciman represent a renaissance of Weberian historical sociology. This intellectual genre recognizably draws upon the tradition founded by Weber in eschewing historical materialism and arguing that global capitalism and contemporary change and processes are caused by the interaction of several irreducibly distinct forms of power and domination. German sociologist Ulrich Beck argues that the contemporary wave of global capitalism produces a "detraditionalized" social life: "Those who live in this post-national, global society are constantly engaged in discarding old classifications and formulating new ones. The hybrid identities and cultures that ensue are precisely the individuality which then determines social integration. In this way, identity emerges through intersection and combination, and thus through conflict and other identities."[26] Weber's intellectual legacy is evident. Beck's analysis of contemporary global capitalism is inexorably paradoxical: society and social action are constituted out of conflictual arenas that are simultaneously closed, national, individualized and transnationally open, and defined in opposition to one another.

Expanding the Canon

In part 3 of *Capitalism and Classical Sociological Theory*, we extended the traditional canon to include the unique cultural and aesthetic contributions of Georg Simmel, and to introduce a selection of early feminist writings. Simmel's work centres on the conflicting, but creative, intersection of individual self-emergence and the self-completion of society, as explained in chapter 11. He warns of the dangers of the unopposed transition to a world increasingly rationalized to the point of complete levelling and meaninglessness. Simmel challenges thinkers to theorize the dynamic interconnections between men's being and women's being, and to practice a sociality that would include both. His vitalistic micro-dialectic produced valuable insights into the interconnected nature of social geometry and social action, urbanization and personality, and the social tragedy of man in the mass. His most compelling concept, perhaps, is "the cultural tragedy" whereby man's response to metropolitan conditions creates a snowballing dynamic that produces the ever greater dominance of objective culture. Simmel challenges us to theorize conditions of transcendence other than war, as metropolis extends into the farthest reaches of the globe.

Simmel held unorthodox views on war. In his early writings on the subject he suggests war, as conflict, would increase social cohesion, and simultaneously it would make choices more meaningful than the endless round of empty amusements characteristic of modernity. In his later writing, however, Simmel shows awareness of the negative side of war. He writes, "Europe stands in the act of committing suicide, and America sees in that the opportunity for itself, to put itself at the tip of world happenings. It [America] stands by this, like the lurking heir at the deathbed of the rich testator."[27] When the war failed to have the effects that Simmel hoped for, he put his faith in an idea of Europe as a bastion against the excessive modernity of America. Simmel's war writings seem inconsistent with much of his previous intellectuality. They are consistent, however, with his constant attempt to find ways to create expanded areas of subjective self-fulfillment and freedom in a world that encourages only the most shallow forms of individuality.

Finally, in chapter 12, we extended the canon further, this time to examine the contribution of women who used their gender as a standpoint from which to expose what they saw as the androcentrism of society and social theory. The chapter shows that many of the educational, legal, and political reforms that have improved the quality of life and opportunities for women can be traced back to the work of the early feminists. For example, Mary Wollstonecraft's *A Vindication of the Rights of Woman*, published 217 years ago, was the first celebrated feminist manifesto.[28] *Vindication* enunciated the principles of emancipation: an equal education for girls and boys, an end to sexual discrimination, and a right for women to be defined by their profession, not their partner. These principles have resonance in contemporary society. While completing this book, we have witnessed two women, Hillary Clinton and Sarah Palin, campaign to be the U.S. Democratic presidential candidate and the Republican vice-presidential candidate, respectively. We witnessed the first African-American, Barack Obama—who made "*Yes we can*" be the leitmotiv of his political campaign and acceptance speech in Chicago—become president. These historic events come forty-five years after the publication of Betty Friedan's *Feminine Mystique* and after Martin Luther King's "*I have a dream*" speech. The early feminist thinkers made a contribution to this episode of American history. Mary Wollstonecraft and Harriet Martineau used the language of slavery to define women's status. As heirs of European Enlightenment, these pioneers blended the oppression of white women and black female slaves, as well as slaves in general, in eighteenth-century America.

Mary Wollstonecraft lived in a society challenged by the ideas of the French Revolution, and prior to the establishment of university-based sociology. She brought to her task a formidable background in Unitarian rationalism and the ideas of radical reformers. Wollstonecraft did not argue for women's essential equality with men. She felt that in fair competition men would still be ahead. But she argued strenuously that women should be allowed to participate, as fully as they were able, in the making of society. Such participation would enhance both male and female virtues and contribute to the progress of society. Her writings were provocative calls to extend the Enlightenment ideals of liberty and equality of opportunity to everyone. Harriet Martineau attained an exceptional education for a woman of her time, and she was also strongly affected by Unitarian rationalism. She was contemporary with Auguste Comte, and translated his major work into English. She was, nonetheless, a very different kind of social theorist. Martineau's books on sociological methods of observation and grounded theory-building, and her critical theorizing about the anomalies of slavery and the political invisibility of women set a standard that remains very high.

Jane Addams was also influenced by Auguste Comte, but only insofar as she envisioned the religion of Supreme Humanity to be something that thinkers such as herself might bring into being. Her intense activism for democratic participation and for peace meant that she was not given full recognition for her sociological ideas and practices. Like Martineau, Addams used methods such as "sympathetic understanding" which brought her close to the subjective realities and social contingencies that shaped the lives of immigrants, prostitutes, criminals, and the poor. Her participation in many co-operative ventures and in shaping government policy accomplished a great deal towards her goal of inducing lateral progress, progress for all, in America's decidedly unequal conditions.

Charlotte Perkins Gilman represents another thread of feminist ideas that were also part of Jane Addams's world. Perkins Gilman's use of evolutionary theory as an argument for the superiority of women and for the implicit inferiority of nonwhites and immigrants from non-Western countries cannot be justified by scientific research. However, her work that is grounded in her own experiences as a woman and as an observer of women in her society contains arguments about the family, education, occupational opportunity, and also the social origins of crime and retarded development, all of which remain significant in sociological theory. We may, perhaps, be criticized for not including the work of Anna Julia Cooper, Nannie Helen Burroughs, and Ida B. Wells, who fought against the horrors of lynching and argued, as their white sisters did, for equal education and opportunity. Women's challenge to the traditional sociological cannon has been carried out, from the beginning, in an activist as well as intellectual way. This intellectual activism of women was grounded in the social experiences that they so eloquently attempted to change.

Our journey through *Capitalism and Classical Sociological Theory* is now drawing to a close. The time has come for you to reflect on what you have learned from this journey. Adult education scholars emphasize the need for reflectivity as a critical component of the learning process. Reflection is like using a mirror to help us look back on our actions and thought processes. Reflective learning occurs when we have experiences and then step back from them to evaluate what we learned from the experience. There are several ways to carry out reflection. One approach is to systematically go through the additional reading list at the end of the book. Further reading, particularly of material that tends to differ with the approach in this book, provides a mirror for us and allows us to look at topics from another perspective. Another way to reflect is to talk to other people—friends, family members, relatives, and co-workers—who provide mirrors for us, allowing us to understand social issues from another perspective. Talk to other people about the topics covered in *Capitalism and Classical Sociological Theory.* Your own experience of life is also excellent material for reflection and can provide insight into many of the topics explored by the classical sociological thinkers. Finally, we hope our guided tour through classical social theory has proved worthwhile, that it helps you understand debates about global capitalism, and that it deepens your understanding of contemporary sociological theory and research.

Notes

1 Noah Richler, "Novel Thinking Needed on Both Sides," *The Globe and Mail*, (October 10, 2006), 11.

2 See Larry Ray, *Theorizing Classical Sociology* (Buckingham: Open University Press, 1999), 8.

3 C. Wright Mills, *The Sociological Imagination*, 40th anniversary edition (New York: Oxford University Press, 2000), 3–4.

4 Naomi Klein, *The Shock Doctrine* (Toronto: Alfred Knopf, 2007), 121.

5 Ibid., 288.

6 Hugh Mackenzie, *The Great CEO Pay Race: Over Before It Begins* (Toronto: Canadian Centre for Policy Alternative, 2007), 3.

7 Peter J. Nicholson, "The Curious Absence of Class Struggle," *The Globe and Mail* (January 5, 2008), A13.

8 See B. Milanovic, *Worlds Apart: Measuring International and Global Inequality* (Princeton: Princeton University Press, 2005).

9 Emile Durkheim, *Moral Education* (New York: Dover Publications Inc., 2002), 26.

10 Ibid., 208.

11 Steven Lukes, "Alienation and Anomie" in *Philosophy, Politics and Society: 3rd Series,* eds P. Laslett and W.G. Runciman (Oxford: Blackwell, 1967), 134–56.

12 Marcel Mauss, "Introduction to the First Edition" in *Socialism*, Emile Durkheim (New York: Collier Books, 1962), 34.

13 Robert A. Nisbet, *The Sociological Tradition* (London: Heineman, 1967), 16–19.

14 Bryan S. Turner, *Classical Sociology* (London: Sage Publications, 1999), 108.

15 Will Hutton and Anthony Giddens, eds. *On the Edge: Living with Global Capitalism* (London: Jonathan Cape, 2000), 1–3.

16 Stjepan G. Mestrovic, *The Coming Fin De Siecle: An Application of Durkheim's Sociology to Modernity and Postmodernism* (London: Routledge, 1991).

17 John E.T. Eldridge, Peter Cressey and John MacInnes, *Industrial Sociology and Economic Crisis* (Hemel Hempstead: Harvester Wheatsheaf, 1991).

18 Peter Scowen, "Wall Street's Causalities Were Too Greedy. Or Were They Not Greedy Enough?" *The Globe and Mail* (September 20, 2008), F7.

19 See Kevin Carmichael, "Global Recession Threatens, U.S. Expert Says," *The Globe and Mail* (September 17, 2008) A13.

20 See, for example, Allan Bryman and James Teevan, *Social Research Methods* (Don Mills, ON: Oxford University Press, 2005).

21 N. Denzin and Y. Lincoln, *Handbook of Qualitative Research* (Thousand Oaks, CA: Sage, 2000), 1048.

22 Ibid., 6.

23 See E.O. Wright, *Classes* (London: Verso, 1985); *Class Counts: Comparative Studies in Class Analysis* (Cambridge: Cambridge University Press, 1997).

24 Alex Callinicos, *Social Theory: A Historical Introduction* (Cambridge: Polity Press, 2007), 175.

25 Quoted by Reinhart Bendix, *Max Weber: An Intellectual Portrait*, (New York: Doubleday Anchor Books, 1962), 464.

26 Ulrich Beck, "Living Your Own Life in a Runaway World: Individualism, Globalization and Politics," in *On the Edge: Living with Global Capitalism*, eds. Hutton and Giddens, 164–74. See also W.G. Runciman, *A Treatise on Social Theory* (Cambridge: Cambridge University Press, 1997); W.G. Runciman, "The Selectionist Paradigm and Its Implications for Sociology," *Sociology* 32, no.1 (1998), 163–88; M. Mann, *The Sources of Social Power* (Cambridge: Cambridge University Press, 1993); A. Giddens, *The Consequences of Modernity* (Cambridge: Polity Press, 1990).

27 Simmel, "Europa und Amerika: eine weltgeschichtliche Betrachtung," first published in *Das Berliner Tagblatt* (July 1915), trans. Austin Harrington, as introduction to Georg Simmel's essay "Europe and America in World History," *European Journal of Social Theory* 8, no. 1 (2005): 63–72.

28 Charlotte Gray, "Feminism's First Manifesto," *The Globe and Mail* (November 15, 2008), D14.

Further Reading and Sources

The Classical Triumvirate: Marx, Durkheim, and Weber

KARL MARX

Selected primary sources

Engels, Friedrich. *The Conditions of the Working Class in England.* Moscow: Progress Publishers, 1973.

Marx, Karl. *Economic and Political Manuscripts of 1844.* London: Lawrence & Wishart, 1974. And in *The Marx-Engels Reader,* 2nd ed., edited by Robert C. Tucker, New York: Norton & Company, 1978, 66–125.

———. *Thesis on Feuerbach.* In *The Marx-Engels Reader.* 2nd ed., edited by Robert C. Tucker, New York: Norton & Company, 1978, 143–45. First published 1845.

———. *Wage-Labour and Capital.* In *The Marx-Engels Reader.* 2nd ed., edited by Robert C. Tucker, New York: Norton & Company, 1978, 203–217. First published 1849.

———. *The Poverty of Philosophy.* New York: International Publishers, 1982.

———. *The Eighteenth Brumaire of Louis Bonaparte,* in *The Marx-Engels Reader.* 2nd ed., edited by Robert C. Tucker, New York: Norton & Company, 1978, 594–617. First published 1852.

———. *Grundrisse.* London: Penguin Books, 1973.

———. *The Preface to a Contribution to the Critique of Political Economy.* Moscow: Progress Publishers, 1977.

———. *Capital, Volume I.* London: Lawrence & Wishart, 1970.

———. *Capital, Volume II.* London: Lawrence & Wishart, 1974.

———. *Capital, Volume III.* London: Lawrence & Wishart, 1971.

Marx, Karl, and Friedrich Engels. *The German Ideology.* New York: Prometheus Books, 1998.

———. *The Communist Manifesto.* London: Penguin Books, 2002.

Selected works

Bottomore, T.B., and M. Rubel. *Karl Marx: Selected Writings in Sociology and Social Philosophy.* London: Pelican, 1963.

McLellan, David. *Karl Marx: Selected Writings.* Oxford: Oxford University Press, 2000.

Tucker, R., ed. *The Marx-Engels Reader*, 2nd ed. New York: Norton & Company, 1978.

Selected secondary sources

Acton, H.B. *What Marx Really Said.* London: MacDonald, 1967.

Barbalet, J.M. *Marx's Construction of Social Theory.* London: Routledge, 1983.

Carver, T., ed. *The Cambridge Companion to Marx.* New York: Cambridge University Press, 1991.

Clarke, S. *Marx's Theory of Crisis.* London: Macmillan Press, 1994.

Cohen, G.A. *Karl Marx's Theory of History.* Princeton, NJ: Princeton University Press, 2000.

Cornforth, M. *Historical Materialism.* London: Lawrence & Wishart, 1962.

Elster, Jon. *Making Sense of Marx.* Cambridge: Cambridge University Press, 1985.

Fine, Ben. *Marx's Capital.* London: Macmillan, 1975.

Freedman, Robert. *Marx on Economics.* London: Pelican, 1962.

Larrain, Jorge. *Marxism and Ideology.* London: Macmillan Press, 1983.

McLellan, David. *Marx Before Marxism.* London: Harper Torchbooks, 1970.

McLennan, David. *Marx.* London: Fontana Press, 1975.

———. *Karl Marx: The Legacy.* London: BBC Publications, 1983.

Morrison, Ken. *Marx, Durkheim, Weber,* 2nd ed. London: Sage, 2006.

Sayer, Derek. *Capitalism & Modernity: An Excursus on Marx and Weber.* London: Routledge, 1991.

Swingewood, Alan. *Marx and Modern Social Theory.* London: Macmillan, 1975.

Wheen, Francis. *Karl Marx.* London: Fourth Estate, 2000.

Wood, Allen W. *Karl Marx.* London: Routledge, 2004.

Worsley, Peter. *Marx and Marxism.* London: Routledge, 2002.

Wolff, J. *Why Read Marx Today?* Oxford: Oxford University Press, 2002.

Online Sources

http://marxmyths.org/chris-arthur/article.htm

EMILE DURKHEIM

Selected primary sources

Durkheim, Emile. *The Division of Labour in Society.* New York: The Free Press, 1997.

———. *The Rules of Sociological Method.* New York: The Free Press, 1938.

———. *On Suicide.* London: Penguin Books Ltd., 2006.

———. *Moral Education.* New York: Dover Publications Inc., 2002.

———. *Education and Sociology.* New York: The Free Press, 1956.

———. *The Evolution of Educational Thought.* London: Routledge & Kegan Paul, 1977.

———. *The Elementary Forms of Religious Life.* Oxford: Oxford University Press, 2001.

Selected secondary sources

Bellah, R., ed. *Emile Durkheim on Morality and Society.* Chicago: University of Chicago Press, 1973.

Fenton, Steve. *Durkheim and Modern Sociology.* Cambridge: Cambridge University Press, 1984.

Giddens, Anthony, ed. *Durkheim: Selected Writing.* Cambridge: Cambridge University Press, 1972.

———. *Durkheim.* London: Harper Collins, 1997.

Lukes, Steven. *Emile Durkheim His Life and Work: A Historical and Critical Study.* Harmondsworth: Penguin Books, 1973.

Parkin, Frank. *Durkheim.* Oxford: Oxford University Press, 1992.

Pearce, Frank. *The Radical Durkheim.* 2nd ed. Toronto: Canadian Scholars' Press, 2001.

Pickering, William S.F., ed. *Durkheim Today.* Oxford: Berghahn Books, 2002.

Stedman Jones, Susan. *Durkheim Reconsidered.* Cambridge: Polity Press, 2001.

Thompson, Kenneth. *Emile Durkheim,* rev. ed. London: Routledge, 2002.

Online sources

British Centre for Durkheimian Studies: www.isca.ox.ac.uk/research/durkheimian/DurkheimResources.html.

MAX WEBER

Selected primary sources

Weber, Max, *The Protestant Ethic and the Spirit of Capitalism.* London: Penguin, 2002.

———. *Economy and Society.* 2 vols., edited by G. Roth and C. Wittich. Berkeley, CA: University of California Press, 1968.

———. *The Sociology of Religion.* Boston: Beacon Press, 1964.

———. *General Economic History.* Translated by F. Knight. New York: Dover Publications, 2003.

———. *The Methodology of the Social Sciences.* Translated by E. Shils and H. Finch. Glencoe, Ill: Free Press, 1949.

Selected secondary sources

Albrow, M. *Max Weber's Construction of Social Theory.* London: Macmillan Press, 1990.

Bendix, Reinhard. *Max Weber: An Intellectual Portrait.* New York: Anchor Books, 1962.

Dawe, Alan. "The Relevance of Values in Weber's Sociology." In *Max Weber and Modern Sociology.* Edited by A. Sahay, London: Routledge, 1971, 37–66.

Eliaeson, Sven. *Max Weber's Methodologies.* Cambridge: Polity Press, 2002.

Hamilton, P., ed. *Max Weber: Critical Perspectives.* London: Routledge, 1991.

Tribe, Keith, ed. *Reading Weber.* London: Routledge, 1989.

Ray, Larry J., and Michael Reed, eds. *Organizing Modernity: New Weberian Perspectives on Work, Organization and Society.* London: Routledge, 1994.

Ringer, Fritz. *Max Weber's Methodology.* Cambridge, MA: Harvard University Press, 1997.

Runciman, W.G. *A Critique of Max Weber's Philosophy of Social Science.* Cambridge: Cambridge University Press, 1972.

Turner, B.S. *Max Weber: From History to Modernity.* London: Routledge, 1992.

———. *For Weber.* London: Sage, 1996.

Turner, S.P., and R.A. Factor. *Max Weber and the Dispute over Reason and Value.* London: Routledge, 1984.

Turner, Stephen, ed. *The Cambridge Companion to Weber.* Cambridge: Cambridge University Press, 2000.

Expanding the Canon: Simmel, Wollstonecraft, Martineau, Addams, and Perkins Gilman

GEORG SIMMEL

Selected primary sources

Simmel, G. *On Women Sexuality and Love.* Translated, edited, and introduction by Guy Oakes. New Haven, CT: Yale University Press, 1984.

———. *The Philosophy of Money.* 3rd ed., translated by Tom Bottomore and David Frisby, edited by David Frisby. London: Routledge, 2004.

———. *The Sociology of Georg Simme1, 1858–1918: A Collection of Essays.* Translated by Kurt H. Wolf, edited and introduction by Kurt H. Wolf. Columbus: Ohio State University Press, 1959.

———. *Simmel on Culture.* London: Sage Publications, 1997.

———. *Essays on Religion.* New Haven, CT: Yale University Press, 1997.

———. "The Metropolis and Mental Life." In *Georg Simmel: On Individuality and Social Forms.* Edited and introduction by Donald N. Levine. Chicago, IL: University of Chicago Press, 1971, 324–39.

Online sources

www.archive.org/stream/sociologyofgeorg030082mbp/sociologyofgeorg030082mbp_djvu.txt

www.brocku.ca/MeadProject/Simmel/Simmel_1897a.html

www.gsz.hu-berlin.de/dokumente/georg_simmel-the_metropolis_and_mental_life.pdf

Selected secondary sources

Axelrod, Charles David. *Studies in Intellectual Breakthrough: Freud, Simmel, Buber.* Amherst, MA: University of Massachusetts Press, 1979.

Frisby, David. *Georg Simmel,* rev. ed. London: Routledge, 2002.

———. *Fragments of Modernity: Theories of Modernity in the Work of Simmel, Kracauer and Benjamin.* Cambridge, MA: MIT Press, 1986.

———. *Sociological Impressionism: A Reassessment of Georg Simmel's Social Theory.* London: Heineman, 1981.

Jaworski, Gary D. *Georg Simmel and the American Prospect.* Albany: State University of New York Press, 1971.

Leck, Ralph M. *Georg Simmel and Avant-garde Sociology. The Birth of Modernity 1880–1920.* Amherst, New York: Humanity Books, 2000.

Weinstein, Deena, and Michael A. Weinstein. *Postmodern(ized) Simmel.* London: Routledge, 1993.

Witz, Anne. "Georg Simmel and the Masculinity of Modernity," *Journal of Classical Sociology* 1 (2001): 353–70.

MARY WOLLSTONECRAFT

Selected primary sources

Wollstonecraft, Mary. *A Vindication of the Rights of Woman.* Edited by Miriam Brody. London: Penguin Classics Books, 2004.

———. *Vindication of the Rights of Men; A Vindication of the Rights of Woman; An Historical and Moral View of the French Revolution.* Oxford: Oxford University Press, 1994.

———. *Ahead of Her Time: A Sampler of the Life and Thought of Mary Wollstonecraft.* Selected and arranged by Ella Mazel. London: Routledge, 1995.

———. *The Collected Letters of Mary Wollstonecraft.* Edited by Janet Todd. New York: Columbia University Press, 2003.

———. *Thoughts on the Education of Daughters with Reflections on Female Conduct in the More Important Duties of Life.* Clifton, NJ: Augustus M. Kelley Publishers, 1972.

Holmes R., ed. *A Short Residence in Sweden and Memoirs of the Author of "The Rights of Woman.* London: Penguin, 1987.

Online sources

Gutenberg project Wollstonecraft: www.gutenberg.org/browse/authors/w#a84

A Vindication of the Rights of Woman: www.gutenberg.org/etext/342

Maria, or the Wrongs of Woman: www.gutenberg.org/etext/134

A Vindication of the Rights of Men; A Vindication of the Rights of Woman; An Historical and Moral View of the French Revolution: www.galloway.1t01.0rg/Wollstonecraft.html

HARRIET MARTINEAU

Selected primary sources

Martineau, Harriet. *Autobiography.* Edited by Linda H. Peterson. Peterborough: Broadview Press, 2007.

———. *Harriet Martineau's Autobiography.* Edited by Maria Weston Chapman. Boston: James Osgood, 1877.

Online sources

Harriet Martineau's Autobiography and Memorials of Harriet Martineau. Edited by M. W. Chapman. Boston: James Osgood, 1877. Vol. 2 accessed from http://oll.libertyfund.org/title/2012/140260 on February 19, 2008.

http://essays.quotidiana.org/martineau/

http://onlinebooks.library.upenn.edu/webbin/book/browse?type=lcsubc&key=Martineau%2c%20Harriet%2c%201802%2d1876

JANE ADDAMS

Selected primary sources

Addams, Jane. *Twenty Years at Hull-House.* New York: New American Library Signet Classics, 1960.

———. *The Second Twenty Years at Hull-House.* New York: Macmillan, 1930.

———. *The Selected Papers of Jane Addams, Volume 1: Preparing to Lead, 1860–81.* Edited by Mary Lynn McCree Bryan, Barbara Bair, and Maree de Angury. Urbana and Chicago: University of Illinois Press, 2003.

Online sources

http://ia331332.us.archive.org/1/items/janeaddamsabiogr006019mbp/janeaddamsabiogr006019mbp.pdf

CHARLOTTE PERKINS GILMAN

Selected primary sources

Perkins Gilman, Charlotte. *The Yellow Wall-Paper.* New York: Feminist Press, 1973.

———. *Women and Economics: A Study of the Economic Relation between Men and Women as a Factor in Social Evolution.* New York: Harper & Row, 1966.

———. *Concerning Children.* Boston: Small & Maynard, 1900.

———. *The Home: Its Work and Influences.* New York: Macmillan, 1903.

———. *Human Work.* New York: McClure & Phillips, 1904.

———. *The Charlotte Perkins Gilman Reader.* Edited by Ann J. Lane. New York: Pantheon, 1980; www.womenwriters.net/domesticgoddess/CPGguide.html.

———. *Charlotte Perkins Gilman: A Nonfiction Reader.* Edited by Larry Ceplair. New York: Columbia University Press, 1991.

———. *The Abridged Diaries of Charlotte Perkins Gilman.* Edited by Denise Knight. Charlottesville: University Press of Virginia, 1994.

———. *Social Ethics: Sociology and the Future of Society.* Edited by Michael R. Hill and Mary Jo Deegan. Westport, CT: Praeger, 2004.

Selected secondary sources

Deegan, Mary Jo. *Jane Addams and the Men of the Chicago School 1892–1918.* New Brunswick, NJ: Transaction Books, 1990.

Deegan, Mary Jo, ed. *Women in Sociology: A Bio-Bibliographical Sourcebook.* New York: Greenwood Press, 1991.

Kelly, Gary. *Revolutionary Feminism: The Mind and Career of Mary Wollstonecraft.* London: Macmillan Press, 1996.

Lengermann, P.M. and J. Niebrugge-Brantley. *The Women Founders: Sociology and Social Theory 1830–1930.* Boston: McGraw, 1998.

Logan, Deborah Anna. *The Hour and the Woman: Harriet Martineau's "Somewhat Remarkable" Life.* Dekalb: Northern Illinois University Press, 2002.

Index

D

F

I

Y

Z